MW01076606

PERSONS OF THE DRAMA

By Stanley Kauffmann

Novels

The Hidden Hero
The Tightrope
A Change of Climate
Man of the World

Criticism

THEATER

Persons of the Drama

FILM

A World on Film
Figures of Light
Living Images

EDITOR

(with Bruce Henstell)
American Film Criticism: From the Beginnings to *Citizen Kane*

Stanley Kauffmann

PERSONS
OF THE DRAMA

theater criticism and comment

HARPER & ROW, PUBLISHERS

NEW YORK, HAGERSTOWN, SAN FRANCISCO, LONDON

1817

Portions of this work originally appeared in *The New Republic, World, Performance, Horizon,* and *The American Scholar.*

Grateful acknowledgment is hereby made for permission to reprint the following:

"On the Acceptability of the Homosexual," "Marat/Sade," "A Note on Program Notes," "Measure for Measure," "The Oresteia," "About Williams: Gloom and Hope," "Serjeant Musgrave's Dance," "The Journey of the Fifth Horse," "Sunset," "Homosexual Drama and Its Disguises," and "Who Did It?" originally appeared in *The New York Times.* ⓒ 1966 by The New York Times Company. Reprinted by permission.

Lines from *The Misanthrope,* by Richard Wilbur, reprinted by permission of Harcourt Brace Jovanovich, Inc.

Lines fom Cascando in *Poems in English,* by Samuel Beckett, copyright ⓒ 1961 by Samuel Beckett. Reprinted by permission of Grove Press, Inc.

"All of That," by Harold Pinter, reprinted by permission of ACTAC (Theatrical & Cinematic) Ltd.

"Pinter and Sexuality" originally appeared in *The American Poetry Review.* Reprinted by permission.

From WNET Channel 13 series of weekly broadcasts: Commentaries on *The Deputy,* copyright ⓒ 1964 by Stanley Kauffmann; on *Hamlet,* copyright ⓒ 1964 by Stanley Kauffmann; on *The Devils,* copyright ⓒ 1965 by Stanley Kauffmann; on "The Moscow Art Theater," copyright ⓒ 1965 by Stanley Kauffmann; on "The Open Theater," copyright ⓒ 1966 by Stanley Kauffmann; on *Macbird,* copyright ⓒ 1967 by Stanley Kauffmann.

To the Memory of Lili Darvas

contents

preface

My three previous collections of criticism are about film and are organized differently from this book. Though they are obviously incomplete records, still they can be read (among other ways) as chronicles of the periods they cover. No such chronicling intent applies here. A full theater record has real value, but this book has a different purpose: to represent one critic's views on some qualities and questions in the theater of the past decade. In addition there are a few relevant biographical and historical articles.

I have tried to be rigorously selective. The reviews deal, I think, with themes or authors or actors or directors—or all four—of continuing interest; the fact that all of these productions are gone ought to be irrelevant. The articles deal with subjects not affected by the life of any one production. The arrangement of the book is by topic, and within each group the order is generally chronological, altered when I thought it might be helpful to place items together—for instance, reviews of the same playwright. Once in a while, therefore, there is a reference to something that in fact occurred later but comes earlier in this book. Many of the pieces have been slightly revised, but no opinions have been altered retrospectively. Postscripts have been added when necessary.

A word about the sources of the material. In 1963 the Public Broadcasting television station in New York, Channel 13, invited me to review plays once a week. In January 1966 I became the theater critic of *The New York Times.* In September 1966 I left that post and resumed as theater critic of Channel 13 for another year or so. In 1969 *The New Republic,* for which I was the film critic, asked me to review plays too, alternating theater and film reviews as I thought appropriate. So the reviews that follow come from television, a newspaper, and a weekly magazine. The source is specified when it is not *The New Republic.*

The articles come from various journals. I want particularly to thank Shirley Tomkievicz and her associates at *Horizon* for their cordiality. Robert Marx helped with intelligent research for the *Horizon* articles.

As in my last previous collection, *Living Images,* I offer a closing essay in place of an introduction. A small portion of this essay derives from some notes of mine in *Yale/Theater.*

Thanks to Nahum J. Waxman of Harper & Row. Thanks, once again, to the editors and readers of *The New Republic.* Thanks always to L.C.K.

S.K.

New York
October 1975

PART I
theaters

american theaters

The Stages of Joseph Papp

(The American Scholar, *Winter 1974/75*)

Everyone who publishes theater criticism in New York has a Joseph Papp story. Here is mine. In October 1970 the late Jack MacGowran appeared in a Broadway play that flopped. Papp knew that Mac-Gowran had done a program of Beckett readings six months earlier in Paris with Beckett's approval; and Papp promptly whisked Mac-Gowran downtown to do the Beckett readings in one of his theaters. I saw the program, enjoyed it greatly, and reviewed it favorably in *The New Republic*. Because I had recently written adverse comments on several Papp productions, I thought it only fair to note in my review

3

that MacGowran was being presented on one of the stages of the Public Theater, "whose producer, Joseph Papp, whatever his defects, is certainly not short on energy and enterprise."*

At 9:00 A.M. on the day that the review appeared, Papp telephoned me and said angrily, "What do you mean, my defects?"

Well, this article is what I mean, but it is also what I mean about his virtues. Whatever one's opinion of this or the other of his many productions, Papp requires serious discussion because he is an insistent cultural phenomenon. He is now unquestionably the most prominent person in the American theater. He operates in New York, which, unfortunately, is still the theater capital of the U.S. and thus the capital of theater publicity. He operates in almost every field of the contemporary theater. He began and still works on Off Broadway. He has produced on Broadway. He is busy in the workshop-experimental sector called Off Off Broadway. He runs a summer Shakespeare festival in Central Park and a mobile theater that tours Greater New York. And, cutting across all these categories, he has long been active as a producer of black theater, presenting plays written, directed, and performed by blacks.

All his activities have been intertwined with a policy of free admission where possible, and low-priced tickets where it isn't, with the theater committed to social relevance and community service. Papp contrasts vividly with the last previous most prominent individual in the American theater, David Merrick, who was in the spotlight during the 1960s. Merrick was the quintessential smooth, clever, ruthless, big-business operator, a rapist of success, a producer whose shows were sometimes mammoth hits (*Hello, Dolly!*) but, in any serious way, were uninteresting even when they were hits. He made enough money to establish a tax-loss foundation that occasionally produced a valuable play that had been proved elsewhere (*Marat/Sade*), but neither in this foundation work nor in his original productions did he show any distinct taste or policy, and his career has had no effect whatsoever except on his and other bank accounts. Papp is a very different No. 1 figure. I think it's fair to say that Papp is more interested in his policy and his goals than he is in any one production. The productions implement the policy—something for which there is

* See p. 211.

no analogy in Merrick. To investigate that Papp policy, how it grew, and where it led, we must begin at the beginning.

Papp was born in Brooklyn in 1921, the son of an immigrant Polish trunk-maker, Shmuel Papirofsky, and a mother born in Lithuania. (Papp used his full surname until he went to work for CBS in the 1950s; they shortened it for him.) He had little formal education —he never went past high school—but in his youth he soaked up the reverence for literary-musical culture that was endemic in Jewish immigrant communities, including reverence for Shakespeare. In 1941 he joined the Navy and spent four years in the Pacific, where he was assigned to Special Services. He wrote and produced and directed shows for servicemen. After his discharge in 1945 he was in California, and he used his GI Bill privileges to enroll in the Hollywood Actors Laboratory. This group had been organized by such actors as Morris Carnovsky and J. Edward Bromberg, former members of the Group Theater in New York during the 1930s, now living and working on the Coast. The Lab was much influenced by the Group's esthetic reliance on Stanislavsky and its view of the theater as a social-political mediator. Papp studied acting and directing there, then became an executive of the Lab. He "also taught acting to working people at the California Labor School." (His words eight years later before the House Committee on Un-American Activities.) In 1951 Papp got a job with a road company of *Death of a Salesman* as stage manager and understudy; at the end of the tour he went to work as a stage manager for CBS TV in New York.

I make no attempt here to psychoanalyze at a remove, but Papp's psyche would have to be prodigiously tortuous to keep one from making a simple inference about what happened next. While he was working in straight commercial TV, Naming the Game and Garry Mooring, he got together a group of actors, in 1953, and began to work on scenes from Shakespeare in space provided by a Lower East Side church. With his childhood background and his six years of conditioning in socially oriented Hollywood groups, it was inevitable that he would be dissatisfied with his bread-and-butter, or milk-and-honey, daily job, that he would find a way to make it subsidize more substantial work.

Why did the group choose Shakespeare instead of more topical social plays? Here are some possible reasons. First and fundamentally, Papp has a genuine love for Shakespeare which I would not want even to seem to deride in anything that follows. Second, working on classics evidently satisfied a cultural imperative that had been drummed into him as into many thousands of children raised by Jewish immigrant parents. To honor the freedom of the New World as against the restrictions of Eastern Europe, the watchwords, brighter than success in a good number of those households, were education and culture. Third, and marrying the two reasons above, there was never any conflict for Papp between cultural obligation and social relevance in his allegiance to Shakespeare, no choice between Ivory Tower and Barricades. This is the man who wrote of *Henry V* twelve years later: "Although this play is a paean to the glory of England, it transcends flagwaving and is transformed into a statement of triumph for all ragged men fighting everywhere against impossible odds." (And by that time, as we'll see, he had changed his ways of *doing* Shakespeare.)

The next step for Papp in those early days was to establish a unique relation with an audience. He began this the following year, 1954, when his group presented its first program free of charge, then got a charter from the Board of Regents of the State of New York as the Shakespeare Workshop. In 1956 they presented their first summer season at the East River Amphitheater, again free of charge. The following summer they played for the first time as the Shakespeare Festival (the name still used) in Central Park in a makeshift theater; the next winter they played indoors in the Heckscher Theater of the Children's Center on upper Fifth Avenue, far above the chic belt, close to Spanish Harlem. (Which is where I first saw them—*As You Like It* with George C. Scott as Jaques.) Consistently they were working with small subsidies and charged no admission.

The following summer, on June 19, 1958, Papp was summoned before HUAC. He denied that he was then a Communist, took the Fifth Amendment twelve times when asked whether he had ever been a Communist, and steadfastly refused to implicate anyone else. That very day CBS fired him. With typical scrappiness Papp refused to accept this decision, took the matter to arbitration, and was reinstated, to enjoy the luxury of resigning in April 1960. (Twelve years after that, he got an extra bit of revenge, eaten fairly hot: he and the Festival were engaged by CBS to do a series of large-scale TV shows. The engagement was short-lived—there was censorship trouble on the second show—but Papp must have had some personal pleasure out of it.)

After his HUAC-related troubles Papp concentrated on his Shakespeare Festival. I omit details of the opposition he encountered, with city officials and with legal tangles.* He overcame them all with magnificent drive, and with something else that was accruing to him. By the time he moved into this phase of his career with and for the Festival, he had naturally begun to get considerable newspaper space, and he began to acquire a persona: as battler for the public cultural weal. Part of this persona was certainly his due: whatever one's opinion of his work, he was unquestionably trying to serve the community. Part of it was because of the press's perennial eagerness to characterize in the large; it gives them an easy way to handle people about whom they have to write often. Part of it, one began to sense quite early, was developed histrionically; Papp had found a role in the Erving Goffman sense and felt comfortable in it, a role that fitted both his aims and his ego.

One result of this tripartite persona was the inauguration in 1962 of the 2300-seat open-air Delacorte Theater in Central Park, where the Shakespeare Festival performs every summer free of charge. Further, Papp soon organized mobile theaters to tour Shakespeare to other parks and to playgrounds.

As he moved into the 1960s some qualities began to come clear in his productions themselves. First, to clarify, not every Papp production is actually directed by Papp. This is a blessing. Some of his productions have been adequate or better, but I have never seen one directed by himself that I liked. From the beginning he has engaged a number of directors to work for him, to handle much of his schedule. Through his choices he has of course manifested qualities in himself, and since every one of these productions has been supervised and ultimately "passed" by Papp, his relation to them has been close. His stamp—at least of approval—is on everything.

That *As You Like It* at the Heckscher Theater in 1958 was directed by Stuart Vaughan. It was fairly early in Papp's producing career, and it seemed to me that, with the unmistakable though then merely eccentric exception of George C. Scott, it was just one more in the long line of dull conventional Shakespeare that had seemed fusty

---

* For these details see Robert A. Caro's *The Power Broker* (Knopf, 1974), the life of Robert Moses, who was Parks Commissioner at the time.

when I first met it in the early 1930s. In those Depression days some unemployed actors had banded together under an experienced Shakespeare exploiter named Percival Vivian, had got some old costumes and scenery and the huge Century Theater (since demolished) all on a percentage basis, and had presented a repertory of miserable Shakespeare productions, calling themselves a Festival for as long as they could persuade high-school and college teachers to dragoon their students into attending. I was then in drama school, therefore more demanding than I am now, and I was disgusted by the argument that at least these students were getting the chance to see Shakespeare, at low prices too. In 1958 at the Heckscher I thought of that earlier Festival.

So I shied away from Papp's Shakespeare for a few years. The next productions of his that I recall were outdoors in Central Park: *The Merchant of Venice* (1962) with George C. Scott as Shylock, now assuredly mad and absolutely irresistible; *Antony and Cleopatra* (1963) with Colleen Dewhurst giving promise of greatness (still unachieved, I sadly think); and that same year another *As You Like It*, with Paula Prentiss, alas. In these productions and others Papp was beginning to show marked changes from Century Theater fustiness. These changes had nothing to do with esthetics: they were demotic, even civic responses that dovetailed perfectly, one may infer, with Papp's interests and bent. It was one of the happiest conjunctures that I can think of in the theater of my time.

Soon after the end of World War II the population of New York began to change greatly. White emigration to the suburbs increased the proportion of blacks in the city, and there was also a great postwar influx of Puerto Ricans. In fifteen years or so the very color of the crowd in the streets had markedly changed. In social dynamics the blacks and the Latins became more self-confident and more mobile. The theater, which had previously been "downtown" and remote for non-white New Yorkers, had now become a possible part of their lives. These changes were hugely important to Papp.

He cared about minorities, quite sincerely, I'm sure, as a citizen and a humanitarian. But these demographic changes also, I think, gave him the perfect opportunity he needed in his theater. Here he was, a producer without any evident shred of artistic mandate, a director of the most pedestrian sort, who had fervent cultural concerns and social empathy. And here he found himself in a city involved in swift social transition, where ethnic minorities were coming rapidly to the fore. Perfect! Now he had a mode, a *mark,* for his Shakespeare. Instead of just bland old "good-for-you" Shakespeare, he could make the classics respond to the topical situation, make them—in the tiredest term of our era—relevant. The fact (for me, anyway) that he had no sheerly creative gifts, no artistic talent, could be submergd in matchmaking between Shakespeare and the several ghettos, by making the theater accessible and enjoyable to *all* previously excluded/ ignored groups.

The first, obvious move was to mix his casts. Increasingly through the 1960s he used non-white actors in white roles.* (The Henry in that *Henry V,* for just one instance, was Robert Hooks.) But the more intrinsic way in which Papp responded to—encouraged—the change in the audience's composition was in his style of production. There seemed now to be one over-arching precept for his work: the play must be made interesting to those outside the cultural elite; the play must entertain a black or Puerto Rican or working-class white who has felt excluded from that elite and now has no ambition to belong to it. His staff reports that in fact Papp's free Shakespeare drew a large proportion of young middle-class whites, people with time to spend on a waiting line instead of money to spend at a box office, but perhaps—particularly in the late 1960s—they too were attracted by Papp's ecumenical intent, an intent inferable from his productions and explicit in his statements. ("The history of my life with the New York Shakespeare Festival has been characterized by confrontations caused by a singular drive—to create a meaningful theater for popular audiences.")

The best-known example of this democratizing process, because it moved to Broadway after its Delacorte premier, came in 1971— Papp's production of *Two Gentlemen of Verona,* directed by Mel Shapiro. It had a Puerto Rican Proteus and a black Silvia and a rock score. The whole tone of the production was: "See? Shakespeare can be fun. Forget all about the poetry and all that Elizabethan stuff. We can make it *now.* Watch. Listen." It was Papp's *Henry V* thesis of

* This was highly unusual but not unprecedented. The first instance that I know, in New York, of a black actor in a white role in a mixed cast was Orson Welles's casting of Jack Carter as Mephistophilis in the Federal Theater's *Doctor Faustus,* 1937. Canada Lee played Bosola in *The Duchess of Malfi* in 1946, but was made up to look white. See my article "En Route to the Future," *The New York Times,* July 31, 1966.

topicality carried to its prosaic extreme. Certainly a lot of people enjoyed the show, but one thing they were *not* enjoying was *Two Gentlemen of Verona*. The same sort of mixed casting and of rock music, the same rib-nudging commonalty could be imposed on *The Bacchae* or *The Sheep Well* and could result in a virtually identical show that would have no more or less to do with Euripides or Lope de Vega than it had to do with Shakespeare. The extrapolations and impositions would meet and fuse somewhere on their own.

But this method was Papp, manifest: Papp doing what he could do: Papp seizing the day. To be just, I must add that occasionally he made a good choice of a director to implement his policy, in which case the transpositions or alterations were locked into place with optimum effect. For instance, Michael Kahn directed *Measure for Measure* in 1966 as a play seemingly about the urban problems of Vienna at the time, but still managed to make the moral-metaphysical dilemmas ring true.* In the best of Papp's Shakespeare that I have seen, A. J. Antoon directed a transposed *Much Ado About Nothing* in 1972, which also moved to Broadway and then to television, as an American play.† Antoon set it in Teddy Roosevelt's U.S.A., which was near enough for recognition, yet far enough for this play's romance. The taking ragtime score by Peter Link seemed paradoxically the opposite of an attempt to modernize: it supplied a leaven of nostalgia. There were chasms in the cast and crudities of execution, but Antoon caught the gradations of the character comedy and a good deal of the poetry; so the production did what "versions" so often try and usually bungle—it brought Shakespeare close. Equal emphasis on the last two words.

By 1966 the Shakespeare Festival at the Delacorte and the mobile theater were not enough for Papp. Apparently he felt that topicality-through-classics, though paramount, was not everything. There was one whole corps of theater workers with whom he had not yet been in touch: playwrights, living working playwrights. He wanted to add to his connection with his audience the instrument of contemporaneity.

He entered a field here—new plays, especially new American plays

---

* See p. 96.

† President Nixon attended a performance on Broadway. No press report that I saw noted the irony: a former member of HUAC attending a play produced by a man who had been an uncooperative HUAC witness. See p. 98.

—that was in quite a different state from the somnolence of "official" Shakespeare which he had disrupted with demographic ideas. The Broadway picture, for new plays, was dim, but Papp was not then interested in Broadway. The Off-Broadway scene was busy; the Off-Off-Broadway scene—often amateur in personnel but unconstrained in content and unconventional in method—was teeming. Through these two channels American playwrights were pouring out works, usually of no great merit but imaginatively ambitious and free-flowing—celebrations, among other things, of the very fact that these relatively new channels for playwrights existed.

One can guess, on the basis of Papp's past and subsequent profile, that one reason he went into the field of new plays was that he chafed at the thought that so much was going on in the theater of which he had no part. Possibly Shakespeare began to seem a limitation to him, not only in contact and topicality but in ambition. At any rate, when he went into new-play production, he went in big, impressively. In 1966 he and his associate producer, Bernard Gersten, raised the money to buy the Astor Library, a beautiful century-old building downtown on Lafayette Street. (By coincidence with Papp's family background, it had for many decades done important service to America as the headquarters of the Hebrew Immigrant Aid Society. If not Papp's parents themselves, surely many of their friends had passed through those doors in search of American futures.) Quite rightly, the building had been officially designated as a city landmark; Papp then converted the spacious interior into four theaters, a film theater, a concert room, galleries, and workshops. Admission was charged, but it was kept as low as possible; besides, there were sub-scription discounts and student rates.

By this time Papp's persona was a part of the metropolitan land-scape. By this time he had not only developed charisma, he was one of the people responsible for the vogue of that word. He was now, in his new field, entering competition with already going non-Broadway theaters like La Mama and Theater Genesis and many others for the best in new plays; and with the help of his persona he quickly surged ahead in that competition. He not only got many of the livelier scripts, he produced them in ways that smacked of daring and adventure. He combined his ambition with a talent for publicity—the best kind of publicity, because in the middle of the spotlight's glare he could appear selfless and dedicated.

The bright ball kept rolling. At the Public Theater, as the downtown complex was collectively named, the first production was *Hair*. The success of that show—there, subsequently on Broadway, then in theaters around the world—needs no retelling. At the Public Theater, allowing for occasional exceptions like a revival of *Trelawny of the "Wells,"* Papp pursued two policies, not mutually exclusive. The first was the production of black theater. He was not limited here, as in Shakespeare, to integrated casting: he could do solidly ethnic work— black plays by black playwrights with black actors and directors. One such play, Charles Gordone's *No Place to Be Somebody,* won the Pulitzer Prize in 1970. That this play, in my view, was of small worth, that the bestowal of the prize seemed a joint confession of that prize's bankruptcy and reverse Uncle-Tomming, is beside at least one point: the Papp tide was swelling, and tides that swell *keep* swelling, at least for a while.* Also a part of his ethnic policy were Hispanic plays in Spanish (which he had also done in the mobile theater), but these never got comparable attention or publicity because of the language barrier.

His other chief policy was his openness to new, young theater people. If I had to choose the pre-eminent contribution that Papp has made, it would be this: the way he has altered the dreadful situation that used to prevail for newcomers in the New York theater. Until about 1950 the New York theater meant, predominantly, Broadway, and to the newcomer Broadway presented a high blank cold wall that only a few could scale or find a crack in. Talent was by no means the prime factor for progress or, sometimes, even a pertinent one. A successful actress in her fifties said to me recently, "I know I wasn't among the most talented of my generation. I just had more stamina and more luck." The situation improved somewhat with the growth of Off Broadway, but Papp made the single biggest change. It began with his Shakespeare Festival; it spread quickly with the Public Theater, naturally, because now he was also open to new playwrights. No, he wasn't merely open to new playwrights and other theater people—he went looking for them. And he found them: not only writers but directors, scenic designers, lighting designers, and administrators. I don't mention names because I can't mention half and

---

* Another Papp production won a Pulitzer Prize in 1973, Jason Miller's *That Championship Season,* another instance of Pulitzer bankruptcy. See p. 228.

because I don't share his high opinion of at least half. My point just here is not to criticize his choices but to praise this impulse of his.

In the early 1970s an altering Papp began to emerge. This is of course inaccurate: people rarely change, they simply become more, or less, what their chromosomes and conditioning dictate as the circumstances of their lives nourish or deprive them. Hegel said that "the organic individual produces himself; it makes of itself what it is implicitly." Circumstances were certainly nourishing some qualities that had long been implicit in Papp. Now he seemed to succumb to the age-old and most dangerous seduction of success, the belief that it couldn't have happened to him if he hadn't deserved it. This is sometimes true; but it's the place in your mind, back or forefront, to which you assign the belief that determines your behavior. Papp now began to seem more and more as if he had judged himself and found himself not wanting. It was as if the servant of the people had begun to spell the operative word in that phrase with a capital S.

He thought of expanding. He formulated the idea of an American National Theater Service Agency, which would tour serious new plays around the country, possibly editing them wherever necessary to accommodate differing intellectual and moral attitudes. The agency would be supported by government and foundation subsidy; the Papp name was now so magical that the Rockefeller Foundation gave him $80,000 just to explore the idea.

This agency idea ran into sharp opposition that anyone else in the field could have foreseen. Papp, intoxicated with his purpose and his persona, declared that his aim was "to break into all that barrenness out there to restore theater to its rightful place as a creative, social force in this country." Never mind that the use of the romantic word "restore" was typical of theater pronouncements even by the otherwise hard-headed; there were some fifty professional resident theaters "out there," as well as dozens of experimental groups and numerous university theaters of at least admirable ambition, some of them with professionals on staff. Many of the directors "out there" did not exactly subscribe to Papp's term "barren," and they read Papp's thesis as deliberate myopia in order to push a plan that proved how much the country needed him. The imperial fit was on him, some of them thought. The scent of Eighteenth Brumaire was in the air; the republican general was en route to becoming First Consul. Reactions were sharp, and Papp's national scheme dissolved.

But possibly he lost interest in it anyway because another addition to the republican empire was in the offing. In March 1973 it was announced that Papp would take over the Vivian Beaumont and Forum Theaters at Lincoln Center in New York.

The history of those two theaters, upstairs and downstairs in the same building, had been brief but full of woe. The Lincoln Center Repertory Company, which in fact had never been a repertory company, had begun in 1964 in a different building while its present quarters were being completed. There and subsequently it had been under three managements: Elia Kazan and Robert Whitehead, who combined '30s directing theories with glitzy Broadway-culture; Herbert Blau and Jules Irving, who, at the other extreme, combined heavy intellectual atmosphere with professional amateurism; and then the solo management of Jules Irving, which was nerveless, improvisatory, devoid of distinction.

The original Lincoln Center aim had been to build a great permanent repertory theater in New York.* Maybe that is impossible. Resident theaters in other American cities, even such cosmopolitan cities as San Francisco and Washington, do not face the two constant pressures of such a theater in New York. First, the choices for New York audiences are much wider than anywhere else in America. Second, New York audiences are more demanding. This is certainly not to say, I add as wryly as I can, that New York has a theater public of epicures, but it does mean that New Yorkers are used to seeing the latest and newest of everything, that they have some standards in physical production, and that they have no gratitude at all for the mere fact that they can see a live theatrical presentation in their city.

To prosper, a "classic" New York resident theater ought to have two characteristics. First, it ought to have a level of production that is never lower than the best in the country. I don't mean the guest

* In 1958 Vivian Beaumont Allen donated $3 million to Lincoln Center for the specific purpose of constructing a theater "designed with primary emphasis on the needs of a company presenting repertory . . . that our country might one day have a national theater comparable in distinction and achievement to the Comédie Française."

appearances of expensive stars and directors. If it is going to bother to be a resident theater at all, it must retain for long periods of time an ensemble of quality under a purposeful, gifted directorate. But the economics of the American theater, the competition from the commercial theater and from films, makes such a condition difficult to maintain.

Second, since it ought to be the best theater in what has been the theater capital of the country for 150 years, it ought to be (as the established theaters of European capitals are) the place where the nation's great dramatic literature is kept alive and visible. But there is little great American drama. After you have pulled out two or three late O'Neill plays, one or two by Tennessee Williams, even strained yourself with an Arthur Miller, you are then stuck, in American fare, with a quasi-pop, somewhat "cute" series of revivals, some of them enjoyable but not exactly a *raison d'être* for a national rep. This is not as much of a handicap for other American resident theaters because they do not bear the "national" onus—except possibly in Washington—and because, still, any good theater production is some sort of manna in some sort of desert. But the resident theater of the nation's theatrical capital does not have, in American dramatic literature, the artistic, the *psychological* foundation that it needs. It can serve as a "living museum" of great European drama, a very important function, but still less than the whole ideal.* Even the National Theater of Reykjavík has in its repertory a large proportion of highly regarded Icelandic plays.

These two problems, one obvious and one subtle, cannot be solved by any manager of the Lincoln Center theaters; nevertheless, they face him, obviously and subtly, if he wants to establish a theater comparable with the famous ones of the world, which had been the original aim. Those problems, added to the various personal deficiencies of the different managers, had ground down the administrations before Papp. So grievously had the theater suffered in reputation that it was in terrible financial straits. Like the New York Philharmonic and the Metropolitan Opera, which are also at Lincoln Center, the theater runs at a loss; unlike the Philharmonic and the Met, the theater attracted relatively little in donations and subsidies because

---

* American symphony orchestras and opera houses thrive happily on mostly foreign repertoires, of course, but then no orchestras and few opera houses anywhere in the world devote themselves largely to domestic works.

no one had much faith in it or got much *réclame* from supporting it. That, quite clearly, was one of the reasons why Papp was chosen. He could attract money.

From that point of view he was unquestionably the best choice. He was hot. He was rising. He seemed, in the public's eye and in the eyes of most of the eager New York critical corps, to be incapable of doing much wrong. He was fast becoming a municipal hero. Little could have pleased Papp more than the *New Yorker* cartoon that appeared shortly after his Lincoln Center appointment. It showed the Manhattan skyline and, arching over it like a rainbow, the legend "A Joseph Papp Production." The cartoon was striking because it made one think that this was what Papp had had in mind all along, particularly since he didn't give up anything to take on Lincoln Center. He just added those two theaters to his string.

One of the first announcements that he made in relation to his new post was about money. In March 1973 he said, "Before we put one foot in the door, we must have in hand or in assurances $5 million." He set a deadline for May. (By May he had done astonishingly well. Mrs. Mitzi E. Newhouse had given him a million—the downstairs Forum was renamed in her honor—and there were healthy assurances and prospects from various foundations and government agencies.)

A second simultaneous announcement was radically more important. Papp exactly reversed previous Lincoln Center theater policy. The larger theater upstairs, the Beaumont, which had lamely been trying to become our leading "standard" theater, would be devoted to new plays responsive to our era and problems. The smaller theater below it, now the Newhouse, which had formerly been used for new plays, would present Shakespeare. Part of the reason for this change may have been that Papp sensed the impossibility of licking the twofold Beaumont artistic problem outlined above. Part certainly was that he had his lines out to new writers and he didn't want to subordinate work in which he had looked good. Certainly, too, part of the reason was that he wanted, on his arrival, to set off a bombshell. The new policy meant that Papp could strengthen his affinities with working writers, could avoid imitation-European booby-traps, and could run a Shakespeare Festival year-round. It was, as theory, ingenious. The policy spelled death, or at least deep discouragement, for any major attempt at a "living museum" of dramatic heritage in New

York, but it was congenial to Papp's temperament and it provided the new-broom impact that he wanted.

Prices at Lincoln Center had to be higher than at the Public Theater, where they are still low and where workshop productions are free. Summer Shakespeare in the park is, of course, still free. And it's possible for anyone under twenty-five or over sixty-five or a full-time student of any age to buy a pass that gets him into plays for $3 each at Lincoln Center. Regular subscription prices go as high as $10 per—not much by Broadway levels but, I'm sure, discomfiting to Papp.

He began his productions at Lincoln Center in the fall of 1973, as the master of six theaters in New York, as well as of various halls and mobile units. The official statement by his press representative said: "Since 1956, the Festival has presented 77 admission-free shows; since 1967 at the Public Theater complex, 59. The first year's budget was $750; the coming five-year projection is $35,848,000." In Papp's own words about himself, he is "in a commanding position to exert an influence on the course of American theater."

His first Lincoln Center production, therefore, was in the eye of the spotlight and the storm. The play was *Boom Boom Room* by David Rabe. Papp had previously produced three Rabe plays at the Public Theater, all of which, as it happens, I had disliked in varying degree. The first two, *The Basic Training of Pavlo Hummel* and *Sticks and Bones,* were "undergraduate" anti-war plays with gimmicks, although the second was occasionally somewhat better than that.* They were cheered and garlanded, and Papp made extravagant remarks about the young author. The third play, *The Orphan,* was a complicated anti-war allegory that to me simply revealed more nakedly the sophomoric mind that had been there all along; and this time the press demurred—though, naturally, Papp was unshaken. More as if to prove his point about Rabe than out of a continuum of faith, Papp chose this new Rabe play to launch the new Lincoln Center. After the premier there were published reports that Rabe himself thought the play was not ready for production—Rabe himself said he wasn't sure he had let the play "gestate" long enough—which lends credence to the belief that the production was more a willed act of personal vindication and suzerainty for Papp than of conviction about the readiness and worth of the play.

* See p. 224.

In the event *Boom Boom Room* turned out to be one more sopho-moric exercise, this time about the sexual victimization of a Philadel-phia go-go girl who ends up as a topless dancer in New York. Rabe had no more to say on the much-mooted matter of sexism than he had to say about Vietnam. Again he had thought of one melodra-matic central image—this time it was go-go girls hanging in cages above the stage throughout the play—and had filled in the interstices, which happened to be the play itself, with adolescent insights and cliché characters. Moreover, it was clumsily directed by Papp him-self, who had stepped in to save the show from the first director, an Off-Off-Broadway amateur named Julie Bovasso.

Much of the critical response was what Papp must have wanted, but among other reviews (including mine) the most influential notice, by Clive Barnes in *The New York Times,* was heavily adverse. When he learned of Barnes's review, Papp went into the most extreme spasm of outrage of his career. As my opening anecdote shows, he has always been eager to contend with critics; he has always felt free to counterattack. This is neither new with Papp nor unwelcome; why shouldn't the subject of criticism have the right to respond? But Papp's responses had usually had about them a sublimation of ego-injury in a glow of civic outrage. The implicit air had been that to attack his plays meant attacking his policy—theater for the people—and was thus a sort of civic treason. Now, on this particularly tender occasion, when people were watching to see (a) whether he had overextended himself and (b) whether he could beat the Beaumont jinx, the Barnes notice provoked responses in him, too trivial to detail here, that indicated a change in Papp—a metamorphosis from daunt-less guardian of public policy to towering egotist outraged by dissent. Suffice it to say that, as a result of the brouhaha, a few months later at another Papp opening there was a reported near-bout of fisticuffs between Papp and another critic, with Barnes figuring in it.

The revved-up aggression—again without long-distance psycho-analysis—is inescapably revealing. It kept revving up: soon after the Rabe opening Papp made a trip to Minneapolis and delivered a speech in which he berated the Guthrie Theater there for its lack of attention to new plays dealing with our lives. Then he came home and, for his next Beaumont production, did *The Au Pair Man,* a feeble allegory about the decline of the British Empire by an Irish writer, Hugh Leonard. This controversion of his own angry pronunciamento is, in its way, a confirmation of afflatus—putting himself above the requirements of his own stated policy, to which he wants to hold others.

As for the following three plays in Papp's first Beaumont season, each of them shows something significant about him. His next was *What the Wine-Sellers Buy* by Ron Milner, a black play by a black playwright, and it contained the first bit of deliberate whoring that I have seen in a Papp theater. The entire movement of that play, which was about ghetto life in Detroit, inexorably predicted a grim ending; in the last few minutes, either with Papp's permission or prescription, the author contrived a happy ending. This was another facet of a new Papp, with concern for a kind of success he had never wooed before. Presumably he was rationalizing on the Broadway and old-Hollywood line that ninety percent truth is better than none. He had never before rationalized or compromised in this way, to my knowledge.

Next came a revival of Strindberg's *Dance of Death,* played for laughs under A. J. Antoon's direction and wasteful of Robert Shaw's power in the role of the Captain. Aside from questions about the performance itself, Papp's third production, despite all the manifestos about new plays and after the excoriation of the Guthrie, was a revival. True, he had said in his proclamation in the Beaumont program: "In some instances a 'great' old play may take the slot of a 'good' new play, but I suspect that this will be the exception, not the rule." The exception had been scheduled pretty early, and again Papp controverted his own dicta with perfect coolness.

The season's last Beaumont production was *Short Eyes,* a new play by Miguel Piñero about a New York House of Detention. I thought that, well as it was directed by Marvin Felix Camillo, it lolled about in what a friend of mine called "the pornography of bad conditions." But what was most interesting about it in terms of Papp's career was the play's provenance. After the production was first done at the Riverside Church in New York, Papp had presented it on his main stage downtown at the Public Theater, where it had made a hit. So he had moved it uptown to Lincoln Center. Later it was reported that a play called *Black Picture Show* by Bill Gunn had been in rehearsal at the Beaumont and had needed to be postponed. To replace it, *Short Eyes* was moved uptown. But, whatever the reason for the move, that vacancy uptown disproved the oft-repeated boast of a superabundance of good new scripts waiting for production.

Further, the move of *Short Eyes* underscored the idea of hierarchy, of comparative rank between downtown and the Big Time. Before he had an uptown station, Papp moved some hit shows to Broadway from downtown or from Central Park so that they might pump money into his Off-Broadway operations. Now, established uptown, he gave grounds for the suspicion that the emphasis had been reversed. By this move of *Short Eyes* and by statements he made later, it seemed that he was beginning to think of his other theaters, either by design or by duress, as tryout stops for Lincoln Center. The reason stated was a policy of "positioning." Papp now had a range of size in his (indoor) theaters from a few hundred to about a thousand. The argument was that the most popular plays, potential or proved, went into the larger theaters. Naturally. But this just provides economic substantiation for a hierarchy with the Beaumont at the top.

His three Shakespeare productions at the Newhouse in 1973–4 were *Troilus and Cressida, The Tempest,* and *Macbeth.* The last of these was never officially opened: that is, it played for some weeks to subscribers and other ticket-buyers, but the press was never invited to review it. I saw some of *Macbeth* and thought it not notably worse than the first two; but the important point is that all three of these productions also showed something new in Papp. With the single exception of a *Hamlet* that Papp himself directed in 1967 in apparent imitation of the absurdist Shakespeare that Peter Brook and Charles Marowitz had done in London, his Shakespeare in the previous decade had been populist in intent. All three of these new productions were mannered and elitist, the work of directors whose ambitions were esthetically pitiful but sheerly esthetic. Again, an overall sense of "uptown" ambition.

Papp's concurrent season down at the Public Theater was skimpier than in previous years because, one can deduce, of his new uptown activities. The only success was *Short Eyes,* first produced elsewhere, which turned into a lifesaving stopgap for the Beaumont. Nevertheless my two most interesting experiences of the Papp year took place downtown.

During the winter of 1973 he presented a musical down there called *More Than You Deserve.* It wanted to be a kind of black humor inversion of *South Pacific* set in Vietnam and was only partially effective; but evidently it was sharp enough to irritate some patriotic folk, because during the performance I attended there was a bomb scare. The theater was cleared while the police investigated. Within minutes Papp appeared, summoned from home, tieless and disheveled. He consulted with the police, then mixed with the audience waiting outside, chatting and explaining. When we were permitted to return to the auditorium, Papp spoke briefly, explaining and apologizing and joking, in the role of Your Friendly Neighborhood Theater Manager, and the audience loved it. They knew him, he knew them, and they had all just been through a common experience. I felt I was seeing the best, purely societal side of the man. It was the quintessential Pappian hour, the fruit of twenty years' public service, and I'm glad I was there.

And also at the Public Theater I saw an unsatisfactory production that was, for me, the most rewarding Papp venture of the year, uptown or down: a dramatization of Norman Mailer's second novel, *Barbary Shore*. It was adapted and directed by Jack Gelber, who wrote *The Connection* and who has since directed frequently, but I had the feeling that it had been done unconventionally—that it had not begun with a neatly typed script which had then been memorized by actors, but that it was a work of exploration. I had the feeling that Gelber had asked Papp for a place and some funds in order to work on a theater version of the novel. Much of the result was valuable. Two of the actors were Estelle Parsons, who could have done the slatternly wife in her sleep but was very wide awake, and Rip Torn as the Irish radical. Torn's Irish accent was pathetic, but he increased my respect for him as a successful actor trying to grow, to extend his imagination, to make demands on himself that our theater generally neither encourages nor permits. (James Earl Jones, who has grown in good measure through Papp productions, is another example.) I had just been greatly impressed by Torn's performance as an egomaniacal country-music singer in a neglected film called *Payday,* and here again I was impressed by the range that Torn was claiming and in good measure justifying, with Gelber's help. I left feeling happy that there was a theater locus where such work could be done by people already well along in their professional lives.

Any comment on Papp is obviously an interim report. This is underscored by two announcements made while I have been writing this article (early summer 1974), all of them sharply pertinent to it. First, Papp announced that he had gone to Oslo to conclude deals with Liv

Ullmann and Ingmar Bergman. Ullmann will play at the Beaumont in the 1974–5 season in *A Doll's House*.* The following year Bergman will direct *Rosmersholm* there. Second, he announced that Al Pacino will play in a workshop production, downtown, of Brecht's *Resistible Rise of Arturo Ui*. "We will evaluate it and then groom it for the Vivian Beaumont," said Papp.†

The first item forecasts the trajectory of Papp's future. His latest subscription mailer has already told us that his exception-and-rule pronouncement about old and new plays has been discarded, that in the 1974–5 season three new plays and one revival will be presented. (This not only fixes the mixture, it reduces by one the total.) Patently Papp's resolute reliance on new works is modified; patently, too, he has seized the chance given by his new post to soar out into international wheeling and dealing. I'll be grateful for the chance to see Ullmann's and Bergman's theater work: that's not what is at issue. The point is the change in Papp, as against his past and his predictions, and what it means for his theater. The Ullmann-Bergman arrangement is a managerial coup, not an act of creative imagination.

The Pacino announcement is less startling as a coup because Pacino has already played at Lincoln Center (wretchedly, in a 1970 production of Williams's *Camino Real*) and, after his first *Godfather* success, played Shakespeare with a small company in Boston. But Papp's comment on the matter confirms the hierarchical feeling prompted by the *Short Eyes* switch. Some of his theaters are now no more important than others. His heart is in the highlands.

The summer Shakespeare Festival in Central Park was reduced to two plays in 1973 and remains at two in 1974. This may be attributable to budget difficulties, but budget difficulties do not explain the faint air of enforced attention, like that of a somewhat bored but faithful husband, which begins to hang over the event.

So. For the first part of our conclusion, some readings can be made on what Papp has done. First, quite apart from his institutionalizing of his theater and theaters, he has institutionalized himself. This is most perceptible in respect of his Shakespeare. By now he has pushed so muscularly through so many Shakespeare plays, some of them

---

* See p. 125.

† *Later note:* the Bergman production did not materialize and the Pacino production did not open.

more than once, a few of them more than twice, that a benign con-
spectus now prevails about his work, even among some of the few
who were critical of individual productions in the past. Mark Twain
said that some German words are so long that they have perspective;
Papp's Shakespearean record, as such, is now so long that it too is
taking on perspective. The mere length of that record is evoking a
rosy glow. Most of the productions, as I have seen them, have been
inadequate and some of them have been dreadful. But Papp has built
his very endurance into a species of critical stature, so that his new
Shakespeare productions, even when they are disliked, are seen as
steps in a grand saga.

To see Papp more clearly—in this one aspect of Shakespearean
institution—compare him with a predecessor. Something over a century ago in London an actor-manager named Samuel Phelps took
over a disreputable theater, the Sadler's Wells, in Islington, an outly-
ing lower-class district. "Legitimate" drama, which meant Shakespeare and the other classics, had become the figurative property of
the upper classes, who cared little about it, attended the major central
theaters very little, and were a poor audience when they came. Quali-
tatively, they were just the sort of audience Papp resents and de-
spises. Phelps made a bet on the clerks and workingmen of Islington,
and between 1844 and 1862 he produced thirty-one Shakespeare
plays (along with many others).* Many visitors to Sadler's Wells
commented on the warm feeling of community between stage and pit,
the audience's sense that this was *their* theater and the actors' sense
that they were working for *their* audience. This feeling of relation is
something that in itself Papp can claim, but there is a decisive difference between him and Phelps. During Phelps's management of
Sadler's Wells, that theater became famous throughout Britain and
Europe for its high and innovative quality of production. The German novelist Theodor Fontane visited Sadler's Wells six times between 1855 and 1857 and wrote about the productions for a German
journal. In the summer of 1859 Phelps took his company, with their
scenery, on a German tour. The enthusiastic critical reception, with
its emphasis on Sadler's Wells ensemble playing and production—a
revolutionary concept then—greatly influenced the Duke of Saxe-
Meiningen. The Duke's principal interest was his court theater, and

---

* See *Samuel Phelps and Sadler's Wells Theatre* by Shirley S. Allen (Wesleyan University Press, 1971).

work from 1874 to 1890; but Sadler's Wells greatly influenced the very idea of "directed" productions as we know them today, in their work from 1874 to 1890; but Sadler's Wells greatly influenced the Duke. Thus, besides the community value of Phelps's theater, it had high artistic stature, which in turn had lasting influence. For all Papp's twenty years of Shakespeare, no remotely comparable claim could be made for his work. He has mixed his casts and given newcomers opportunities, but the level of work has been low and the identifiable artistic tone, as against social utility, has been non-existent. There have simply been a lot of productions.*

Apart from his status as institution, Papp has also made a mark as a kind of theater savior-cum-apostle. In this regard, compare him with Jerzy Grotowski, the leader of the Polish Laboratory Theater. I don't for a split second equate the two men as intellectuals or artists; still there is a relation between them. Grotowski has said explicitly that the prime purpose of his work is to find reasons for the theater to continue to exist, to find its irreducible and irreplaceable essence. Papp, in his way, has been engaged in a twenty-year campaign to make the theater "important," available, necessary. Grotowski's way has been through art, profound and seminal. Papp's way has been through sheer activity and through hospitality—to theater workers and an altering audience. In religious analogy, it's the difference between St. John of the Cross and Billy Graham.

Admittedly it's arbitrary of me to compare Papp with Phelps and Grotowski, but is there an apt comparison that would do better for him? None that I can think of. And, quite precisely, that leads to the crux of the matter.

If we disregard the big commercial managements as irrelevant to our discussion, then Papp is the only person who has made a considerable mark in the theater—in any American or European theater that I have seen or read about—without extraordinary talent, without exemplary taste, without an esthetic imperative, without intellectual distinction. If I run through all the names that come to mind—Barker and Copeau and Reinhardt, Baylis and Strehler and Lady Gregory, the directorates of the Provincetown Players and the first Washington Square Players, of the Edwardian and latter-day Royal Court—a

---

* And they have been free. But even that is not an innovation. In the 1930s I used to see Shakespearean and other plays at the Free Theater run by Butler Davenport in a converted brownstone on East 27th Street.

random list, very extensible—I can find no one who has had as great an effect on the theater of his time as Papp for whose talent and taste I have so little respect.

Perhaps it is this very attribute, this consummate *lack* of attributes, that makes him a man for our season. I mean this not cynically but clinically. Papp began from a base of radical political convictions and moved into a time when such convictions became less germane to the country and to him but which left him with undiminished social concerns. In this new de-politicized society, with his social dynamics, with an inheritance of veneration for culture and especially for people's culture, he found a happy conjuncture. He met the accelerated growth of an esthetic view founded on (in the traditional sense, anyway) anti-esthetics, the arrival of pop art, of junk art, of pop '60s non-political political revolution, a general turbulence not only anti-intellectual in tenor but revisionist of the belief that art requires cultivation in both the maker and the appreciator, a new view holding that extraordinary talent and extraordinary discrimination are divisive, inhibiting, and exclusive. (I heard the word "fascist" used at public meetings in the '60s against those who believe that art depends on talent and taste.) In short, it was the perfect atmosphere for a man whose past had given him communal and cultural hungers, whose ego gave him tremendous itches, but whose composition provided minimal artistic gifts. His personality and makeup have fitted the times so well that he has become a figure of major stature in an art without one single achievement of major stature in that art.

From all this it could be argued that Papp was destined for Lincoln Center. That Center, as Robert Brustein once remarked, is the sort of thing that America produces instead of culture. Papp is what the American theater has produced, in the same period, instead of a great creator. What Lincoln Center theater needs, at almost any figurative price, is success; and that is what Papp has had the most of, in the theater.

Still, it's undeniable that he has made the theater throb and bustle. And he has opened doors for young people. Ironically, it may turn out that the best contribution of his ego was in helping others to contribute. In any event, it's better, heaven knows, to have a Papp dominant than a Merrick, or better than having unruffled blandness.

To balance our gratitude we can remember a fact of history. In the theater's worst moments, the audience rules; in its best moments, the audience still rules but good artists induce it to rule differently. The great theater people have extended the theater's power to affect the audience's imaginative resource. Papp, at his best, confuses imagination with information; at his best and his worst, he aims straight for the center of the audience's resource as it now is, and hugs it.

POSTSCRIPT, June 1975. Papp's second season at the Beaumont, 1974–5, was disastrous except for the revival of *A Doll's House,* and that was notable only for Liv Ullmann's performance, a jewel in a tin setting. The Beaumont season also included three new American plays, Burr's *Mert and Phil,* Gunn's *Black Picture Show* (whose postponement had brought *Short Eyes* uptown in the previous season), and Scully's *Little Black Sheep.* These works demonstrated Papp's continuing appetite for plays with striking social themes and his continuing myopia to the quality with which they are written.

His Newhouse season began with a production of *Richard III* starring Michael Moriarty, directed by Mel Shapiro, which showed that good actor paralyzed within a sterile concept. This was followed by a flashy but dull production of *A Midsummer Night's Dream.* The next scheduled production, *Julius Caesar,* was canceled. The Newhouse season was filled out by bringing in a non-Shakespeare production from another theater, *The Taking of Miss Janie.**

The whole Lincoln Center season concluded with another statement of policy change. In March 1975 Papp clarified the trajectory in his career that had been discernible earlier. Blaming the Beaumont audiences for their discomfort with his daring productions, omitting to mention that their discomfort might have been at least partly because those plays and productions were poor, he renounced his new-play policy for that theater. The Beaumont season of 1975–6 would consist of traditional plays with international stars, like Liv Ullmann, and "traditionally styled" contemporary plays with established American directors and actors. The new Newhouse policy was not clear, except that it would no longer include Shakespeare and might concentrate on lesser-known classics with small casts.

Papp's 1974–5 season downtown at the various halls of the Public

* See p. 251.

Theater had seemed makeshift. Many of the productions had been by outside organizations to which he had merely given space. His own productions were mainly experimental workshops. Most of these, as I saw them, ranged from the unremarkable to the unspeakable. One such production, which was worked on for many months, turned out to be both good and phenomenally successful, *A Chorus Line*.* Papp's relation to this production, however, was apparently that of host and enthusiast—helpful functions but hardly those of a producer in anything but the nominal sense. (This show moved to Broadway and proved a money-spinner for the Festival.)

The "uptown" shift of Papp's interests was further underscored when he announced in May 1975 that he was taking over the Booth Theater on Broadway for a season of new American plays—by writers whose work he had done previously. He saw this season as his alternative to the traditional policy he had already announced for the Beaumont, and he justified the locus by saying, "There's more receptivity on Broadway than at the Public Theater and at Lincoln Center." This was the first time he had included the downtown complex in his indictment of stodginess. He said further about Broadway: "It's a marketplace. I believe in the marketplace." That too was a new facet of Papp pronunciamento, or at least a new admission.†

My point is not to harry Papp for inconsistency or change. Doubtless there will be other policy shifts by the time this sees print, depending on success or failure, not principle. Nor do I disregard the budget problems that he, like everyone else, is facing. (One argument he makes on this score is irrefutable: the costs of Off-Broadway production have zoomed past reasonable expectation of return in houses limited—by city-licensing and union regulations—to 299 seats.) My point is to indicate that the man who once bustled because of populist interest is now more interested in the bustle than the populism. He now rides on the back of the tiger and not only loves it, he claims to be controlling it.

Even this might be a mere academic discrimination on my part were it not for the paramount consideration. The vast majority of his productions were and are quite poor. An exception like *A Chorus Line* is inevitable, but what an average.

* See p. 266.
† *Later note:* the Booth season lasted for one short-lived production, Dennis J. Reardon's wretched *Leaf People*.

When the preceding article was published in *The American Scholar*, a loyal member of Papp's staff wrote a protesting letter to the journal which concluded by calling Papp a "brilliant producer." Surely a brilliant producer is one who does brilliant productions, not one who merely does a large number of productions. I greatly respect Papp's courage and enthusiasm and good will; but I think it cruelly typical of American culture that the mere bulk and busyness of his career have raised him to an artistic status for which he has neither the artistic qualifications nor the artistic accomplishments.

The Open Theater

(Channel 13, New York, November 18, 1966)

Two recent Off-Broadway presentations form one extraordinary theatrical event. The first is *America Hurrah* at the Pocket Theater, the other is *Viet Rock* at the Martinique. They are offered as separate productions by different producers. This is nonsense. There *are* different producers, nominally, but both plays are the work of the same group—the Open Theater. Both plays were written by members of the Open Theater for that company, and after varying metamorphoses have now reached Off Broadway as separate productions. In reality, they are both manifestations of the work of one group.

The Open Theater was founded in 1963 by an actor-director named Joseph Chaikin, not as a place of performance but as a workshop. He founded it, he says, because he wanted to teach a more eclectic technique than anyone had taught him. He didn't want to be bound by Stanislavsky or his American revisionists, he didn't want to be bound by the Actors Studio, he didn't want to be bound by anything. He wanted to draw strength from all of them, and particularly from the Living Theater of Judith Malina and Julian Beck. He wasn't interested in a theater of behavioristic psychology. He wanted to draw from all the most sophisticated disciplines and use them to reach elementals.

His group has performed often at various Off-Off-Broadway theaters—the Café La Mama, the Judson Church, and elsewhere. They have always been interesting; now, at the Pocket and the Martinique, they seem to me more than that.

The authors of these two plays, Jean-Claude van Itallie and Megan Terry, have been members of the Open Theater since its beginning; have been writing for and with the group, adapting, improvising, being improvised upon. Their plays have been criticized in New York in the conventional manner: as two scripts that were produced with different casts at different theaters. Again this is superficially true but fundamental nonsense. Their scripts are by now as inseparable from the entity of the Open Theater as the hydrogen from the oxygen in water. One has only to read the script of *Viet Rock* to see this.

America Hurrah has been generally praised, *Viet Rock* generally dispraised. I think both the praise and dispraise are misconceived.

America Hurrah by van Itallie consists of three one-act plays: *Interview, TV,* and *Motel.* In the first two, a group of eight actors moves through a constantly flowing series of imaginary scenes, choric movements, choric pronouncements, skits, and vignettes that deal with such aspects of American life as the impersonal job interview, the hurrying horror of crowded city streets, psychiatric jargon, the Niagara of television twaddle. These banalities, as objects of parody, are themselves banal; and van Itallie has little more to say about them, *as author,* than, for instance, *The Mad Show** has said. But the Open Theater—as a performing ensemble of vitality, unity, and freedom, under Chaikin and his co-director, Jacques Levy—has a great deal to say about these subjects that *The Mad Show* could not approach. Van Itallie has simply provided them with subjects and lines, adequate enough. The third short play, *Motel,* is really a black blackout sketch. In a grotesque motel we see a female motel-keeper, about the size of a figure in Macy's Christmas parade, who moves about while a recorded woman's voice drones on about the services and virtues of her motel. A man and a woman, equally outsize, come in and strip to their papier-mâché bodies; then, while this dull woman's voice drones on and on, the man and woman scrawl obscenities all over the walls, break up the furniture, and demolish the hostess as the record keeps babbling advertising vacuities.

That whole production was generally hailed as inventive and ad-

---

* A satirical revue of the previous season.

venturous. *Viet Rock* by Megan Terry was generally considered a disappointment. It had been anticipated as an anti-war play—anti the Vietnam war, of course—and, as such, was called unoriginal, obvious, insufficiently partisan. Some thought it failed to strike decisively against U.S. militarism. These criticisms seem to me entirely true and entirely irrelevant.

Viet Rock is not propaganda against the Vietnamese war. It is a free fantasia on the theme of war: a fantasia using the bodies and voices and the concerted and individual energies of thirteen performers in a montage of scenes—usually incomplete, flowing ahead or back or around or contrapuntally—using materials drawn from the draft, the training, the killing, the pacifist resistance, and it includes Hanoi's activities as well (although I should have liked to see more of the last). Its methods are identically the methods of *America Hurrah:* only its themes are different.

Certainly it will disappoint those who, like me, object to the Vietnam war and who are looking for a single-minded blow against that war. But that is not its intent. It is a rhapsodic and imaginative theatrical exercise on the idea of *all* war—using performers and words and music as an abstract painter or film-maker might use lights and sounds and objects.

As a demonstration of the horror of war, it is juvenile. But who needs to go to a play in 1966 to learn that war is horrible? As intellectual argument on the rights and wrongs of Vietnam, it is entirely negligible. But Terry and the Open Theater have discarded any propaganda or polemic purpose to make a strong, free-moving theatrical composition on the persistent verities of war—using the Vietnam war as a basis.

Not all of the evening is equally good. The songs are dull; some of the satire is heavy; some of the emotional moments are gross; but the kaleidoscopic effect—the sensation of a whole theater whirling around a theme—creates the texture of a poem on war, not all of it successful but all of it poetic. Again this is not the performance of a script by actors in the usual sense. It is a theatrically composed work, *founded* on a script, using every imaginative and physical resource of the actors, who have often contributed material through improvisation. The director is the author herself.

The limitations of the techniques of the Open Theater seem already apparent. It is surely a very different kind of theater from the traditional literary one and will inevitably be constricted by this fact. But it is surely vital, in a theatrical world that is generally stale. To see *America Hurrah* and *Viet Rock* on successive nights, as I did, is not to see two plays by two playwrights but two demonstrations of one dynamic theatrical idea.

POSTSCRIPT. With no pleasure to me or to anyone else, my prediction came true. The Open Theater reached the limits of non-literary theater, as all such theaters seem to do by whatever avenue they travel: thrashed about at those limits for a time, then declined into dissolution. Its high point for me was its beautiful production in 1968 of *The Serpent,* with a text by Jean-Claude van Itallie based on Genesis. As the decade ended, the Open Theater became more and more introverted and began to elevate certain kinds of theater "games" and attenuated exercises into productions. The theory took the place of the work. In 1973 the Open Theater was dissolved. But its career, particularly the influence of its director, Joseph Chaikin, left many young theater people invigorated.

Chaikin continues his own career elsewhere.

The American Conservatory Theater

(November 1, 1969)

The American Conservatory Theater of San Francisco, which is run by William Ball, has played a season of three plays in New York, opening a long season of visits by resident theaters arranged by the American National Theater and Academy. The ACT began with *Tiny Alice.* I'm not going to re-review Albee's script. Five years ago it seemed to me a piece of arrogant, pseudo-literary pretentiousness, flung in our faces with the usual blather of a desperate author that those who don't appreciate it are either stupid or malevolent. Five years later it seems worse.

According to published reports, Albee insisted that Ball modify his production for this New York visit. I don't know what was changed, but what remains is a thundering vote of no confidence in the play by the director. Ball has loaded and larded the play with devices, physical and mechanical, to plead for our attention: grotesque "business" (in the first scene the lawyer blows smoke in the cardinal's face), grotesque action (one character leans forward accusingly while the other leans back), grotesque organ stabs out of the dark before each scene to assure us that the subject is God. In the lengthy death speech at the end, one of the most gratuitous jobs any playwright ever assigned an actor, Julian rushes up some stairs, gets hit in the face with a loud bit of the *"Tuba mirum"* from Verdi's *Requiem,* then falls backward in the flashiest circus act since Kenneth Haigh dived off a tower for Sidney Lumet in the latter's production of *Caligula* (1960). At the start Paul Shenar, the Julian, has some appropriate lyric eagerness, but consistency is impossible in a part that is an author's conceit. DeAnn Mears, the Alice, plays competently but is so sexless that I thought Ball's "new interpretation" might be that Alice finally whisks off her wig and gown and reveals herself as a transvestite.

Georges Feydeau's farce *A Flea in Her Ear,* written in 1907 and recently butchered on film, was staged by Gower Champion, a guest director. This has been called a "great comic play." It isn't; it's a marvelously designed laugh-machine that can be made to hum by a good production. We are told that Champion's black-and-white production, his strobe-light act-openings, and Keystone Kop makeups were wrong because we can laugh only at real people. Well, so much for the Keystone Kops—not to mention the commedia dell'arte and three or four centuries of its descendants. Was Bobby Clark or Bert Lahr "real"? I would love to have seen either of them in this double leading role. (Mistaken identity is the chief plot gimmick: a rich insurance broker and a drunken porter in a shady hotel are lookalikes.) Champion now understands the staging of farce—something he was still fumbling when he did *Three Bags Full* on Broadway three years ago. He knows that one essence of this kind of farce is motion, even in the moments of seeming quiet. Quiet makes for verticality; farce exists horizontally. And Champion, choreographer that he is, has spun an unbroken web of interlocking large and small movements for this play. But all he could do was drill the cast in the movements, he could not supply the requisite comic talent. For another essential of farce is that the performers themselves have to *be* funny; there is no time or chance or reason to create comic characters. Neither Clark nor Lahr was an actor; *they* were funny. (The last good farceur I saw on Broadway—Ian Carmichael in *Boeing Boeing* a few years ago—made me smile when he opened the door and came in.) No one in the ACT company is himself funny except Michael O'Sullivan, who does his familiar hysterical scarecrow act, this time as the cleft-palate cousin, and is the only performer who manages to get some laughs. The others are merely obedient to Champion's ballet.

The Three Sisters, directed by Ball, has a few good moments. This beloved play, which grows more important every year, is easy to make "look" good, like all of Chekhov. The moody lighting, the snow, the Victorian clutter, the picturesque groupings, all these are accessible even to a modest directing talent. Ball seizes his opportunities. It seems a bit odd that the Prozorovs have a stage batten dangling across their living room with clusters of spotlights on it, just past fingertip reach; still, with the help of Paul Staheli's settings, Ball makes some nice pictures. But not much more. Where were the actors? What is the point of producing this masterwork merely to make pretty Russianoid tableaux? Can the grossly inadequate performance of a great play be justified on the ground that it is part of a repertory effort by a permanent company?

Paul Shenar, the Tusenbach, is quite affecting in the early acts, but his last act is somewhat coarse. Kitty Winn, the Irina, is bearable. Angela Paton, the Olga, might be bearable except for her flat Midwestern accent. (Ball's ear is not his best asset.) Masha and Vershinin, without whom there cannot be a play, are performed by two seeming undergraduates, (Miss) Michael Learned and Ken Ruta, and the rest of the cast seem stale old-stagers, no matter what their ages.

One possible audience benefit of repertory was lost in the ACT season—the chance to see actors in several parts. Only Philip Kerr and Harry Frazier were in all three plays. The former was negligible, and the latter proved only that there is always work for spherical actors.

Much of the reaction to the ACT visit has been disappointment. I don't share it. Partly this is because on visits to San Francisco in the last two years I have seen two of their productions: a muscular, crude *Hamlet,* directed by Ball, with Paul Shenar, and a somewhat better but rather farcical *Man and Superman,* directed by Jerome Kilty, with René Auberjonois as Tanner. (Auberjonois, the ACT's best actor, has left the company.) But Ball's excesses and defects were visible, to some, in his New York productions before he founded the ACT. In 1963 his production of *Six Characters in Search of an Author* had characters running around the back of the auditorium and other excrescences. In 1965 his production of *Tartuffe* (with the Lincoln Center company) began with a barbarous distortion—Tartuffe on stage at the start, despite the fact that Molière (poor boob) designed his work so that Tartuffe is talked about for half the play before we set eyes on him. And then Ball proceeded to have Michael O'Sullivan, in the title role, walk on his ankles and flap about like Milton Berle on a bad day. Here clearly was a director who looked on the text as opportunity for display—and not even in the Tom O'Horgan sense. At least one can rationalize that O'Horgan has a theory of theater he is trying to advance. Ball, an essentially traditional director, simply twists tradition to suit his egocentricities.

Well, hope limps eternal. The ACT is a quite mediocre company at best, but it has aroused devotion in many of its members, and their continual training is part of its purpose. Hence the word "conservatory" in the name. Ball has serious ambition, the evident gift of leadership (not irrelevant in the director of a permanent ensemble), and some vivid theatrical imagination. Perhaps the company will expand in its powers and he will stop sprawling in his. But, with all good wishes to them, I think their worst luck has been the high praise that some people have given them.

(December 15, 1973)

The American Conservatory Theater, one of the leading resident theaters in the U.S., is presenting a new production of *The Taming of the Shrew* directed by the head of the theater, William Ball, at the Geary in San Francisco. The outstanding success is the physical production. The single set by Ralph Funicello—well lighted by F. Mitchell Dana—has a sharply raked stage with a scaffolding above it which gives the effect of an improvised theater in a public square, with space at both sides for "townsfolk" to watch the play. The costumes by Robert Fletcher are exquisite. Almost all are in the same shade of buff, which changes in the varying lights. Distinctions between characters are made in the cut and in the way that touches of red are used—in belts or buttons or slashes or leggings. Although I can't quite understand why the "actors" and the "townsfolk" watching them are dressed in the same color (and although I felt sorry for those poor extras who had to sit motionless at the sides for hours), the effect is ingenious and lovely.

For all the rest, one overriding reservation. If a director doesn't really want to do *The Shrew,* this is a pretty good way to not do it. Ball has opted for the fast and physical, with the text as a trampoline for antics. Some of the minor characters are handled as commedia dell'arte types, others are treated more or less as Shakespeare's characters; all are rammed into a brisk wrestling match in which the text goes down under Ball's cleverness. I doubt that *The Shrew* is anyone's favorite Shakespeare, and physical farce is surely part of its process; still it *was* written, and written pretty well, and even its best scenes, like the first meeting of Katherine and Petruchio, are handled here solely as opportunities for leaping, catching, swinging around poles—quasi-judo and quasi-Tarzan displays in which the audience is meant to gasp at the acrobatic precision and the risk of injury more than anything else. (The two leads, Marc Singer and Fredi Olster, come off breathless but unbruised.) The result of all this is that when the show reaches the one uncircumventable moment of *text*—Katherine's last speech of contrition—it seems to come from a different play. It sticks out so egregiously, without psychological preparation, that, after its knowingly humble finish, the only way that Ball can "save" the moment is to have Katherine look at the audience over Petruchio's shoulder and give us a broad wink. Bankruptcy.

It's long been clear that Ball treats plays in an appropriative, self-displaying manner, although in some productions the process has been more subtle than here. He is not a commonplace director, but he is a thaumaturge of the second-rate.

Ontological-Hysteric Theater

(January 27, 1973)

Early last year I began to hear about an experimental group called the Ontological-Hysteric Theater, headed by Richard Foreman, and a few months ago I went to a production of his with some expectation.

He conceived, staged, and designed *Dr. Selavy's Magic Theatre,* at the Mercer-O'Casey, which is a musical entertainment with songs by Stanley Silverman and Tom Hendry. (Selavy is Marcel Duchamp's old pun on *c'est la vie.*) Some of the songs are good and, for a change, some of the singers in an Off-Broadway show actually can sing. But where was the ontological hysteria? There were some heavy comments in the program, reminiscent of Arthur Miller, and there was some heavy religious parody on stage, but the (presumable) idea of a patient entering an asylum and being cured by a theatrical experience, with music, was utterly absent. I saw a pretty good parodic revue, with some nice anti-theatrical theater: things fell down at odd moments; when the actors went out, they didn't disappear, they just stood at the sides waiting to return; a little girl wandered through occasionally, chewing gum; and so on. Bright undergraduate nonchalance, but not much more.

Then I went to see Foreman's own group, not a group he had assembled for a show, the Ontological-Hysteric Theater in their own place (the Cinematheque). I saw that Foreman had commercialized his ideas for *Selavy* and that here was the thing itself. Now, although I don't know what his group's name means (anyone can conjecture about it, even without seeing them, but I still don't *know*), they have a good deal of my interest and respect.

The title of the piece I saw is no less pretentious than the group's name: *Sophia = (Wisdom) Part 3: The Cliffs.* If Parts 1 and 2 were ever performed, the fact that I missed them didn't seem relevant. It's not a play, it's a theater piece, worked out by the director and the company—of six principals and six others. The setting, designed by Foreman, has a black curtain at the back of the floor (it's not an elevated stage), on top of which are some doll houses each with one side missing. Actors sometimes stick their heads up into those houses, as if their heads alone lived on top of a black cliff. I had no clue as to the meaning of this. It also came as a shock, toward the end of the long evening, to learn that Sophia was Saint Sophia and that some mystic significance was said to be lurking under all that had happened. This had quite escaped me, like the pertinence of the *Selavy* program notes.

What held me for much of the two and a half hours, including intermission, was the feeling of highly intelligent play—in the sense of playfulness. The action falls into phrases, and the phrases are built around a simple arrangement of furniture or a door that is brought in or a large piece of cloth, for instances. The first instinct, each time a phrase starts, is to look for "meaning" or payoff, in the punch-line sense; then it dawns that they are simply imagining things to do with these objects and each other, as a child might, but a very logical and sophisticated child.

Sometimes there are passages of dialogue on a tape recorder, previously recorded by the people we see before us, who now mumble a few of the words from time to time, belatedly, as if they were being reminded of their words. One of the women in the group is naked most of the time, but there is nothing overtly sexual in the evening (she rolls about a few times with a clothed man, but there is no sexual miming). The fact that she is naked and that nothing sexual happens contributes to the underlying mode of the evening: wit. (This is supported by some legends that are flashed on screens by projectors.) Foreman says, in effect, that he knows we expect some sex play because of her nakedness, even knows we suspect him of exploitation, and he does absolutely nothing in that direction. The nakedness certainly helped to keep me watching intently, but that soon became a valid theater device on Foreman's part, because of his attitude. By and by, it was as if a woman had turned up naked at a dinner party and behaved exactly like all the clothed people. It was not unnoticeable, but was predominantly funny.

The effect—of her actions and the whole evening—immediately suggests surrealism, but it doesn't work out that way. The point of surrealism is, through non-sequential arrangements of objective reality, to reach flashes of the "marvelous." No such aim here, that I can see. The O-H Theater seems interested only in exploring objective reality, the sensory and sensual. Simply by the intensity with which they all play, by the sequence of the actions within a phrase or by their counterpoint, they seem determined to refresh our basic powers of observation and response; and they (often) give delight just by doing what they do. Foreman seems essentially concerned to discover what simple, overlooked things one group of people can do in front of another in order to hold interest and tickle imagination.

What is it all for? One thing it is not for is the training of performers. These people, as far as I can see, are just "civilians" who have put themselves at Foreman's disposal with devotion; they are not technically equipped in any discernible way. This, too, is an interesting anti-conventional move, anti even the usual anti-conventional ensembles like the Performance Group. This amateurism has pluses and minuses: it keeps the work from being a solipsist theater-game; yet it circumscribes the whole project, in my view. It becomes an area of experimental probe by which other companies can be stimulated. Still, if that turns out to be all, it is certainly far from nothing.

Foreman and company will be off after January to work on a new theater piece. (They are supported by state and federal subsidy.) But they will be back. And the viewer who can overcome his mistrust of arty experiment—oh, so well founded—might just take himself down to their theater when they return, put himself in front of them, and get some amusing, refreshing exercise of his responses.

(February 8, 1975)

Two years ago Richard Foreman had two shows running Off Off Broadway, a musical and a "pure" production of his Ontological-Hysteric Theater. Now he has done this double play again.

The musical, *Hotel for Criminals,* has an attractive score by Stanley Silverman (who also did the score for Foreman's last musical), with sympathy for the period of the piece and with smart orchestration of eight acutely chosen instruments. (A tuba, for instance.) Foreman's book is a whimsical mélange of elements from the celebrated French films of 1913–14 by Louis Feuillade dealing with the adventures of the master criminal Fantomas. Using elements of his Ontological-Hysteric techniques, Foreman has arranged (the key verb in describing his direction) a series of scenes and tableaux that are always immediately striking and sometimes interesting for more than the first glimpse. There is a wispy semblance of story. The costumes by Whitney Blausen are mostly black and white and gray to suggest old films. The whole effect of the show is of an "in" joke by cultivated people, kept going by good music and good taste but ultimately flat.

Pandering to the Masses: A Misrepresentation (a typically reticent Foreman title) is another in his series of explorations in O-H theater, done without any of the concessions to convention in *Hotel.* The music here is all recorded (as in previous O-H productions). So is most of the dialogue; the actors from time to time mumble along after it. The setting is long and steeply raked, with a doll's house at the end. And once more (as with *Hotel*) a few zebra-striped strings criss-cross the front of the stage. Foreman sits before the audience running a couple of tape recorders, ending sequences with a loud buzzer and/or a shout of "Cue!" Once more there are quasi surrealist, even dadaist compositions using actors and a lot of sliding scenery and a great many props. Once more there's a lot of nudity, most of it female.

The audience gets a long explanatory Foreman essay in the program, which tells us that the play is in a prologue and nine acts and that, in gist, the hero, a writer, learns to cast off "the habit of thinking we think in logical, linear, monophonic ways." Presumably Foreman needs to believe he is accomplishing this thematic end in order to create his pictures. Fine. For myself, I only experienced a series of effects, visual and aural, many of which were ingenious and amusing, none of which was moving or mind-blowing, and the total of which was much too long—an uninterrupted 105 minutes.

Unquestionably Foreman has made a contribution to theater possibilities with his O-H work, but I still feel that this work is much more stimulus than accomplishment. He has shown other theater artists how things can be done that they may not have imagined and has provided materials for use elsewhere—indeed, he himself has used them elsewhere in his musicals with Silverman. But on the basis of four O-H productions, I would say that he has now reached the limit of his contributions in this vein. His work and my experience of it keep reminding me of Donald Barthelme's fiction and collages—intelligent, tart, unconventional, and rather quickly finite. Foreman has had some new ideas; now, like most innovators in art, he soon shows the need of newer ones.

The Performance Group

(March 24, 1973)

Sam Shepard is, to put it somewhat inaccurately, the Tennessee Williams of today. He is the most talented of his generation, he relies heavily on language to make his drama, he has a vivid theatrical sense, his subjects tend to be non-urban, he strikes toward elemental passion, and he sometimes makes you impatient with his fooling around. He got extravagant praise for his best play so far, *La Turista,* he wrote (or wrote on) the poor script for Antonioni's *Zabriskie Point,* he has torn off strips of fitfully effective rhetoric about aspects of our apocalypse, but (unlike Williams) he has not yet worked hard enough to produce one fully realized play.

Shepard's latest is *The Tooth of Crime,* and it's just one distended metaphor. A big pop-music star feels he is getting old and slipping (although of course he's young by any standard other than the pop world's). A younger singer comes along and displaces him. This changeover is put in an old gangster-film framework: the hood in his lush hangout with his henchpeople, the challenger who is taken on as favorite disciple and finally kills the boss. The language—so far as I, in my ignorance, know—is that of the pop world, but the shapes and currents of action are pure *Little Caesar.* The final "shootout" is a verbal duel, in which each of the two contenders take turns at extended rhetorical arias. The young man beats the star, who then puts a pistol in his mouth.

The theme clearly is that the blind but powerful forces of our age have hyped everybody up, have turned entertainers into ravenous beasts because they sense the ravening bestiality of the fickle public, and that the inhabitants of the pop-music world have become, in their desperation and grab, a species of archetypal criminals without crime. (Something like the theme of Rip Torn's film *Payday.*)

This is the material for a good short play—half-hour, perhaps forty minutes. In this production it runs two and three-quarter hours, including intermission. Partly this is Shepard's self-indulgence. Partly it's the doing of the director, Richard Schechner, and his company, the Performance Group.

Schechner's Group, which in recent years has toured a good deal through this country and abroad, plays in New York at a place called the Performing Garage—a big bare floor, differently used for different productions, with a narrow gallery running around all four walls. For this play there is a tall free-standing constructivist set occupying most of the floor space, designed by Jerry Rojo, who is called the environmentalist, not the scene designer. The audience is invited to sit or stand where it will and is warned in advance that it will have to follow the action around, either on the floor with the actors or on the gallery, as the play moves around the bays and towers.

Schechner's work, as I have seen it, is absolutely devoid of any recognition of the concept of talent, any need for it. He conceives ideas, then applies them; that's all. That these are often dry critical exercises—possible to any theoretician, talented or not—never seems to matter to him. His cast reflects this. They too have no talent; they are simply willing and committed, inflated with a kind of confidence in the venture. In Foreman's Ontological-Hysteric Theater, the absence of competent actors doesn't matter; no characters or passions are involved. In Schechner's Group, the attempts at theatrical effect are simply pathetic. Still, without any talent or even personality, with enormous pauses as the actors move around the set and wait for the ambulatory audience to catch up with them, with Schechner's huge barrage of trite "experimental" effects and underscorings, some of Shepard's stinging vulgar ecstasy sears through from time to time.

For me the center of attention shifted from the play to the audience. The most consistently interesting aspect of the evening for me was the willingness, the eagerness, with which the (predominantly young) audience accepted its assignment of following the actors and forming circles around them during every scene. At least it provided dramatic action of a sort, delegated though it was from the production to the audience.

Robert Wilson

(January 5 and 12, 1974)

For the last three years I've been hearing and reading about Robert Wilson and his extraordinary theater productions, which have been seen fitfully in New York, Paris, Iran, and elsewhere. *Deafman Glance,* done in Brooklyn two years ago, ran three hours. Another production, with a complicated title, was done on a mountain in Iran and ran 168 (*sic*) hours. Wilson's latest production, in Brooklyn, is called *The Life and Times of Joseph Stalin* and was announced to run from 7:00 P.M. to 7:00 A.M. I don't usually review productions I haven't seen completely—I'm told that *Stalin* actually ran until 9:00 A.M. and that 100 people sat through it all—but I would like to comment on the two and a half hours that I saw.

When one enters the old opera house, one sees Queen Victoria standing motionless at stage left. The forestage, right and left, is covered with sand on which various objects are strewn and through which some people's heads poke motionless. High over the audience a wire is strung with some large metal hoops on it. Victoria is immobile while the audience seats itself and waits; then, as the lights dim, she begins a series of Gertrude-Steinian utterances. The curtain rises on a stage covered with sand and backed by a blue sky-drop. A large photo of (I think) the young Stalin hangs from the flies but is soon hoisted up. A woman is reading something incomprehensible offstage, and continues throughout. Victoria disappears, two other regally dressed characters appear, then take seats in an audience box. A red-clad runner jogs back and forth across the stage from time to time. Two young women and a man, all stripped to the waist, do a series of dance attitudes. (The pace of these actions, and of almost everything, is very, very slow.) A black youth (male? female?) in Victorian woman's dress is seated, holding a stuffed raven. A chair dangles by a rope from the flies. A man comes down the theater aisle with a long pole and moves two of the high-strung metal hoops slightly. A man and a boy come on stage and talk about television. A stout black man in a white suit bounds in and does a lot of pirouettes across the stage. Toward the end of the act, twenty or twenty-five people dressed like stereotype black mammies come out and do slow gyrations to the Blue Danube Waltz.

This act, called "The Beach," ran an hour and fifteen minutes; my itemization above is drastically incomplete. After a fifteen-minute intermission, Act Two began, with a prelude called "Victorian Façade," then shifted to "Victorian Drawing Room." I left some forty minutes later. There would be five more acts and five more intermissions of fifteen minutes each.

Two points are immediately clear: narrative is not the object; and the title, despite the photo, is irrelevant to anything I saw. (I'm told that, some hours after dawn, there were specific references to Stalin.) More important, the first glance—but only the first—makes us think there are connections here with the surrealist theater of the 1920s. In fact, after Wilson's last Paris show a commentator wrote: "One convert to [Wilson's] style was Louis Aragon, who saw in Wilson the logical heir to the Surrealists." Heir, perhaps, but with a distinct difference. The surrealist theater for me—archetypally, Artaud's *Jet of Blood*—is usually one of speedy bombardment, a rapid series of disjunctive phenomena making their effect as much through their speed of sequence as through their contents and disjuncture. Wilson's tempo is *largo*. His intent is not the surrealist fracture of our "defenses" with speedy sequences of illogic. He wants us to savor pictures. He wants to create picture after picture with theatrical means, but not *tableaux vivants*—he wants them to flow or melt into one another, to move. He wants to connect them more by visual themes than by verbalizable ones, to provide combinations of people and lights and things and sounds that are striking. Perhaps they will stimulate the viewer to invent his own play; perhaps not. No matter.

Wilson creates these pictures, ingeniously, delicately, wittily. Now twenty-nine, he's been trained as a painter, has worked with deaf children, and knows how to speak to the eye. He has great skill in using theater means to present a (let's call it) flowing gallery of pictures. This does not keep the performance from frequently being boring; I have more expectations and interests in the theater than to see a series of pictures, however good. But paradoxically, a certain quotient of boredom seems part of the plan. Wilson, though serious, is not solemn. Members of the audience are encouraged to change seats, to leave and return, to treat the presentations on stage as a sort of visual buffet from which they can help themselves as they choose.

My own reaction in sum: Why shouldn't there be a Robert Wilson? (Several foundations agree with me; and many prominent theater and dance people are impressed with his work.) Why shouldn't the theater's means be used by a painterly sensibility to thrust pictures into the element of temporality—of duration and motion? In film many painterly talents have tried it, though rarely at this length or with Wilson's invention and humor. His theater work is more difficult and in some ways more rewarding than the film attempts because he's doing it before us, with real people (some 150 of them, all told) and animals and lights and scenery and sounds. Boring as it is residually, his work is nevertheless authentic and authentically daring. I would hate to see Wilsonism take over theater and dance completely (small risk), but I'm glad he exists. I think I see why he is stimulating other and (to me) more congenial theater artists, and I would gladly go again for two or three more hours of boredom.

(*May 31, 1975*)

Robert Wilson, the creator of *The Life and Times of Joseph Stalin,* has changed status. In a short time he has moved from underground hero of the avant-garde to darling of the chic. This is not because of any cheapening he has done; his "frame," as Erving Goffman would say, has changed. *The New Yorker* has run a long profile on him, his next show was put in a Broadway theater, and many reviewers seemed to vie for the number of times they could call him a genius.

Now that he has produced still another show, at the Brooklyn Academy of Music, it's worth taking another look to see what he's doing and what's happening around him. At the ANTA a couple of months ago he presented for four weeks *A Letter for Queen Victoria.* This mere three-hour show (as compared with his fourteen-hour *Stalin*), with good music by Alan Lloyd, was suggested to Wilson by an eccentric letter that Victoria had once received, though of course that letter could hardly have been more incidental to what we saw and heard. *Stalin* had frequently been effective because it had essentially been painterly: with an immense cast, mostly of volunteers, Wilson had created a series of often exquisite pictures that melted into one another. *Victoria* was predominantly literary: with a much smaller cast and fewer pictures, Wilson leaned heavily on dadaist dialogue with a lot of screaming. Some of the pictures were fine, like one of aviators against a wall in Chirico light (no point in trying to *explain* that), but the verbal emphasis made it all much less appealing. Besides, the very fact that we knew in advance that the show ran three hours, and so could actually be sat through entire, made it more tedious than the several hours of *Stalin* that one could slice out as one wished. Prominent in the *Victoria* cast was Christopher Knowles, a thirteen-year-old boy "with severe brain damage" (says *The New Yorker*) who had also been in *Stalin*. I felt as if I were often intruding on therapy which was going well but which might better have been private. Between discomfort and boredom, I had a poor three hours.

Then a few weeks later I happened to hear a painter and a poet discussing *Victoria,* enthusiastically identifying for each other the artistic source of this visual effect and the literary source of that verbal one, though neither of them said much about what Wilson had done with these influences, what work he had created. (This is in marked contrast with Andrei Serban, whose *Trilogy* surely also showed influences but who summoned those influences into a new, cogent, forceful work.*) I began to see that *Victoria* had served as a test of in-ness.

Wilson's latest piece is said to be written and directed by the boy Knowles and Wilson. *The $ Value of Man* is done in the Lepercq Space of the Academy, the same huge, high-ceilinged room in which Peter Brook's company last appeared. Tiers of seats are placed at the narrow ends of the rectangle, seats on the floor along the sides. It begins with a man coming out and, in a spotlight, whirling a bit (Wilson is big on whirling), then falling down for a while as in acting class practicing falls. Then a singer leads out a file of sixteen or eighteen people. The singer does (I think) an Iranian song, beautiful, with delicate quarter-tone flutings—irrelevant to what follows but the most beautiful element of the evening. The group whirls, waves, kneels, stretches, etc.—the whole oxymoronic free routine that Brook's group did on that spot two years before.†

Still, despite this beginning, *Value* is the most thematically concentrated Wilson work I've seen. At a microphone on one side young Knowles then recites, so far as one can understand the boy's impaired speech, a TV commercial; then there is some action about it by the group. This happens three more times, while at a microphone across the floor Wilson prompts the boy's memory. (My discomfort with the boy has certainly not decreased.) Wilson also reads snippets from a newspaper account of an experiment in ethics that a philosophy professor conducted with his class, from which the show gets its title. The stage actions, meant to symbolize the commercializing of modern man, include some group movements, roughly choreographed, of some sixty people wearing white dresses or trousers, usually barefoot, with dark suit jackets and wide-brimmed hats, carrying cigars and pistols—both men and women. (That's how you tell crass people, by their cigars.) The best picture of the evening is done twice, once at either end of the space. High green squares are erected with lights

* See p. 108.
† See p. 58.

inside them; the black-suited people stand on ladders around the squares with playing cards, as if around huge gaming tables, chattering sporadically while violins drone a country-music vamp. It's a good theater cartoon of money madness.

After some two hours of the scheduled two and a half, the audience, which had been urged to move about freely, was milling around the floor between the "games" and a table where a man was working an adding machine, while smoke pots began to fill the air. As the audience milled, I milled out.

Wilson has the asset of a cultivated sensibility (the analytic painter and poet were right) married to a great innocence. Nothing is too complex, too venturesome, or too familiar for him to attempt it. His cultivation gives his productions their sporadic beauties; his blitheness in the face of theater obstacles gives him freedom. I sense that the audience is responding to a kind of cultural flattery as much as to achievement, to his lack of inhibition as much as to his accomplishment.

My own trouble with much of Wilson's work is not the quiz-show aspect, which is as flattering to me as anyone when I can "pass," nor his ingenuousness, which I too find disarming to a degree. My plaint is that when his work takes me, I feel, as with much avant-garde work, that I have seen a live nerve extracted from a body and laid on a lab table. Much of what Wilson was doing with language in *Victoria* was overshadowed for me by Peter Handke's plays.* (I doubt very much that Wilson was "using" Handke, by the way.) Handke's inquiry into the relation of language to chaos and order, to purity of feeling, is *included* in his organic plays that are full bodies of theatrical experience. My difficulty with *Value* is Antonioni: his stock-exchange sequences in *Eclipse,* including the one-minute silence for a deceased broker, gave me much more of the maniacal ballet of money-chasing, of the pathos of greed, than Wilson could approach. (Again I doubt that this film was a specific influence.) And Antonioni gave it to me as part of a large, beautiful, humanist work into which those anti-human sequences fed.

A major impulse of this century's art has been toward literal and figurative abstraction, as hundreds of painters and writers testify. They have tried to pluck out and present in isolation the states of

* See p. 195.

feeling that more traditional artists have arrived at through complicated design, through implication. Sometimes the result is wonderful. In *Endgame,* for instance, Beckett abstracts at once and dramatically crystallizes a state more or less equivalent to what *Uncle Vanya* reaches at the end of a long and complex "story" play. Beckett's journey through and around this state of being is so exquisite and profoundly articulate that it is something more than satisfying. But with lesser abstractions, like Wilson's, after the first shock of impact, I think, "Well, what next? What is he going to do with it? When X or Y or Z presented that feeling or view in his painting or play or novel, he did it en route, it was part of something. What are we en route to here?" Usually, in an organic sense, very little, or nothing. We get just a gallery of abstracted feelings, some more effective than others.

Can Wilson continue to produce theater pictures, independent of large organizing form, sufficiently striking to keep him generally interesting? That's the chief question—the fountain flow. Will the compliments that he implicitly pays the cultivated, the convention-wearied, inflate their estimate of him? That's a question too, and, for the health of contemporary judgment, almost equally important.

foreign theaters

The Moscow Art Theater

(Channel 13, New York, February 15, 1965)

The world-famous Moscow Art Theater is at present paying us a four-week visit, a highly interesting one. Not interesting in all the ways one might hope, still an occasion well worth attention. The first point to make clear is the status of that theater in its own country. The Moscow Art, for several reasons, some of them quite sound, has become a hallowed name in the theatrical profession here, but when any foreign company visits us, we have difficulty in judging it in its national context. Our assumption might be, understandably, that this is the leading theater of the Soviet Union. But an article on this group by Andrew Field in the February 1 *New Leader* makes clear that what we are seeing here is an animated museum. Mr. Field, an expert on Russian culture, says:

The Moscow Art Theater, in spite of its grand history, is the object of widespread scorn among sophisticated Russian theater-goers. . . . Perhaps the kindest way to view the Moscow Art is as an historical institution. . . . Which are the exciting theaters of Moscow today? For the general high level of their acting the Vakhtangov and Maly Theaters enjoy very good reputations. . . . For freshness of repertory the small Theater-Studio Sovremnik. . . . Let me stress that my comments are not intended as an attack on the Moscow Art. They represent, rather, the common opinions held by knowledgeable Muscovites themselves. . . . The American cult of Stanislavsky and the Moscow Art Theater is about thirty years behind the times. . . . It is unfortunate that these cultural exchanges are arranged by impresarios, by State Department officers, by everyone, in short, except those who are capable of rendering some sort of informed judgment.

Let's look now at the three productions thus far disclosed. The first is Mikhail Bulgakov's dramatization of Gogol's *Dead Souls,* and, whatever else is true, it was a mistake to begin with this show. First, it's not a play but a series of scenes from a novel, some of them merely tableaux. The curious point is that although this is by far the most recent of the productions—it was created by Stanislavsky thirty years or more after the Chekhov plays we saw—it's by far the most old-fashioned, theatrically speaking. It's in the style that I call zoological caricature. We all remember fairy-tale illustrations of animals in human clothes: the fox, the rooster, and so on. One feels that each of these principal characters thinks of himself as an animal: a teddy bear, a walrus, a lion. The acting technique is what I call two-handed: gestures tend to be made simultaneously with both hands. Anyone who saw productions of the Yiddish Art Theater on Second Avenue when it was at its best under the late Maurice Schwartz— such plays as *Yoshe Kalb* and *The Wise Men of Chelm*—saw this style of production done better. The worst things about *Dead Souls* is that it diminishes Gogol. Most of the bite is gone. Chekhov once wrote, "People's theaters are just foolishness, something to sweeten up the people. Gogol should not be lowered to the level of the people, but the people should be raised to Gogol's level." Not here.

This brings us, naturally, to the two Chekhov productions, *The*

Cherry Orchard and *The Three Sisters.* They are both better than the Gogol, but both are unsatisfactory—they give the impression of talent frozen and tradition domineering. I found *The Cherry Orchard* better than *The Three Sisters,* which skated on the surface of its feelings and themes and ended as a complete disaster. The last act of *The Three Sisters* is surely one of the most moving half-hours in all dramatic literature, and during this performance all I could think of was the measured steps that were being taken to this side or that, the obvious preparations for outbursts that were merely vocal display or superficial hysterics. Even the last act of last year's Actors Studio production was better than this. Kim Stanley was much more affecting than Marguerite Yureva. In the early part of *The Three Sisters* there were some evidences of the best element that this company can provide—which grows out of its long history of ensemble playing and the fact that they are recreating something of their own country and cultural tradition: a sense of eavesdropping on society distilled. And this, I must add, in spite of settings which are quite shabby and unimaginative by our standards. But the high points in *The Three Sisters* are blunted. The outburst of the drunken doctor in the third act, played here by Alexei Gribov, was a poor, pallid vaudeville act compared with the blazing moment of futility and self-disgust that Edmund Gwenn gave us in the Katharine Cornell production in 1942.

The Cherry Orchard was far more satisfactory, despite the fact that Madame Ranefskaya was played by Alla Tarrasova, who seems a heavy-handed peasant of an actress. Whoever saw the great Alla Nazimova in this part some thirty years ago knows what it is supposed to be: a woman of truly fatal charm, insidiously enchanting, irresponsible and irresistible, the product of centuries of fine breeding, together with centuries of grave immorality. With Nazimova, you felt that you were lucky that she was not in your life or she would charmingly ruin it just as she was ruining her own and others. With Tarrasova, I simply wondered why this healthy woman was dallying. Why she didn't put on her leather cap and jacket and get to work with her tractor to put the estate on a paying basis?

But around her there was some good if quite conventional acting. Trofimov and Semonov, Charlotta, Varya, and Anya were well played, and my favorite performance in all three plays was that by Mikhail Zimin as Lopakhin. It was perhaps a more polished Lopakhin than Chekhov planned, not enough of the rude *nouveau riche,* but there are as many kinds of *nouveau riche* as anything else, and I found Zimin making the world of his person true, appealing, appropriately disturbing.

Of Stanislavsky's work we know now little more than we did before. *Dead Souls* is based on his conceptions, but a production can change from night to night, let alone in thirty years. *The Cherry Orchard* has been restaged by Victor Stanitsyn, *The Three Sisters* by Josef Raevsky. I suppose in this company we can find some of Stanislavsky's general ideas: e.g., the production of plays like Chekhov's ought to seem elements in a continuum of life that has just flowed into the rooms at these times—large themes articulated in well-wrought domestic details. But I'm afraid that we also see traces of the state of mind of the D'Oyly Carte Gilbert and Sullivan company: the "business" was set many years ago, and new incumbents of roles simply learn them by rote. Tradition is a very valuable quality in art, but it needs to be challenged constantly and to answer those challenges satisfactorily or be changed. It seems easy to understand why, as Andrew Field implies, cultivated Muscovites feel that this company is more a morgue than a living theater.

Peter Brook

NOTE: The first two of the following three reviews of Peter Brook productions do not deal with his own theater group; they are placed here because they show his movement toward the matters discussed in the third review.

(The New York Times, *January 9, 1966*)

The full title of Peter Weiss's play must be stated once because it is itself a synopsis: *The Persecution and Assassination of Marat as Performed by the Inmates of the Asylum of Charenton Under the Direction of the Marquis de Sade.* It was originally produced in West Berlin in 1964 (with a setting designed by the author) and is seen here in the production of the Royal Shakespeare Company of London directed by Peter Brook.

Weiss, a German-born writer who lives in Sweden, has based his work on fact. Sade, during his long confinement in an asylum at the end of his life, wrote plays (none of which survives) and produced them with the inmates; these plays were often attended by visitors from nearby Paris. Weiss has imagined that one of these plays, performed in 1808, dealt with the murder of the Jacobin Marat by the Girondist Charlotte Corday fifteen years before, and the result is played for us by the patients, with the "author" at one side of the stage and the benevolent director of the asylum, his wife and daughter at the other. But it is not a conventional play-within-a-play. Weiss has used the device as an element of the drama itself: the principal ideological tension is between the "author" and his own leading character, Marat. This suggests a Pirandellian ambiguity, but the drama moves out of even unconventional expectation—to thrust, discover, astound. Because of the ambition of Weiss's imagination and the dynamics in his concept, the result is generally gripping and intriguingly disquieting, if at last unsatisfactory.

The concept is in a sense deceptive, for the play is not neatly symbolic. Our possible assumption that the madhouse is the world or that the madmen, portraying figures of history, are comments on the deeper lunacy of the seemingly sane—these patterns are too thin for the author's intent. He uses his startling setting and device simply as an impulse to launch his work, not as a control. He is out to reach our subconscious and keeps clawing his way toward it. But—and this is the work's contradiction—he is also out to reach our intellects, and the freight of ideas qualifies the play's free flight. This is not primarily because of the ideas themselves but because of a conflict between two theatrical philosophies. Let us look at those ideas before describing the conflict.

Marat is the voice of violent action, a believer in perfectibility through the guillotine, who thinks that only through erasure of the tainted can the less tainted improve—in short, an idealist. Sade, his "creator," is repelled by the vanity of rigid belief, is appalled and humbled by what he finds in himself and others, is a believer only in his life as he continually discovers it—in short, a species of existentialist. The gentleman Duperret, with his cries of "Freedom," is less a pleader for a return to the past than a spokesman for bourgeois, property-protecting liberalism. The mob is, through centuries of training, the professional poor. (Thus they are Marat's instrument.) The play's ideas are as graphically simple as posters. Possibly excepting

Sade, no personage can seriously be called a character. Marat is not comparable with Büchner's Robespierre; the quartet of clown-faced singers, the mob are mere abstracts of *The Threepenny Opera*. The tantalizing dimensions of most of the persons come from the fact that—within Weiss's play—they are all acting roles and the actors are all mad.

The several ideas and colorations are offered up with no clear indication of the author's preference and, what is worse, no conviction that this irresolution is the point. There are some lines spoken near the end by Sade (omitted from the published version) in which he says that the play may have planted seeds and we may not know yet what they are, but this sounds less like the apex of a design than uneasy justification. The play's indecisiveness in this area can be construed as intellectual shilly-shallying, as the author's unwillingness to opt for one or the other of his two chief ideas, individualism (Sade) or proletarian revolution (Marat); but in my view Weiss's equivocation is not ideological, it is artistic. He is essentially a revolutionary playwright, or would like to be, but he is also a contemporary artist, aware of contemporary sensibilities and modes. Artistically, he starts from a Brechtian position, equipped with some of Brecht's apparatus: the herald who announces scenes with chapter headings, the songs as gloss or gibe or dilation, the drama intended to involve us less in present anguish than in the historical causes of the anguish. But very soon another and antithetical mode breaks in: that of the visionary French actor-critic-theoretician Antonin Artaud—Artaud, the enemy of literature in the theater, of ideology, indeed of speech, who sought to purify the theater to essential emotion. (Is it mere coincidence that Artaud himself played Marat in Abel Gance's film *Napoleon* in 1926? Possibly Weiss, who is also a film-maker, was stimulated by this fact.) The influence of Artaud is in such elements as the quality of Sade himself, the mock flagellation and executions, the knife-worship, the tidal swells of the insane mob. There is a fundamental discord between the social Brecht method and the instinctual Artaud approach, between straightforward ironic vigor and the flickerings of the unnamed and unnamable.

Weiss is torn. The Artaud process appeals to him in its search for indefinable truth beneath credo and behavior, but he cannot divorce himself from the programmatic. He fights the subjective with the explicit, and vice versa. This imperfect alliance nags at his play, particularly diminishing its tensions in the middle—the end of Act One, the beginning of Act Two; and this play must live by the tensions it generates as it goes, not by plot or by character revelation. The uncertainty continues right to the very end, where the lines are revolutionary slogans, the action is maniacal and anarchic. Compare Genet's *The Balcony,* which also takes place in a house of fantasies— a brothel—and which also contains a fantastic charade of power and revolution. By holding to one mode, the Artaudian, and exulting in it, Genet conveys huge implications about the nature of power and of reality. (It is noteworthy that Peter Brook directed the first French production of *The Balcony.*) But I must emphasize that, with its flaws, *Marat/Sade* is easily the most interesting play to appear in New York since the Lincoln Center production of *Danton's Death* and is very much more rewarding to see—not because Weiss is in the same class with Büchner but because of Brook's stunning production.

I have not before been a warm admirer of Brook. On the basis of five plays and one film, I have thought him a gifted but flashy virtuoso, the kind of director who looks for what he can do to a play. But Weiss seems to have written with dependence on precisely this sort of virtuosity and has provided the right opportunities for Brook's temperament. In this case the director's flamboyance enriches texture instead of competing with it. The production surges, opens and narrows like the iris of a camera, using its members in mad, stuttering, but carefully composed movement. Also, as I have never seen anywhere before, Brook has even made actors of his musicians. (Vice versa?) Occasionally there are touches that seem less Artaudian candor than Brook's ostentation: the glimpse of Marat's bare behind, the bulging and stained trousers of the satyriast. But this play is magnified through its production, greatly aided by Sally Jacobs's cold setting and monk's-cloth costumes and Richard Peaslee's wry music. The translation by Geoffrey Skelton, with verse adaptation by Adrian Mitchell, is biting and bitter. There are some long lunges for present-day connection (terms like "the final solution" and "technocratic"), but perhaps they are in the original.

In an excellent cast, Ian Richardson, as Marat, is outstanding: burning intensity sustained through a difficult monodic role. Patrick Magee, handsome, square-jawed, white-haired, plays a silken, tenor Sade. One can imagine a style in the part other than Magee's—he seems to sight the lines a little ahead of and above him, then purrs up to them—but he has the requisite elegant oddness. As Corday, Glenda Jackson, though she reminds us more than the others that she is contemporary and English, quivers with insanity-dedication. All the mad men and women are well played. They create a hell in which they are bound to one another with invisible bonds that all of us can feel.

(February 20, 1971)

Peter Brook's production of *A Midsummer Night's Dream* accommodates two views. If there is a cast album of this Royal Shakespeare Company show, it sounds, I'm sure, pretty much the way Shakespeare sounded in 1890. Barring a few instances, the verse is read with classical intent, and the comedy lines are treated in a style that would have pleased Beerbohm Tree. But for the eye it's a different, contradictory story.

As usual with Brook productions, the curtain is up when we enter (and the play begins before the house lights lower). The setting, by Sally Jacobs, consists of three high white walls with parapets atop guarded by black rails, with two swinging doors in the back wall, with a narrow black vertical slit in each side wall. There's a white overall carpet. Hanging from the flies are some trapezes and an affair covered with red ostrich feathers (Titania's bower, as we learn). Musicians and sound implements are atop the walls at the downstage corners. The lights, by Lloyd Burlingame, come up—blazing white, not one touch of color in the dozens of lamps. The entire cast bustles through and off, then Theseus and Hippolyta begin.

The costumes are also by Jacobs, with strong colors mostly reserved for the fairies; the mortals are mostly dressed in white with spots of color, the women in vaguely Greek dresses, the men in trousers and blouses. After the opening minutes of drenching white, Egeus bursts in wearing a rich blue surplice, and the effect is so startling, you can almost hear the blue. Pace, vigor, contrast, fun, even occasional loveliness, the production dusts us with them all like a low-flying plane. When the action moves to the forest, the trapezes and ropes come into swing, for use by the fairies. Meyerhold has always been big in Brook's mind, and circus elements were big in

Meyerhold's mind. The hoisting and swinging give the fairies a pleas-antly obvious way to become unearthly, accompanied by Richard Peaslee's teasing music and sound effects.

And Jan Kott still haunts Brook's stage. Eight years ago, with *King Lear,* much was made of the fact that Kott's new book *Shakespeare Our Contemporary* had influenced Brook. Few have noted that Kott's (questionable) chapter on the *Dream* has touched this show. Kott says that this is "the most erotic of Shakespeare's plays" (so much for *Antony and Cleopatra!*), and there is some crotch-grabbing and noisy nuzzling. The funniest use of this raunchy motif is at the mo-ment when Bottom is transformed into an ass and Titania, under the influence of a potion, falls in love with him. The gross suggestion of a donkey phallus may indicate what was really on both their minds, and as they proceed to her bower, we hear the only touch of Mendels-sohn in the show—the "Wedding March," which is usually reserved for the court.

There is some doubling of parts. The actor who plays Philostrate, the Duke's master of revels, also plays Puck, the master reveler. The Theseus doubles as Oberon, Hippolyta doubles as Titania. These latter two doublings have comic point because Oberon and Titania accuse each other of dallying with the mortal ruler of the opposite sex and because it adds to the important duality of the play's world, and because it helps the plot's one sore point. At the start Theseus says the law forbids him to interfere with Egeus' marital plans for his daughter; but at the end Theseus simply says, "Egeus, I will overbear your will," and matches the daughter up with the man she had wanted all along. If, between those two statements, the actor who plays Theseus has been the Oberon who caused the amorous mix-ups in the woods, the director has at least given a wry razzberry to the otherwise arbitrary switch. But I don't understand why Egeus doubles as Quince.

And that's the least of the things I don't understand in this produc-tion. In *Lear* the unvarying white light at least conveyed a supra-real idea of pitiless pressure, even when it contradicted some of the words. Here the white light seems merely an attempt to smash the moon-lighty stage conventions of the play. (Which takes some doing, because "moon" is one of the most frequently used words in the *Dream.*) The empty-warehouse feeling of the *Marat/Sade* setting suited the play's void; here the white emptiness suggests an inappropriate cross between an operating room and Avedon's studio at *Vogue*.* And what about the spectators on the parapets—often characters who have just finished a scene below? The *Dream* contains a play-within-a-play; is this spectator device meant to make the whole evening seem a play within some larger cosmic play? Why do Egeus and the young lovers, in the first scene before the Duke, keep their eyes straight front, looking neither at him nor each other? Why has Brook cast Lysander and Demetrius with two young men of outstanding homeliness? If he is cutting against *jeune premier* convention, then why isn't he consistent in the other casting?

In his stimulating and well-written book, *The Empty Space,* Brook says: "Our work on Shakespeare production is always to make the plays 'modern' because it is only when the audience comes into direct contact with the plays' themes that time and conventions vanish." But the "modern," in all the visual aspects of this production, is merely negative: he has stripped away the two usual ways of producing this play: Attic attitudes or Mendelssohn meringue. But he spends the whole evening just stripping them away. The very intelligence that is evident in that stripping, together with the patterned *sound* of the play, make me search for a pattern in the *look* of it. Without success. The point of his *Lear* was clear, whether one agreed with it or not: waiting for Beckett. The point here seems only a series of points.

Some of the cast are very good. Frances de la Tour is a perfect— and perfectly traditional—Helena. John Kane's Puck, larger than usual, has impish spirit. David Waller, the Bottom, has bumptious solidity; he lacks, though, the necessary asinine charm. Barry Stanton, the Snug, is more winning in his one line about being "slow of study" than Waller is in his whole part.

The most attractive actor is Alan Howard, the Theseus/Oberon. He is a highly accomplished speaker of verse, with a good stage voice, unfruity but musical; he has presence and command. But he's on the verge of self-infatuation. I estimate, to judge by the ponderous rate at which he speaks the Duke's casual asides in the last scene, that his Hamlet (which he plays with this company) must take a week.

I note, too, that from time to time Brook has a character sing

* Subsequently I discovered, if not an explanation, at least a precedent. Granville Barker, commenting on his famous production of the *Dream* in 1915, said: ". . . what is really needed is a great white box. We set our scenes in a shell—it's blue now [because the designer thought it too cold], but it was white once." See p. 317.

his/her first lines after an entrance to guitar accompaniment, which is agreeable enough. But the First Fairy's "Over hill, over dale" speech has been broken up and given to the four mod youths who play Titania's attendants, which is puzzling because the four of them look as if the only way they could get over hill and over dale is on a Honda.

For me, this has never been a play of two worlds but of the interweaving of two modes of consciousness. If you like, you may call the fairy world either aspects of the immanent divine or aspects of the subconscious, always lurking, waiting to pounce, to disturb. Either way the *Dream* is a testament, in ravishing language, to the power of the invisible and the silly cockiness of our seeming self-governance. Brook's production frequently touches this idea, tellingly, but I can't say that this is his realized theme. He wouldn't have needed all his new apparatus to do that.

His method here is like an unresolved figure in dialectics. The thesis is the generally traditional sound; the antithesis is the anti-traditional look; but the synthesis?

(October 20, 1973)

Peter Brook, the English director, is best known in this country for his productions of *King Lear, Marat/Sade,* and *A Midsummer Night's Dream,* which have been widely discussed as unconventional but which are really among his more conventional activities of the last decade. He has been experimenting and probing in the time between his more "visible" works. In 1964 he helped found a Theater of Cruelty in London, inspired by the writings of Antonin Artaud, and for the last three years he has been the leader of a group, based in Paris, called the International Center for Theater Research. Brook was, earlier, one of the first to tell the West about the work of Jerzy Grotowski and his Laboratory Theater, to insist that Grotowski's work be seen outside Poland, for which we are all in his debt.* Brook's ICTR is unabashedly obligated to Grotowski's group for more than its name.

* See p. 63.

In 1971 the ICTR produced a work called *Orghast,* written in a new language devised by the poet Ted Hughes and performed in the ruined palace of Darius in Persepolis. In December 1972 Brook led the ICTR on a motor-caravan tour through Africa, south from Algiers in a great loop down through Nigeria and back, doing improvisatory shows spontaneously in towns and villages, on a carpet in marketplaces. Recently they spent eight weeks with El Teatro Campesino playing in California farm communities. They are now based for five weeks at the Brooklyn Academy of Music, working there and in parks roundabout.

I went to the Academy to spend a morning at an open demonstration of the group's exercises, then returned in the evening for a performance. (A good many people also attended the afternoon demonstration as well, spent the whole day there.) We sat on low bleachers ranged around three sides of a huge room. When we entered for the demonstration, ten of the group were kneeling at the far end of the room chanting a song from a Noh drama, led by the one Japanese in the company. (Among them there are two blacks and François Marthouret, who was in Tanner's recent film *Le Retour d'Afrique.*) Then there was a short talk by Brook, an articulate and engaging man, explaining that what we were going to see was the process of "tuning up."

Accompanied by drum beats, the group then went through a series of exercises familiar in outline, if not in specifics, to anyone who has read Grotowski or seen the Open Theater or any of the many performer-centered companies—movements and "games" designed to heighten and control physicality, the power and presence of the body. These were followed by vocal exercises designed to "realize" the voice, to make sound a part of one's organism, not just something that is shoved out of the throat. Later the audience, mainly theater people and theater students, was asked to join in some vocal exercises.

What struck me most forcibly about these exercises was not that they were unoriginal, that Brook had devised nothing new; this was disappointing but not central. What bothered me was that after three years' work (and a reported million dollars of foundation funding), these performers had achieved such a small degree of physical and vocal control—stratospheres away from Grotowski's company. For all the air of adventure, for all the gnomic remarks by Brook at the beginning and subsequently, everything in all this work is also part of the accomplishment of the good traditional actor—which, again, is not true of Grotowski's company.

Well, I thought, proof of the pudding. I came back that evening to see a performance. (The afternoon, I'm told, was devoted to improvisations.) The play is called *The Conference of the Birds* and is arranged from a twelfth-century Persian poem—a series of episodes with accompanying music, interwoven by a narrator, like Story Theater. It has very little to do with birds and a great deal to do with glib mystic episode and spurious spiritual insight. At one point the narrator, a gigantic woman, says portentously: "I prayed to God to open the door for me to Him. A man passed by and said, 'You idiot, what makes you think the door is shut?'" An hour and forty minutes of that sort of stuff would be suffocating even if performed by the greatest company of the ages.

The play obviously has a script and obviously also has opportunities for nightly improvisation. In the latter the company showed moderate invention and skill, related to what I had seen earlier in the day—particularly an episode of "birds" on a scaffold—but nothing equal to the sacerdotal air that the group surrounds itself with. The tone, if not the point, of the enterprise is in the very opening and the closing. At the start, a drink—tea, I suppose—is brewed on stage, then poured into two big bowls that are passed around to be shared by the audience. (Sitting in the back, I missed my sip.) At the end the narrator asked the audience to come up and join hands with the company in a large circle. Dozens did. I left, shocked by this Julian Beck–Judith Malina cheapness in a Brook group. Perhaps they are all still standing there, locked in a new community.

Brook, anxious for communion with audiences, has done what Beck and Malina and many others have done in the past ten years: he has gone to the audience overtly. He doesn't want to entertain audiences, he wants to make partners of them. He thinks, with something more than justice, that our theater in general, produced by a sick society, is laugh-or-cry consumer fodder unrelated to the psychic and spiritual pollution of that society. But in his fully justified revulsion he has succumbed to a current common fallacy: that the way to break through to the audience is to talk to them, to approach them physically, to mingle with them. Only very rarely has this method had more than a merely physical effect. In the best works of Joseph Chaikin with the Open Theater, even in rare peak moments of the Living Theater under Beck-Malina, the fracture of traditional performer-audience "roles" has made a union like that of the traditional theater at its best. But virtually nowhere in that Brooklyn day did Peter Brook show that he had the right talent for this untraditional work. He has miscast himself. His best productions have been those, like the ones named above, that made the *theater* move with adventure; he has no apparent gift for taking the theater outside the theater. All through the Brook evening I got sad reminders of Jean-Louis Barrault, a splendid actor-director, with his production of *Rabelais* a few years ago, a free-form affair in which he tried desperately to "swing."

But there is a larger issue beneath the specifics of Brook's failure with the ICTR—the issue of elitism.

Unquestionably the theater of the Western world is elitist. Ever since Athens the theater has existed for a relatively small proportion of any country's population, either by reason of class or money or simple lack of physical availability in most parts of any country. Brook's travels to African villages and Chicano communities and Bedford-Stuyvesant parks are, quite apart from their content, efforts to break the theater out of its elitism, to take it across physical chasms, as well as socio-economic ones. I believe that such efforts, full of instant gratifications, are delusory and eventually harmful to the very institution he means to revivify.

The primary purpose of the theater, as of any art, is to be the best it can be. And the plain fact—not snobby but experiential—is that the public for the best art is usually small. For an artist of Brook's refinement to revolt against numerical limitation and bourgeois consumerism by sentimentally debasing his work is to strike a blow at the very art for whose sake he has been disgusted. Society should provide every possible means, educational and economic, to make every person a potential member of the theater audience; that is democracy. But within that society the theater should do everything it can to be as aspiring and profound as possible; that is art. Brook, like others before him, has confused the political issue of equality with the esthetic issue of quality.

Brook reports, in *The Drama Review* (September 1973), his happy reception in those Nigerian villages. Recently I saw a helicopter shot on TV of hundreds of thousands of Koreans cheering Billy Graham. Does Brook think he can compete with this? More to the point, in terms of effect, does he think that Graham's "crusade" made Korea a truly Christian country? Or if communal fun and pleasant memories are what it's all about, why not send Graham to those Nigerian villages instead of the ICTR?

The matter was fixed for me by the sight of James Earl Jones in that Brooklyn audience. I remembered Jones and Ruby Dee and Zakes Mokae in Fugard's *Boesman and Lena,** and I'm convinced that their wonderful performances in a magnificent play contained infinitely more communion and exaltation than all the facile embracing and mysticism that were going on this evening. I'm not at all sure that a Nigerian villager (allowing for language) would respond to *Boesman*. I *am* sure, in my bones, that *Boesman* had an incomparably greater effect on its audience than ICTR had on its villagers. It is risky to apply a utilitarian standard, but I would venture further that theater at the *Boesman* level will do more for the betterment of society than communal noise-making and drink-sharing. The latter improve society about as deeply and lastingly as Billy Graham does. (One of his best friends is President Nixon!) But as for *Boesman,* I know for myself—as some others know for themselves—that I am in some degree different because I saw it.

It is the fate of the theater to be elitist. The task is not to trifle with that fate, to fiddle with it ashamedly because of society's corruption, but to fulfill it as finely as possible. This is a task in which Grotowski, whom Brook so rightly admires, has never faltered; in fact, Grotowski has been slated because his productions—coming from a Communist country, too!—are elitist. And he keeps on doing them, aiming for the deepest, not the most.

Brook says he has not turned his back on the theater as he used to practice it and will eventually return to it. Soon, I hope. Five years ago he published an interesting book called *The Empty Space* in which he said he could take any empty space, call it a bare stage, have people walk across it and engage an audience. In essence that's what he tried in Brooklyn, but in this case the space remained empty.

* See p. 204.

Grotowski's Theater

(*January 3, 1970*)

The full name of the group is the Laboratory Theater of the Institute of Actor's Research. It was founded in Opole, Poland—a town of 60,000—in 1959 by Jerzy Grotowski (then twenty-six) and Ludwik Flaszen, who is the literary advisor. In 1965 the group moved to Wroclaw—a city of half a million—and in *The New Republic* of July 30, 1966, Andreas Freund reported from Paris about the group's performance there of *The Constant Prince.* Now the Polish Laboratory Theater, under Grotowski's direction and very much with his presence, has performed a season of three plays, including *The Constant Prince,* at a Greenwich Village church, sponsored by the Brooklyn Academy of Music. These three plays—together, more than as separate entities—were a major theatrical experience in my life, and this article is an attempt to understand why.

Preliminary Matters

Many people, including me, were irritated by the handling of tickets and of spectators. Having finally got in to all three productions, I can now be Olympian and ask others who were less lucky to understand something that is fundamental to a Polish Lab performance. Grotowski has written of his theater: "Here the producer always keeps in mind that he has two 'ensembles' to direct: the actors and the spectators. The performance results from an integration of these two 'ensembles.' " For each production he changes the shape of the theater itself—the arrangement of seats in relation to setting and action (as described below). For each production the seating capacity changes—diminishing, in fact: only forty were admitted to a performance of the last play. It is not Grotowski's fault, it is his stubborn virtue that more were not admitted. Freund reported that the Théâtre de France shut its main entrance when the Polish Lab played there and admitted only sixty spectators through the stage door into a cordoned-off space. This is not Grotowski's trickery but his *method.* I don't know about Paris, but in New York this method was immediately taken as clever show biz or the snobbism of a smart restaurant. The color of the irritations, particularly in the face of the wholeness of the Grotowski enterprise, is largely a reflection of New York consumer attitudes toward the theater.

Productions

First, *The Constant Prince,* taken from the play by Calderón. There are 100 spectators, arranged in two concentric groups around a small rectangular arena, looking down on the actors. (This is intended to suggest a Roman circus or an operating theater.) In the arena there is only a wooden slab, at one end; there are two entrances diagonally opposite each other, though only one is used. Two spotlights at opposite ends are the only lighting. (These were the only lights for each production. Grotowski, who sits at the side during every performance, adjusted one light slightly during the performance that I saw of this first play.)

Calderón's verse drama, a work of genius, concerns a Spanish prince captured by Moors who refuses to be ransomed by the surrender of Spanish territory in Africa. In Calderón's typical "aria" style, it must run over three hours, and it has a large cast. Grotowski's version runs a bit less than an hour (every one of these three productions ran just that length) and has a cast of six. Is it Calderón's play? I read the original only after I saw the Polish production, and although Grotowski does not present anything like the fullness of Calderón's work, the images of his production, its temper, illuminated my reading.

Five of the actors (one of them a woman) are in black, the prince is in white, and he is soon stripped to a loincloth. A crown, a red cloth, an umbrella, a beret are the props. The actors intone, whisper, keen, chant, pantomime, dance. (Martha Graham and Merce Cunningham are names frequently used in comment about this company.) Rituals are arranged, like a sequence in which each of the captors bites the prince's neck, afflicting him and being nourished by him. Yet characters and reality are not strict: it is a "play." When the captors are miming a struggle against the wind, it is the prince, prone on the slab after torture, who supplies the wind effects with his voice. When the captors waltz in ecstasy, it is the prince's full-throated bellowing in three-quarter time to which they dance. (The prince is their principal actor, Ryszard Cieslak. I don't know whether he is even an "actor," in anything like the representational sense to which we are accustomed; but in his expressiveness of body, range of voice, and intensity of *union* of the physical and emotional, he is titanic.)

There were program notes, as there were for all the plays, outlining the principal sections. But in this play, language is no barrier. A Polish friend told me that he understood three words, two of which were *"Kyrie eleison."* Voices—wonderfully modulated and controlled —are used here as a medium of sound, not words.

The prince suffers agonies at the hands of his captors, triumphs, dies, and triumphs further. A few days later I saw a rehearsal of Beckett's *Endgame* elsewhere, and a line of Clov's threw a backward light on the prince: "I say to myself—sometimes, Clov, you must learn to suffer better than that if you want them to weary of punishing you—one day. I say to myself—sometimes, Clov, you must be there better than that if you want them to let you go—one day."

Acropolis

Ninety spectators. The setting is a jagged series of platforms in the middle of the large church floor. There are short double rows of seats for spectators—three or four in a row—fitted into the crevices of the platforms. (Some others were seated in the oval balcony of the church.) Over the platforms a wide-spaced network of cables. On the center platform a pile of sections of stovepipe and a battered iron bathtub. Again the two spotlights at opposite sides.

The production is based on a play by Stanislaw Wyspianski, written in 1904, which takes place in Cracow on the eve of the Day of Resurrection. Statues and figures from a cathedral tapestry come to life, all personages from Homer and the Bible. The play, says the program, "is conceived as a total vision of the Mediterranean culture" and it closes with "the resurrection of Christ-Apollo."

Grotowski and Flaszen have shifted the scene to Auschwitz. Seven prisoners take an hour on the way to the ovens to slip in and out of Homeric and Biblical characters, summing up the roots of Western culture on their way to incineration, not resurrection. As the six men and one woman play their little episodes, they hang up the stovepipe on the cables (building their own oven), they work with a heavy wheelbarrow, one of them occasionally picks up a fiddle and plays sentimental tunes, including "Thine Is My Heart Alone." (Banal music figures in all the plays.) All of them wear patched burlap tunics and brimless black hats. Their legs are bare, and they wear heavy workman's shoes, on which they sometimes perch tiptoe. Much of the time they move squint-eyed, as if blind. They work in balletic spurts, they sing and orate and chatter and mourn. Language seems more important here than in *The Constant Prince;* at least such names as Jacob and Priam and Helen of Troy are easily recognizable.

At the end the oven has been symbolically constructed, and the central platform is bare. They lift a trapdoor and descend into that platform. The last one in is the woman, who pulls the door closed after her.

Apocalypsis cum Figuris

Forty spectators. The large church floor is bare. Benches are ranged along two walls for the audience. The same two spotlights, only this time they are next to each other, resting directly on the floor, casting shadows upward. Before the forty spectators are admitted, the lights are dimmed in the foyer where they wait, so that their eyes are attuned to the lighting inside. When they enter, they find six actors lying on the floor, five men and a woman. One of them (Cieslak) is in a black gown; five are in white modern clothes of various kinds. (This was the first time that, on entering, I felt a sense of Off-Off-Broadway cliché. For me the production had to overcome that feeling and fight its way to freshness; it soon did.)

Apocalypsis "was evolved by its performers under the guidance of the director by means of acting exercises and sketches." Words were improvised as needed, and later when the framework was ready, literary material was found to replace the stopgap words—selections from the Bible and *The Brothers Karamazov* (the Grand Inquisitor), bits of T. S. Eliot and Simone Weil. This time the language seems really germane, because all the important passages were translated for the program, which the audience was asked to read beforehand. I lost track of them in the course of the play, but the general flow is clear. The characters have Gospel names—Simon Peter, Judas, Lazarus, Mary Magdalene, John. Jesus is called the Simpleton. The program says that in Polish this name "suggests certain associations: an innocent, gullible half-wit, living outside the accepted conventions, gawkish, often deformed, but in mysterious communion with the supernatural. The demoniac and the village idiot are familiar figures in Slav tradition."

This is a free-flowing modern allegory of the Crucifixion, with the others putting their sins on and venting their angers on the Simpleton-Christ, with (again) some ritual eating of the hero's body and some banal tunes, and the symbolic use of a loaf of bread. There is some broad sexual pantomime and some grossness, presumably to interweave the presence of the brutal peasantry. About halfway through, the spotlights go out, and an actor brings in lighted candles. At the end, after this very earthy Christ has whipped the money-changers from the temple and has been crucified, the last remaining actor puts out the last candle.

Style and Sources

Grotowski is the author and subject of a collection of articles and interviews (and acting exercises) called *Towards a Poor Theater* (Simon & Schuster). He is using "poor" in the religious sense, a stripping-off of rich trappings to discover internal richness. In it he describes his basic motive as a search for a *via negativa,* an attempt to define by negation, to eliminate everything that film and television can do, to find out whether anything remains that the theater alone can do—as a justification for its continued existence. A coincidence helped to show me that he has succeeded in finding those singular theatrical essences.

In 1968 the Public Broadcasting Laboratory filmed *Acropolis* in London and then broadcast the film over NET. The film was made intelligently and sympathetically, and Grotowski himself came to New York to help edit it. The result, for me who had read so much about the Polish Lab and had hoped so high, was painful; I got some data, not much more. The difference between the theater performance of *Acropolis* and the PBL film was the difference between an event and the report of an event. Every good film esthetician since Vachel Lindsay has been concerned with the differences between—not the ranking of—film and theater; here the event was so utterly theatrical that film was utterly irrelevant. To sit *amidst* those Polish actors at *Acropolis,* almost to smell them, to see them setting down the wheelbarrow an inch from my foot and find myself not flinching because I had *confidence* in them, a knowledge that they knew I was there and were doing it all for me and at the same time that they didn't care whether I was there or not—all this seemed to certify Grotowski's "negative way." It was not merely the patent fact of their and my physical presence, it was a sense of not being acted *on* but of collaboration. A thousand light-years away from the Living Theater's childish "participatory theater" and self-indulgence and adolescent anarchy, this intensely disciplined company had made me a member of one of their "two ensembles."

Grotowski writes of his sources:

. . . We consider the personal and scenic technique of the actor as the core of theater art. It is difficult to speak of the exact sources of this approach, but I can speak of its tradition. I was brought up on Stanislavski; his persistent study, his systematic renewal of the methods of observation, and his dialectical relationship to his own earlier work make him my personal ideal. Stanislavski asked the key methodological questions. Our solutions, however, differ widely from his—sometimes we reach opposite conclusions.

There are also, it would seem, some other roots. Artaud is one—at least in the sense that he, too, was searching for a *via negativa,* for absolutely prime, "ancient" sources. (In one of the lectures that Grotowski gave while his company was in New York, he said that he went to an art gallery in London which was showing "packages" and "objects," and he thought that the plush rope to keep visitors back was one of the exhibits. In contrast to this avant-gardism—with which in general he is fallaciously linked—he cited the work of Henry Moore, which, he said, is so modern that it is ancient. "It is difficult to think who created his work." This goal of the "ancient" is clearly an aim of Grotowski's, as it was of Artaud's.) Some Asian dance and theater have plainly contributed to this theater. But a central concept seems to me to come from Meyerhold. In *Meyerhold on Theater* (published by Hill and Wang) he writes of two distinct theatrical approaches. The first is the concept of the triangle: author and actor at base angles, the director at the apex, and the spectator behind him, getting the play through the director. Meyerhold prefers the "Theater of the Straight Line," which runs from author to director to actor to spectator:

The director, having absorbed the author's conception, conveys his own creation (now a blend of the author and the director) to the actor. The actor, having assimilated the author's conception via the director, stands face to face with the spectator (with director and author behind him) and *freely* reveals his soul to him, thus intensifying the fundamental theatrical relationship of performer and spectator.

(It is worth noting that in 1915 Meyerhold did a production of *The Constant Prince.*)

There are some paradoxes. This theater, interested in the clarity of self and supreme subjectivity, a theater that would have shocked Lenin and disturbed Brecht, is supported by a Communist state. Also, it is an elitist theater—in two senses. It cannot be a people's theater because of the limited number at each performance. It cannot be popular because only an art-experienced spectator can respond to it. At that lecture, when Grotowski was asked about the theater's serving others, he replied, in effect, "The theater is not the practice of medicine. Why always this concern about doing for others? Do for yourself. The theater is a place where some people reveal themselves to others. Either those selves must be worth revealing, or the theater is nothing." Communist countries often permit fluctuations from didactic art and social realism, but usually, as with some Polish and Czech films, it is within "safe" limits. The stark interiorism of the Polish Lab is extraordinary in the current Eastern European cultural landscape.

Effect

I cried at the film of *Goodbye, Mr. Chips;* I did not cry at *Acropolis.* Nor was I exalted, as I was at the three performances of Olivier's *Oedipus* that I saw in 1946. I was more emotionally involved at *Acropolis* than at the other two plays, but I know that this was because of the word "Auschwitz," because the actors may have had relatives who died there, and *because Poles themselves often have been oppressors.* But all three of these productions, in net effect, were simply placed in front of me. No one was out to "get" me. Something was being shown. Only later did I come to "feel" something about them: suffering as language (*The Constant Prince*), human history strangling and consuming itself (*Acropolis*), religion certifying and becoming the mundane (*Apocalypsis*).

I was reminded of the novelist Jerzy Kosinski, Polish-born, whose early life has many (presumable) parallels with the lives of these people. Kosinski's first novel, *The Painted Bird,* was a terrible and moving account of a homeless, persecuted child in Eastern Europe during World War II. His second novel, *Steps,* disappointed some admirers of the first book who wanted to cry some more over the persecutions. For me, what happened in *Steps* is analogous to what has happened in the Polish Lab, a refusal to play the old game of heart-tug, no matter how wonderfully it has been played in the past, a refusal to rely on the traditional acceptances of a world that produced the horrors, in order to make you cry about those horrors. Kosinski has published a brochure about the writing of *Steps* which he calls *The Art of the Self* (a title that is stunningly relevant to Grotowski), in which he says:

> The reader may perceive the work in a form of his own devising, auto-matically filling in its own loose construction with his own formulated experiences and fantasies. . . . This reception runs counter to that of the conventional contemporary melodrama which gains its effects from pre-determined emotional group response.

Similarly, Grotowski's actors simply place crystals before us, reductions, moment by moment, episode by episode. We may make our own connections, or not. We are in charge of ourselves; they are in charge of themselves. There is no attempt at seduction. They present their credentials, and leave the rest to us. All that we can be absolutely sure of as it goes along—to quote *Endgame* again—is that "something is taking its course." Something that is still alive and breathing after descents into profound depths.

Point

T. S. Eliot says somewhere that a writer writes for himself or for one other or for God. The last two alternatives have been eliminated by many modern artists. Much of the result is so non-lingual, so frag-mented, that it is hermetic and solipsist; one can at best recognize its sincerity and move on. Grotowski is an exception. His self (figuratively) is all he will work with, the actor's self is all that he wants the actor finally to know. But he perceives that if art is to provide order in chaos, then it must itself have order; if the self is to be explored in anything more than self-aggrandizement or varieties of masturbation, then the ability to *realize* what one has found is essential. Grotowski turns inward; but with such stern consecrative technique that he makes it possible for others—us—to follow. (Possible, not obligatory.) The rejection of old modes does not result in no mode.

Any comment on the relation of his theater to literature—whether it is "anti-literary" or is fed by the language they speak—can be made only by someone who knows Polish.

I don't think that Grotowski—or any other man or group—is "the" theater of the future. I don't even think it likely that his visit here will bear much real fruit in our theater—unless others are stimulated to find their own ways. (An American actress who has studied with Grotowski told me that when a student leaves, Grotowski says to him, "Now go home and destroy me.") I don't think it probable that the total commitment of his company is likely in the Western world outside a Communist country. (An irony to add to the ones mentioned earlier.) Only in some of the dance and drama of the East can one find parallels with this company, which rehearsed its latest production, *Apocalypsis,* 400 times before they presented it. (And they were a unified company when they began rehearsing!) What has that to do with the random and dispersed efforts that produce most of our theater, on or off Broadway?

There is still another reason why this company is unlikely to produce any real fruit in this country. American art has shown little ability to take the full measure of tragedy, of the American fate, to confront and acknowledge the past and present without either moralistic self-justification or mere self-flagellation. All these Grotowski productions are rooted deep in the history of Poland and of Poland in the world. Where is the American theater that—just for an instance —can really face the truth and implications of My Lai? Where is the American Cieslak to exult in the anguished innocent-guilty song of a Lieutenant Calley? The journalist John Osborne recalled a few weeks ago that, when he was in a Vietnamese village three years back, he saw a villager running to warn the Vietcong of the Americans' presence, and he confesses that he thought that "somebody ought to shoot the goddamned gook." Where is the American theater company to embrace the whole truth of that statement, to hold it out steadily before us?

Nothing less than the ability to confront bone-deep truth interests Grotowski. He is in a third way an elitist—in the theater world— caring only about a theater that is totally committed. He says repeatedly, *"Why* must the theater continue? What would be the difference if it disappeared? Either it is important, or it is nothing. If it cannot be important for me, I will do something else."

Finally, I think that this is what I am left with: his productions were *totally* important to those concerned with them. And their commitment involved me. Beyond that, not much certainty, except that —certainly—"something is taking its course."

The Comédie Française

(*February 28, 1970*)

The Comédie Française is now touring this continent in a repertory of Molière and recently played in New York, where I saw one of the productions, *Dom Juan.* (Molière used the Portuguese version of Juan's title.) This was by far the best Molière I have ever seen—including some previous productions by the Comédie itself. Partly this is because *Dom Juan* does not often try to be funny. There are a few attempts to make you laugh, like the tedious scene with the tailor, but for the most part it is comedy in the philosophic sense and much the better for it. Nothing withers more surely than old jokes, and when they are in another language, fed into one's ears by transistored translation, they drone like funeral rites.

The play lives. "Modern" sounds patronizing, and "relevant" sounds hygienically nutritious, yet both those words apply to this drama of a man with the courage of his short-range convictions and the wit to make himself dangerous to those with longer views. At one revealing point this conflict is localized in the don himself. After he reveals to his servant that his confession of remorse to his father was all a sham, he says: "I take you into my confidence deliberately, Sganarelle, because I like to have one witness to my real feelings and my motives for acting as I do." There is a bone for theologians to pick on!

This production was directed by Antoine Bourseiller and was put in the repertory in 1967. I don't care much for the sets and costumes by Oskar Gustin. The settings are metallic abstractions, presumably intended to "psychologize" the piece, but they look like 1925 *moderne*. The costumes have little to do with the sets, and the use of the same leatherette suiting for master and servant hurts the necessary class difference. Apparently Bourseiller has used this décor to jar the audience into awareness of a new approach, but that approach would be hard to miss in the most conventional décor.

He has had the world's best bank-account of classical acting on which to draw: productions of the Comédie are sometimes fusty, but individual technique and style are rarely bad. Georges Descrières makes a cool, elegant, steely don, an actor whose baroque gesture is always under fine, sardonic control. Jacques Charon, the Feydeau specialist who directed the recent sad film of *A Flea in Her Ear,* is obviously much more at home on the stage, and he plays Sganarelle with humorous servility nearing the end of its centuries-old tether.

The production is held firmly in Bourseiller's view of the play as an ironic, quasi-existential statement: the pace and, above all, the stage movement support this view. He adapts the spacious classic movement of the Comédie to a contemporary use, in something of the way that de Chirico adapts classical perspective to statements of bleakness. Note, for instance, the way that the visit of Don Juan's father is staged. The father comes in upstage right, almost straight downstage, then across left to a position below that of his son; his movement describes a sharp angle as he speaks, implying dislike and then an overture toward intimacy. The don, as he speaks, then comes downstage toward us, brushing right past his waiting father, almost to the footlights without stopping. The movements have sweep, but more; a large stage and a large style have been used to speak of interior distances.

I wish I had been able to see the other plays in the repertory (not directed by Bourseiller), but certainly if the Comédie performs anywhere near you, this *Dom Juan* is worth traveling for.

(August 7 and 14, 1971)

Paris

At the Comédie Française I saw their 1144th performance of Beaumarchais' *The Marriage of Figaro*. It looked like the 10,444th. What a lot of circus horses plodding obediently around a ring. What abominable character-actor buffoonery, in the worst tradition of opera-house comedy. What spiritless gaiety. What a miscast Susanna (more regal than her mistress). What a charmless Figaro. If Figaro doesn't ingratiate, what the hell are we all doing there?

The only exception to the incompetence and the mere competence is Georges Descrières, who played the title role in Molière's *Dom Juan* in New York last year. Descrières, who looks like an elegant George C. Scott, is an actor of carriage and wit.

The tattiness of the French theater is proverbial, but this production, at what is supposedly France's first house, would disgrace the West Englewood High School Varsity Show. The designs are childish and the construction amateur. Every time—I repeat, every time—someone opens or closes a door, the entire room shakes. When scenery is changed between acts, a flap of cloth is left projecting in the join between two flats.

Ideally, repertory life is the best life for an actor, but I can't imagine a worse fate for an intelligent French actor than to be a lifelong member of the Comédie. (Some get trained there and escape —Jeanne Moreau, for instance.) The "museum" function of a repertory theater is invaluable, particularly in a country with a rich dramatic literature; but a good museum doesn't show its treasures under inches of dust. My opinion of the Comédie has changed.

Report from Germany

(July 10, 1971)

One of the nice things about going to the German theater is that you don't need to know German. (Mine is sketchy.) If you have some knowledge of dramatic literature, you can go to two or three plays a week; the repertory theaters are always doing some familiar works. I'm in Europe for two months, courtesy of the Ford Foundation, to look at theater and film and allied matters, and am spending the first five weeks in Germany. Herewith a report.

Frankfurt

I begin at Experimenta 4. This is the fourth biennial festival, in Frankfurt, of new theater and film and music from all over (West) Germany. I see three plays and parts of two film shows. The latter seem to be groping their way upward toward the lower reaches of the American Underground. Only one of the plays is worth comment, *Heimarbeit,* which means *Homework,* but not in the schoolboy sense. It's by Franz Xaver Kroetz, a relatively new and rapidly rising playwright, and it's performed by the Munich Kammerspiele. Kroetz has focused on the poverty that still exists under the postwar Economic Miracle. There are only two characters, a Bavarian husband and wife, and their scenes are interwoven with film clips shot in that very stage setting with the same two actors plus one other. The materials are out of Büchner and Hauptmann—the enforced, empirical morality of the poor—but Kroetz's tight, modern structure, with everything understated, gives the play both pertinence and a sense of history. The poor we have always with us. And because of this play I run straight into the hottest current controversy in the German theater. After the ovation for *Heimarbeit,* one of the two excellent actors tells the audience that this is a sample of the work that Heinar Kipphardt did as *Dramaturg* of their Munich theater (a job that Brecht once held). More applause, for Kipphardt has just been fired, and the papers are full of uproar. He's in the audience and comes up to answer questions—a stocky, mustached, gentle man, trying to tell his truth, not whip up sympathy.

I'd better explain the term *Dramaturg.* (It will occur again.) We have no such function in the U.S., though several resident theaters claim to have Literary Managers. The closest parallel I know is Kenneth Tynan's job with the British National Theater. It's the primary task of the *Dramaturg* to provide his *Intendant* (Managing Director) with a choice of plays: not merely to read such scripts as are submitted, but to scout the world for good new plays, to commission works, to suggest relevant works of the past. Sometimes he helps administer the theater, and he is usually a close collaborator with the *Intendant* on the general artistic tone and policy.

Kipphardt is also a playwright, best known in the U.S. for his "documentary" *In the Matter of J. Robert Oppenheimer* which was produced in Los Angeles and New York. During his years at the Kammerspiele, where there has apparently been cool respect between him and the *Intendant,* his views and recommendations have brought him into conflict with the governmental agencies that subsidize the theater. Lately the Kammerspiele presented Wolf Biermann's *Der Dra-Dra* (a child's word for dragon). Biermann is an East Berliner, unpopular there because of his anti-Stalinist Marxism. Kipphardt prepared a program booklet for the Munich production, as part of his job, in which he reportedly implied that Biermann's East German dragons had their counterparts in some West German figures like the Munich mayor and Willy Brandt.

Enter Günter Grass, the famous novelist, who is very active in the Social Democratic Party (of Brandt). Grass, who in the minds of many has become an Establishment fat-cat, attacked Kipphardt in the press; by coincidence, Kipphardt's contract, just terminating, was not renewed. Now the feuilleton sections of newspapers are full of the affair, and the latest issue of *Die Deutsche Bühne,* a monthly about the German theater, devotes its first four pages to it. I've just seen the draft of a letter, to be sent to the press, signed by ten prominent directors who promise never to work at the Kammerspiele unless Kipphardt is reinstated. (Which isn't likely.)

The day after *Heimarbeit,* I lunch with Kipphardt, and we converse in his German and my English. As delicately as possible, I ask whether there isn't a certain naïveté in the reaction to the government's reaction—in fact, a false naïveté. Don't radical artists pretend shock and outrage when things like this happen, although they are inevitable? More courteously than I probably deserve, he replies that even if this is true, the outrage is part of the process, and in any event a theater man of certain convictions must deliberately set out to reap the result of his convictions. What's his future, I ask, besides writing? He thinks he might work through television. The funds for German TV come directly from the public, in license fees, not from advertisers or government. The TV people might give him funds to do plays, in return for the right to film the productions for broadcast. This method of TV subsidy, as I've seen, has already worked effectively in Britain.

Later, a prominent young critic tells me that the "Kipphardt case" is only the latest symptom of a recurrent trouble. Almost all significant German theaters receive substantial support from city or state government or both, so artists who are radical politically or esthetically have their troubles. Strangely, his remarks make me envious. Compared to the U.S., this seems a healthy way to have theater troubles. At least they occur in a theater *system,* in a society that is committed to concern about its theater.

Hamburg

A poorly acted production of Shaw's *Heartbreak House* at the Thalia, also afflicted with "designer-itis," the compulsion to use startling settings, whether or not they are apt.

A dress rehearsal of Molnár's *Olympia* at the same theater, with two old favorites, Hans Jaray and Paula Wessely, playing with the ease that looks easy to almost everyone but actors; and who help to keep this old soap-bubble afloat.

A charming evening at the Hansa, the last variety theater in Europe, which has been going for seventy-five years. Biedermeier furnishings, steeply banked rows of armchairs with small tables before them, on each table a button to summon your waiter. When the curtain rises on the small stage, the first thing you see is a painted drop, advertising the theater's huge and inexpensive open sandwich. Then the long show begins (with dancing bears) and, like the sandwich, is very good. Have *you* ever seen a man stand on his head, then spin like a top?

A fascinating production of Aristophanes' *Lysistrata* at the Schauspielhaus. Here the original scenery and costumes, by Erwin W. Zimmer, help the concept enormously. We see a huge curtain of unbleached muslin that drapes forward over the apron, completely hiding the stage. When it rises, we see wide steps leading up to a sort of low rectangular tunnel, all covered in leopard skin. The general effect is rough, strong, primal, an environment that blends perfectly the necessary sophistication and rudeness. This is further borne out by the costumes, which look like weathered ritual garments, and the half-masks that all the actors wear. Dieter Dorn's direction is particularly fine with the two choruses, the old men and old women. I could have done without some cuteness supplied by two non-speaking *compères,* but generally this was a vigorous, unified performance.

I note (as I'm to note again elsewhere) that this complex production is only one item in a busy season's repertoire.

Like many large theaters, this one has a smaller theater in which experimental work is done. The Malersaal of the Schauspielhaus presents two short plays by Wolfgang Bauer, who, like Peter Handke, is a young Austrian and whose name is often coupled with Handke's at the head of the list of important young dramatists.* *Film und Frau,* the longer piece, is too long: a sometimes funny comedy about Hollywood's effect on sex fantasy and sex life, with some striking visual images. *Party for Six* (the title is in English) is set in Graz. The dialogue is in thick Austrian dialect and quite beyond me, but everything is clear enough anyway. (As a German friend confirms later.)

The set is a dowdy living room. A young man is giving a party. His guests arrive, two men and three girls, and they all go into the next room and shut the door! We hear music and talk and laughter. Occasionally one of them comes out to go to the bathroom, and we see a small upstairs window light up. Or more bottles are fetched. Or a boy and a girl come out to grapple, the boy is repulsed and lies on the sofa in the dark, sulking, till someone else comes out.

It's a series of short scenes, no story, just trivial incidents; but by the oblique view, the sharp selection of detail, and the tart curtailment of scenes, Bauer builds a mosaic of minutiae—a witty, sympathetic picture of small-town frustrations. For the curtain call I see only five of the six actors. Puzzling. Then I notice that the bathroom window is lit up.

(July 24 and 31, 1971)

Düsseldorf

The Schauspielhaus, like many other German theaters and opera houses, was built after the war. This is one of the handsomest new theater buildings I've seen anywhere, set on the edge of a park filled with great trees.

The building is better than the show. I see Molière's *Tartuffe,* in a shabby production, poorly lighted, and routinely acted. The one interesting element is the Tartuffe himself, played by Karl-Heinz Martell (directed by Werner Kraut). This Tartuffe glides, his torso

---

* See p. 195.

seeming to follow his legs, and he is wigged and bearded to look like a sick Karamazov brother. Without losing the comedy of hypocrisy, Martell suggests that Tartuffe is not an utter faker, that he at least had some weak ambition toward a religious life. In the entrapment scene with Elmire, his anger at her for exciting him gives the part an added dimension. Stanislavsky said that when you play a miser, you should look for his generous moments. Martell has heard.

In contrast with this production, *Eugene Onegin* at the Opera is incredibly lavish. (And proves again that Tschaikowsky, whatever his lack as a symphonist, was a masterly theater writer. The duel scene, for instance, is a moment of genius.)

Next day I meet Wilhelm Berner, the *Dramaturg* of the Schauspiel-haus. A tall, worried-looking man wearing formal tie and informal windbreaker. He tells me that this is the busiest theater in Germany. They give two performances a night—at the Grosses Haus and the Kleines Haus (their experimental stage)—seven nights a week. They also play a circuit of ten towns roundabout. The state contributes to their budget, as well as the city, so they have to play throughout the state. Sometimes they have four different companies playing four different plays on the same night. They give children's matinees as well. (Sixty-six actors on the payroll.)

Berner works very closely with the *Intendant,* Karl Heinz Stroux, and is proud that during their years there—he ten, Stroux fifteen—they have given many premieres of German plays, German premieres of foreign plays, and even some world premieres of foreign plays. Ionesco and Neruda, among other authors. They are now preparing the German premiere of Berrigan's *The Trial of the Catonsville Nine,* the first play of the new season, in late August. (They take six weeks off a year.)

But—Stroux and he are leaving Düsseldorf at the end of next season. The theater trustees are catering, he says, to the demands of young "communistic" elements and of older people, including some critics, who pander to the young. Berner is bitter because he feels that he and Stroux have worked hard to keep their theater vital and con-temporary.

When I leave, I pass the stunning new Thyssen skyscraper just across the street and wonder about the "communistic" influence in this industrial capital. Maybe there's another reason why Stroux and Berner are leaving? That night I see Stroux's production of O'Neill's

More Stately Mansions. The sets are deplorable, the direction largely pedestrian. The mother is played by Elisabeth Bergner, still a star. And still clever, still slim, still appallingly affected.

Cologne

Klaus Schöning is a different kind of *Dramaturg*—for the Third Program (serious material) of the Westdeutscher Rundfunk (radio network). On the way to the Rundfunk building I cross the square in front of the great cathedral, which took 700 years to complete and survived the war virtually intact. Schöning's office, decorated with pop art, looks out on the cathedral front.

He is congenial, young, long-haired. He tells me that he's responsible for finding 100 plays of varying lengths for each six-month season. He has been at WDR for eight years and has edited two volumes of radio plays, which he shows me. Their typography alone confirms what I've heard of his interest in the avant-garde. He also confirms that many poets and novelists are more eager to write for radio than for TV or film or theater. He commissioned Peter Handke, among many others, to write his first radio play, and has just commissioned Robert Creeley, the American poet. (And has the right translator, he says.)

Now he's starting a series of what he calls *Hörspot*—literally, hearspots—five-minute plays to shove in at odd moments in the schedule. For instance, after the news, a quick political satire just so people won't take politicians too pontifically. Won't there be opposition? I ask. He shrugs. All the political parties want to influence the media, he says, but their chief interest is in programs of comment, particularly on TV, which has the biggest audience. So he is relatively free. "For the moment," he adds with a laugh.

I see two plays in Cologne. At a tiny café-theater called the Senftöpfchen (the Little Mustard Pot) I see a dress rehearsal of a likable two-character trifle with an untranslatable punning title, by Karl Wittlinger. It's played by Curt Reich, who directed, and his wife, Ruth Köppler. She, pleasantly bare-bosomed most of the time, is skillful. Reich, round-faced and slightly beefy, is a born comic actor, immediately winning. Maybe it's the "continental" circumstances, but this slight, one-joke play (too trivial to explain) amuses me throughout.

And next night, at the Schauspielhaus, Tolstoy's *And the Light Shines in Darkness!* Designs and textual adaptation by the novelist Heinrich Böll. Another overwhelming physical production—and, again, just one item in a big repertoire. Constructivist in style, the show has large units that roll in and out, turntables, even a complete field of wheat! The asylum scenes suggest that the director, David Esrig, has seen Peter Brook's *Marat/Sade,* and, throughout, his direction is rather italicized, but he and Böll have done their damnedest to keep Tolstoy's late, tractarian play from being a bore. They almost succeed.

It strikes me that, where these old city-states used to compete in trade and in war, they now compete in the lavishness and novelty of their theater and opera productions.

Stuttgart

Jörg Wehmeier, gray-haired and courteous, is the *Dramaturg* of the Staatstheater. Every theater has its particular pride; his is that this is the most political theater in Germany. I comment on the astonishing way that the Germans insisted on having new theaters (where old ones had been destroyed) and subsidized companies so quickly after the war. He is less impressed. He says it was just bourgeois pattern, what we would call culture-vulturism. As proof, he cites the trouble they have here whenever they do anything daring, the hundreds of letters they get demanding mere entertainment. He and the *Intendant,* Peter Palitzsch, are so fed up that they are leaving at the end of next season. Going to Frankfurt.

I report that Berner says he and Stroux are leaving Düsseldorf for just the opposite reason—they're not radical enough to please. Wehmeier replies skeptically: "So he says."

Palitzsch joins us, a lean, energetic man with a frequent, quick smile. He was a colleague of Brecht's in East Berlin (as were several other men I've met). He has just come from a rehearsal of *Hölderlin,* a new play by Peter Weiss, the author of *Marat/Sade,* which deals with the corruption of revolution. Stuttgart will have the world premiere in early fall.

I ask Palitzsch what I know is an old question, still relevant—about the political efficacy of the theater. Can an instrument that grows out of a certain society change the society that was its source?

He answers that he is not interested in direct propaganda but in providing a philosophic "model" in the theater. His chief motive is to fight the fascist influences he senses in German society. He makes quite clear that he doesn't mean Nazi: fascist with a small f.

For this work he needs actors who are completely committed, not ones who are only professionals, however good. The actor can do no more than he is and must not do less. He will take some of his present company to Frankfurt and has invited others. He hopes to build a philosophical-political theater, to play not only in the main Frankfurt playhouse but in workers' halls in the suburbs.

Privately, despite his conviction, he makes me feel a bit depressed. I know this is because of my uncertain belief in political theater—my feeling that, one way or another, I've heard all this many times. Still, I know that Palitzsch too has heard it before. So perhaps . . .

Unfortunately, the one production I see at his theater is not by him. It's *Uncle Vanya,* directed by a young associate—and crammed with every glibly melancholy Chekhov cliché. I hope that none of these actors will go to Frankfurt with Palitzsch. His job will be difficult enough.

Munich

The Taming of the Shrew at the Residenztheater is an "underplayed" production, modern and internal, lacking high spirits and a grasp of physical comedy. The sets are dull and based on a dull concept— turning leaves of scenery like leaves of a book. But within its limits it's decently acted, and the director, Otto Schenk, has put a valid base under his view of the play: sex. When Petruchio and Katharine first see each other, there's a moment's sexy silence—as they are simultaneously struck—before the fights begin. It's a good sounding-board for the scrapping. At the end, when she "puts her hand beneath her husband's foot," he bends to the floor and kisses it. So Schenk's idea is completed. If only there were some juice in the show.

In a tiny basement theater "off Broadway" I see a two-character play "on motives from Jules Feiffer," with Gisela Hagenau and Sepp Holstein. The latter directed, imaginatively suggesting cartoon strips of naturalism. Bernard and his girl eventually marry, have children, grow old, but still fence and "explain." There are only ten people in the audience, only eight of whom really understand German. But those eight enjoy themselves, so apparently the sex troubles of Feiffer's New Yorkers strike responses in Munich. Glands across the sea.

Joachim Kaiser is the widely respected theater critic of the *Süddeutsche Zeitung*. (Several German newspapers, like this Munich paper, are read nationally.) He writes about films and music as well, and he says that his readers seem much more concerned about music than theater. "If I say *Hamlet* has four acts instead of five, no letters. If I get wrong the key of a Bach duet, a dozen letters."

But he indicates that the theater public's taste has sharpened in at least one way. I mention that young German actors seem to me to be technically well equipped, whatever their degree of talent. Kaiser says that ten years ago they were not so good, but the rise of university theaters has helped to train them, and the growing impact of TV—which, he says, is usually decently acted, whatever else may be wrong with it—has made even provincial audiences more demanding of actors.

And, of course, the organization of the German theater makes it possible for at least some young actors to work steadily. How do newcomers get in? I ask. Kaiser says there are auditions. If a young actor is unlucky, he gets taken on by a big theater, and ten years later may still be playing small parts. If he gets taken by a provincial theater, he may soon get to play good parts and can work his way up to a big theater. (The old Edmund Kean–Henry Irving pattern.)

A couple of coincidences. I heard the name of Karl Valentin a few weeks ago for the first time. He was a Munich cabaret comedian, tall and gangly, whom the city treasured and whom intellectuals took very seriously. Brecht adored him. He died some twenty years ago. Wandering about Munich, I come to a surviving tower of the old city wall which has been made into a Karl Valentin Museum. I go up the narrow winding stairs to a room filled with photographs, old comic props, programs, and a phonograph to play Valentin recordings. Everything to keep this man from dying.

And today I see a review of a new "opera-sketch" about Valentin, in which he is hailed as a spiritual ancestor of Beckett and Ionesco. I wonder whether those authors ever saw him. Anyway, I feel I've stumbled on something good that, paradoxically, I'll never know.

Berlin

Theater in West Berlin is pretty well over for the season by the time I get here. Biggest disappointment: I won't see the most discussed play in Germany, Peter Stein's production of Ibsen's *Peer Gynt* at the Schaubühne am Halleschen Ufer. This is a Maoist theater, so naturally it cannot be in the East, but, curiously, it's subsidized by the West.

So across the Wall to the jewel in East Germany's theater crown, the Berliner Ensemble. I see their production of Brecht's *Arturo Ui,* a play I dislike. First, its pattern—a Chicago-gangster parable about the rise of Hitler—is utterly predictable after the first few minutes. Second, it's historically vicious: it says that Hitler and pals are gangsters who muscled in on Germany. As if there had never been a cheer or a vote for the Nazis. Besides, there is something grimly funny about seeing a parable about machine-gunning politicians in a city where you can also see soldiers on street corners with submachine guns.

But the production, first done in 1959, directed by Manfred Wekwerth and Peter Palitzsch (now of Stuttgart), is splendid. I had heard that the Ensemble had been running down; tonight, at any rate, their work is crackling and fine. Ekkehard Schall (Brecht's son-in-law) is as magnificent as reported, a man whose body is as good a comic instrument as any I've seen since the films of Keaton. Schall is said to spend two hours a day training. Not rehearsing, training. Rehearsals are something else.

Benno Besson, artistic director of the Volksbühne in East Berlin, is a French Swiss who looks like an older Jean-Louis Trintignant. He used to work with Brecht—in fact, collaborated on an adaptation with him—and has been at the Volksbühne for four years.

Contrary to most observers in the West, Besson reports that in the East young people are very interested in the theater. (Friedrich Luft of *Die Welt,* the well-known West German critic, told me that he's gloomy about the audience's continuing "connection" with the theater there.) But Besson says that, contradictorily, few young people want to become actors—although he says there are three good acting schools, in (East) Berlin, Dresden, and Babelsberg.

Predictably, Besson says that his audience is intellectually sharp but esthetically retrograde. Avant-garde theater is unknown. Criticism is bad. No interesting new playwrights—yet.

He adds four new productions to the repertoire each year, two of which he himself directs. Why does he choose to work here? His answer parallels answers I've heard from film directors in the Soviet bloc. There are restrictions, but so long as one is in favor, there are enormous resources and facilities. The balance comes out the same as in the West, he says, although the specifics are different. Besides, he likes the idea of working in a community, with an audience that shares certain beliefs and attitudes. He has missed this very much when he has worked in the West.

I tell him that after our talk I'm going to see Shaw's *Caesar and Cleopatra* at his theater. He winces. An old production, he says, done before his regime. I go to it; and I wince.

Fiddler on the Roof, at the Komische Oper (East Berlin), was directed by the legendary Walter Felsenstein. A Berlin friend who knows Felsenstein's work well is as dismayed as I am by *Fiddler*— says he can't understand why Felsenstein wanted to do it, and that I mustn't judge him by this production. O.K. But it certainly makes the Robbins-Mostel show on Broadway look even better in retrospect. *Fiddler* needs a Robbins and a Mostel to be bearable, let alone enjoyable.

I found no Parnassus in the (West) German theater, but I didn't really expect one. What I did find was a rather nice love-hate relation between that theater and its intelligent public. That public is irritated, impatient, sometimes bored; but would, I think, be terrified if the theater were to disappear. Meanwhile, if only by rote, each city of any size pays to keep a theater or theaters going; and at least provides a continuum; and an *occasion* for possibility.

Report from Iceland

(*July 15, 1972*)

Reykjavík

Gudlaugur Rósinkranz is the director of the National Theater in Reykjavík, therefore the theatrical dean of Iceland. One of the things

I like about him is that it never occurs to him that Iceland's theater is less important than any other. There is no touch of "We're only a small country, but . . ." He is white-haired, slim, dignified, energetic. Now sixty-nine, due to retire in September, he has been director here since this theater was built in 1950. I have seen pictures of him through the years, in one of those books that permanent theaters produce regularly, and he looks substantially unchanged since the beginning except for his hair.

Did he run a theater before he came to this one?

"There was no theater to run. No professional theater. This is still the only theater in Iceland."

But there must have been some theatrical activity?

"Very much. Here in Reykjavík there is a fine amateur theater, much older than we are, and every town, every village has some sort of amateur theater. In fact, they are subsidized."

Amateurs?

"Absolutely. If people start an amateur theater, they get some money for their expenses from the state and from the community. It is a law. Oh, no great sums, but something."

So at least he had a strong interest on which to build.

"A strong *tradition,* I would say. And many plays. Some of our best writers have always been writing for these amateur groups."

Did he begin with a company of amateurs?

"Some, certainly, but even they had been training. I had been a headmaster in a school where we did many plays, and I believed in training. While they were constructing this building [his office is a large room with a fireplace in a suite of offices backstage] we were training a company. In 1949 and 1950. Then we rehearsed three plays, so that we would open with a repertory. And here we are, ever since."

Some of the same people are still in the company?

"Many of them. And many of them are wonderful actors."

Does he direct plays himself?

"No, no. We have directors, some Icelandic, some guests from other countries, even one from America. I sit here. I have enough to do. But I watch it all carefully."

And the training school continues?

"Not at the moment. We are awaiting a new law which will combine our school with some private schools that were started, and then we will proceed again."

How many in the company and how many plays a year?

"We have three directors and two designers and twenty-five actors —besides a few others we get for this or that—and we now do ten plays a year."

The permanent actors have seasonal contracts?

"Longer. We have three kinds of contract—I won't go into all details—but the best is for almost a lifetime, with all pensions and insurance and so on."

Has the audience changed in twenty-two years?

"Very much. Much more demanding. Films and television have helped with that."

Do they like what they see?

He smiles. "They come. We have almost always a full house." (Later I see that this is true; and that there is a much greater proportion of young people than I saw in German theaters last year.)

The repertory seems eclectic. This year they are doing both *Othello* and *Oklahoma!*, among others. Any Icelandic plays?

"Many." He is very firm. "Every year we do at least one Icelandic play, this year one by Halldór Laxness, our Nobel Prize winner. One season we did nothing but Icelandic plays, old and new."

Do Icelandic authors write often for his theater?

"I have statistics that I made because I am finishing here soon." He consults some papers. "In twenty-two years we have done forty-four Icelandic plays, and twenty-eight of those were new ones."

So, in the largest sense, it is a community enterprise.

"This is our national theater. And we are a national people."

The theater itself is a moderately ugly modernistic building, on a hill dominating the small city, and is equally unattractive inside. Smallish: it seats about 675. The lounge is decorated with busts and paintings of Icelandic poets and dramatists, none of whose names I know. It feels like being dropped into a fictional country where the novelist has invented everything, famous poets and all.

My first night there is a bill of two short plays by one of the theater's designers, Birgir Engilberts, who also did the décor. I see the first, *An Ordinary Dream,* which is funny from rise of curtain.

The set is a tabletop with a potted plant that towers over the two actors and an ashtray with a cigar butt that is almost the size of a man. The dwarfed man in the ashtray and the woman next to the pot are evidently waking with hangovers after a party. They accuse one another of various misdeeds at the party, and as the fantasy progresses, they grow increasingly uncertain that they are one another's spouses: they may have each passed out in the wrong apartment. (I've been told the story.) The two actors are quite competent, though they seem to be trading just a bit on the audience's affection for them.

The next production I see at the National is Goethe's *Faust,* directed by a guest, Karl Vibach from the Lübeck theater in West Germany. Fascinating. The three angels of the prologue are golden, with golden faces too, on pedestals against a black backdrop. Vibach has cast them with an acute ear: their voices orchestrate well.

After this baroque opening like souvenirs from an Austrian church, Vibach slips us into a moderately mod scheme. As Faust makes his way (on a revolving stage) down the university corridor to his study, he passes students lounging against walls, reading, inspecting posted grades, all dressed in contemporary boots and pullovers that seem somehow timeless. Among the delights that Mefistofeles shows him later are hippies and rock music and female nudity, but the production never seems to slide into mere cleverness.

The chief reasons for this, stronger even than Vibach's grip, are the two principal actors. Róbert Arnfinsson, the Mefistofeles, is outstandingly able, intensely and enjoyably theatrical, intelligent, musical. The Faust, Gunnar Eyjólfsson, a handsome man, is among the best classic actors I have seen in my life. Of course, I don't literally understand a word of his, but I know approximately what he is saying, can relish his vocal address and variety; and can certainly see his ability to move and to time his movements, and his power to hold the stage through that beautiful combination of self (Eyjólfsson) and self's emphases provided by an author (Goethe) that are usually at the root of fine acting.

Two extraordinary actors, presumably not the only ones in that theater, playing out their careers in a language understood by only 200,000 people on an island that most of the world flies past on its way to culture.

PART II

productions

revivals

Hamlet

(Channel 13, New York, April 14, 1964)

In the current production of *Hamlet,* Richard Burton gives a lot of evidence that he is very well qualified for the part. Then why doesn't he satisfy?

Look first at his merits. First, Burton has a natural affinity for verse. He speaks it like a man at home in it, not—like so many contemporary actors—like one who comes at it from the outside and is trying to paw his way in. His voice is not seductive in itself—like Peter O'Toole's or Fritz Weaver's, for example—but it has compass, power, stamina, and a good theatrical cutting edge. He has the assurance that comes not only from long stage experience but from specific experience in poetic drama. I saw him thirteen years ago at Stratford-on-Avon as Prince Hal, and though he was miscast in that part, even then he gave a sense of belonging in Shakespeare. This considerable range of feeling and perception helps him to deal with the range of Hamlet. He has sheer presence, easy and attractive, and it has nothing to do with film-star glamour or his recent wave of notoriety. He had that quiet, melancholy strength of personality in 1950, in *The Lady's Not for Burning*. And at various moments through the evening he is, to put it simply, simply beautiful. For instance, I have never heard the most famous soliloquy spoken better. It achieved the perfect state; suddenly, softly, we seemed to be able to hear the young prince thinking. Yet there was no prosaic trickery: the line of the verse, the richness of meaning were not lost. I'll never forget it.

Why, then, is Burton unsatisfying? A large part of the trouble is explained by the following quotation: "It is a temptation for the actor of Hamlet to develop the possibilities of each scene instead of presenting a complete basic character in which the part may progress in a simple convincing line." Who wrote that? John Gielgud, the director of this production; and that is exactly the basic fault of Burton's performance. There is not from first to last a clear image of who this Hamlet is. I do not dictate what that image should be, though, like everyone who cares for the play, I have my own image of the part. All I ask for is Burton's image; and it is unclear. One may almost say nonexistent.

Seeking for effects, scene by scene, without overall design, he often misses effects—falling back on the loud-soft syndrome: shouting for a bit, then suddenly speaking quietly, or vice versa. He falls into the trap, always waiting for Hamlets, of taking the audience too much into his confidence when he mocks Polonius, or Rosencrantz and Guildenstern, inviting us too heavily to wink with him at these characters, making us too aware that he knows we're there. Some of his scenes lack rationale. For example, after the ghost scene, when he asks Horatio and Marcellus to swear secrecy, he plays the Ghost's subterranean "Swear" for laughs. It's incomprehensible.

Then, too, he doesn't move well, and that distracts us. In his first soliloquy, "O that this too too solid flesh would melt," his shambling about the stage fights what he's working for in the lines. Often, and I think unconsciously, he uses a sort of bridesmaid's hesitation step, drawing one foot up to the other. He's not keenly enough aware of the visual as enriching or hindering other matters. There is no grace and very little tension in his body, little princeliness in his bearing. Also, he is over-addicted to patting the faces of other actors in affection or disdain.

Some of these defects can be attributed to Gielgud's direction, which is extremely disappointing from an artist of his caliber. Gielgud's voice, incidentally, reads the Ghost's lines in a recording—and he proves again that he is just about the best speaker of Shakespeare alive. But his staging is poor. The play-within-a-play scene, for example, is merely a jumble. In the closet scene he has the murdered Polonius tumble out on stage and lie in full light, right behind Hamlet and his mother. So while Hamlet berates the queen for making love over the nasty sty, he himself is scolding her practically over a well-illuminated corpse. Much of the stage movement is cramped and awkward, but partly this is due to Ben Edwards' setting, which is a triumph of mismanagement.

None of the other actors is worth comment in this brief time except George Rose, the First Gravedigger, who certifies what he showed in Dogberry a few years ago—that he is a wonderful Shakespearean clown. And Hume Cronyn as Polonius. He is an obvious carpenter—you can see him busily sawing and hammering for his effects—but he builds them.

The conceit of this production is that it is a run-through. No costumes. A run-through is a rehearsal after some weeks' work without interruption by the director, so that he may see the play as a whole, make notes, give the cast criticism. Well, this cast badly needs those notes. But in Burton it has a Hamlet of considerable potential. The next question is whether the conditions of modern stage and screen life will ever let him realize it.

A Note on Shakespeare Program Notes

(The New York Times, *June 23, 1966*)

Is Shakespeare our contemporary? A lot of program notes want us to think so, particularly those in the programs of resident theaters and festivals. Often those notes are written by the directors of the plays; and sometimes they contradict the productions that we see.

For instance, the program of the Shakespeare Festival at Stratford, Ontario. Their present repertory contains a production of *Henry V* that has been directed by Michael Langham with all the evocations of Shakespearean stage life that we have come to expect from him. Whatever flaws it may have, there is never any question that he understands the play in essence and style.

In his program notes Langham asks what "this jingoistic national anthem of a play" has to do with our age, a play that "glorifies war, exploits the inanities of nationalism, is offensively class-conscious, and . . . is patently and exultantly anti-French." His answer: "Though the above view of the play is widely held, it does not necessarily represent Shakespeare's intention. . . . Frankly, I believe that our age of disillusionment is closer to his than any that divides them."

Langham adds that the Chorus does NOT (his capitals) express Shakespeare's own attitude, that it "represents the popular view, the national press so to speak," and that the play invites us "to examine the difference between the popular myth and the truth."

I would set out to rebut these assertions, which strike me as amiable nonsense, if they had not already been excellently rebutted by Langham himself. There is no slightest trace in his good production of what he says is the disillusioned truth of the matter. The Chorus enjoins us to imagine a real war taking place on the stage, and the play supplies the stimulating symbols of that war for our imagination. The fact that the Chorus omits mention of the cowardice and knavery of some of the lower-class characters does not negate the unswerving loyalty of other lower-class characters or the unquestioned acceptance of class structure and militaristic patriotism. Unlike his notes, Langham's production is set firmly in the ethical atmosphere of the age in which it was written.

The Festival is also presenting *Henry VI*, which has been impressively directed by John Hirsch. Again the production is excellently Shakespearean. Again some odd program notes. For instance, Hirsch quotes, as appropriate to the play, eight lines of W. B. Yeats's poem "The Second Coming," which tells us that anarchy is loosed upon the world, the ceremony of innocence is drowned, the best lack all conviction, and the worst are full of passionate intensity.

This, I think, is a philosophical fast-shuffle—to equate the era of the Wars of the Roses with the era that followed World War I, about which Yeats was writing. People have been butchering people with diligence ever since Cain, but the spiritual atmosphere of the mid-twentieth century is unique in Western history.

Now the point of all this is not to subject the talented Langham and Hirsch to extraneous literary criticism. What concerns me is that they felt the need for this quasi-apologetic insistence that Shakespeare is contemporary.

If their productions had dramatized a specifically modern approach, like Peter Brook's existential *King Lear,* then their notes would at least be appropriate to the case. But these artists presented relatively orthodox productions. "Orthodox" does not mean unoriginal or imitative, it means simply that, for all the color of the director's individuality, each production lies within the mainstream of Shakespearean stage tradition, that each director rendered his play as a work of its time, made timely to us by the universals reached through the particulars of that time.

The peripheral worry about Shakespeare's pertinence contradicts the perception shown on the Stratford stage. We see there that Shakespeare is *not* our contemporary—not in any congruent, ideological sense. He was, to hammer the obvious, a genius who comprehended more about human life than any other man who ever wrote (peace to the partisans of Dante and Goethe) and who thus inevitably comprehended a great deal about us. But he was, in his mortality, a man of the Elizabethan age, when bear-baiting and atrocious executions were popular spectator sports (and no one can prove that Shakespeare did not enjoy them as much as any other Londoner); when Drake's defeat of the Spanish Armada was a national joy; and when, despite any incidental grumblings, monarchy and a strict class system were taken as the order of the universe.

To believe that the soldierly loyalty of Fluellen in *Henry V* is less true than Pistol's cynical opportunism is to try to convert Shakespeare into an anachronism. The man who wrote Henry's St. Crispin's Day speech, about the privilege of fighting at Agincourt, is the same man who wrote Falstaff's speech about the emptiness of military honor. To insist that he meant the latter and not the former—just because you or I may mean the latter and not the former—is to diminish Shakespeare, not to prove that he is modern.

Certainly every age sees Shakespeare through its own eyes. Apart from an era's specialized readings, like Ernest Jones's Freudian study *Hamlet and Oedipus*, orthodoxy itself changes. The term has to mean something different to a man of 1966 as against one of 1866, even of 1936. But this is largely because of psychological and social conditioning that manifests itself willy-nilly.

Langham and Hirsch are needlessly worried. Shakespeare is working on us, through their productions. Besides, by insisting that despite all the stuff about kings and glory the author is still meaningful, these program notes perform two disservices, I think.

First, they encourage others, especially lesser directors, to chase the silly phantom of literal timeliness in Shakespeare. (Which is not synonymous with individual interpretation.) Second, they may lead to some audience bewilderment about these exceptional productions. Hirsch's *Henry VI* does not take place in a "world devoid of hope" as he says it does. Langham's *Henry V* is not a contrast between a propagandist Chorus and a play that tells the truth. Their author, as they themselves produce him, is larger than they claim.

Measure for Measure

(The New York Times, *July 14, 1966*)

Good news from Central Park. After a dullish *All's Well That Ends Well* by the New York Shakespeare Festival and after an execrable *Macbeth* in its mobile theater, I expected little of the new production. But a hefty measure of praise for *Measure for Measure*.

This latest production, which opened Tuesday night at the Delacorte Theater, has been directed by Michael Kahn with understanding and a sense of form. Kahn stumbles when he tries for arty effects. There is an opening pantomime of wretches, prostitutes, and crippled beggars that is cut-rate Marat-Sadism. (It is not only irrelevant but contradictory. The Duke in this play, whom we are supposed to admire, talks about loving the people while he is surrounded by this horrible oppressed mob.)

But once the Peter Brooklets have flowed into the background and Kahn concentrates on the play—the realization of characters and the structures of speech and scene, the meat of direction, not the garniture—he does commendably.

This "dark" comedy, set in Vienna, tells of young Claudio, who is condemned to death for getting his fiancée with child. (This was *old* Vienna.) Angelo, who is ruling the city in the Duke's absence, will pardon the prisoner if Claudio's sister, Isabella, will sleep with him. She refuses—and her refusal has caused a centuries-old critical controversy. Is she a prig to prize her chastity above her brother's life? The flip, hip answer is yes. But one virtue of this production is that it makes her refusal quite understandable and austerely admirable in the religious context of the play. Is she any more priggish than Sophocles' Antigone, who made all that fuss about a funeral ceremony? To both ladies the formal matter is real; to us the form is no longer real but is still a valid symbol of principle.

At any rate, for those who disremember this rarely performed play, it ends happily. Shakespeare uses the same "bed trick" as in *All's Well That Ends Well*. Another lady substitutes for Isabella in the dark. The Duke, who has actually been present all along in disguise, sorts everything out in the final scene.

Barbara Baxley is emotionally credible as Isabella, but her intonations bind her to mid-century Manhattan. Tom Aldredge, as Angelo the temporary tyrant, is thin; one never believes that the Duke would have had enough initial confidence in him to test him with office.

But there are some exceptionally good performances. Shepperd Strudwick has the work-horse part of the Duke and distinguishes himself in it. He looks fine, reads intelligently, and plays with authority. It is the best performance by Strudwick that I can remember, and it shows that his maturity may prove his most interesting period. Al Freeman, Jr., plays Lucio, a too clever courtier, with an elegance and wit he has not shown before. Moses Gunn gives solidity to the Provost. Warren Wade has an amusing orotund aria as an eccentric prisoner.

Claudio is played by Christopher Walken, who won a Derwent Award this year for his performance of the young French king in *The Lion in Winter*. He is an extraordinary talent. His attractive voice could use some widening of range and finer control. (He tends to end lines on the same note.) Occasionally he luxuriates in emotion—a bit more concerned with moving himself than us. But he is a natural actor, with a highly expressive face, immediate conviction, and quick sensitivity. As with Peter O'Toole, whom he resembles somewhat in quality, there is a suggestion of the feline and feminine about him that makes him all the more subtly masculine. Walken should go a long way—to the benefit of us all.

The costumes by Theoni Aldredge cannot have taken much of that gifted designer's time. Ming Cho Lee's permanent set has to do multiple duty, including use as a prison; but I still don't know why it had to look like the balcony scene in *West Side Story*.

Measure for Measure is the best of the many productions I have seen in this Festival. It is good enough to make us wonder why this iron and ironic comedy, cascading with some of Shakespeare's best language, has been so much neglected.

Much Ado About Nothing

(September 9, 1972)

I haven't seen all the productions of the New York Shakespeare Festival, which are presented free in Central Park, but I've seen a great many in the last decade or so, and the most enjoyable is A. J. Antoon's production of *Much Ado About Nothing*. There is no single performance in it like the crazy, glittering Shylock that George C. Scott once gave on that stage, but the whole show knits together better than any other I have seen there. Many Festival productions seemed to aim at low common denominators in the audience. Antoon works in very American style but with very Elizabethan intent: that is, he wants the production to be all things to all men, as it was in the Globe. He is not interested exclusively in those who may be frightened by the author's name, he wants to affect the entire audience; and, barring some very patent lapses, he has covered the spectrum.

For openers, Antoon appreciates the peculiar genius of this great play. Many commentators have pointed out that the chief action of the drama is the story of Claudio and Hero, and how their marriage is almost wrecked by a villain's deception, but that Claudio and Hero are only the juvenile and ingenue in the cast. The leading roles are Benedick and Beatrice. Not all commentators have gone on from these facts to see that *Much Ado* was a daringly unorthodox, brilliantly new use of the theater: a mode in which some characters provide the basic motor force of the play so that two other characters can idle against it, can have a kind of moving belt on which to perform a different, subtler drama: of character, intellect, and wit as a medium for sex. The playwright tips his hat to all the theatrical necessities, but says in effect that the theater can be something other than those necessities and that people can be theatrically interesting when they are trying to do something other than kiss or stab one another. Along with *Julius Caesar,* which may be the first Christian-era drama without a villain, *Much Ado* is one of Shakespeare's esthetically radical works.

Antoon seems to have understood this, and in order to convey the radicalism in theater dynamics, has shifted the setting from Renaissance Messina (where, as with many Shakespeare locations, it never really took place; it is hardly a Sicilian play) to the United States around 1900—close but not too close for romance. Benedick and Claudio seem to be returning from the Spanish-American War, Don Pedro becomes Captain Pedro (a rhythm change easily assimilated because so much of the play is in prose), and Ming Cho Lee's lovely unit set suggests a Victorian pavilion that has proliferated upward, with a permanently waved American flag at the top. Peter Link's brass-band music underscores the period amusingly, and Theoni V. Aldredge's costumes are clever. (One anachronism: Benedick puts on trousers at one point and there's a zipper in them, about thirty-five years too soon.)

This transposition, unlike so many wearisome gimmicks inflicted on Shakespeare, serves some real purposes. First, it changes the Beatrice-and-Benedick backchat into very recognizable Yankee sass, without altering a word. In spirit—not language, of course—it is the same sharp verbal dueling one can still hear in village stores and at small-town dances. By making those comic tensions highly recognizable, Antoon centers us, makes us see the *raison d'être* for this eccentrically shaped play.

Second, the transposition helps him to glide easily over the abrupt change of key that has often bothered directors, the scene in which Beatrice asks Benedick to prove his newly confessed love by killing Claudio for his insult to her cousin, Hero. Up to then Beatrice has been thoroughly civilized, a high-comedy creation, a true Adversary

Woman. Suddenly she behaves like a woman in a Spanish tragedy of honor. Shakespeare was presumably trying to show that underneath the silk in all of us lies a savage and we kid ourselves by dubbing him Honor. Antoon, however, has laid his groundwork; and instead of having Beatrice play that scene like an outraged noblewoman out of Lope de Vega, he has her throw a tantrum, like a Yankee shrew. It fits the Beatrice we have come to know, this tone of "All right, if you're so wonderful, let's see you do this, and if not, just don't bother to come back"; it satisfies the action; and it keeps the scene within the precincts of comedy.

Third, this Americanized setting helps Antoon to make a strength out of a weakness. It enables him to use American actors as Americans instead of as fake Britishers and failed classicists. Sam Waterston is stratospheres away from John Gielgud, the best of the few Benedicks I have seen, but in this production Waterston succeeds. His voice is very limited. (Let's hear more than four notes next time, Waterston.) But his humorous intelligence, his comic timing, his lanky Yankee form make him a satisfying Benedick for this production, a non-gulping Jimmy Stewart.

The Beatrice is Kathleen Widdoes. She lacks innate command, but she is becoming a more healthy and attractive actress. Her Polly in *The Beggar's Opera* last spring, though still touched with conscious sensitivity, was a step ahead of her tremulous past. Her Beatrice has vitality and freedom, if not complete control. She may never acquire some gifts that she was not born with, but Antoon has helped her to the best performance of hers that I have seen. Certainly she is growing, and that's not exactly common among American actors.

And Antoon has got a beautiful performance from Douglass Watson as "Captain" Pedro. Watson has always fluctuated between the almost fine and the somewhat forced. His Pedro comes out a solid, gentlemanly, conventional officer, with the warm-heartedness to be credible as a matchmaker and the well-meaning blindness to take part in the shaming of Hero. We understand why he would do it and why, eventually, he should be forgiven.

The great gaps in the cast—and they are sore ones—are the Claudio and Hero. Glenn Walken (Christopher's brother) is pleasant enough but is utterly without technique. April Shawhan has a small bag of tricks, not technique, and is not nearly as pleasant. Claudio and Hero are relatively stock characters, so designed that their troubles and the solution of them can be taken as patterns in a ballet, not deeply wringing anguish. But Walken and Shawhan lack the ability to present even stock characters convincingly.

On the other hand, Mark Hammer is exceptionally lucid as old Leonato, and Jerry Mayer is nicely saturnine as Don John. My only quarrel with Mayer—with Antoon, really—is that the base for his comic fit of rage, rolling all over the floor, was not established earlier. He begins like Iago and ends like Chaplin's Hitler.

With Dogberry and Verges and their squad of police, Antoon has opted for the Keystone Kops, with Barnard Hughes, the Dogberry, made up like Ford Sterling. Admittedly, *something* has to be done with those scenes. The lines aren't hilarious, they are simply scaffolding for comic performers who are themselves funny. Hughes, a good actor, has no native well of comedy bubbling in him and just moves competently through some careful designs. Here, as in other places, the director errs in prodigality. There is too much slapstick, along with the assumption that anyone can do it, that it is not a difficult craft.

Antoon's prodigality works both ways. It bathes the play in warmth, in affection for the characters, to which the audience responds happily. He has a rich sense of period. He knows that when men went picnicking in those days, with their feet bare and trousers rolled, they wore jackets and ties and starched collars. He has a nice sense of action-as-décor. Just as Balthasar finishes his song, which is a lilting music-hall setting of "Sigh No More," a champagne cork pops. But if Antoon uses good things well, he also uses them ill. The revolving stage is charmingly used to bring Benedick out paddling lazily in a canoe; it is obtrusively used to bring out the ladies on carousel horses at the end. (Why? In the logic of Antoon's own production, where did those horses come from?) Benedick's cigars go with his action; Beatrice's secret cigarette-smoking—with other ladies —stops the action.

Still, prodigality of spirit and fertility of imagination are not bad curses for a director, and Antoon will just have to bear up under them, refining them as he goes. And I hope he will become harder to please in his casting, less willing (apparently) to settle for more bad actors than good.

This is his fourth New York production in two years. One of them, *Cymbeline* in the Festival last summer, was a fumbling attempt at fairy tale. The other three, all very different from one another, were all done exceptionally well. *Subject to Fits* crackled with high-voltage arcs of surrealist electricity. From *That Championship Season* he drew a keenly tempered realistic production much better than that humdrum play. And now *Much Ado*. If he were a film director, the *auteur* mills would already be grinding. (For instance, he is distinctly more gifted and original than his film coeval, Peter Bogdanovich, about whom the gas is already billowing.) He has shown wide range, intense theatrical imagination, a power to perceive and to conceptualize his perceptions, a taking sense of rhythm and phrase and movement. (I haven't even discussed the movement and compositions of *Much Ado*.) I came away from the show with double elation: glowing from the play and thinking about Antoon's future.*

The Oresteia

(The New York Times, *June 30, 1966*)

Majesty is our theme—majesty in Michigan. The Ypsilanti Greek Theater opened its first season last night with a production of the only extant Greek trilogy, that titanic masterpiece *The Oresteia* of Aeschylus; and across 2500 years from the Theater of Dionysus to the converted baseball field of Eastern Michigan University, huge dark voices seemed to sound. Time contracted as we came closer to our fountainhead, and expanded in mysteries that we know can never end.

The founding of this festival, intended to be annual, is a tribute to the citizens of this small city near Detroit. But the hero of last night's opening was Alexis Solomos, the artistic director. Solomos was for fourteen years the director of the National Theater of Greece, and he has conceived this production—whatever the flaws along the way—in a high arch of tragic style, with imaginative response to the work's poetic and primitive demands.

His prime collaborator is the composer Iannis Xenakis, who has provided ultra-modern music—of dissonances, taps, noises. Together with the stage direction, Xenakis' score creates the first essential of a

* See pp. 216 and 228 for comments on previous Antoon productions, p. 19 for a subsequent one.

Greek revival: the illusion of tradition. We know virtually nothing of the music and movement of the original productions; we ask to be convinced through inner consistency and aptness. We must feel that this is how an Athenian tragedy should sound and look; and in this regard, the director and the composer have succeeded unforgettably.

Aeschylus' trilogy consists of *Agamemnon, The Libation Bearers,* and *The Eumenides.* The story, which in original and paraphrase is woven into the thought and dream of the Western world, tells of the murder of King Agamemnon by his wife, Clytemnestra, because, in time of war, he sacrificed their daughter to the gods. In turn, Clytemnestra and her lover, Aegisthus, are killed by her son, Orestes, with the support of his sister, Electra. And, in turn, Orestes is vindictively pursued by the Furies.

A principal theme is the question of where vengeance ends and justice begins. At the last, Orestes is tried, with the young gods presiding and with mortals casting the vote. He is acquitted. For the Greeks, an era of humane reason begins, and the Furies become the Eumenides—the Kindly Ones.

Richmond Lattimore's translation is direct and flexible, but sometimes mundane. (The last dialogue between Pallas Athene and the Furies almost has echoes of labor arbitration.) The condensation of the work—essential if it is to take less than a full day—deals least justly with the third play, I think. But overall themes are delineated and concluded.

As the Clytemnestra, this festival is blessed with Judith Anderson. There are very few living actresses who could, from the first moment, encompass the immensity of this role and this play. In stature and voice, gesture and movement, Dame Judith is magnificent. There are moments when there seems more emphasis on sustaining the line than on emotional penetration. She gives us all the grandeur of the role, though not always all the passion. Yet her performance is possible only to a large talent used by a large spirit.

Donald Davis is a royal and stubborn Agamemnon, but Davis is even better when he reappears in the third play as Apollo, lucid and golden. Frederic Warriner colors the Aegisthus trenchantly. John Michael King has an understanding of Orestes and some grip of the role; he is not yet fluent in movement, and his agonies are sometimes more vocal than real.

Ruby Dee is asked to play Cassandra as an ecstatic visionary.

Dee's voice is not quite adequate to the almost inhuman demands, but her physical intensity, sustained in the middle of that enormous stage, is extraordinary. Karen Ludwig looks well as Electra and performs feelingly. Jacqueline Brookes looks even more striking as Athene, but she uses only a few of the higher notes in her voice.

The body of the drama—on which all the other characters depend —is made by the two choruses, sixteen men and sixteen women. Under Solomos' excellent direction, assisted by Helen McGehee's choreography, these choruses move, chant, speak singly, together, and in counterpoint, with astonishing beauty and power. Every single one of these ladies and gentlemen is giving a good performance. It is the texture of their work, as much as anything else, that establishes this festival as a serious and promising enterprise.

The costumes, designed by Solomos, are clean and flowing. Eldon Elder's single setting is simple. The lighting by Gilbert V. Hemsley, Jr., is serviceable but unremarkable.

Also, it must be noted that there are some small defects in audibility. Despite microphones hung above the covered stage, some of the lines spoken far upstage and on the parapet are hard to understand. Doubtless this can be corrected. (Besides, there are plans to build a permanent theater.)

But all reservations must be taken as comments on a production marked generally by sureness of style and fine execution. I look forward to the other play in this year's festival, Aristophanes' *The Birds* with Bert Lahr, which opens tonight. Meanwhile it is clear that, despite any shortcomings, a few of the Olympian gods survive and have smiled on Ypsilanti.

POSTSCRIPT. *The Birds,* with the beloved Bert Lahr, was an underrehearsed disaster. The "annual" Ypsilanti festival did not continue.

Antigone

(*June 12, 1971*)

The *Antigone* of Sophocles was Hegel's ideal of tragedy, and I'm not about to quarrel with him, although I expect to go to my grave without deciding whether *Antigone* or *Oedipus Rex* is the best play ever written. *Antigone* is the great work about choice (the conscious), *Oedipus* the great work about fate (the unconscious). Hegel esteemed the former because *Antigone,* which was 440 years old when Christ was born, epitomized for him the human condition as he saw it around him. He saw that the conflict between men is not between good and evil (how many men are consciously evil?) but between opposing visions of good. People behave according to what they take to be truth, not according to what they take to be falsehood, but each man's view of truth is necessarily partial. And each man takes his partial truth for the whole. Hence our disasters.

Creon, though hot-tempered, is a king obeying tradition, law, and the duties of kingship, rigorously free of favoritism to his family. Antigone obeys the obligation of sacred family ties at the expense of law and continuity and peace. Their conflict kills Antigone and Creon's son, affianced to Antigone, and Creon's wife, and it ruins Creon; yet which side was (in Hegel's terms) without spiritual value? The issue here is the burial of a dead rebel, but it is prototypical of virtually every divisive issue in human affairs. If Creon had wavered, it would have been corruption to him; if Antigone had wavered, it would have been corruption to her. The play ends with Creon desolate and repentant, seeing that the truth he thought whole was only partial. But if he had spared Antigone and condoned her law-breaking, she might well in time have come to see that her own truth was limited.

The chief conceptual defect of John Hirsch's production with the Lincoln Center Rep is that it takes sides from the beginning, thus subverting Hegel (let alone Sophocles!). Creon is fierce, Antigone is fine, and that is more or less that. A heroine and a heavy are created, in post-classic sentimental vein.

There are some other flagrant faults. Although Charles Cioffi speaks well as the chorus leader, most of the chorus members are dreadful and are badly managed by Hirsch. The choruses become a posing, patched-up bunch of interludes, nothing choric at all about them in speech or movement, quite unlike the choruses staged by Michael Cacoyannis and Alexis Solomos elsewhere.

The setting is a huge frieze by Douglas W. Schmidt with gigantic figures that have pieces missing from them. Does Schmidt think that the Greeks *erected* ruins?

But there are assets. The translation by Dudley Fitts and Robert Fitzgerald is springy and live, immediate yet not vernacular. The music by Lukas Foss sounds Greek. Almost nothing is known of ancient Greek music, so if it sounds Greek, it's Greek. The costumes by Jane Greenwood have good, thick, sculptural feeling.

As Antigone, Martha Henry shows intensity and intelligence. Her face is notably undistinguished, but her voice pounds with some force. (Tandy Cronyn, the Ismene, has an excellent theater face but an undeveloped voice.) Henry has little fire or commanding stature, but in a modestly competent, resident-theater way, she gives a credible, clear performance.

Many have said that Philip Bosco overdoes Creon, that he starts too high. Academically, that's true. But the part has apparently been designed by the director as a villain of sorts, and Bosco is fulfilling the design. The really astonishing thing about his performance is that, though he does start high, he doesn't run down; he can sustain it. I can't think of many other American actors who have Bosco's vocal range and stamina, or his feeling for style. Here is an actor who can be a king without silly pomp, who knows how to carry in his dead son's body and lament over it. Bosco lacks certain refinements of artistic intelligence, particularly in realistic drama; his performance in *An Enemy of the People* this year was almost monochrome. But he is one of the few Americans really at home in classic and romantic drama. (What a curse!)

Medea

(June 24, 1972)

For sheer visceral excitement, the high point of the 1971–2 season was a stretch of ten minutes or so in the middle of a forty-minute production of *Medea* at La Mama Theater Club. Everything I had heard about this production prejudiced me against it. It was in Euripides' Greek, with some choruses in Seneca's Latin; only a small audience was allowed, and they went through an extended ritual of admission. It sounded like stale Off-Off-Broadwayfaring.

The first moments confirmed prejudice. We were ushered into the ground-floor theater of La Mama, where I thought we were to see the play. Then, after about fifty people had arrived, we were conducted downstairs, past actors in costume holding candles and reciting lines in Greek or Latin, along a cinder-block corridor to the basement. Here we were seated on facing benches against the long sides of the rectangular room, with members of the chorus interspersed among us. At each of the narrow ends of the rectangle were some steps and a simple doorway. The ceiling was covered with billowing burlap. I was ready to leave.

Very soon I was rooted. The director, Andrei Serban, was moving to a simple, strong idea: that the core of *Medea* is primal stuff, that comprehension of each utterance—when the play is known and the motions are elemental—is no more necessary here than in great opera. In both arts, cognition of language may even be an impediment to full release. All that we need, in giant drama, is the impassioned sound of words whose general meaning we know. Details of verbiage can sometimes weigh us down.

One need not take this approach as a fiat for all classic productions in order to see how it worked in this instance. During the minutes when Jason and Medea faced each other at opposite ends of that small room, storming full-throatedly at each other in a completely foreign language, I felt the blood of this ancient drama quicken as I have rarely felt it in productions of large plays.

Serban prepared for these moments with intelligent patterns of movement; with Elizabeth Swados' music-and-sounds, to create a barbaric aural atmosphere; with careful dynamics of the chorus; and, chiefly, by his work with his principals, Priscilla Smith and Jamil Zakki. Smith looks more like Smith College than Colchis, but she and Zakki transcended themselves. Their bodies were completely invested in what they were doing, their voices were two full, round columns battering at one another.

All the cast, even the children, were caught in Serban's intensity, and made a seamless fabric of conviction. I keep thinking even now of the children's dangling legs as, after being slaughtered, they were handed down through a gap in that burlap ceiling to their horror-struck father below.

Serban is a Romanian, a student and associate of Peter Brook, and is now director-in-residence at La Mama. Productions there don't "run": they appear, disappear, and often reappear. *Medea* has since gone touring in Europe and may be back. Serban will presumably be back and must be watched. The stuntishness in him is much less than his main thrust: quintessential guts and revelation.

Trilogy

(November 23, 1974)

Two years ago a young Romanian named Andrei Serban directed a production of *Medea* at the La Mama Theater, in the East Village, that signaled the arrival of a unique talent. That production then toured "Off-Broadway" theaters in Europe and, somewhat revised, has returned to La Mama's new annex, next door to its first building. With an expanded company Serban has now added productions of *The Trojan Women* and (Sophocles') *Electra*. Two plays are performed in an evening, so on two successive evenings one can see all three plays plus a repeat of one. To see these productions is to have the wonderful double experience of reaching back into something old and venturing forth into something new.

Serban's drive, throughout these plays, has been toward their mythic essences, to distill and crystallize the subconscious, even preconscious elements that made them part of our communal heritage centuries before the plays were written down, the elements that have kept them vital through the centuries since. I know that to describe his method is a risk because it sounds arty: it *would* be arty if it were not art. Serban doesn't use languages known to the audience: the plays are performed mostly in mixtures of the original Greek and some Latin. Also, as a result of some recent travels and studies, he has blended in elements of Asian and Central American Indian cultures. (His support has been from National Endowment and other foundation grants.) He has fused all these materials to move the performance from the plane of mundane daily recognitions to the elemental; and, to further this "submersion" process, he has not told complete stories (except, nearly, in *Medea*). For each play he has selected a series of important episodes, bursting them into life with music and light and setting and intensity of performance.

The quality of all four of these factors is what transforms mere theory, which it was in the experimental work of Peter Brook (with whom Serban has worked), into accomplishment. The music by Elizabeth Swados (who has also worked with Brook) is magnificent. It ranges all the way from solo unaccompanied voice to polyphonic choral singing, from a complex of instruments including the gamelan to mere percussive sounds on wood blocks, from the shining sound of hand-bells rung by the chorus at the end of *Electra* to something like Gregorian chant. Swados' music is most present in *The Trojan Women,* which is in fact subtitled "An Epic Opera," but in all three plays her sounds keep every moment out of the vernacular.

The lighting by Laura Rambaldi serves the same purpose. It is always simple, always stark and vivid. Sometimes she uses torches, alone; sometimes a single spotlight from high overhead, thus transforming the huge room into an even huger cavern; sometimes—rarely —an "effect" like the rippling light waves at one point in *The Trojan Women.* The structural settings by Jun Maeda—gaunt steps and platforms scattered as needed—seem to grow out of the occasion. One cannot think of these productions apart from the sound of the music and the look of the lights and scenic pieces.

Or apart from the nature of the performances. The most casually overlooked element of Serban's productions, in the generally enthusiastic reviews that I've read, is his ability to choose and teach actors, to raise them all to a level of naked power. Every reviewer mentions that Aegisthus in *Electra* comes down the steps with a live snake twined around his neck, but few mention that William Duff-Griffin, the Aegisthus, pours forth a rough river of sound from his throat as he descends that validates the snake as part of an ancient mystery. Every performer in every one of the plays is at least good, except the new Jason in *Medea,* who is not as strong as Jamil Zakki was two years ago. There are four children in the plays, and all of them too speak the old languages and comport themselves at the same level of conviction as the adults. If one actor must be specially praised, and she must be singled out because she has two leading roles, it is Priscilla Smith, the Medea and Electra. Utter subscription, to a director who is worth it, has transmuted Smith from a gifted young woman into the creator of elemental figures, large and passionate.

Here is a taste of one of the productions, *The Trojan Women.* The audience is made to wait outside in the lobby, which gets crowded. The lights dim, a costumed man appears through the theater doors and plays a passage on a horn, and the entire company comes down a flight of stairs into the lobby, singing a beautiful song of sorrow. They move slowly through the crowd in the lobby to the farther end, then they turn and go back into the theater itself, and we follow them into the virtual blackness. There, under dim, high light, they form a circle and finish their song. The light fades; beyond a black curtain that cuts across the middle of the hall, torches flare up, wild music starts, and a voice sings in strange, ecstatic lament. The curtains part, and we move into the other half of the big room (actually a former ball-room) with a stage at one end and two-tiered wooden galleries on two sides. At the far end of one gallery is Cassandra, a stunning black actress (Valois Mickens) naked to the waist, a rope halter around her neck, singing and dancing her despair to torchlight. Then she is led down and away through the crowd (us), her voice fluting into half- and quarter-tones as she goes.

Andromache (Priscilla Smith again) appears on the gallery opposite and anoints her small son, Astyanax (Ted Lambert), for his death, intoning the while in a strange, nasal voice. The boy is lowered into a cage and borne off, through us, by Greek soldiers. (The actors move back and forth to play Trojans or Greeks as needed.) Then Helen (Joanna Peled), the cause of the war, is brought forth in a tumbrel. Women pelt her with straw, climb in and shave off her long curls (figuratively: they take off her wig, revealing her shaved head), and strip her naked and smear her with mud. Then they set a bear on her to violate her, as the citizens scattered among us incite and exult. . . .

At the end of an hour or so (the audience long since cleared off the floor and seated in the galleries), the captive women move down the center of the hall to the stage, led by a man carrying a tall pole with a looped banner. They are singing softly their song of farewell. Up on the stage they gather in golden light around the upright pole, which begins to sway slightly, thus becoming the mast of the ship that is taking them into exile. Their voices die and the light dies on them, so slowly that we think we can still see them in the black after the light has gone.

I have had no theater experience comparable to this trilogy since the first production of *Boesman and Lena* in 1970, have seen nothing that struck so boldly into the past and the future since the Grotowski company in 1969. But I must note that these three productions are tragedies only for those who already know the plays as tragedies. Few could miss the power of these productions, but what makes the originals great tragedies, as against great scaffoldings for tremendous Jungian images, is their characters, their language (as rendered in our own), their linkage of poetry and inner action. None of this is given to us here. What Serban has done, with superb theatrical imagination, is to scrape down to the psychic-tribal essences that made these legends material for tragedy in the first place. For me his work doesn't supplant the best traditional tragic performances of these plays (if and when they are available), but it is a brilliant revolt against the drudgery and trudgery of the merely conventional, a refreshment of the theater's bloodstream at the source.

The Time of Your Life

(*November 22, 1969*)

In the year in which Samuel Beckett wins the Nobel Prize, the Lincoln Center Repertory Theater revives William Saroyan. Surprisingly, it turns out to be a good idea: not because of any nostalgic contrast between a rosy past and a bleak present; not because Saroyan contends in a 1966 preface that (believe it or not) he was a predecessor of Beckett's in altering our view of the human condition, but because the passage of time lets us see that *The Time of Your Life* is not exactly the warm-hearted American vaudeville it has been called.

Saroyan's comedy is one of the last items in the two-decade era of the Well-Patched Play. For about a hundred years the stage had seen the Well-Made Play, which is not dead yet, but between the World Wars we got a spate of American plays that depended less on intricate plots with surprises and reversals and precisely spaced "big" scenes, and more on a parade of minor characters, each with a tiny "turn" of his own or a bit of subplot. Such an approach enabled an author to give his work a feeling of verism on the cheap (life was being sliced) and also freed him from certain demands of the Well-Made form. That form was not abandoned by any means, but the profligacy of the '20s induced the writer to fill it out with a series of vaudeville acts, rather than to dwell exclusively on his central characters, to develop them and his plot further. A prime exponent of this approach was the witty George S. Kaufman, any number of whose collaborations are samples. Of course this ragbag method ("The show sags here, Max, let's throw in a funny two minutes for a window-washer") was tied to the prevailing economics of the theater: actors were cheaper then. But it was that current mode of show biz which Saroyan used and expanded in his poetically intended work. His play is a rather patently conceived Grand Music-Hall of Life.

The setting (except for one short inset scene) is a honky-tonk saloon in San Francisco, 1939. A consciously mysterious character named Joe sits there, drinking champagne, dispensing unexplained money, dispatching messengers, ordering and arranging the lives of people who pass through. There is a carefully balanced assortment of characters: a whore with a soul, a young man and his idealistic girl, a tall-tale-telling hobo, a good-hearted cop, a "thinking" longshoreman (as vapid as Eric Hoffer), a kid who wants to be a tap dancer, a hungry Negro piano-player, two rich slummers . . . well, to complete the list would be almost to mock the play. But that would be misleading, because Saroyan has the ability to write sharp vignettes for many of them, which takes the curse off the arranged feeling and instead gives the play a comfy sprawl. Occasionally there is the oppressive feeling that we are being consciously shown America-1939, but most of the time the solos, duets, and trios are quite entertaining.

The play's theme—*In the time of your life, live*—is not new in the American canon. For instance, in almost exactly the same words, it's the advice that Strether gives Bilham in James's *The Ambassadors*. As Saroyan uses it, the theme combines a diluted descent from Thoreau with an augury of hippiedom—another American lunge at Edenic bliss. But contradictory things grow out of that free-living belief (as they do now in some hip films and novels). First, the world is made up of Good People and Bad People. There are more Goods than Bads, there is instant communion between the Goods, and there is instant hatred of the Goods by the Bads. *The Time of Your Life* has only one Bad, the vice-squad detective, Blick, and he really has to do yeoman service for his nasty cause. He is the only evil in the play and his part is small, so, as written and played, he has to cram an awful lot of badness into a little space. My heart went out to him as he sweated away to supply the necessary wicked contrast.

Then there is the character of Joe. He has a certain resemblance to

Giraudoux's Madwoman of Chaillot. He sits in one place, more or less, the world comes to him, he rewards virtue and punishes vice (after deciding which is which), and dispenses largess as he talks about money like a minor Proudhon. The only difference between Joe and the villainous Blick is benevolence and malevolence—the despotism in them is exactly the same.

And the play ends with as prime a bit of lynch law as I have ever seen on stage. After we hear a couple of shots, the old hobo comes in and says that he has just killed Blick and has thrown away his gun. Then Joe gives the old man another revolver, presumably to carry on his good work.

The real fairy tale about this play is that it is a sentimental fairy tale. Underneath the boozy friendliness, its basic view is rigidly moralistic, with a view of Paradise as a place where everyone behaves in the way that the Good (self-appointed) order it, and where the Good have the right to kill the Bad but not vice versa. What makes the play specially interesting to see again is that this tension, between superficial humanism and underlying puritanism, is now more apparent than before. But also, to be sure, Saroyan's gift for cutting disrespectfully right to the core of every new situation is as humorous as ever, and some of his fancies still glisten untarnished. This is the best production I have seen at the Vivian Beaumont since *The Caucasian Chalk Circle* in 1966, and the company is more comfortable with Saroyan than with Brecht.

Douglas W. Schmidt, the designer, had the problem of converting the huge thrust stage into a cozy saloon, and he solved it principally with colors, décor, and the aid of John Gleason's friendly lighting. John Hirsch, the director, was nevertheless left with the space problem: getting his actors in a front door, down a flight of steps, and across to somewhere near the center—a distance that seems the length of a football field. But Hirsch has a sense of pace that helps reduce the yardage, which means attack of speech as well as physical speed. He also has the sense not to use the Peter Glenville cliché of holding exit lines for delivery just before the exit; actors get their last lines off generally before they start the long ascent to the door, and before they are up the stairs the focus has shifted elsewhere and the play continues.

Joe is a role that George M. Cohan might have wanted to write for himself. It needs that sort of full personality to keep it from being somewhat domineering and intrusive. James Broderick, who is probably tired of being told that he resembles Norman Mailer, is a careful and intelligent actor. I saw him last as Richard in Joyce's *Exiles* with the Trinity Square company in Providence in May. (Not counting his performance as Ray in *Alice's Restaurant*.) He showed understanding and control, but he lacked quite the presence to make Richard a center of gravity for the play. His Joe, equally intelligently played, lacks the teasing flavor, the unction, to keep him from sounding peevish sometimes.

Robert Symonds is an ideal "company" actor. He seems able to do anything at least adequately and some things excellently. Here he plays the old hobo so credibly that, from the middle of the auditorium, you both chuckle and wish he would take a bath. Philip Bosco, one of my favorite American classical actors, has a fine time —and gives us one—as the tough-but-tender saloon-owner. Leonard Frey, who was the pock-marked "queen" in *The Boys in the Band,* is winning as the young hoofer—and shows surprising range. Gene Troobnick, always welcome, gives nice touches to the good-hearted cop.

Lincoln Center continues to have hard luck with ladies. Susan Tyrrell, Priscilla Pointer, and Laura Esterman (as Kitty, Mary L., and Elsie the nurse) are so incompetent that to criticize them might discourage people from seeing a production which is, on the whole, worthwhile.

Trelawny of the "Wells"

(*November 28, 1970*)

The Public Theater is now doing *Trelawny of the "Wells"* on one of its four stages. Pinero's play, written in 1898, was an interesting choice for revival, and its importance was generally missed by reviewers who saw it only as cute or creaky.

The Bagnigge Wells is a theater in an unfashionable part of London; time, the early 1860s. Rose Trelawny, the young leading lady, falls in love with a young aristocrat, is disliked by his family because of her profession, gets a probationary term of living in the great house, cannot live as stuffily as the great family, and returns to the stage. The young aristocrat becomes an actor too, and eventually joins her in the new theater to which she has gone.

Here and there in the British and American nineteenth-century drama, choked as it is with upholstered trash, is a play that, despite its mechanics and bathos, is clearly yearning toward the serious. Pinero was saying something in this play about the cruelty of class strata in Victorian England, but he was also saying something about art. He had himself been an actor twenty-five years before he wrote *Trelawny,* and he knew its theatrical milieu at first hand. Tom Wrench, the rebellious young actor-playwright of the "Wells," was modeled, we all know, on T. W. Robertson, author of *Society* and *Caste,* who initiated realism in the English theater. But Pinero openly admitted his debt to Robertson, and there may be something of himself in the role.

Equally important—and generally unremarked—is the change in Rose Trelawny. After her tribulations in the aristocratic house, she returns to the "Wells," only to flop. She can no longer manage the fustian style at which she had been successful; her personal experience has made it seem empty, emotionally false. Only when she goes to the new theater, in Wrench's new realistic play, can she act again—truthfully and well.

Pinero, in his limited way, is making a statement about psychological and emotional verity in art. *Trelawny* is a tiny harbinger of modernism; and, by having a young aristocrat go on the stage, is also socially revolutionary. All this is encased in a thoroughly antiquated play, but that fact makes it even more interesting.

The performance is slovenly. Only Valerie French, as a successful alumna of the "Wells," has any style. Robert Ronan, who plays Wrench like an East Villager, has directed the theatrical material patronizingly, with a range of "ham" clichés. One would think that actors would have some interest in *understanding* actors of the past, instead of mocking them in stereotypes. The most egregious waste is of Grant Code, who plays a footman in the noble house. With his few lines, Code shows the authority and flavor that were needed in the role of Sir William Gower, the crusty old head of the house, qualities that are out of the question for the present actor in the part.

The Good Woman of Setzuan

(*November 28, 1970*)

Here comes the Lincoln Center Repertory Theater again, plodding patiently toward the altar of Culture. Their first offering of the season is Brecht's *The Good Woman of Setzuan,* and everything, from the choice of the play onward, extends that company's walking somnolence.

The Good Woman is one of several Brecht works (*Arturo Ui, A Man's a Man*) that are painfully two-dimensional. When Brecht's bitter didacticism is amplified into full-blooded cynical-meliorist art, we get works as good as *Mother Courage* and *Galileo* and *The Threepenny Opera,* or even the youthful *Baal;* but when he points his finger at us and tells us not much more than that the heart of man is desperately wicked, the play is over—in theatrical dynamics—about seven minutes after it begins.

Shen Teh is a good-hearted prostitute in the China that Brecht invented for some plays, as he invented an America for others. In return for a kindness, three visiting gods reward her with money. The money brings trouble, and she has to assume a tough alter ego—a fictitious male cousin—in order to protect her good self. The final chorus asks us, please, to find some way to make the world safe for the good. (Ralph Manheim has done a pliable new translation.)

The play has modest, bland narrative interest, shallow dramatic depth. This production does everything to emphasize the blandness. Robert Symonds has staged it adequately but has not really directed it—there is no tonal center. Elizabeth Wilson, a very good comedienne, is vivid as the vinegary neighbor Mrs. Shin, but Colleen Dewhurst alternates between Joan of Arc (as Shen Teh) and a "camp" gangster (as her own tough cousin). Presumably there's a way to get a comic-ironic tension out of this double role, but Dewhurst, for all her gifts, has not found it.

I know a German actress whose former husband was once a leading actor for Brecht himself, so, with him, she went to many Brecht rehearsals. She told me recently, "You people have it all wrong nowadays. Brecht was a genius of a *director.* He wrote the plays for himself to direct, and now you have only the plays." Surely the point is arguable; but surely, to judge by the little I've seen of the Berliner Ensemble, he *was* a directing genius, and surely there is a galloping thinness—in the theater—that is overtaking many of his plays. Unless *The Good Woman* is superlatively done, so that its moderate chances for virtuosity are fully exploited, it's hardly worth doing. It was highly important that Brecht become part of our cultural consciousness (a debt we owe largely to Eric Bentley). It's highly debatable that much of Brecht's large output will remain theatrically vital.

The Playboy of the Western World

(January 30, 1971)

Philip Bosco, as the drunken farmer Jimmy Farrell, bumps against the door as he lurches out of the Mayo tavern. The cant of Bosco's body in this small part and the transformation of his tongue into Mayo liquid—these are some of the theatrical high points in the Lincoln Center production of Synge's play. What Bosco gives us here, what he has often given us before, is the embodiment of repertory acting standards—an honorable ideal of authenticity, not flaming inspiration. Acting like Bosco's tells us only what we know already, but tells it truly; and his ability to tell us many kinds of truth, at this enjoyable level, is what repertory production usually comes to mean—at its best.

Bosco's soundness was foreseeable; there are also a few pleasant surprises. Stephen Elliott, who gave rather a cheap performance as Mr. Shu Fu in *The Good Woman of Setzuan,* is good granite as Old Mahon. Frances Sternhagen is wrong in quality for the Widow Quin, but she is such an intelligent and witty actress that she wins us sheerly with her understanding of the part.

John Hirsch, the director, has also had fair success with that unexciting young actor David Birney, bringing him up to a reasonable facsimile of Christy, the Playboy. But he allows Sydney Walker to cavort like an old-stager as the innkeeper, and he has not been able to bring out much power or charm in Martha Henry, the Pegeen Mike. I saw Henry's Viola at Stratford, Ontario, in 1966 and since then she seems to have grown only in confidence. The Irish accents come and go throughout the evening, which is not a matter of mere verbal décor, since the play lives in its words—its Irish words.

On balance, the production is better than most of the Lincoln Center productions: it is mediocre. This is not meant as a smart crack but as a statement of what seems to be true about this company and about most of our resident companies, as I have seen them. The best we can rationally expect of them is acceptable mediocrity, and it's the loss of that useful level of production that is a present danger.

To explain, circuitously, with Synge's play as instance. *The Playboy* is now part of the world's drama heritage, particularly to speakers of English. If it no longer looms as a major or revolutionary work, it is still a vivid example of the ethnic mode that was one way of revolt against the commercial theater at the turn of the century. (Although Synge wasn't precisely going back to his roots. He was a Dublin Protestant, like Shaw; and his best work was about the relatively wild, fiercely Catholic west of Ireland.) His folklorist approach influenced Brecht and, apparently, Lorca, and although his simplicities look different to us now (since the cultural environment has altered), they are never simplistic, never quaint.

The play's symbols too have been altered by time. Young Christy kills his father, he thinks, and becomes a hero in a strange village by telling the tale; when the father appears, Christy "kills" him again and "eats" him, in effect. A Jungian might say that in 1907, when Synge wrote the play, he was reacting to deep unconscious patterns. Since Freud, the father-killing takes on more conscious meanings.

Even more pertinent to me at this juncture is the view of the "murder" itself. When Christy arrives and reports the killing of his father, he is idolized because these people believe that only great emotions can drive a man to crime and they admire great emotions. But when the wounded father tracks him down and Christy tries to kill him again, the villagers reject him. Pegeen Mike, the girl who once wanted Christy and now turns on him, says that "there's a great gap between a gallous story and a dirty deed." So the play not only dramatizes the contrast between the opium of fantasy and the bread of reality, it is concerned with the dominant theme of this century— the increase of consciousness and its burdens. In the very last line, Pegeen Mike mourns the loss of the Playboy, whom she has lost only by clearer perception of him, by an increase of perceived reality.

All right, then. As I've tried to show, *The Playboy of the Western World* is of sufficient intrinsic interest so that everyone ought to have the chance to see a decent performance of it at least once in his life. This is true of hundreds of plays that none of us will ever see—even done badly—but that doesn't lessen the argument for *The Playboy*. (The immediate occasion here was the hundredth anniversary of Synge's birth.) The question for the future is whether any remnant at all of that drama heritage is going to be preserved *in performance*. Anyone can read *The Playboy* and get much from it, but, figuratively, Philip Bosco's lurch is the completion of Synge's work. The problem is not the same as in musical performance because of the availability of the LP and the tape, and because as long as instrumentalists continue to be trained at all, they will be able to play Bach as well as Berio. In the theater, the quest for relevance among many young theater people, for contemporaneity, is taking many young actors and directors away from tradition, perhaps enabling them to play the theater's Berio but not its Bach.

Anyway, not as Bach. Every age does its revivals in its own way, but this age often seems to do its revivals not to keep classics alive and to connect us with history but to disconnect and appropriate them. Few today would argue that there is one right way to do a play, but at any given moment there is a consensus about the difference between a traditional revival—well or ill done—and a revival done according to some concept of specially modern relevance. Valuable juices would drain away if the latter died off; but our identities may wither if the former dies off. I'm not arguing for such mummifying as I've seen in the Moscow Art Theater and most of the Comédie Française. I would hope for such revitalized tradition as I've sometimes seen in the Royal Shakespeare Company, the National Theater of London, and the Stratford (Ontario) Shakespeare Festival. But I would settle, if forced, for the acceptable mediocrity of this *Playboy* production.

The question is by no means exclusively American. West Germany has 170 theaters, most of them subsidized by states and cities, and François Bondy reported recently (*New York Times,* January 4, 1971) that those subsidized theaters are moving in three directions. One of those directions is particularly German: plays examining the national conscience *vis-à-vis* the Hitler experience. The other two directions are parallels of the American schism: one toward the living museum of the drama heritage, the other toward experiment. Of the second, Bondy says:

> The fashion now is for classical plays, from Aeschylus to Goldoni, turning them inside out in order to reveal their unsuspected revolutionary message and to give the spectator a thrill by having him discover that the best-known old plays can be made into something new and unfamiliar.

They surely can be, in Germany and elsewhere, and sometimes stimulatingly, but if there is no tradition, no museum, what are they being "new" against?

The difficulty in the theater, obviously, is that its museums are not a matter of purchases that virtually settle the matter, as with paintings, but of living people continuously "making" the collection with live work. Even if videotape cassettes preserve plays in performance, trained people will be needed for them, and none of the best plays will be settled once and for all by one cassette any more than the *"Eroica"* was settled by one recording. The ultimate purpose of our resident theaters, as it's turning out, may be to serve as competent living museums—if they can survive the disappointment of our expectation that they were going to serve more purposes; and if succeeding generations of good actors and directors and designers want to devote themselves to sustaining the viable past.

Every age gets the theater it deserves, I guess, but use every age according to its deserts and which should 'scape whipping? Every age doesn't always get the theater it needs or wants, and I'm not overjoyed by the thought that we may be the last generation to see even a mediocre production of *The Playboy*. It's not that we must pray for future Oliviers; there doesn't seem to be too good a prospect for future Boscos.

A Doll's House / Hedda Gabler

(March 13, 1971)

The battle for Ibsen has been waged well by a few critics in the last generation, the fight to free him of the trappings of the Social Problem playwright, to reveal him as a Faustian poet for whom social problems are only the visible data of larger struggle. By now every college student should, or could, know that *Ghosts* is not about syphilis and *Rosmersholm* is not about politics. What is emerging now, from this rightly revised view, is the stature of Ibsen as hero.

The artist-hero, of the last century and this, is the artist who not only has the vision and courage to oppose the currents of his time; he also sees that, by his faith to his vision, he is imperiling the very art in which he expresses that vision, is testing the survival power of his art; and knows he must proceed—as Joyce did with the novel and Picasso with easel painting.

In his early verse dramas, *Brand* and *Peer Gynt,* one hears Ibsen saying to the theater, "Serve the freedom in me or die." The theater did neither; *Brand* had to wait almost twenty years for production, *Peer Gynt* eleven, and the old theater persisted. So Ibsen (one may say in a simplified way) decided to strike for freedom from within the old forms, using the skills he had acquired in the entertainment theater from his many years as a director. He began to do his revolutionary work within the shape of the well-made play.

The result is a combination of tedium and fire, an obeisance to Scribean mechanics as his passport for a voyage into truth. What a lot of *arrangements* in these two plays under review, what a lot of fussing just to get the right people for a scene on stage together, what trickery to convey information and delay discoveries. But the predominant sense in them is that Ibsen was challenging these forms as he used them, was demonstrating that they were inadequate to new consciousness, to new demands on the idea of art itself.

A Doll's House and *Hedda Gabler* are now playing alternate weeks with the same company at the Playhouse in New York. The first play is a clanking piece of stage machinery for seven eighths of its length, fairly indistinguishable from other domestic dramas of the day except for the famous tarantella scene. The real difference, of course, is the last scene: in itself, plus the fact that it was written in 1879.

That last scene is retroactively explosive, in two intertwined ways. A seemingly conventional marriage has moved to a contradiction of its social conventions; a seemingly conventional play has moved to a contradiction of its theatrical conventions. Everything we have seen up to the last scene becomes different after we have seen the end; the conclusion alters *the whole work.* The play can be seen as a struggle against the niceties of theater carpentry, along with its struggle against strangulation by the niceties of marriage.

In some degree *Hedda Gabler* is the same work rethought and recast twelve years later. Ibsen's beating at the form of the play can be sensed, this time, from the start. Hedda seems imprisoned in its one-two-three-four sequence of scenes, as much as in the one-two-three-four sequence of the hours of her existence; one feels she wants to tear the linear shape of the play as well as of her life, because one mimics the other. The theme now is not equal marital respect and dignity but the sources from which the disrespect originally comes: the quality of a civilization, the sterilities in it that make a sterile life-style its apogee, that warp and embitter its best people. Hedda keeps saying she is bored, but the truth of the matter is that she is numbed, a paralyzed idealist. To triumph over this society requires a titan. To see what is wrong with it, to hate it, and yet *not* to be a titan is to be Hedda. The dammed energy in her gets perverted into diabolic romanticism, with death, decked in vine leaves, as the ultimate purity.

In the present productions, what do we get of these two complex plays? A spoiled, flibbertigibbet wife who suddenly becomes a premature member of Women's Lib; and an idle, vindictive fool whose neurosis drives her lover to death and herself to suicide.

Basically this is the fault of the director, Patrick Garland, who has slammed these two plays onto the stage as if they were workaday revivals of *The Second Mrs. Tanqueray* for a summer tour. (During an intermission in *A Doll's House* one of this country's best Ibsen scholars told me he thought he could hear Garland at rehearsals saying, "Let's pick up those cues, kids.") On the conceptual level, these productions simply don't exist; and in terms of felicitous staging, they are ludicrous. For just one example: when Helmer makes his first entrance in *A Doll's House,* he comes downstage center to Nora, and they *stand* there, close together, face to face, talking that way for at least a full minute, in the middle of their own living room. I expected them to burst into "Sweethearts," with full orchestra, at any moment.

Claire Bloom has almost always been good in films, intelligent, fresh, true. She might have played a good Nora under a director who saw what she was leaving out (the subtext under the first seven eighths that connects the play to its conclusion) and the falseness she was inserting. Her chance of success with Hedda was much slighter and her failure there is much greater. She lacks stature and command, any of the authority that comes from concealed torment. Her speech has lost some of its distinction, her voice has lost a great deal of its flexibility, and she settles for a number of unsubtle readings. When Lövborg and Mrs. Elvsted are about to seat themselves, Hedda says coyly, "I want to sit *between* you," with all the subtlety of a truck.

And some of the casting is odd. Patricia Elliot, the Mrs. Linde and Mrs. Elvsted, not only gives better performances than Bloom (admittedly in easier parts) but towers over her physically. When Hedda affectionately calls Mrs. Elvsted "little idiot," she's addressing someone who not only is stronger but taller.

Donald Madden, the Helmer and Tesman, is a puzzle, the wrong kind: where did such an old-fashioned actor come from, in this country at this time? (I've seen him before; the question is rhetorical.) With his vocalizings, conscious nasal resonances, posings instead of passions, his air of sensitivity-for-sale, Madden is giving the best of old-style acting a bad name.

John Bury's settings are astonishingly undistinguished—he has done good ones—and the set for *Hedda Gabler,* in funeral-parlor gray, is about as discreet as Garland's staging. The best elements in these productions are the new adaptations by Christopher Hampton, a young English playwright. Hampton's *When Did You Last See My Mother?* was presented here a few years ago and, I thought, imperceptively reviewed. His Ibsen adaptations are generally limber without being jazzy. One test is in *Hedda Gabler,* when Judge Brack reports the location of Lövborg's fatal wound. Brack says that Lövborg was not shot in the chest, as first reported, but—translations vary—in the stomach or abdomen or bowels. It's perfectly clear what Ibsen was implying, and Hampton handles it simply and well by having Brack say that, instead of the chest, it was "somewhat lower."

Hedda Gabler

(July 22, 1972)

London

When London theater is good, it is very, very good; when it is bad, it is at its usual level.

Americans tend to imagine a glory about the London theater that, as a level, simply does not exist. We need to shed our theatrical inferiority complex *vis-à-vis* London. Broadway is no worse than the West End. In some ways it is preferable—musicals, for instance.

The English exceptions are treasures. Last year I saw a production of Gorky's *Enemies* by the Royal Shakespeare Company under David Jones that was beautiful. This year, amidst a lot of trash, another treasure: the Royal Court production of *Hedda Gabler* adapted by John Osborne, with Jill Bennett (Mrs. Osborne), directed by Anthony Page.

Alan Tagg has designed a setting, lighted by Andy Phillips, that transforms the small Royal Court stage into a large Nordic nineteenth-century mausoleum. Osborne has rendered Ibsen as he should have done: which is to say, he has not wrenched the play to fit a theory or serve as hobby-horse, he has simply seared the dialogue into language that shows why he admires the play and was attracted to it. It is urgent, supple, *useful* theater writing. For example, after Hedda has offended her husband's aunt about her hat, she says, "These things just seem to wait for me to do them."

The line is not only a sample of Osborne's diction, it is a clue to Hedda and to Jill Bennett's performance. (She is best known in the U.S. through her film performances: as the aunt with the heart attack in Bette Davis' *The Nanny,* as Trevor Howard's lady friend in *The Charge of the Light Brigade.*) This Hedda comes in finished, though only subconsciously aware of it, gliding airily to an end that is in her own nature and of her own doing. Some of the London critics complained that Bennett's performance was not tragic, but *Hedda Gabler* is not a tragedy, it is the *dénouement* of a tragedy. Gooses were cooked long before the curtain rises. Hedda never tries to change her life, to pry herself free, to leave her husband or take up again with Lövborg. She simply toboggans down the slope on which she has already started, and vindictively—she would say idealistically—she takes Lövborg with her.

The *prior* tragedy is essentially one of gender. Hedda has the impulses and imagination of a man—romantic but male—in a society that provides no place for a woman other than the conventional one. Her father, the General, is often mentioned; her mother never. Her father's pistols (phallic symbols, need one point out?) are pivotal in the story. Her frigidity, her boredom, her loathing of her pregnancy, her terrible vengeances are all unwitting functions of a biological doom that has condemned her to a role for which she is not psychologically or temperamentally fitted. This production even suggests, quite aptly, a lesbian touch toward Mrs. Elvsted. All these matters Jill Bennett encompasses admirably.

For American theatergoers, who recently had Claire Bloom's inept Hedda visited upon them, here are a few comparisons to help make matters vivid. Bloom was a petulant, grown-up schoolgirl striving for glacier force; Bennett is gracious, humorous, easy with superficial facets that contrast ironically with her depths. Bloom strove pathetically to be commanding; Bennett never bothers—her rich voice, her lynx-like presence allow her, figuratively, to do as she pleases, yet never lose us. Bloom wanted not to lose our sympathy; Bennett doesn't care if we hate Hedda—she seems to understand that what Ibsen is after is something larger than having us like a star, he wants us to loathe a certain world, the one that made her.

Ronald Hines is a perfect Tesman: we can understand how Hedda might have slipped into marriage with him. Brian Cox, the Lövborg, plays with a hulking Marlon Brando solidity, rather than the usual poeticizing ethereal quality in the role. Denholm Elliott, long a favorite of mine, plays Judge Brack like a sadistic surgeon.

Anthony Page's direction bothered me at the outset, with its linear, angular movements and compositions, often quite neatly parallel with the footlights. Then these patterns began to suggest the corsets and stays of this society. At only one point would I quarrel: he has Hedda downstage of Brack when he tells her of Lövborg's suicide. The focus should be on her, not on Brack. As is, she has a difficult time controlling the moment.

Bennett has a few other tonal difficulties toward the end. But if she doesn't quite fulfill the desperate self-immolation feeling, she has been so captivating until then that we are willing to rationalize on her behalf: perhaps Hedda is so trapped in a mingy world that large-size Medea movements are impossible even at the finish.

A Doll's House

(March 29, 1975)

No question that the most hotly awaited event of the New York theater season was Joseph Papp's production of A Doll's House, with Liv Ullmann. The last ticket for the eight-week engagement was sold three weeks before the first performance. I'm happy, for once, not to be the bearer of deflationary tidings: in terms of Ullmann's performance—and that alone—the anticipation is justified.

She has the first line of the play, offstage, and I didn't recognize her voice. It sounded a bit hoarse and a bit lighter than I remembered. Maybe she was a bit hoarse, but as the evening wore on, the voice acquired more color. I, possibly besotted with love, now think that the light timbre at the start was part of her design. I liked her performance while I was watching it, have liked it more and more as it keeps coming back to me, and am now convinced that it will stay alive in me—as, to put it minimally, the best Nora I have seen.

First, a few reservations, if only for their sobering effect. It's obvious that no one will ever know Ullmann's acting at its best unless he understands Norwegian or Swedish. (A Swedish expert tells me that Ullmann, who is Norwegian, has no accent or difficulty in his language.) She has an odd accent in English ("toime" for "time") and there's a soft plosion at the end of every sentence, of every substantial phrase—a last little push—that I don't remember in her films. But aside from such details, she doesn't have the utter control, the *being* in English, that she has in her own language(s). Listen to Peter O'Toole or Glenda Jackson or George C. Scott, and you hear how an actor who is *of* English uses the language both unconsciously, without thought, and very consciously, with subtlest design. Ullmann will never be able to use English with that combined carelessness and care. On the other hand, her English here is stratospheres above that in her English-language films because she is playing a part with which she is thoroughly familiar in Norwegian. She has played Nora often in Ibsen's own words and therefore has a great deal to model this performance on.

Still I had the sense that her performance is built in units—the way a ballet dancer does a *pas de deux,* then a solo, etc., all in a performance that's unified overall but is made up of discernible segments. I think this effect, of moving from one portion to the next, is partly due to her not-quite-comfort with English.

Partly it's due to the physical disposition of the play by the director, Tormod Skagestad, head of the Norwegian Theater in Oslo, who has previously done the play there with Ullmann. I hope that his shortcomings too are due to language and cultural unease, or else it's bad news about the Oslo theater. Skagestad has accepted some poor casting of other roles here, and has pulled and shoved and nagged the action of the play without much sense of inner dynamics. Granted that the Beaumont's thrust stage is hell for a "living-room" play, Skagestad has made the worst of it. I've rarely seen actors who seemed less to be living in their living room.

In spite of all these things—*because* of all these things—the rest is praise for Ullmann. I've written so much about her radiance that I'm glad the reader has been able to see it on film so that I stand a chance of being believed. A woman who can make that wretched Beaumont glow with her presence—without staginess or affectation, simply by concentrating on her performance—must be naturally and overflowingly beautiful. Ullmann is. She doesn't exploit that beauty, although in a practical way she relies on it. (How could she not know that she is beautiful?) With her beauty as base, she builds a character design and a dramatic experience. This is the only Nora I've seen who seemed to me in genuine pain, under the smiling and skittering, from the very start: a woman who loves her husband insofar as she then understands him and the meaning of love, who loves her children and the idea of family life, but who is in a twofold anguish: fear of blackmail, for the forgery she committed out of love, and discomfort with a society that has made her desperate action the only way she *could* act, that has emphasized her inferior position as woman.

When Claire Bloom played Nora—I choose her because she used the same Christopher Hampton translation—the "squirrel" cutenesses in the early portions were an obvious game, masks worn to make life livable and to be dropped later when the life was changed. But Ullmann doesn't do "squirrel" acts. Through those early parts she plays Nora as a sexual being whose sex is important to her and her husband; the squirrel and lark and other nicknames become living-room metaphors for bedroom memories and anticipations. The occasional early glints of Nora's clearheadedness fit this full woman better than they do Bloom's slave-girl coquette. This unforced sexual atmosphere—a woman who needs this man who needs her—makes her anguish all the more real.

The last act, the last scene flower out of this sexual ambience. When what Nora calls the "wonderful" doesn't happen, when her husband, Torvald, doesn't step forward to protect her, at least to share the blame because she committed the forgery for his sake, it is of course a blow to her opinion of him, but its immediate effect is on her sexual being. We see her figurative colors change before our eyes. This Nora changes in spirit, mind, and gonads. The sexual bonds that had linked her and Torvald, that had made her inferior cadging position just bearable, have snapped. The last scene, so often critically debated, has never seemed more humanly prepared and resolved, more credible and courageous and lonely. If we add the innumerable lovely details, like the pitifully graceful moment when she takes off her wedding ring and then holds out her hand for Torvald's ring, we have a performance that is a realized theatrical joy.

But if we add, we must also subtract. The rest of the cast ranges from mediocre to worse. The best of them is Barton Heyman as Krogstad, the blackmailer. When Krogstad is adequately played, I always feel sympathy for him: a man who collapsed when he was jilted by the woman he wanted, who married eventually, and who now wants to fight back to respectability for his children's sake. The fact that he is not a villain makes Nora's drama with him sharper, and Heyman states Krogstad's case solidly enough. Unfortunately, Barbara Colby as Mrs. Linde doesn't convince us that her jilting of Krogstad would have shaken his life; it's a knobby and untaking performance. Michael Granger as Dr. Rank, the dying family friend, is beneath comment.

The crucially bad performance is Sam Waterston's as Torvald. Is this the best that the American theater could come up with to play opposite Ullmann? Waterston has occasionally been good, as in Antoon's Americanized *Much Ado About Nothing* (1972). Since then he seems to have become egregiously introspective. Last season he struggled to play Hamlet as Prospero in *The Tempest* downstairs at the Newhouse; upstairs now he seems to be struggling to play Hamlet as Torvald, self-displayingly moody and "sensitive." His voice still barks (as in the film of *The Great Gatsby*), and the net effect is of a neurotic whippet yelping stridently. The solid male whom Nora needs is not there, the man honestly trying to do his best for wife and family according to the conditioning of a male-oriented society. Waterston is lightweight, insufficient, off-key. If there had been a good Torvald, Ullmann would naturally have been even better. As it is, she seemed to spend some of her time "building up" this weak actor.

Apart from the colors of Santo Loquasto's set, which are blatantly chosen to suggest a depressing atmosphere, the shape of it is unhelpful. The two most important doors, the front door and the one to Torvald's study, are parallel to the "footlights," so they provide the actors with the dullest possible entrances and exits.

The School for Wives

(May 8, 1971)

I go to Molière reluctantly. Two reasons. First, fascinating as old comedy often is in several ways, it's not often funny. (I except most of Shakespeare and some Restoration plays.) Performance rarely helps matters.

Second, connected with the first, the comedies that still live do so by reason of their language. Translations are never good enough, in comedy. I assume that Molière, for the French-speaking, lives as Shakespeare does for me. In English, stripped of his language, Molière reduces to linear plot, in most cases, with commedia characters and last-minute mechanical resolutions. The clear exceptions are *Dom Juan* and *Tartuffe,* whose thematic and character complexity come through in competent translation. Otherwise, with verbal richness gone, the diet is mostly thin.

Richard Wilbur, one of our best poets, has now translated several Molière comedies. French scholars call his work fine. All I hear is his English, and, reasonably deft as the verses are, the translations are just an endless series of rhymed iambic couplets, often with feminine endings, that jingle on and on. I don't have the text of his *School for Wives,* but here's a random sample of Wilbur's *Misanthrope:*

> It's true the man's a most accomplished dunce;
> His gauche behavior charms the eye at once;
> And every time one sees him, on my word,
> His manner's grown a trifle more absurd.

For two and a half hours? Probably the above is a just rendering of the original. Nevertheless it's jejune English prosody—with the strained placement of "on my word" to provide a rhyme. It would be inappropriate to compare these translations with Wilbur's serious poetry; but compare them with his lyrics for the musical version of *Candide* and hear the difference between a poet writing light verse in his own tongue and a translator gathering up a lot of little packages while trying not to spill any. Wilbur has said that he believes verse is essential in translating these plays. That's because he knows the French so well. I have the bliss of ignorance in the matter, and that bliss is disturbed by Wilbur's tackling this insuperable task. My point is not that he could have done better but precisely that he could not.

Brian Bedford has been hailed for his performance of Arnolphe in this Phoenix production of *The School for Wives,* and in one way he deserves it. With the help of the director, Stephen Porter, he has attacked the jigging couplets in an attempt to overcome their greeting-card rhymes—with run-on phrasing, pauses, and comic inflections. Bedford has an enormous role and, vocally, falls just short of success: he never completely "digests" the couplets, but at least he makes a skillful try at it.

Otherwise his performance is more mannerism than style. He looks and behaves (sometimes sounds) like a younger, slimmer Charles Laughton. Someone says something distressing to him, but he must not reveal his distress. He listens deadpan. Count of three. Then a swift toothy grin. Numerous times.

The story of the middle-aged man who has raised a girl in innocence to be his bride is a not very ingenious farce (in English). It's not helped here by a graceless juvenile, David Dukes, and by an ingenue—named Joan Van Ark!—who has a Betty Boop voice and is about ten years too old for her part. The setting by James Tilton, with its garden walls that swing open for scenes inside, repeats the idea of the Christian Bérard set that Louis Jouvet brought here in his production of this play in 1951; but Tilton's set is not nearly as pretty.

Scapino

(June 22, 1974)

Scapino is an adaptation of Molière's *Les Fourberies de Scapin* produced by the Young Vic of London under the direction of Frank Dunlop. The Young Vic is, roughly speaking, the young people's division of the National Theater, which itself used to be called the Old Vic. The Young Vic was founded by Dunlop in 1969 and has got a reputation for juice. *Scapino* came briefly to the Brooklyn Academy of Music last winter, where I missed it. Then the Circle in the Square in Manhattan, short of funds to produce its own last play of the season, invited the production to return. It came; it was seen; it conquered. But not this column, I'm afraid.

And not because Dunlop has taken lots of liberties. When we go to a revival of a classic comedy these days, we know in advance that we're probably not going to see *it*—we're going to see a version of it, adapted to the times. The modernization of serious plays, tragedy or drama, is often egotistical intrusion by a director who feels compelled to have a "concept" or else is an implicit confession of inability to handle the play in period. And certain comedies, those of wit and character like *The School for Scandal* or *The Way of the World,* don't often fare well when altered because their language is untransportable and their finesse depends on period style. But where there is more humor than wit in a comedy, along with a lot of physical action, then updating is not only possible but sometimes necessary. Lower kinds of comedy, down through farce, frequently depend on topical reference more than societal framework, and a good dust-up helps to keep them funny. When the late Bert Lahr played Aristophanes' *The Birds,* he slipped in a paraphrase of a potato-chip commercial with which he was then closely associated—and got a laugh. Not very Athenian but, in spirit, perfectly Aristophanic.

So it's not the liberties in *Scapino* that bother. It's the fact—for me, anyway—that they don't quite work.

The setting, as in Molière, is Naples, appropriate for a play whose characters come from commedia dell'arte, but now it's Naples more or less today. The first thing that happens, before the play begins, is trite: a young bootblack wanders through the audience, asking for cigarettes and kissing ladies' hands. When I see actors mingle with the audience, I immediately suspect the director of bankruptcy or cultural time-lag. The next thing that happens is not much fresher; still it's funnier. Jim Dale, the star of the show, the Scapino, appears in mod clothes on a small balcony and, strumming a guitar, sings a soulful Italian song whose words come from the menu of any Italian restaurant.

Dale is not only the star, he is the show. It stands—or doesn't, quite—through him. He is an actor, dancer, singer, composer, British TV music star, and he takes the stage with vigor and address. His role is the clever servant of old comedy, progenitor of Figaro and countless others, and the plot tells how he helps two pairs of lovers against parental opposition. (Part of the plot hinges on the gimmick that the parental opposition turns out not to exist, so we get a fore-taste of Sheridan's *The Rivals* and Rostand's *The Romantics*.) In the course of his conspirings Dale leaps, sings, bounds into the audience over the backs of their seats, does trick voices and frenzied series of impersonations, etc., etc. There is a lot of phallic play with a big sausage—another classic device—and a good deal of crotch humor. But none of all this, by him and by others, made me laugh much.

In this kind of show, when it's weak, a conspiracy is entreated between stage and audience. We are doing a lot of comic things, say the actors, you can see that they're comic, and since we're doing so many of them so quickly and so energetically, it's your part of the bargain to laugh. Which, to be honest, many do here. But the cast didn't often force me to laugh; I simply *watched* them doing all these fast and purportedly zany things. After that opening song, the only other real laugh I got was from the first entrance of Ian Trigger, one of the fathers, a diminutive white-haired eccentric actor who came in like a crazy dwarf going several ways at once.

What's at stake in this kind of show, I think, is innocence. The great physical comics—Chaplin, Keaton, Lloyd—and the good smooth farceurs—early Jack Lemmon and Ian Carmichael—play with a conviction that has no slightest touch in it of letting hair down, no hint of condescending let's-all-be-kids-for-the-nonce. They are what they are and do what they do with utter subscription, with *purity*. But all through the antics of Dale and friends I had a slight feeling of patronization, of serious minds unbending graciously. In fact, after the show Dale led the audience in that archetypal English exercise, a community sing (of that opening song, which runs through the show), and he said, "Be a kid for two minutes. It's marvelous fun." Chaplin or Keaton could never have said or thought that; the idea would have insulted them. The pervasive scent of that idea made *Scapino* a synthetic experience for me.

Early in 1973 a musical called *Tricks,* based on the same Molière play, was brought to Broadway from the Actors Theater of Louisville and the Arena Stage of Washington. As a script and score, it was intolerable—cutesy and quaint and quintessential 1920s little-theater. But the performance of René Auberjonois as Scapin was intricately designed and neatly executed, more varied and less self-admiringly pre-emptive than Dale's. *Tricks* was painful to sit through, *Scapino* merely non-amusing; but Auberjonois was more engaging than Dale.

Long Day's Journey into Night

(June 12, 1971)

Long Day's Journey into Night is, by uncommon consent, the best play ever written on this side of the Atlantic. Compared with the greatest work I know about the birth of an artist, Knut Hamsun's novel *Hunger,* O'Neill's drama is somewhat naïve and idealistic. But he casts his net wider than Hamsun, and the doggedness with which he clings to his four characters, as if his life depended on chewing the life out of them and onto the stage, at last overcomes the touch of the poetaster.

The recurrent dynamic device of the play is outburst and apology. Over and over a character explodes, provokes an angry response, then subsides and recants. By this method O'Neill reveals things that would otherwise lie hidden and also provides a texture of conflict for a day's events that are not in themselves highly dramatic. The figurative shape of the play is thus a series of arcs, but the base line of the arcs goes deeper and deeper. Although the play is rarely moving and never exalting like the great Greeks, its utter commitment and its absolute insistence take it past its faults, even past its virtues, to the place of great art: the place where we look *back* at life.

The present production is sketchy. First, the setting is maladroit. The Promenade Theater has a fairly shallow stage, and the designers, Elmon Webb and Virginia Dancy, make it shallower. They have put a staircase at back, thus shifting the playing area even farther downstage. Why wouldn't it have been possible to simulate the staircase behind a center entrance, thus adding a good four feet of depth to the playing area? As is, the drama seems to be taking place on a furnished shelf.

And Arvin Brown, the director, underscores the narrowness from the first moment. James and Mary Tyrone enter arm in arm, then they have to part so that she can go ahead, single-file, into their own living room!

That's not the last of Brown's clumsy staging, but his chief defects are in the character concepts, out of which the "arcs" arise and which thus make the play. Centrally, the trouble is with Robert Ryan, the Tyrone. If Tyrone is not the personification of an old romantic actor, then he is neither himself as a man nor the source of much of the bitterness and gesture of the play. The primary point about those old actors is that they were conscious of style offstage as well as on, that they considered themselves a race apart from other mortals. In fact, it was O'Neill's hatred of that theater in his father that made him the kind of writer he was; and certainly the attitudes behind the father's life-style are essential to the play's tensions. Ryan just slumps around in a concave way, without any richness of physical or vocal line, and leaves the part bare, theatrically and thematically. (Philip Bosco might make a fine Tyrone!)

James Naughton is a moderately pleasant Edmund, but has no touch of the buried blaze that O'Neill was celebrating in himself. Stacy Keach works well as James, Jr., handicapped by our memory of Jason Robards in the one part that fitted him. Keach is good enough, but never gets the heartbreaking acid of Robards' ambivalence toward his kid brother.

The exception to all the above, and a very happy surprise, is the Mary of Geraldine Fitzgerald, an actress whose past performances had not raised expectation high. Here she is lovely. Her defensive web of smiles and her sense of being lost within the mazes of herself create this sad woman for us. In the very last speech of the play, the drugged and dreamy Mary remembers her girlhood in the convent, how her youth and religious vocation ended: "I fell in love with James Tyrone and was so happy for a time." Fitzgerald pauses slightly before the last three words; and the way she speaks the final phrase is what I'll cherish from this production.

A Moon for the Misbegotten

(*January 26, 1974*)

Strange to remember, these days, that Eugene O'Neill's *A Moon for the Misbegotten* ran into censorship troubles when it was first toured in 1947. Written in the early '40s, set in the early '20s, it seems such a period piece of sin and suffering now.

Aside from that aspect, *The Misbegotten* is an anomaly: a kind of postscript to *Long Day's Journey into Night*. If you don't know the earlier and infinitely better play, *The Misbegotten* must seem only a drawn-out series of skits and arias, chiefly concerned with a sentimental Irish-American boozer. If you know the other play, which O'Neill evidently assumes you do, then the last days of Jamie, the older Tyrone son, take on both pathos and clinical significance—particularly if (*pace* the New Critics) you also know the facts behind both plays.

From biographies one learns that the playwright's older brother, a terrible drunk, sobered up when his father died and he went to live with his mother in blissful "marriage"—apparently the (sexless) union that he had wanted all his life and whose impossibility had made him an alcoholic. When his mother died, Jamie hit the whiskey slide again, steeply, and died a year later. The key speech in *The Misbegotten,* the only genuinely interesting scene in this long play, is Jamie's description of the death of his mother and his whiskey-sex spree on the train bringing her coffin back East from California.

He reveals his secrets to Josie, the Amazonian daughter of an Irish tenant farmer on the Tyrone place in Connecticut, whom he visits regularly to josh and drink with and to blather about purity. The only shred of interest in Josie is her lie about herself (another of O'Neill's necessary "pipe dreams"): she spreads the story that she is loose, although she's a virgin, because she needs at least imaginary desirability. Jamie spends one moonlit night in her arms—innocently, despite a great deal of frenzy on the subject of sex—and then leaves, presumably to die soon.

Now this minor tangential play has finally been "placed" in the theater, after several lesser attempts, thanks to Jason Robards' performance. Essentially this is the fourth installment of Robards' performance of this O'Neill character: it's virtually the same man he played in *The Iceman Cometh, Hughie,* and, of course, *Long Day's Journey*. Robards does it superbly. It's the only character I've seen him do superbly, but he makes it a small cosmos of European heritage versus American values, of religion versus unwelcome liberation from it, of Oedipal tangle further tangled by booze and binges. If you want an object lesson in the art of acting, read Jamie's prosy speeches about his mother's death, then go to see Robards. It's one more proof of the selfhood of the actor's art.

Colleen Dewhurst, the Josie, is still a failed great actress to me. She ought to have been great, that's easy to see; but she's fat, she swings that saccharine smile like a club, and she sounds like a worn 78-rpm recording of a magnificent voice. I can't share the enthusiasm for Ed Flanders as her father. He's supposed to be a tough, sly Irishman with a grudging soft spot, but Flanders seems to have strayed in from *Finian's Rainbow*.

José Quintero, who has a long experience with O'Neill and with Robards in it, had his lapses here with Dewhurst and Flanders, but helped bring Robards to perfection. Ben Edwards' setting looks more like scene designs of the twenties than like the twenties themselves.

Ah, Wilderness!

(October 11, 1975)

Eugene O'Neill dreamed this play one night in September 1932. The next day he wrote out the entire scenario and within six weeks the play was finished. Only one other play, *Desire under the Elms*, had come to him in a dream. *Ah, Wilderness!* is a quite different kind of dream, and not just because it is a comedy (O'Neill's only one).

First, to refresh you, it takes place in "a large small-town in Connecticut" on July 4 and 5, 1906. It centers on the family of Nat Miller, a 57-year-old newspaper publisher; the main action concerns his 17-year-old son Richard who, because of seeming rejection by his girl, goes to a saloon, gets drunk with a prostitute (though he doesn't go to bed with her), and learns a lesson from his experience. The boy is reunited with his girl, swears purity, and is set for Yale. Others are other Miller children, Nat's maiden sister, and his wife's bibulous brother who has often been rejected by Nat's sister.

Many commentators have pointed out the similarities between this play and *Long Day's Journey into Night*: the location, the family-as-arena, the hoverings of sin over the house, the power of the father, the subtler power of the mother, the young character who is more or less the author's vicar. (O'Neill was Richard's age in 1906 and

Edmund Tyrone's age in 1912, the year when *Journey* takes place.) They tell us that *Ah, Wilderness!* is his contrasting bright version of his past, a comic mirror-image of his great tragedy. But the commentators usually omit important points. First, *Ah, Wilderness!* was written nine years before *Journey;* so the past that had haunted O'Neill all his life, that terrible past, surfaced from his unconscious for the first time in pleasant and nostalgic vein. Second, it came out Protestant. No hint is given that the Millers are Catholic, and there surely would have been such a hint if we were to think so; because, otherwise, given the time and place, we must assume they are not Catholic. The elimination of religious difference with the community is one of the elements that makes the just-folks atmosphere *possible* in this New England of 1906. Third, that year is in a different era from 1912. For well-dramatized evidence of that fact, see E. L. Doctorow's novel *Ragtime*. Fourth, neither of the parents has the slightest personal anguish of any consequence, as compared with James and Mary Tyrone. Nat Miller's worst problem is that he thinks, mistakenly, that bluefish will poison him. O'Neill, according to Louis Sheaffer's solid biography, gave himself different parents for this play. He patterned Mrs. Miller on the mother of four of his boyhood chums, a Mrs. McGinley, who may herself have been Catholic, to judge by her name; and he based Nat Miller on a New London newspaper editor who had befriended him.

Two conclusions emerge, personal and artistic. Personal: the play is an exercise in wish fulfillment. O'Neill himself said that the play is what he "would have *liked* my boyhood to have been." Later, in the dedication to *Journey* he said that he was able "to face my dead at last." Not here, not yet. He wanted happy conventional parents in his dream, he wanted to be Protestant in a predominantly Protestant community, he wanted to learn early not to be a drunkard and to avoid sins of the flesh, and early he wanted to find pure love.

All of us are plagued consciously or otherwise all our lives by the idealism of adolescence. But the artistic use that O'Neill made of his unfulfilled adolescent yearnings is, to me, shocking. He didn't see his dream in any kind of perspective; he took it straight and put it down without comment. To use that dream without framework, without mediation, was to falsify. O'Neill lied. He contravened the major theme of his whole body of work—the attack on materialism and sanctimoniousness, the spiritual confusion and sloth, the provincialism that he found in American life. Many of his plays are strained and bloated, but their falseness comes from the juvenility of their attempts to tell the truth. Those were all dramas, at some level or other of seriousness. Comedy, to O'Neill, evidently meant a commission to falsify. The play is one long ode to middle-class respectability, the whitewashed sepulchre whose emptiness he so fiercely exposed elsewhere. *Ah, Wilderness!* doesn't merely alter the biographical data of O'Neill's past to conform to that adolescent dream, it posits that dream as a worthy ideal. So it is not only his one comedy, it is—by his own standards—his one deliberate lie.

How chuckly and quaint it all is now—the old slang, even older than in 1933 when the play was first done, the jokes with the greenhorn Irish maid, the male-oriented universe, the Currier & Ives view of sex. And yet (the play implies), darn it all, wasn't there something *to* all that? Didn't their lives back there make more *sense?*

They didn't, no more than ours anyway, and O'Neill knew they didn't. What, in a lesser writer, would be merely romantic is in him meretricious. The aspects of American life that he took pains elsewhere to show as mere façade, he shows here as the whole noble structure. In his hands comedy became exactly the opposite of what it has been for most other great dramatists in history.

The Circle in the Square, which has lately taken to presenting other theaters' productions—*Scapino* by the Young Vic of London, *The National Health* by the Long Wharf of New Haven*—now presents the Long Wharf production of *Ah, Wilderness!* Arvin Brown, the artistic chief of Long Wharf, is one of the few directors who can cope with the Circle's ungainly oval playing space, but he has been less successful with his casting and performances here than in *The National Health*. Richard Backus, the Richard, is an earnest young journeyman-actor, but he has little appeal or force; he simply supplies what is required, like a recruit obeying a sergeant. Geraldine Fitzgerald has charm as his mother, but her acting has been more closely controlled in the past. Here her performance resembles an etching that has been somewhat carelessly printed. John Braden is miscast as the drunkard. O'Neill specifically asks for a man who is "short, fat, bald-headed, with the puckish face of a Peck's Bad Boy who has never grown up." (Remember Gene Lockhart, who first played the part?) Braden is tall, angular, lantern-jawed. Certainly a director can

* See pp. 130 and 242.

disregard an author's request if he then succeeds in his own way; but Braden doesn't look like a man who has been trading all his life on his puppy-like playfulness, seems to know he's wrong for the part, and consequently pushes very hard. Teresa Wright plays the spinster; it's the theater's version of the mimetic fallacy to cast a colorless actress in a colorless role. Suzanne Lederer is clumsy in every way as the prostitute. Swoosie Kurtz—that's her name, I assure you—is too old for Richard's girl but plays it with some delicacy.

The one joy of the evening is William Swetland as Nat Miller. What a good actor. To see Swetland's name on a program—and I have seen him now in other O'Neill, in Shaw and Storey and Gorky and other plays at the Long Wharf—is to know that in one role at least you are going to get tactful imagination, skill, and unimpeachable validity. What a rare, fine thing these days to be a good "company" actor.

The first Nat Miller was George M. Cohan. (It was the first play by an author other than himself in which he had appeared.) Cohan objected strenuously to the saloon scene because—this was not so strange forty years ago—he didn't want to be in a play that had a prostitute in it. He was right about wanting to cut the scene, even though he had the wrong reason: the saloon episode is superfluous. So is the reunion scene between Richard and his girl. Both scenes could be cut without harming the play in story or in characterization, and the cuts would greatly help this long day's journey into the next day. But of course the two scenes get lots of patronizing chuckles, which makes them and O'Neill even more suspect. (I'm not arguing against audience enjoyment, just noting O'Neill's odd function in this one instance as crowd-pleaser.)

For the program and ads of this production the title is printed in stars and stripes. I suppose this is to help celebrate the Bicentennial. No comment.

The Crucible

(*May 27, 1972*)

This revival was doomed to inadequacy with the casting of Robert Foxworth as Proctor. He is an actor of ability, but he is grossly miscast. He suffers from a management at Lincoln Center that has, once again, chosen a play with a crucial leading role and, apparently, only afterward thought about casting the role. It has happened often before; this time the afterthought is Foxworth.

Even if every other element in Arthur Miller's play is rendered perfectly—and some of them here are rendered well—it cannot succeed unless Proctor is authentic. Foxworth is physically unconvincing: when he talks about farming, he looks and sounds like a man home from a hard day on Madison Avenue. He is temperamentally unsuited, unable to suggest the dark Hawthornean doubts and hungers that Miller would like. The role is meant to symbolize archetypal puritan American conscience, flaws and all; and if the actor cannot encompass that size, there simply is no show, no matter what else is good.

Some of the rest *is* good. Pamela Payton-Wright, whom I have admired since her Kattrin in a Milwaukee *Mother Courage* six years ago, is perfect as the sex-driven Abigail. Philip Bosco wrestles credibly with new ideas of duty as the Reverend Hale. Nora Heflin is fine as the muddled, malleable Mary Warren. Martha Henry, not an actress to enchant audiences but a competent and intelligent one, is strong as Elizabeth Proctor, the cold woman who moves through pain to admiration of her husband.

John Berry, who directed *Boesman and Lena* excellently two years ago and has done lesser work since, does only fairly well here. If he had a hand in the good performances noted, he also had a hand in the poor ones and the miscasting. If he treated some scenes dynamically (like Elizabeth's unwitting betrayal of her husband), sometimes I was aware of people standing around in semi-circles as in a Shubert operetta; and his sense of vocal levels occasionally confuses volume with drama. Jo Mielziner designed good lighting and suggestive sketch-sets, but it's difficult to handle the acreage that actors have to traverse on that stage before they get down to where it matters.

As for the play itself, when it was first produced in 1953 Eric Bentley, a radical, had the courage to point out that it was analogically dubious. The Salem witchcraft trials of 1692 were used as a parallel with Joe McCarthyism, but Bentley noted that witchcraft is imaginary and Communism is not.

Now Joe McCarthy is dead, though not very deeply buried, and *The Crucible* must live, if it can, without patent reference. In one way, time has helped it. It was a thematically schizoid play: its last act was a moral-metaphysical drama. Now the political underscoring is less heavy in the first three acts, and it becomes an imperfect drama of an imperfect man driven by his imperfections to a chance for purification. His sin, of adultery, makes him the victim of a plot, and that plot gives him a chance for a redemptive action.

Those first three acts are too plotty to be deep and the plotting sometimes creaks: the business of the needle in the doll, for instance, or the speed with which Governor Danforth changes (in Act Three) from a keen legalistic mind to a credulous believer in hysterical girls' accusations.

Still, for me, it is Miller's best play. Those first three acts have some motor force, the language steers most of the time between mouthy archaism and modern vernacular, and the character of the Reverend Hale is possibly Miller's best dramaturgic stroke: a shadow protagonist, a "safe" man undergoing an empathic crisis, something like (excuse the profanity) Nicodemus against Jesus.

One can understand, watching those first three acts, why Miller has become the most popular social dramatist of his time, not only in America but in the world. He deals exclusively with received liberal ideas. The best social dramatists, and many inferior ones, have usually dealt with dangerous ideas. In Ibsen's worst social plays, this is true; the basic theme of *An Enemy of the People* is that the majority is always wrong. Miller adapted that play (and lessened it), but he could not have tackled that theme himself. Ibsen wanted to show his audience its failures: Miller makes enlightened folks feel even better about themselves.

Except for the last act of this one play, *The Crucible*. Proctor can sign a false confession and live, if he chooses, and with this choice the play moves out of the political analogy of the "old" version or the plottiness of the "new." Proctor wants to live, naturally, but he also thinks it would be fraudulent to die for his beliefs, a kind of moral arrogance. Then, by refusing to name accomplices and by refusing to sign a confession that would be used by the state to blacken his name and bludgeon others, he *becomes* good enough to die for his beliefs.

It is the largest subject raised in all of Miller's works. In language and in its wholeness with the preceding acts, this last act is far below the scene that might have been Miller's model: the trial scene of Shaw's *Saint Joan*. Still it is the one moment in Miller that does not stroke our superiorities or tug our humane-decent hearts. It asks whether a man can rationally give his life for something that he can be aware of only while he is alive; or, if he believes in a higher Judge and a greater consciousness, whether he has the right to martyr's robes. And by implication it also asks something else: if there is nothing a man will die for (I don't mean kill for), if there is nothing at all that he will maintain to the uttermost limits, is there a genuine foundation to any of the values by which he lives?

It is the progress to these questions and the embodiment of them that Foxworth cannot manage. Without them, what does all the rest matter?

Death of a Salesman

(July 19, 1975)

Death of a Salesman contains the idea for a great play, and I would maintain that its immense international success comes from the force of that idea prevailing over the defects in execution. The force takes hold with the very title, which is highly evocative, and is amplified by the opening sight of Willy Loman coming in the door. That sight is a superb theater image of our time, as unforgettable an icon as Mother Courage and her wagon (another traveling salesman!): the salesman home, "tired to the death," lugging his two heavy sample cases, rejected by the big milk-filled bosom of the country from which he had expected so much nourishment.

The force of the play's idea continues fitfully to grasp at us: the idea of a man who has sold things without making them, who has paid for things without really owning them; an insulted extrusion of commercial society battling for some sliver of authenticity before he slips into the dark.

But to see the play again is to see how Arthur Miller lacked the control and vision to fulfill his own idea. First consider the diction of the play, because a play is its language, first and finally. *Salesman* falters badly in this regard. At its best, its true and telling best, the diction is first-generation Brooklyn Jewish. ("Attention, attention must be finally paid to such a person.") But often the dialogue slips into a fanciness that is slightly ludicrous. To hear Biff say, "I've been remiss," to hear Linda say, "He was crestfallen, Willy" is like watching a car run off the road momentarily onto the shoulder. (I've never heard anyone use the word "crestfallen" in my life.) Then there is the language of Willy's brother Ben, the apparition of piratical success. He speaks like nothing but a symbol, and not a symbol connected with Willy in any perceptible way. Miller *says* he's Willy's brother, that's all. The very use of diamonds as the source of Ben's wealth has an almost childishly symbolic quality about it. When Miller's language is close to the stenographic, the remembered, it's good; otherwise, it tends to literary juvenility, a pretended return from pretended experience.

Thematically, too, the play is cloudy. It's hard to believe that, centrally, Miller had anything more than muzzy anti-business, anti-technology impulses in his head. Is Willy a man shattered by business failure and by disappointment in his sons? Then why, when he is younger and at least making a living, when he is proud of his sons and they of him, does he lie about his earnings to Linda and then have to correct himself? Why, at the peak of his life, does he undercut his own four-flushing to tell her that people don't take to him, that they laugh at him? The figure that comes through the play is not of a man brought down by various failures but of a mentally unstable man in whom the fissures have increased. Willy is shown to be at least as much a victim of psychopathy as of the bitch goddess. When was he ever rational or dependable? Is this a tragedy of belief in the American romance or the end of a clinical case?

But assume, for argument, that Willy is not a psychopath, that he was a relatively whole man now crushed by the American juggernaut. What is the play's attitude toward that juggernaut, toward business ideals? There is no anagnorisis for Willy, no moment of recognition: he dies believing in money—in fact, he kills himself for it, to give his son Biff the insurance benefit as a stake for more business. His son Happy is wedded to money values and says over his father's coffin that he's going to stick to them for his father's sake. Biff was so aggrandized by his father that he became kleptomaniacal as a boy and even now, after his father-as-idol has collapsed, can't resist stealing a successful man's fountain pen as a niggling vindictiveness against that man's success and his own non-success. The only alternatives to the business ethos ever produced in the play are Willy's love of tools and seeds, building and planting, and Biff's love of outdoor life. As between romances, I'll take business.

Miller confuses matters even further by the success of young Bernard next door as a lawyer in the Establishment world, a success for which Willy feels envy. What we are left with is neither a critique of the business world nor an adult vision of something different and better, but the story of a man (granting he was sane) who failed, as salesman and father, and who made things worse by refusing to the end to admit those failures, which he knew were true. That is one play, and possibly a good one if it were realized; but it is quite a different one from a play that, in its atmosphere and mannerisms, implies radical perception about deep American ills.

Some other points. When I saw the film in 1952, which made the environment more vivid, I couldn't help wondering why Willy had money worries: he had almost paid off the mortgage on his house, which was a piece of real estate in an increasingly valuable and desirable section, to judge by the building going on all around it. I don't think this is a petty literal point in a realistic play whose lexicon is bill-paying. Further, all the dialogue about Willy's father, with his wagon-travels through the West and his flutes, seems falser than ever, Miller's imposition on this Brooklyn play to give it historical base and continental sweep. As with the character of Ben, there is a schism in tenor between this material and the rest of the play. Last, a point that is strangely more apparent now than it was in 1949 when *Salesman* first appeared: the play is set in the late 1940s and reaches back some fifteen years, yet there is scarcely a mention of World War II. How did Biff and Happy escape it? If they didn't, wouldn't the re-united brothers have had something to say about it? And wouldn't the war have had some effect on Willy's past-cum-present view of promise-crammed America?

Some of the play is touching still: Willy when he is at his most salesman-like, the Requiem over his coffin, and much of the material on Miller's favorite theme, the love-hate of father and son. But these are sound moments in a flabby, occasionally false work. Miller had gift enough to get the idea, but then settled for the dynamics of the idea itself, supported by a vague high-mindedness, to write his play for him. As the world knows, many viewers and readers have taken the intent for the deed. Some have not. And for one viewer this new production only emphasizes the gap between intent and accomplishment.

Emphasizes it grossly. Except for Willy, the cast of this Circle in the Square production is at best inoffensive, something that can be said only of a few of the women in smaller roles. Most of the leading actors are varyingly deplorable. Teresa Wright (Linda) is a dry stick. James Farentino (Biff) is a gallery of Actors Studio attitudinizings. Harvey Keitel (Happy) is weak and keeps gesturing simultaneously with both arms like a puppet on a string. The neighbors Bernard and Charley are played by black actors who are utterly inept. "Colorblind" casting is theoretically admirable; but when black actors in white parts are as bad as these two, they only make you wonder doubly why the director used them. You wonder, too, why the director inserted a second intermission, harming the flow of the play, and why he had the two scenes of the Woman in Boston played by two different actresses. It makes Willy a womanizer, instead of a family man with a "family" away from home.

That director was George C. Scott. If it had been someone else, Scott's own performance as Willy might have been memorable. Now it is patently contrived. He uses two principal modes. He smiles a lot during the "depressed" passages. (This playing against the lines is something he also did in Astrov's opening scene in *Uncle Vanya.**) And he erupts. The Smile soon becomes an obvious set-up for the Fury. As for the Fury, Willy's outbursts are surely those of angry frustration, affecting in their impotence. But Scott, a powerful actor, gets so strong that the Fury connotes a man too imperious to have lived Willy's life. Another director might have seen this and might have helped Scott to a characterization out of which self-kidding and explosion grew organically. Inevitably an actor of his ability must have some moments that burst through even a merely technical conception, but in general Scott plays Willy like a crafty boxer, smiling along softly until he sees a chance to sock.

* See p. 146.

Uncle Vanya

(June 30, 1973)

Mike Nichols has directed a production of Chekhov's *Uncle Vanya* with George C. Scott as Dr. Astrov and Nicol Williamson as Vanya. (Williamson is best known in the U.S. for his film of *Inadmissible Evidence* and his theater and film appearances as Hamlet.) I've been waiting eagerly, ever since the first announcement, to see these two fine actors in these roles, but even more eagerly to see Nichols' work. Through his directing career in the theater, he has borne the indictment of refusing to face challenges. Virtually everyone has acknowledged his gifts, but many have accused him of choosing easy plays to work on. The best play he has directed before this, that I have seen, was Ann Jellicoe's *The Knack* (done excellently); his last previous play was his fourth Neil Simon comedy, *The Prisoner of Second Avenue* (done soporifically). In every production except the last, he has shown uncanny skill, particularly in timing and inflection, all lavished on easily accessible work.

His film career began with *Who's Afraid of Virginia Woolf?* and *The Graduate,* both of which were cinematically competent and in both of which he triumphed with actors. His two subsequent films, *Catch-22* and *Carnal Knowledge,* were lesser. But the standards for judging a film director's career differ substantially from those that apply in the theater. Film directors start from scratch. (Remakes don't figure importantly; and adaptations of classics don't figure importantly with serious directors.) For a theater director, as with a theater actor, the question sooner or later is one that could not signify in film: how does he measure against the great works?

Now Nichols has measured himself: and he shows that in Chekhov he is still a director of Neil Simon. Does Nichols see *Uncle Vanya* as a comedy? It is apparently a myth that Chekhov thought of his plays as comedies (see the excellent new edition of his letters, edited by Karlinsky and Heim), still Nichols doesn't even clearly follow the myth. Does he see the play as revolutionary dramaturgy (which it is) where the moment of Aristotelian recognition *changes nothing?* Does he see it as a prophecy of our world? Does he see it as an engine of irony in which the caprices of falling or not falling in love blight lives? Does he see it as a pre-ecology ecological warning? (Chekhov's first version was called *The Wood Demon,* because of Astrov's passion for forests and their preservation.) Tatters of all these ideas float through, but the only really clear idea is that Nichols wants to be "Chekhovian"—that is, have some guitar-strumming and yawning and samovar-tapping and twilights.

So, although he handles movement deftly on the abominably designed stage of the Circle in the Square's new theater, although he achieves some mildly daring compositions (two characters sitting at opposite ends of that racetrack stage conversing easily through projected imagination), although there is one good performance and an occasional good moment, the result is a ragbag, not a production. Against Chekhov, Nichols measures small.

Equally distressing, he has done some bad casting. Julie Christie, star of such films as *The Go-Between* and *Darling,* is Elena, the beautiful, trapped, young wife of the aging professor. Possibly Nichols thought he could repeat the magic he demonstrated with Katharine Ross in *The Graduate* and Candice Bergen in *Carnal Knowledge*—getting a performance from a non-actress. But Elena, to put it mildly, is a more subtle role than the other two, and it has to be created whole in front of us. Christie, who is not even strikingly beautiful anymore, has all the impact of a faded fashion model. Chekhov said he agreed with a correspondent's view that Elena is "a thinking and decent person," not "an apathetic, idle woman, incapable of thinking or even loving." Christie doesn't even come close enough to miss the mark.

Elizabeth Wilson (who was Benjamin's mother in *The Graduate*) is a very good comic actress and conceivably could do a certain kind of serious, thin-edge, near-hysterical acting as well. Here she is Sonya, Vanya's patient niece, in love with Astrov, and is quite wrong at once because she is too old. We can feel no slightest hope that Astrov might marry her, so there is no blasted possibility, no anguish. What is worse, Wilson has been directed to play such moments as the confession of her love to Elena like a giddy comic spinster, so that Sonya is left without pathos, without dignity, and without "position" in the play. Then when we arrive at her famous last speech, in which she tells her uncle how they will work together and rest at last, we get the mirror image of the earlier giddy comedy—a tear bath that would float a cruiser. In both cases the character is adulterated because the director is reaching for effects, not fulfilling a design.

Cathleen Nesbitt, an old beauty, is Vanya's mother. Lillian Gish usually plays the nurse, but was out of the performance I saw. Barnard Hughes, as the pedantic professor, is merely a fussy old crank, devoid of benevolent pomp and unctuous oppression. Without those qualities, the Aristotelian recognition referred to above falls flat.

George C. Scott, a magnificent actor, is poor, not even magnificently poor, as Astrov, the lonely idealist doctor, who echoes Chekhov's own medical experience of epidemics and his social concerns for Russia's future. Scott is now a bit fat and the night I went was very hoarse. But, more important, like his director he has no *idea* of the part, no intent or subscription; he just scans the surface for chances to score. He smokes cigarettes and cigars very nicely from time to time, and he finds a few places in which to slam the table in Scottish fury. (There's not much of that fury in Astrov.) In the opening scene he plays "against" the lines very effectively, with breeziness and no self-pity, as he tells the nurse how he has changed in ten years, but this approach soon dribbles into a muddle of differing tacks.

The one impressive performance is Nicol Williamson's Vanya. Williamson—to complete the gamut of this aspect of miscasting—is too young! He doesn't remotely look the forty-seven he is supposed to be. And he sometimes grinds his lines to a conclusion like a terrier shaking a rat. But he has a vision of Vanya, as a man with abilities and with shackles, a good farm manager and a poor social operative, a good mind and a poor ability to advance his ideas; and Williamson has lovely vocal color and a power of emotional conviction to bring the above to flower. I believed his love for Elena, his loathing of the professor, I believed in the man who believed them. The outburst in which he takes the two wild shots at the professor is the most difficult scene in the play and, paradoxically, it's the most successful scene in this production, because of Williamson.

Nichols apparently wanted an all-star cast, but he has proved a poor astronomer. Some of the stars are cold, some are wrongly constellated, and the astronomer is flying too high. At the moment, anyway, theater Nichols, as distinct from film Nichols, seems to have been right to stick to lightweight plays. Here even his customary skill seems inhibited—possibly by awe.

Ulysses in Nighttown

(April 6, 1974)

Last week *Candide,* an Off-Broadway hit of 1973 that moved to Broadway.* This week *Ulysses in Nighttown,* an Off-Broadway hit of 1958, now reproduced on Broadway.

Once again Zero Mostel is Bloom, once again Burgess Meredith has directed, and they use the adaptation by Marjorie Barkentin. (This time, however, the program doesn't note that she prepared the script under the supervision of the late Padraic Colum.) I saw the show in 1958, liked most of it greatly, had reservations. I saw the new production, liked most of it less, had more reservations. I don't think it's just because sixteen years have passed, but, in patent ways and in one subtler way, the sixteen years have something to do with it.

The adaptation draws mostly on the brothel dream-nightmare of Joyce's titanic work, with bits spliced in from before and after that sequence. I couldn't see in 1958, and can't see now, what the play would mean to someone who had never read the book. References are fast and generally unexplained; the language—and this was one particularity of Joyce's genius—is composed for eye *and* ear, not for ear alone. (Compare it with the "ear" language in his superb, under-rated play *Exiles.*) But for those who have some experience of the novel, this adaptation has moments of vivid refreshment, like good illustrations. The center is the passage through the Dublin night of Bloom, the pathetic middle-aged slave of his wife and of himself, and of Stephen Dedalus, the young teacher, to a point where they become, if only briefly, vicarious father and son to each other. Much has been done with music and lights and setting and costume and in-floating, out-floating characters to make the play hover between fantasy and revelation; but the core of the trouble is that Joyce's use of the drama-dialogue form in the Nighttown sequence, together with stage directions, has misled some people into thinking that the sequence is dramatic. It's not: it's a black and painful poem—a series of transformations and evolutions that body forth the past actions and fantasies

* See p. 263.

that Bloom doesn't want embodied and that he suffers under as they assault him. This, need it be said, has huge interest for a reader; on stage it eventually sags because the director has to keep trying to top one "effect" with another, not hew to a line of dramatic progress.

The Broadway producers, aware of the need for "effect" and in any event wanting to glitz up a poor little Off-Broadway show, have put *Ulysses* in a big musical house and have budgeted it to fit. This is one of the clear markers of the sixteen-year time lapse: the avant-garde now being expensively "produced." Another marker is the new permissiveness: the whores are naked to the waist and Molly Bloom is naked to the toes. Many have commented on this as mere exploitation: I, no doubt perversely, disagree. The bare bosoms of the tarts harmonize with the mood, and Molly's nakedness becomes utterly appropriate because of the performance by Fionnuala Flanagan. This Irish actress, new to me, is exceptionally good. Parts of Molly's closing soliloquy have been stitched into the Nighttown episode; and when you see Flanagan sit naked on a chamber pot in the middle of a big stage in a big theater, then loll around on a bed fondling herself, and when you consider that very very soon after this display begins, Flanagan convinces you that you are peeping and eavesdropping on *privacy,* then you know you are dealing with a genuine actress who has exceptional powers of concentration and imagination and a full range of techniques to express them. There is not one iota of skin-show in it. It's not only the best performance in the play, it's the purest Joyce.

Which is, of course, a comment on Mostel. My memory of his 1958 performance is of general subscription to Bloom with only a few moments when Mostel cracked through—a moment, for instance, when he was executing actions under the narrator's command and was ordered to kiss a leper's feet. His slow double-take was vaudeville, not Bloom. Now in 1974 that double-take is exaggerated, yet it stands out less because the overall proportions have been exactly reversed. Now there's a lot of Mostel and not much Bloom. Once in a while, as the sexual indictments are read out against him, Mostel gives us humble pathos, as if the luridness of secret thoughts and actions were the burden that every suffering human must carry—almost a pantomime of the doctrine of original sin. But those moments are rare. What we get for the most part are the fruits of a sadly misguided career.

This, I think, is the more subtle reason for the failure of the revived *Ulysses*. The show depends on Mostel, and increasingly Mostel has misused himself in his professional life. There's no need to expatiate on his immense gift of pantomime, the comedy in that worldly baby face, the delicacy with which that elephantine body can poise itself down to a feathery pinpoint; all these are his talents and his curse. He now uses all these gifts very glibly. He is never happier as Bloom than when he has nothing to say, and since Bloom has a great deal to say, Mostel is not often happy. His speech has become labored, his delivery flat; he has got by so long and so easily with mugging (unconnected with anything) that his pantomime has become facile and his whole vocal ability has retrogressed.

But it's even more melancholy than that. Mostel, despite all the extravagant encouragement he used to receive to attempt great classic roles, was never an actor in the traditional sense. Although he has tried some acting, particularly in films, his whole road, I think, lay elsewhere. Compare him with Chaplin—a comparison that his original gifts merit—and you see the difference in choices. Chaplin realized early that he was a clown: that is, a performer of *one* comic character, whom he then put into various stories. His early search was to realize that character; once he had the character tailored to temperament, then, with that base, he could act. Few who have seen the last moments of *City Lights* would say that Chaplin is not a great actor; few who have seen *Monsieur Verdoux* or *A King in New York* would think him even a good actor when he is not first the Tramp.

Mostel hasn't realized a clown persona. Instead he has tried to work more or less like a traditional actor, in different parts. But the gifts that could have made him a great clown kept erupting into those parts, blemishing the characters without establishing the clown. And he's aggravated matters by mugging for laughs. After you've seen pages of Mostel face-making in books and magazines, it's hard to believe in the "sincerity" of the face he gives you in Bloom. You feel that Bloom-Mostel could just as easily be making a different face.

In the last sixteen years, with all his shows and films, he has only twice (to my knowledge) come close to fulfillment: in *A Funny Thing Happened on the Way to the Forum* (on stage, not film) and *Fiddler on the Roof*. They were neither Plautus nor Sholom Aleichem, but at least they came close to the Mostel ideal—Zero the Clown as Pseudolus and Tevye.

Still I wouldn't want to see him again in those parts. Mostel is now too far away from Zero.

Cat on a Hot Tin Roof

(October 19, 1974)

This production, nineteen years after the premiere, confirms that Tennessee Williams is one of the two American dramatists of enduring substance and that this is not one of his best plays. The other man, obviously, is O'Neill, and his later plays are well above Williams'; still *A Streetcar Named Desire* is truly an American tragedy and *The Glass Menagerie* stands, even if a bit unsteadily, as one of the few successful poems in our theater. *Cat* is significantly less than either.

It came after the two best plays in Williams' very prolific career, and it's among the first in a series that, though laced with fire, nevertheless declines toward a mere rehash like *Small Craft Warnings* and a feeble protest against its author's sterility like *Out Cry*.* To say that Williams' career describes an arc is too neat. For one thing, it isn't over; for another, such plays as *Period of Adjustment* and *The Gnadiges Fraulein* show a largely untapped spring of humor in him. But nothing since *Streetcar* (1947) has so beautifully fused the elements of the Williams "mainstream" in so beautiful a form.

Cat deals with that mainstream. This means, on the surface or near it, such matters as loneliness, buried and released violence, sex, and "difference"—the last often signified by physical difference, like lame Laura in *The Glass Menagerie* and injured Brick here. More deeply, Williams has been concerned with American change, with the extension of the Civil War by other means, with the course of our history as we have moved from a nineteenth-century society of adventure and idealism circumscribed by puritanism to a twentieth-century society that is increasingly liberated and increasingly devoid of appetite for adventure or ideal. Fundamentally *Streetcar* is about the end of a romantic America that had rot under the romance, and the onslaught of a brass-and-beer America that has mere bareness where the rot

* See pp. 168–171.

used to be. *Cat,* taking another tack on the same theme, deals with questions of continuity, with death and birth. The play asks: isn't death, as much as sex, a prerequisite of birth?

Big Daddy, a nineteenth-century figure, built his 28,000-acre plantation with guts and drive (on a start given him by two homosexual planters!). Now he has cancer. The grim news is first sugar-coated, then delivered full. (The romance of circumlocution makes the truth worse when it comes, makes gentility seem mendacious.) His favorite son, Brick, is a former athlete who became a sports announcer, then a drunk. (An actor become spectator, then not even a spectator.) Brick broke his ankle the night before the play begins, fooling on a playing field while drunk, and has become a drunk because of the specter of homosexuality. And his drunkenness puts in question his inheritance of his father's fortune, which, in one sense, was *founded* on homosexuality. Brick's wife, Margaret—Maggie the Cat—unintentionally helped to confirm the fear of homosexuality in his former football pal, now dead of drink. Brick is punishing her by refusing to sleep with her—a punishment that quite clearly relieves him of unwanted obligation. But Gooper, Brick's busy lawyer brother, has lots of children; Gooper is ready and anxious to inherit from Big Daddy. Brick, whom Daddy prefers, is not only childless but indifferent.

The main action of the play is Margaret's struggle to bring Brick back to her bed, which occupies the center of the stage. She will be, if she can, the nexus between past and future, between Big Daddy's full-blooded past and the future, between Brick's once-high spirits (symbolized by his feeling for sports) and their possible revival.

Female fecundity thus becomes the essential element in the continuity of the past, but (as in *Streetcar*) it is harassed by the puritanism of the past. Some sorts of death, including the death of Brick's friend and the death of Brick's disguised guilt about him, are essential before Margaret can give birth. If Brick can be brought to Margaret's bed, there is a chance for a future better than Gooper's, more humane —if less forceful—than Big Daddy's past, a future relieved of some puritanical spasm. A German friend who saw this revival with me called it a dated chapter in peculiarly American history. It's dated as far as the sheerly theatrical impact of Brick's latent homosexuality is concerned: that subject has become common theater and film fare in the last eight years. But the psychic drama of Brick in his society's transition is still very valid.

If only Williams had realized the play sketched above. But his articulation of these themes is clumsy. Much of the first act is laborious exposition, cramming us with facts while pretending not to know that we are there. And it's particularly tortuous because Brick is mostly restricted to cynical taciturnity and bourbon-pouring; thus a huge burden falls on Margaret. Brick's little nephews and nieces, the "no-neck monsters," are cartoons; their parents, Gooper and Mae, are barely two-dimensional; Big Mama is not much more; the preacher is out of a revue sketch. Notoriously there are two third acts: Williams revised his own third act to please the first director, Elia Kazan. He brought Big Daddy back on stage as he had not intended to do, and he gave Brick and Margaret a last scene that promises procreation. This production uses a version of the revised version. Big Daddy comes back in, principally to tell a long joke that wasn't new in 1955; but the happy ending has been tempered somewhat by keeping the couple out of bed and by adding a few final ambiguous lines from the original version. But no matter how you slice these versions, it's still a weak act. The best scene in the play is the long one in Act Two between Big Daddy and Brick, but that scene is all revelation and exploration. The dynamics of the play depends on Margaret, who is offstage for most of Act Two.

The dialogue is garlanded with litanies of repetition, apt enough for characters who enjoy speaking, but sometimes Williams intrudes into their rhetoric. For instance, Brick says that he and his football friend used to toss long high passes "that couldn't be intercepted except by time."

Within this unwieldy play of erratic dynamics, the director, Michael Kahn, has worked hard for centralizing currents, flowing from and to that big bed. He is greatly helped by Elizabeth Ashley, absent from the New York stage since *Barefoot in the Park* (1963), who is lithe and silkily strong, more vaginal than Barbara Bel Geddes in the first production, more feline than Elizabeth Taylor in the film. Speaking of which, by odd chance I came home from the theater to see a clip of the *Cat* film on TV which, alas, finished Keir Dullea's Brick for me. Thirty seconds of Paul Newman in the part underscored that Dullea had been only an earnest yeoman. Fred Gwynne as Big Daddy is rumbly and good enough but not awesomely powerful. Kate Reid is a disaster as Big Mama, flopping around the outside of the role. Two versatile actors, Joan Pape and Charles Siebert, do well enough as Mae and Gooper—and Siebert has the most convincing Mississippi accent of the lot. The bedroom designed by John Conklin fulfills Williams' request that it look like "a set for a ballet," but he has overdone the ruin-and-decay effect of the breakaway ceiling and walls.

London Assurance

(January 4 and 11, 1975)

Apparently the Royal Shakespeare Company moves its most successful productions out of rep into the West End and elsewhere to spin money for the mother company. Whether this hurts the artistic ensemble one can't say from here, but it certainly sounds risky. I saw *London Assurance* (half of it) two years ago in its West End run. Since then members of the cast have done other things and have now reassembled for the U.S.

I despise this show (all of it now). Ronald Eyre, who adapted and directed, seemingly decided that he, his company, and his audience are very much superior to this 1841 play and staged it just to prove the point. Not a cranny that could be stuffed with gags, not a line that could be kidded, not a character that could be cartooned is left untouched. They do it all moderately well, but what fundamentally sickening work.

I'm not calling for protest marches against the violation of minor Victoriana. But Dion Boucicault, the Irishman who wrote this successful play at twenty and then had a long career as actor and director, playwright and adapter (he did Jefferson's version of *Rip Van Winkle*), was not a fool. He wrote this play as an amiable satire on the follies of his day. A middle-aged aristocrat is besotted with the vogue of estheticism and also with a plan to marry a young girl for her property. He loses her, after much pother, to his son, who is one more version of the reformed wastrel we know from *Love for Love* and *The School for Scandal*. Along the way father, son, idle friend, and sharp lawyer get a nice roasting in dialogue that is always curlicued and occasionally elegant. It's hardly a work of much consequence, but neither is it utter hokum.

In a well-known lecture on the art of acting that Boucicault gave to London professionals in 1882, a still-valuable talk, he mentions that the actor who first played the foolish aristocrat came to him for advice and Boucicault gave him the names of "two old fogies" on whom he had based the role so that the actor could study them. Donald Sinden, the gifted man who plays the role now, has studied only gags. He mugs at the audience, dislocates his false teeth when he trills the French "r," and so on. Of course there are laughs; there would also be laughs if he split his trousers when he bowed. Eyre and Sinden and many of the others are satirizing the satire, and it's cheap. It's as if an orchestra were to revive a Raff symphony and sob in the violin passages. Why bother with it at all?

A few of the actors survive this smart-assing, possibly because Eyre couldn't think of any way for them to foul their particular nests. For instance, Sydney Bromley, as the elderly husband of a hyperactive horsewoman, plays straight and sweet. But the air of Eyre pervades, and really suffocates at the very end—which I had been lucky enough to miss in London by leaving at intermission. All problems have been solved, all principals are present, and the aristocrat, chastened and enlightened, delivers the closing speech about the qualities of the true English gentleman. The sentiments are certainly somewhat remote from us, but if the play had been done straight, the speech would carry its own self-satire, because of changed attitudes, and might have some lace-and-lavender charm. Instead as Sinden sings away, overdoing it ostentatiously, the other characters yawn and the lights dim on them, and the play ends with Sinden yattering in a spotlight with everyone else asleep. It doesn't even fit the kind of gagging Eyre has used up to now, but it makes the audience, fresh from the heights of Neil Simon, feel lucky to be living now and not then.

Of Mice and Men

(January 25, 1975)

How do American actors manage to grow? Anyone who knows anything about theater/film life in this country and how haphazard, unfriendly, ungrateful that world is, must be amazed that at least some actors develop. All the odds are against their growth, and in a way things are even more difficult for them if they become successful, because then there are a lot of people making money on them who don't want them to take chances. If the American theater were as well organized as American baseball, an actor who came up from the bush leagues to the majors would be welcome but not necessarily heroic. In the theater as is, an actor who develops artistically is, in some degree, necessarily heroic.

So James Earl Jones and Kevin Conway are, in differing measure, heroic to me. Both have grown. Jones became visible in the early '60s, a big black man with a big voice who barreled along on his physical attributes. He did a Macbeth in 1966 that was only a lot of bellowing. (Something he reverts to in Shakespeare. His Lear two years ago wasn't a great deal better.) But, just to touch highlights, his subsequent performances in *The Great White Hope, Boesman and Lena, The Cherry Orchard* (Lopahin), the film *Claudine,* and now in *Of Mice and Men* show immensely increased control and range, show Jones making demands on himself that are increasingly austere and imaginative. His Lennie is the simple naked core of that retarded giant, strong and helpless. The Jones of 1965 could not have done this beautiful work.

Conway has up to now been largely a boisterous Off-Broadway nuisance. In *One Flew over the Cuckoo's Nest* he pushed his potbelly around aggressively, enjoying his slovenliness, and did more or less the same thing in *When You Comin' Back, Red Ryder?* Clearly, Conway had force, but he was giving us self-display masquerading as freedom. And now here he is as George, taut, underplaying, manly, no sense of wallowing, every sense of serious intention. It's not merely a difference of roles: I've seen Conway in non-swagger parts. It's a matter of growth. Now Conway, who might have gone on to sell just one line of goods like Al Pacino, has become an actor of possibilities.

Praise to Edwin Sherin, the director, who surely had a hand in these performances and in the casting of Conway. But also some dispraise. I can't remember a Sherin production—*The Great White Hope, Find Your Way Home,* others—without good news and bad news. John Steinbeck's play is a work of sentiment, so George S. Kaufman, who directed the first production (1937) and is said to have worked on the script, played against the sentiment more or less astringently. This gave the play an almost naturalistic tone and made the sentiment effective. Sherin, on the other hand, underscores the sentiment, particularly grossly in the casting and direction of Candy, the crippled old swamper. The only other good performance besides the principals' is David Gale's as Slim. (Even Jones has a tough moment, because he is black, when he has to face the isolated black man in the barn. The racial difference gone, Jones apparently tries to think of Lennie as a privileged child.)

Sherin's staging is never easy and is sometimes clumsy. For instance, he puts the final moment smack downstage, with Lennie kneeling facing us, George behind him facing us, gun in hand. We know, just from their positions, that the lights are going to fade before the shot. Result: we wait for the fade instead of the shot. As I remember, Kaufman put the scene upstage in the tall grass, facing offstage, less blatantly appealing for sympathy, theatrically more evocative.

Kaufman also had more realistic settings, which this play needs, and offstage effects like the sounds of horses tramping into their stalls, blowing, jingling harness. This is a penny-pinched production.

Steinbeck's play is one of the American best, alas. I can't imagine a list of, say, Twenty Best that could omit it. The tragic inevitability at which Steinbeck aimed is dimmed by the creakiness of the arrangements. We know with somewhat pleasant ironical foreknowledge in the first scene, when the two friends discuss their plans to have a place of their own, that they will never get it; but Steinbeck ensures the grim ending with the nervous young husband at the ranch and his arbitrarily restless wife. Besides, Lennie's feeblemindedness mitigates the tragedy. He is a "case" on the loose, not a man susceptible to trouble. If he were only slow-witted, instead of defective, there would be some hint of what his life might have been. With the idiot Lennie there are no alternatives.

Still Steinbeck touched some deep American themes, the great myths of the road and of the two male companions. (There are snickers in today's audience at the lines about two men traveling together; the ceremony of innocence is drowned.) And there is a strong residue of nineteenth-century feeling about the land—working on the land is the basic good, owning some of it is salvation. I can't think of another successful American play since 1937 with that feeling, or even one centered on rural work. Because of what has happened since it was written, *Of Mice and Men,* with its faults unchanged, has became a play about the end of something in America and in American drama.

The Dethy

(Channel 13, New York, February 28, 1964)

The first point to be made about *The Deputy* by Rolf Hochhuth is that it is not about Pope Pius XII. International uproar has centered on the one scene in which the Pope appears. But this play is about a young Italian Jesuit named Father Fontana and his road to martyrdom—in fact, an ancient story in all organized religions, the story of a communicant who takes his beliefs too seriously for the security of his church. Before the Church can canonize Joan of Arc, it has to burn her. Tolstoy was excommunicated by the Greek Orthodox Church for excessive Christianity.

In *The Deputy* Father Fontana discovers in Berlin in 1942 that Germans are murdering Jews daily by thousands. He happens to be the son of a Vatican counselor and can take the horrible news directly to the Supreme Pontiff. He implores the Pontiff to cry out in a worldwide voice against these horrors. The Pope declines on several grounds: Hitler is engaged in a war against Communism; a papal edict might spur the Germans to intensify Jewish murders; the Church must have regard for German Catholics; the Church's ancient role is mediation and neutrality. All the Pope feels he can do is to issue a general denunciation of bloodshed. The young Jesuit, soul-shaken by the refusal, cries that God shall not destroy his Church because a Pope shrinks from his summons. The play ends with Fontana joining a file of Jews as they trudge to the ovens of Auschwitz.

So what we have here is not a play about the twelfth Pius, but about a young priest who learns of the most enormous crime in the history of Christian civilization—most enormous because it is happening 1940 years after Christ's message was supposed to have altered human conduct; a priest who wants the Vicar of Christ on earth to stand against that crime and, when that does not happen, who joins the victims. And he does this not with presumption or rebuke but with love and despair. "My God, my God, why hast Thou forsaken me?" becomes for Father Fontana "My Church, my Church, why has thou forsaken my God?"

It is a titanic theme. But, regrettably, I have to point out that the execution does not match it. Of the eight scenes in the play as presented here, the first five deal primarily with the growing impact of the horror on the priest, but those horrors are very familiar to the audience, which is far ahead of the priest—and has been for decades—in its revulsion. There is not enough richness of character or language to compensate for this. For example, Fontana's courtly father and a genial wine-bibbing cardinal are stock figures. A scene in Gestapo headquarters is little different from dozens we have seen in which a bored Nazi inquisitor toys with his prisoners.

The key scene is the one between the priest and the Pope, and here Hochhuth uses what I consider the one unworthy, almost cheap touch in the play. It opens with the Pope's concern about money. The most saintly of popes has had to concern himself with such matters, and in the one scene that the author gives to the Pope in this play, the touch seems facile mockery.

In fact, the whole scene presents an incomplete portrait of the Pope, even though Hochhuth makes no accusation without historical basis, even though he mentions the shelter that the Vatican gave thousands of Jews. For Fontana has told us that he kept a portrait of Pacelli over his bed as a boy, that because of this prelate he himself entered the Church. There is no hint of such qualities in the Pius drawn here.

The last scene at Auschwitz, which ought to be the climax, is the very weakest: a long dialogue between Fontana and a German doctor. The doctor is a cliché portrait of the dehydrated intellectual Nazi seeking rapport with a victim he considers superior to the rabble. The scene lacks development and simply postpones the inevitable end.

Part of the theatrical trouble with this scene is the setting, a wall of barbed wire which forces the two actors downstage, where they cross and re-cross like a pair of vaudevillians. This is the worst of Rouben Ter-Arutunian's poor settings, most of which are suggestive fragments decorated with dangling loops of rope that give a feeling of a deserted circus arena. Herman Shumlin's direction is merely workman-like, rarely touched by more than tractarian urgency.

As Father Fontana, Jeremy Brett is never false, though occasionally lightweight, and sometimes achieves real intensity. In his one scene as the Pope, Emlyn Williams can do little more than play him as an ivory chessman. Fred Stewart is competent as the cardinal. James Mitchell is thin and inadequate as the doctor.

Thus the bulk of *The Deputy* is preparation for and epilogue to one crucial scene. None of that preparation or epilogue is sufficiently penetrating and powerful to compensate for the familiarity of the material or to create a burning epic of a latter-day saint. The monumental drama on humane responsibility in Nazi Europe remains Jean-Paul Sartre's *The Condemned of Altona*. Hochhuth wanted to dramatize the actions of the Vatican *vis-à-vis* Hitler. His method, I believe, should have been to concentrate on the Vatican: to draw Pius as a fully developed character and give us the fullest confrontation between him and this possibly decisive crisis for Christianity. Instead he has cast the Pontiff for a minor role in a probing but unsatisfactory play about a heroic young priest. The profound play on the complex and important subject of the Pope and Adolf Hitler is yet to be written.

The Devils

(*Channel 13, New York, November 17, 1965*)

The English dramatist John Whiting, who died two years ago at the age of forty-five, was often called "the last romantic." He rose to prominence in the age of Osborne and Pinter, was directly opposed to them, and, indeed, in a famous lecture at the Old Vic in 1957, declared that he thought the grubbiness of social realism would be the eventual death of the theater. Whatever the merits of the argument, the effect on a writer of being deliberately anachronistic can be dangerous unless he is a giant; in Whiting's case it led to a cultivation of abstract characters, symbolic action, and doggedly heightened language that gives even his better work a faint aroma of the hothouse.

By far his best play is *The Devils*. It's based on the factual materials in Aldous Huxley's book *The Devils of Loudun,* which relates the occurrence in seventeenth-century France of an outbreak of hysteria in a nunnery, beginning with the young prioress. She claims that the devil has invaded her body and committed lewd acts with her, in league with the handsome priest of the town, Father Grandier, who has never even met her. Her accusation eventually brings about the torture and death-by-burning of Grandier.

The thematic resonances of the story are large. They were well realized in a Polish film, seen briefly in New York a few years ago, called *Joan of the Angels,* directed by Jerzy Kawalerowicz. He saw it as a tragedy of two lives rigidly enclosed in dogma—and, by implication, that dogma could have been Polish Communism as well as Renaissance Catholicism—a tragedy that brought two people to a kind of sublimity by accepting the dogma both as burden and as surety. The restrictive faith that caused the hysteria of Mother Jeanne and the death of Father Grandier was also the faith that beatified both of them and made them able to bear these burdens.

Whiting has elected a narrower concept. He clearly selects the priest as the protagonist and makes Mother Jeanne only an instrument of Grandier's fate. This is emphasized by making the prioress and the nuns conscious fakers, not helpless victims of hysteria but dogged wallowers in it. In Jeanne's case it is also an act of revenge on a man to whom she is attracted but who has, without knowing it, spurned her. This fakery makes the story less interesting, but the

difference of emphasis is justified by making Grandier a figure familiar to us from Graham Greene—the corrupt priest: no less devout
because he happens to be a sinner. Thus Mother Jeanne, unconsciously, becomes God's punishment of Grandier's sexual sins as she
is driven to false sexual accusations out of hysteria. And Grandier is
purged and scourged by his trial and torture. He dies in faith and
love.

Powerful stuff, even in this version. Whiting was not completely
up to it, but he made a very respectable, sometimes deeply touching
try. I dislike the character of the sage sewerman, the priest's confi-
dant, bcause the contrast is too heavy: the earthy man who deals in
excrement as the only person who understands the priest. The language, generally, is that mixture of meaningful understatement with
occasional bursts of rhetoric that seems to have started in the historical plays of John Masefield. Whiting is better at the understatement
than at full-flowered aria. But there is consistent intensity in his tale
of the sinning priest cleansed of his falsity and brought nearer to God
through a false accusation of something he has in fact been doing
with others.

I'm speaking of the published book. The produced play disperses
and attenuates the drama. And, also, the script is cut. This dispersal
begins with the very theater chosen for the play, the Broadway, which
is much too large. Then there is the mechanics of sound amplification; all voices resound through loudspeakers. Michael Cacoyannis
has directed it to suit—as if it were a major musical: everything is
italicized, brassily spaced out, showily choreographed. There are lots
of actors and an immense set, but never in the course of the evening
is one convinced that the life of a town or a time or a religious epoch
is on the stage: only a series of more or less effective numbers. This
show-shop abstraction is emphasized by the abominable setting of
Rouben Ter-Arutunian—scaffolds which, in their size and their texture, diffuse feeling that ought to be distilled. And, as usual, he is
obsessed with wooden slats and venetian blinds, whether they are
appropriate or not.

As Mother Jeanne, Anne Bancroft is strong and graphic, once we
get used to her speech, which still has strong vestiges of pure Bronx.
It's curious that an actress of her talent should be content to let her
speech sound so common—which she did not do in her British film,
The Pumpkin Eater.

But the failure of the evening begins and ends with the casting of Grandier. Jason Robards is probably the most over-estimated actor of our time. He made a success, deserved, in two O'Neill roles, in *The Iceman Cometh* and *Long Day's Journey into Night,* in both of which he played variants of saloon toughs with well-buried hearts of gold. In any other kind of role, where he was supposed to have apparent attractiveness and convincing sympathy, where he has had to make us believe in directly stated depths, not obliquely implied ones, he has failed. Here he is shallow, perfunctory, uninteresting. In a part that calls on its performer to enrich its spaces and silences, Robards has very, very little to supply. Physically, there is nothing of the King David public beauty that is supposed to affect women; and spiritually his performance is flat and sterile. It seals this production into its overblown, big-business emptiness.

Of the other performances there is, I'm happy to say, no time to speak. Among the competent few is eighty-one-year-old Edgar Stehli, who is valid and moving as a priest.

John Whiting's play *The Devils* is worth knowing. You can get it at a paperbound bookshop for $1.45.

About Williams: Gloom and Hope

(The New York Times, *March 6, 1966*)

Forgive, please, a quotation from myself. In 1960 I wrote, in another place: "Is there a future for Tennessee Williams? Or is there nothing ahead of him but his past? His second film of the season, *The Fugitive Kind,* raises more than a suspicion of bankruptcy of material, of his feeding on himself." Now, six years later, the question of limitation and self-cannibalization is raised again—by two one-act plays recently presented under the joint title *Slapstick Tragedy,* and particularly by the first, called *The Mutilated.*

Two New Orleans tarts, in the 1930s, have been friends, are now enemies, and are reconciled at Christmas by a religious vision in a seedy hotel room. The atmosphere is out of *A Streetcar Named Desire.* The facile religious portentousness is out of *The Night of the Iguana* and other Williams works. One of the tarts has had a breast operation, and her physical imperfection, as a symbol of spiritual isolation, reminds us of Laura in *The Glass Menagerie*. There is even a verbatim quotation of a joke about bosoms from *The Milk Train Doesn't Stop Here Anymore*.

But textual detective work is unnecessary. Any theatergoer who has followed Williams' career does not need documentation. He recognizes the environment, the materials, and the devices.

What has kept the theatergoer interested through the years—and what should never be slighted in any discussion of these plays—is Williams' superb theatrical talent: his eye for stage effect, his skill in scene construction, his gift for dialogue that can cut to the bone, that can use cliché with humor and poignancy, and that can combine the odd floridness of lower-class characters with his own rich rhetoric. He is one of the most popular playwrights in the world—literally—because, whatever the faults of his works, he has written parts that actors want to play and with which they can move audiences. That is a prime fact.

But there is another fact. He began brilliantly with *The Glass Menagerie* and continued well with such plays as *A Streetcar Named Desire* and *Summer and Smoke,* but his subsequent work, effective as much of it has been, has been heavily streaked with disappointments.

It is not merely that he repeats himself and reworks material. Serious writers often treat the same material and themes over and over. In fact, it could be said broadly that only a hack's subjects are always novel because he has no real affinity or commitment to any subject. But Williams has little new to say about his subjects, characters, and themes. The re-use in thinner and thinner disguise is becoming threadbare. What once might have been agreeably shocking is now becoming tame and self-consciously squalid. What once passed for sexual candor, poetic evocation, and religious response has taken on taints of merchandising for the Williams market.

He has been the chief exponent in the theater of the school of Southern writers that began to flourish in the early 1930s. Aside from the large talents of some of the writers involved, that school was successful for some other reasons. One of them was that from the heights of William Faulkner to the depths of latter-day Erskine Caldwell, the South had become the American image of those tropical climes where sex is easy, frequent, and intriguingly various.

Williams developed some characteristics of the Southern school in ways that were theatrically vivid and philosophically slick: intercourse as the equivalent of self-fulfillment, and a steamy blend of religion and sexuality. Now, because time has passed and contexts have altered, and because Williams has not much altered or deepened, the audience has had, I think, what they wanted from him. They are not tired of shock, but he is no longer shocking. His glandular pietism is more transparent. His lyrics of human isolation— which, to him, usually means no mate for the night—are less affecting. His new work seems dated, and so does his older work that hangs on sensation.

This article is not an attempt at a burial service. Nothing would be pleasanter than to recant all the above because of a new Williams play as good as his best, either in his familiar vein or a new one. We are simply forced to doubt that such a play will come in his familiar style, because of its long, continual deterioration; but we can hope for a Williams renascence in another vein.

Throughout his work he has shown a strong gift for comedy: not the tidy little jokings of *Period of Adjustment* but raffish, slashing comedy such as that in his screenplay *Baby Doll* and in the first act of *Sweet Bird of Youth.* He takes that gift to a new frontier of caricature in the second of his two new short plays, *The Gnadiges Fraulein*— which is a kind of cosmic comic strip about human flotsam on the southernmost island of the United States.

It begins with an amusingly wild monologue by a sleazy gossip columnist, and a slatternly rocking-chair dialogue between her and a burlesque boardinghouse-keeper. The play soon runs out of genuine impulse, becomes heavy in word play, lame in invention, and disintegrates in pointlessness. But, seen against the element of humor that has wound through his plays, this wild work makes us wish that he would write more uninhibited comedy—either realistically "black" like that in *Sweet Bird* or circus-clownish like *The Gnadiges Fraulein,* or both if he can combine them. There is an insufficiently tapped Williams here—free of the simplistic credo of sex-as-solution served up with a garnish of Spanish moss, hollow prayers, and poeticizings.

In outrageous comedy, it seems to me, there is at least one valid hope for his future. The possibilities are of course wider and are known, or perhaps not yet known, to Williams himself. He is only fifty-five. It was Scott Fitzgerald, I think, who said that American lives have no second acts. Williams' life has already been an exception, but the figurative second act of his career has not been up to the level of the first. All those who are appreciative of his extraordinary gifts will hope for a third act—fresh, powerful, and, very possibly, comic.

Small Craft Warnings

(April 29, 1972)

It's unpleasant to write about Tennessee Williams these days. If he was often overpraised, still he was at one time a first-class writer of theater pieces, works that had their natural and fulfilled life—sometimes splendid life—on the stage. Now he is no longer himself. What is worse, he knows it. What is even worse, he implicitly begs for mercy in newspaper and TV interviews. And when the suggestion arises that he might perhaps stop writing, he says with a pitiful grin, as he said on TV the other night, that some people wish he were dead.

But he is a writer of immense reputation. (A reputation launched by critics, the breed of whom he now complains . . . that's a familiar contradiction.) He may wish that his work could now pass directly from his desk into canon without scrutiny, but the canon wouldn't exist if there had never been any scrutiny, and, with all gratitude for his good past work, here is some more scrutiny.

Small Craft Warnings is a vapid play. The scene is a bar on the southern California coast. The cast is a collection of human flotsam, including that old reliable, the drunken derelict doctor. (We haven't seen him for a whole month, since the Australian film *Out-back.*) The only exception is a shining young bisexual youth who passes through on his way to Mexico, possibly to join a road company of *The Milk Train Doesn't Stop Here Anymore*. Each of these wretches has a problem—some variant of essential human loneliness—and each of them gets at least one moment quite literally in the spotlight, when the rest of the stage is dimmed, for a solo. The mechanics of this process, and its predictability, and the emptiness of the utterances make the play feel well-finished by intermission time.

Williams was never a really intellectual writer, but he used to have a finely tuned sensory system that could transmute intangible feelings into tangible dramatic patterns: a talent for converting sexuality and despair into strong theatrical colors. A writer who could simply provide the opportunity for Marlon Brando to bite his fingernails idly in the shadows while his sister-in-law (who lusted for him) railed about him to his wife in the next room—that writer knew something about image and space and time on the stage.

But now Williams writes plays about plays. Life hasn't been consulted in *Small Craft Warnings,* only a file marked "Loneliness." The title and the setting are as heavily indicative as silent-picture subtitles. The dialogue and structure can thrive only by our assent, not our conviction. Williams is asking us to be kind to him *during* his play, as well as before and after: asking us to watch his play rather as a Victorian audience watched a melodrama, as a knowing display of known devices, rather than an artist's honest direct statement about humanity.

With consistent ineptness, the director, Richard Altman, has underscored every defect; and together he and Williams have cast the play to its disadvantage in every role. But there are two points of interest.

The *shapes* of the roles, though certainly nothing else, show some theater dexterity. An actor friend who saw the play with me said, rightly, that Williams can still write seductively for actors, if not for audiences.

And Williams can now write openly about homosexuality. His writing on this subject is by now as stale as everything else he touches, but it's fascinating to speculate what his career might have been if he had had this option of frankness from the beginning.*

Out Cry

(March 24, 1973)

When realist playwrights die, they become symbolists. Among contemporaries, Edward Albee is only one who proves this historical principle. Now Tennessee Williams, a much more romantic realist

* See p. 291.

than Albee (and a much more gifted one), moves from his familiar terrain of seamy rhapsody to the gauzy blue blue sky. His last play, *Small Craft Warnings,* was a sterile reworking of his lyricism of the lonely; his new play, *Out Cry,* changes style but has much smaller craft.

Two actors, a brother and sister, are stranded in a "state theater of a state unknown." Their company has abandoned them as insane. There is no one else backstage. Ostensibly an audience—ourselves— has gathered in front, though this is not definite. Brother and sister are forced to perform for us; they do something called *The Two-Character Play,* moving in and out of it so that there is no clear border between the play-within-a-play and their private realities. Doubt gathers about their sanity. They may not even be in a theater; the whole setting, Jo Mielziner's airy sketch of a theater, may be part of their fantasy. They may really be the children of the two parents described in the "play," the man of whom has just shot his wife and killed himself.

On paper it suggests, inevitably, Pirandello, and sounds intriguing. In proof it is an excruciating two-hour bore because Williams had only vague ideas about why he was bothering to write it. There is no affective design, no tension, no *point,* not even any stimulating ambiguity. We are given only a series of data, arbitrarily streaked—like a larded roast—with stripes of passion and torment. None of this anguish or heat ever has the slightest power on us because no ground is laid with us for sympathy or expectation. Williams simply provides a sequence of arbitrary moments, enclosed in a fancy: symbolism that asks for effect just because it *is* symbolism, rather reminiscent of little-theater pieces of the '20s.

The most grievous disappointment is in the writing and in the roles as theatrical entities. Up to now, as we watched Williams' sad descent, we have usually had the consolation that he still had a gift for good theater language; but the dialogue in this play is on the level of "You have the face of an angel." The roles, both of them, are just bundles of spurts and relaxations, unrelated to facts as we can see them or fantasies as we can follow them.

I suppose that Williams has earned the right to have everything he writes produced—the idea of an unproduced Williams play still seems somehow discourteous—but he is trying this right severely.

The producer is trying it too. One of the two roles, the brother, is well cast. Michael York is a good actor (he was the best one in the film of *Cabaret*) with a striking theater face and a useful voice, but I wish I hadn't seen him in this play. It's like hearing a pianist, after a moving recital, expend the same emotion on empty exercises. The other role—fifty percent of the cast—is given to Cara Duff-Mac-Cormick, who is incompetent in every possible regard. Peter Glenville, the drayhorse director, plodded true to form; but in this case he did have a fearful burden to carry.

Serjeant Musgrave's Dance

(The New York Times, *March 9, 1966*)

Almost seven years after its premiere in London, one of the most discussed modern plays arrives in New York. *Serjeant Musgrave's Dance* has been hailed as the best postwar English play and has been derogated as murky. To me, there seems to be good argument on both sides.

John Arden, who has had two previous Off-Broadway productions, shows immediately in *Musgrave* his strong, arresting talent. He is not an original in the sense of having invented new techniques, but he combines many of the resources of the theater into modes that are attractively his own.

The play is set in England about a hundred years ago. Musgrave and three of his troopers have returned from service in an unnamed colony. They have all deserted, and they are on their way, under the serjeant's firm, visionary leadership, to a Midlands colliery town. In a crate they have the skeleton of a fellow soldier who came from that town. All four men are sick of war, and, while ostensibly on a recruiting mission, they hope to strike a blow at the powers whom they hold responsible for war. They find the town embroiled in a bitter strike, which complicates their evangelism. They kill one of their own number in a squabble, which complicates it further. Musgrave's climactic appeal in the town square comes to nothing. At the end he and the only other survivor of his group are bound for the gallows.

The "dance" of the title is Musgrave's desire to let God's word "dance on this earth." In the last scene, however, he makes the word literal by dancing as he exhorts.

This touches the matter of the play's realism. In the published version Arden has called the play realistic. His use of the term seems elastic. Many of the characters veer into rhymed verse and song to enlarge on their feelings. The dialogue is realistic in a highly selective way, as if it were made of kernels only—tough, chewy, but the heart of the matter. But the realism does not extend to the plot, which surely is symbolic. For, by any realistic test, either Musgrave and his men are conscious martyrs—doomed as deserters even if their propaganda plan works—or they are mad. Since they are shown as neither, their action must be metaphor.

The author has complicated this metaphor by having one soldier kill another in a fight over running away with a girl. Arden does this, I think, to make a deliberate moral ambiguity: pacifists are as fallible as anyone. But, dramatically, it badly muddies matters. Would the killer have been part of a pacifist expedition? And why kill a man for trying to desert when all of them are deserters anyway? This murder is the cause of Musgrave's ultimate failure; he is accused of having used Army methods to attack war. But this is not what we have seen. The killing wasn't discipline; it happened in an accidental brawl, and Musgrave wasn't even present.

Still the play's central image has power, even if it is diffused toward the end. Arden is often called Brechtian. He resembles Brecht in no way more than his ability to conceive a dynamic central image and to use it like a diamond bit to cut through the rock of circumstance. The trouble is that as he cuts he tends to wobble and finally to slip awry. The image of the soldiers secretly returning with their dead fellow is compelling. The strife-torn town makes a resonant context. But we feel that all the design is in the first two acts, that the third act is simply the author's somewhat patchy attempt to deal with forces that he has unleashed earlier. We miss particularly a clear sense of what would have happened if all had gone well for Musgrave's plan, a sense of what has been defeated.

The production, too, is decidedly mixed. Dudley Moore's music, presumably from the original production, is perfect. Ed Wittstein's scenic elements are excellent. The design of the performance itself by the director, Stuart Burge, is imaginative, but its execution by his actors is spotty. John Colicos, whose Caliban and Petruchio I have admired at the Canadian Stratford, is not completely successful as Musgrave. He has bearing and Scottish iron and fanatic zeal. (Musgrave has some resemblance to John Brown.) But in high emotional moments we get from Colicos a feeling of strenuous externals rather than internal agony.

The would-be runaway soldier is fuzzily played by Terry Lomax. Leigh Wharton is effective as one of the other soldiers, and Roy R. Scheider is less effective as the third. David Doyle overacts as the crookbacked chorus; so does John P. Ryan, the constable. The best-realized acting comes from Jeanne Hepple, a tavern tart, and Charlotte Jones, her boss. Thomas Barbour's parson is exactly what the author warned against—a stage clergyman. Dan Durning's mayor and W. B. Brydon's labor leader are adequate.

Thus, unintentionally, Burge's direction underscores the mixed quality of the play itself.

This exceptional work could have been written only by an author of Arden's freedom—free in theatrical and human spirit. Yet *Serjeant Musgrave's Dance* remains both an outstanding play of its generation and a cloudy one.

The Journey of the Fifth Horse

(The New York Times, *May 8, 1966*)

In all arts, new work sometimes derives from older work; and in the theater this is custom probably more honored in the observance than in the breach. Not to mention Shakespeare, such quick examples come to mind as Shaw, whose *Man and Superman* is his version of *Don Giovanni*, and Brecht, who used the process numerous times—most famously in *The Threepenny Opera* that he derived from John Gay's *Beggar's Opera*.

Ronald Ribman, a young American, has tried this procedure in his play *The Journey of the Fifth Horse*, which is partly based on Turgenev's story "Diary of a Superfluous Man." Turgenev's hero is a nineteenth-century landowner named Chulkaturin whose life is irrelevant to those around him. After his death, even his diary is rejected—by a publisher's reader.

Out of the few final words that note this rejection Ribman has conceived his play. He has imagined the publisher's reader, Zoditch, as a man whose life has parallels with that of the person he is reading about. The play moves on three interweaving lines: Chulkaturin's life, from Turgenev; Zoditch's realities; and Zoditch's fantasies, the latter two invented by Ribman.

Some of the actors glide from one story to another. Susan Anspach plays Chulkaturin's beloved, whom he loses twice, and she also plays one of the two women whom Zoditch loses. Lee Wallace plays the successful rivals of both Chulkaturin and Zoditch.

The structure is inviting, but the result is disappointing. Essentially, Ribman has reduced Turgenev and has not compensated with Ribman. This is not glibly to batter a young author with a great name. Ribman is a writer of serious intent and some ability. But his Zoditch is "superfluous" for reasons quite different from Chulkaturin's. Zoditch is a man frustrated in acquisition—of power and sex; Chulkaturin is defeated in his attempts at union—in love and in a sense of social pertinence. And the lesser and less interesting man takes over much of the play.

Even this might be a trenchant opposition—an insectile man crawling over an aspiring man—except that Zoditch does not deepen in character or engage in action. Quite early in the play we know all that we ever know about him, and, unlike Chulkaturin, he has no story. His life is largely fantasy, and the fantasies are highly repetitive and predictable, the common stuff of a petty, pettifogging clerk.

In raising Zoditch to equal partnership, Ribman has been forced to diminish Chulkaturin, to "state" him merely. Turgenev did not provide a detailed psychological dossier, but he did give his hero space and texture in which to exist dimensionally. In the original, we are convinced of Chulkaturin's own conviction that he is disconnected—in a way that anticipates the consciousness of disconnections in the modern temperament.

Flaubert, another maker of the modern temperament, wrote to Turgenev after he read the story: "How many things which I myself have felt and experienced I have rediscovered in your pages!" Many of us might say the same, but not about the Chulkaturin at the American Place. He is synopsized, rather than dramatized, and this vitiates both our interest in him and Ribman's intended counterpoint.

One example of how the character has been stripped. The "fifth horse" in the title refers to an anecdote about an extra horse tied on to a four-horse carriage. In the Turgenev story, Chulkaturin himself recalls the incident and applies it to himself. "I, too, have simply been tied on! . . . But," the dying man adds, "thank goodness, the post-house is not far away now." Ribman, however, brings in a character, not seen before or after, to tell the fifth-horse anecdote. Thus it becomes an italicized, clumsy insert, and Chulkaturin is robbed of an enriching insight about himself.

The fundamental flaw of the play is that the basic device remains a device. We are never persuaded of Ribman's *purpose* in creating the character of Zoditch and the play's intricate structure. All that really grows out of it is the irony of Zoditch's sneering at Chulkaturin, as he reads, when his own condition is really no better than the other man's and his personal stature is much less. But this irony is quickly perceived, and is not furthered.

Over all, too, there hovers an assumption that the very choice of this period, with Ribman's reasonable facsimiles of period characteristics and details, automatically supplies seriousness, merely because that age is associated with so much great literature. It seems an attempt at profundity-by-association.

Ribman has ambitions that are out of the playwriting ordinary. He has some gift with words and some ingenuity. What he does not show is a grip of dramatic character: character not merely as portrait but as dynamic and interacting organism. After getting his initial idea, he enjoyed it at considerable length, I think, rather than utilizing it dramatically; then he simply forced a thematically intertwined ending. His play, instead of being an illuminating expansion of the original, is itself a kind of fifth horse to Turgenev.

The production is outstandingly happy in two elements. Kert Lundell's setting is almost miraculous. It converts the relatively small stage of the American Place into a number of widely varied playing areas, and it expedites the play's transitions in time, place, and reality.

Dustin Hoffman's performance of Zoditch has the vitality of the born actor and the fine control of the skillful one. With sharp comedy techniques, he makes this unattractive man both funny and pathetic. Hoffman is only in his twenties. Perhaps—the insanities of the theater world permitting—we will be allowed to watch an extraordinary career develop.

Sunset

(The New York Times, *May 13, 1966*)

A producing company called Transcenics, Inc., gives with one hand and takes away with the other. Last night that organization presented the overdue New York premiere of Isaac Babel's *Sunset,* a play teeming with vitality; but their production is hollow. The 81st Street Theater on upper Broadway has been renovated from film use for the occasion. Across this stage Babel's colorful comedy-drama of Jewish life in old Odessa is stretched out and bleached white. Aldo Bruzzichelli's direction runs as counter to the spirit of the play—indeed, counter to its specifications—as if that were the purpose of the evening.

Sunset, translated into vigorous English by Mirra Ginsburg and Raymond Rosenthal, deals with characters known from Babel's *Odessa Stories.* Mendel Krick is a roistering old giant of a carter who bullies everyone, including his family. When his daughter shows signs of getting married and obliging him to pay a dowry, when his two sons grow restive under his yoke, he plans to sell his carting business and run off to Bessarabia with a young girl. But his sons—particularly Benya, an embryo gangster—frustrate this plan and wrench the business from the old tyrant by physical force. Mendel's sun sets; power changes hands; life goes on.

As readers of Babel's stories (and of this play) know gratefully, what this author is interested in is the full flood of living: juice, tenderness, nastiness, sex, revenge—all the blessings of family and community life. He tells the riotous truth about the Jews of Odessa at the turn of the century, who were by no means all quavering peddlers or Talmudists. Supremely, even in his heart-wrenching moments, he is a man who never loses sight of the essential ridiculousness of man. When the blood runs—and Babel saw plenty of it in his life, including, at the last, his own—he can never quite forget the silliness of it all. Men are always dear to him, but they are always small against the stars. In a cosmic sense, he is a comedian.

But Bruzzichelli, imperceptive to the marrow, has seen this play as Stark and Sad. No one can fool him, least of all the author. What, a play set in old Russia? About Jews? Why, it must be sad and slow. Each scene must end with a picturesque tableau seen through a tristful gauzy scrim. Stage-convention Jewishness must be crammed in at every chance, and the author's wishes, which the director obviously thinks are mistaken, must be disregarded.

For example, the scene between Mendel and his tootsie, Marusia. As she undresses to make love, she babbles, according to the author, "in a ringing voice, full of gaiety and good health." While she talks, "Mendel looks at Marusia adoringly." At the end of the scene when she pulls him to her, he is "half crying, half laughing."

Not for the humorless Bruzzichelli. It's Russia, isn't it?—and therefore must be played *à la Russe*. The girl behaves like the pathetic Sonia in *Crime and Punishment,* speaking in broken arcs of rue and brave cheeriness. Mendel stands stolidly with his back to us, never once looking at the girl while she undresses, staring at the floor until the last desperate moment. What is intended as a scene of chattery blithe sex on the girl's part and an old man's somehow admirable refusal to let go of anything in life, even his sins—all this is turned into dank neurological dissection.

Throughout the performance, the tone and the pace and the staging itself are so turgid that when an unwreckable funny line or action occurs, it seems out of place. (And even in this production some of the play would be funnier if all the words were clear.) Thus we are surprised when we laugh—as Babel meant us to—at the cantor who pulls out a pistol and shoots a rat in the middle of the service in an old synagogue.

A few of the smaller roles are acted passably—Geraldine Teagarden as the daughter, Henry Ferrentino as a servant. Most of the actors are inadequate, and the leading actors are the worst.

Much of the sententious distortion in Martin Rudy's performance must be ascribed to the director, but hardly a word Rudy speaks is minimally credible. It is all measured and affected, an inappropriate attempt at Lear plus Old Karamazov that never touches reality. Benya, the older son, ought to be flashy, serpentine, dynamic, a prince both rightful and usurping. In this excellent part Michael Wager is almost invisible.

The settings by Kim Swados are succinct and nicely suggestive, but Gary Harris' lighting is either cold and too dispersed, as in the first scene, or trite, as in the tavern scene.

Bruzzichelli's Off-Broadway production of *The Maids* a few years ago left much to be desired. This production leaves just one thing to be desired: that he had never touched *Sunset*. Now he has only made it difficult for anyone else to produce this lovely play for some time to come.*

Macbird

(*Channel 13, New York, February 27, 1967*)

Macbird has now officially opened at the Village Gate on Bleecker Street—a cabaret, not a conventional theater. First, for those viewers who may have been spending the last few months in Tierra del Fuego and have not heard of *Macbird,* I'll describe it briefly. It's a political satire, in Shakespearean style and roughly based on *Macbeth*. The principal characters are the three Kennedy brothers, including the late President, and Mr. and Mrs. Johnson. The play very heavily implies that the Johnsons engineered the assassination of President Kennedy and the airplane accident of Edward Kennedy, in order to reach power and secure it. *Macbird* was written by Barbara Garson. She and her husband are residents of Berkeley, both radical political activists, and this play—Garson's first—grew out of her participation in an anti-war rally. By a slip of the tongue she referred to Ladybird Johnson as Lady Macbird. This gave her the initial idea.

When the script was finished a little over a year ago, plans were set in motion to get it produced in New York. Meanwhile it was declined by several publishers, and Garson's husband decided to publish it himself in brochure form. Here begins its amazing history. This small publisher—non-publisher, really—sold 105,000 copies of the play before it was taken over by a commercial publisher, who continues to sell lots of copies. Word of mouth had started about the manuscript, including some large recommendations by well-known figures. Newspapers and magazines have devoted great space to it; the *Partisan Review* published an article about it which, it says, may be the first of a series. Productions of the play have been set for a number of other countries. Two weeks ago the *Times Literary Supplement* of London devoted its editorial to *Macbird*—a completely adverse comment, by

* It was produced six years later by the Chelsea Theater Center, again poorly.

the way. Penguin Books is going to publish the play in Britain. And so on.

Well, now it's been produced, and what about it? Two points at once—based on a prior reading of the play. When I read it, I felt strongly that it would play well, and it does. Second, I regret that I had read it. *Macbird* is simply not a multiple occasion. I laughed a number of times when I read it; but at the performance I knew the funny lines and the Shakespearean burlesque, and they raised only an occasional smile in me. *Macbird* is fairly funny—once.

This result is not especially the fault of the production. Roy Levine, the director, is no paragon of imagination—in fact, it's when he tries to supply directorial flourishes that the play really limps; still the staging is adequate. The actors run the usual café-theater gamut, beginning at the lowest level of inept amateurism. But the gamut runs up through a passable imitation of Bobby Kennedy by William Devane to a quite competent Southern-drawl performance of Lady Macbird by Rue McClanahan to an absolutely first-class performance of the title role by Stacy Keach. He transcends some excellent mimicry of President Johnson to create a figure of power and menace. I believed him at the same time that I knew it was a lampoon, and therefore the lampoon was even more effective.

In fact, I'm genuinely sorry for Keach. He has the misfortune to be playing the leading role in a play that, as a script, is a center of controversy; and in the middle of that brouhaha the excellence of his performance is being generally ignored or undervalued. If, figuratively, he were giving this performance in a less controversial play, his extraordinary work might receive the attention it deserves. It doesn't detract from his work here to say that his Macbird made me want to see his Macbeth. He is technically sure, imaginatively free, has large and easy force and an unusual sense of style. The only previous time I saw him in a major role, as Horner in the Lincoln Center production of *The Country Wife,* he had surgical incisiveness but seemed constricted. But then most gifted persons seem constricted at Lincoln Center, and Keach is highly gifted.

As for the play itself, it seems, as it did when I read it, a bright undergraduate's *jeu d'esprit.* It is the kind of pastiche of Shakespeare that many clever college students have done—through the years I have seen a number—on various themes. I'm speaking now merely of its literary and dramaturgic qualities. The remarkable point is that someone with no experience of the theater, like Garson, could have contrived to make a piece so actable. The deplorable point, again speaking dramaturgically, is that she didn't follow her model closely enough. She abandons the parallel with *Macbeth* in the second part to include something of the play-within-the-play idea from *Hamlet,* and other ideas; the result is that the shape of *Macbird* gets flabby in the last third and the satirical interest gets dispersed.

But what distinguishes *Macbird* from similar efforts is its insolence, which is its real point. After all the arguments about moral irresponsibility have been chewed back and forth, one fact remains: the play germinates from one line, spoken by the First Witch: "Trouble stirred is always for the good." Garson believes in stirring up trouble. She wants to stimulate distrust in the administration, to make us question its sagacity more and more. To that end, insolence is essential and she supplies it; but that is not quite the same thing as moral irresponsibility.

She has been accused by some of grossness because she makes game, to an extent, of President Kennedy's assassination. The outrage of this play—and its purpose is to be outrageous—would be lily-livered if it left untouched matters that have truly moved us, if it only made fun of (say) Mother's Day. By the nature of her intent, Garson had to include matters that we take seriously.

She has been accused by many others of scurrility, of irresponsibility, for implying clearly that the Johnsons were involved in the Kennedy murder. This accusation seems to me misconceived, not to say inconsistent. Everyone talks about that point; but few talk about the fact that in the play Bobby Kennedy brings about the death of President Johnson by a tussle that induces a Presidential heart attack. If the first is taken as a serious indictment of conspiracy, why isn't the second a libel on Bobby Kennedy? The distinction betrays a certain sentimentality in the accusers, I think, based on the fact that the first relates to a past action and the second to a hypothesis. But one of these elements is intended no more literally than the other. Both are the fantasy goads of a political activist, not a political scientist. Garson is not a reporter, or an analyst; she is an agitator. To judge her play as one judges those interminable commentaries on the Warren Commission Report is a complete misconstruction.

She *has* agitated people, obviously. Thus she has achieved her primary end. She *has* written a generally clever Shakespearean pastiche that wobbles badly toward the close. What she has *not* done, in my view, is—as some have claimed—to reveal any kind of genius as a writer. The overpraise of this play, as a literary achievement, is to me only a facet of the most interesting aspect of the whole *Macbird* affair: the hunger in this country for a play of this kind, the ravening hunger, particularly among many students and intellectuals, for a loud bray of "no confidence" in the face of our present government. Gratitude for this play's daring has, I think, swayed opinion of its artistic merit. The importance of *Macbird* to me, a very real and urgent factor, is outside the theater and literature: it's a revealing social phenomenon.

A Patriot for Me

(November 1, 1969)

A Patriot for Me is a promising title, but it has little connection with the play. The idea of the play is also promising, but it is bleakly unfulfilled. John Osborne has based this work on fact: the life of Alfred Redl, an officer in the Austrian army from 1890 to 1913, how his homosexuality made him prey to blackmail by Russian spies, how it resulted in his suicide. What themes are involved!—the decay of heel-clicking Europe, the bulldog blindness of the officer caste, the cruelty of ostracism for sexual choice, the revenge of the ostracized, the fate of millions hanging on the psyches of the few, the whole horde of sorry ghosts behind the portraits on the palace walls. And what themes for Osborne, who, whatever his weaknesses, has incisive diction, an appreciation of elitism, and a gift for theatrical metaphor (like the music hall in *The Entertainer*). But over and over through the twenty scenes of this lavish play, I thought, "Ah, so that's the idea of this scene. Good. Now will Osborne kindly write it?"

The drama is not joined; only the plot is worked out. The character of Redl is followed, not explored. The themes, large and relevant, are left waiting in the wings; we catch glimpses of them once in a while, but they never emerge. Redl's personal problems are not made terribly moving and, worse, their pertinence to us is missing. Everything is taken for granted, not implied (something quite different). And after all the dallyings and missed explosions, the play arrives at no terminus. For the American production Osborne has added a brief speech by a general, plus a comment over the p.a. system (which has been commenting throughout), to try to fix the play on a target, the war of 1914 and the subsequent, continuing results. But these are only last grasps.

The first scene is excellent: an early-morning duel, with Redl as the second of a doomed young officer. (One of the few realized elements in the play is Redl's revenge, years later, on the officer who kills the youth, to whom Redl was attracted before he knew he was homosexual.) But then there follows a plateau scene, facts with no dramatic advancement, then more scenes that are especially disappointing in Osborne because they are conventional concepts: a prostitute's room, the schemings of Russian agents. I have no idea of how military spies really speak, but I can recognize the motions of the movies. The scene of the drag ball, now famous beforehand, has no element of necessary surprise; besides, it too is a plateau scene. Moreover, the subject of homosexuality has traveled so far in the New York theater since this play was produced in London five years ago that we don't even get much titillation from these boys in the Bund.

Some critics have slated Osborne for not doing what he has done before—create one central caustic Jeremiah, a mouthpiece for himself, with attendant creatures flitting about. On the contrary, I rather admire his effort to break loose, to try a different, more distanced dramatic shape. But the effort at transformation is fuzzy. There is some hard *previous* work—before writing (for which in itself his gift has always been extraordinary)—that Osborne has not done. Homosexuality as escape-cum-aggression; or as a locus for the Pharisaism of a Europe riddled with decay; or as a metaphor for matters of psychical and social difference in our own times—none of these, or any other approach, is realized. Osborne simply seized the incident of the Redl scandal too quickly and wrote, no matter how long it took him, too easily.

But I must add that the play is probably better than it looks in New York. The settings and costumes are passable, like *Die Fledermaus* at the Met twenty years ago. But with the single exception of Maximilian Schell, the performance is deplorable. Peter Glenville's casting, staging, and directing of actors strike a new low in a career not noted for heights. Schell has what I would not have expected: modesty; and a force that comes from inner focus, instead of his usual display of fancied superiorities. He played Redl in the London production, and I infer that he benefited from his work with a better director, Anthony Page. Dennis King's staginess at least fits the drag baron he plays. But the rest! Salome Jens, as the seductress in Russian pay, is still gassily "sensitive," she still semaphores gestures with both arms simultaneously. She still has not spoken a word on stage or screen that I have believed. Stefan Schnabel makes an Austrian general behave like Mack Swain in an early Chaplin short. Staats Cotsworth, a colonel, bumps along from line to line as if he were falling downstairs. Keene Curtis plays the Russian agent like Akim Tamiroff's understudy. Glenville's direction misses no chance for cliché of movement: the standard retard-and-turn before an exit; the quiet moment with a guitar-player after a violent scene, just before the curtain falls. Whenever a playwright gives his director a scene with extras dancing upstage behind a row of arches while a few characters converse downstage, you can bet that the director will be praised for brilliant staging, no matter how cloddish he is. It happened again here.

And a word about the amplification. The Imperial Theater often houses musicals, so, as is now the questionable custom, it is equipped with amplifiers. The idea is utterly ridiculous for a straight play in what is merely a good-sized house. Worse, the sound equipment is tinny. The voices sound as if you had entered a small-town movie show in 1930 with a banner outside saying "100% All-Talkie."

Indians

(November 8, 1969)

Oliver Smith has designed a setting for *Indians* that tries to open the proscenium stage into large and ambiguous possibilities. Arthur Kopit has tried much the same thing with the shape of his play. Smith's design fulfills itself, but Kopit's play remains an intention.

Kopit is dealing with the white man's treatment of the American Indian and has used, in musical terms, a rondo form. The recurring theme, the enclosure of the work, is the Wild West Show run by Buffalo Bill Cody. Within it, by the interweaving of flashbacks and fantasy, Kopit tells of the last meeting between Sitting Bull and a Presidential commission of three senators in 1886 to improve the Indians' lot; the failure of the meeting; the subsequent assassination of Sitting Bull and other Sioux; and other outrages against Indians. Kopit's underlying theme would be obvious even if he had not publicized it elsewhere: he is attacking American treatment of all "inferior" peoples, Indians, blacks, Vietnamese, and others. Equally important, Kopit is also attacking the neat moral transformation that America applies to these brutalities. (Jefferson Davis wrote that one of the benefits of slavery was its introduction of the benighted African to the blessings of Christianity.) The white American's way is the right way, and those who disagree are not merely enemies of America but of Good.

It is a familiar charge, not the less true for that. To vitalize it, Kopit has used a familiar device, a theatrical form within his own theatrical form. His device, the Wild West Show, is particularly apt, not only because it grows directly out of his material but because it symbolizes a national attitude toward that material—a conversion of history into show biz in order to settle it, to fix the roles and the moral values forever. If history is written by the survivors, so, certainly, are the fictions, like the Wild West shows and the Westerns. The process long antedates Cody. For instance, in 1829 Edwin Forrest produced and starred in *Metamora,* a play about a noble red chief murdered by whites. It is as if an Elizabethan dramatist had written a play for Richard Burbage about a noble Irish king in order to demonstrate the English sense of fair play. America's "aboriginal dramas" (as they were called), in which the red man was often heroic, were attempts to cash in on melodramatic subjects, but they were also attempts to expiate guilt through facile theatrical tribute.

Kopit's device, then, is rooted in a valid theatrical-psychic base. His theme is pertinent. But from the very start his play begins to fail. Glass museum cases containing effigies of Buffalo Bill and Sitting Bull rise into the flies. (They have been visible since we entered; there is no curtain.) The "real" Buffalo Bill enters, riding one of those fake horses, on his own two feet, that clowns sometimes use and that were used in *Becket.* It is a promise of flight, of lift-off, but it fizzles quickly as Bill's opening remarks sag and, to bolster them, Kopit involves him in labored chit-chat with a voice on the p.a. system that urges him to hurry along. A suspicion of strain, of herniated imagination, assails us right away.

Even this scruffy p.a. device might work, or be tolerable, if one essential element—good writing—had been present, there and throughout. But a good writer is precisely what Kopit is not. The best prose in the play is an actual speech (I believe) of Chief Joseph's. If none of the characters is deeply realized, that may be a penalty of the fantasy form. But this form can be realized, can *exist,* only through the quality of its language. No one who saw *Oh, Dad* (to abbreviate that sophomoric title) and Kopit's bill of one-act plays a few years ago would expect much from him in language. He is still a deviser of clever ideas who thinks, apparently, that he can fill in the words later. Which is exactly how the words sound. After Sitting Bull is killed, Cody reproaches his ghost, "You were very unrealistic." The quality of that line, at such a moment, is typical. Kopit's language not only deadens the drama, it collapses the play's form.

Then there are the moments when Kopit the Poet feels that he must gambol, and can afford it. A Russian grand duke, on a hunting trip with Cody, calls him "Buffalo Billovitch." A Wild West melodrama is performed in the White House, with Cody and Wild Bill Hickok, in a travesty of hokum like the end-of-season romp at a summer camp. The playwright who could sink to such depths has a foggy conception of the heights.

The director, Gene Frankel, who did the first and excellent American production of Genet's *The Blacks,* has tried to supply a dream tegument: interludes are covered with strobe lights while actors float in slow motion. But Frankel is stuck, despite these and other devices, with a leaden work that will not respond to levitation. There is a Sun-Dance, devised by Julie Arenal, that is a good deal more pounding drums than dance. For the most part, the Indians are just a lot of Equity members making like Indians. Only Manu Tupou, the Sitting Bull, manages to crack through the pretense to touch a primal nerve. Tupou is a native of Fiji who has appeared in *Hawaii* and other films, and he manages to convey a sense of the Natural Man, communicant with earth forces to which civilized man is blind and deaf. (But Kopit lets him down too. When Sitting Bull asks the senators angrily whether they know whom they're speaking to, we expect a grand answer from him to his own question, but Kopit gives him only a few piddling phrases.)

Stacy Keach is Buffalo Bill. Keach is a young actor (twenty-eight) of whom we have almost every right to expect almost everything. Two years ago he played Coriolanus with the Yale Repertory Theater, and the moment he stepped on stage—leaped on, actually—it was clear that he had misconceived the role and also that he was probably the only young actor in America who could play it. In *Indians* he gets the role right, but there is just not much role to get. The lack is not in psychological complexity, which this kind of play usually prevents, but in poetic richness, which it demands. From the beginning Keach conveys a sense of desperate uphill fight: an artist's fight to sink feelers and feeders into a center that will not respond, to draw fire from a piece of writing that simply rolls over flabbily the more he shakes it. Only at the end, when Cody, now dimly aware of what he has been part of, kneels to us and tries to peddle trinkets and souvenirs to help keep the Indians alive, is there a touch of the performance that Keach might have given if the part had ever been written.

Kopit's play was first produced in London last year by the Royal Shakespeare Company. Earlier this year it was produced at the Arena Stage in Washington under Frankel's direction with Keach and some of the same actors. Now Broadway is taking *Indians* to its bosom as its Serious Play of the Year. (Last year it was *The Great White Hope,* an overpraised but much better play—also from the Arena.) I do not argue backward from Broadway's patronization that the Kopit play cannot be good. But to see even its good moments—the five or six replicas of Buffalo Bill dashing off to impersonate him on stages around the world, the stripping of masks from Bill's face as he recites betrayals of the Indians—to see them plunk to the ground without a work of current or rhythm or depth to bear them along is to understand Kopit's real failure. His play must become a crystallization of the unconscious, an externalization of the dark in us, or it is nothing. It must fulfill Jung's injunction to "dream the myth onwards and give it a modern dress," or it is only one more pretentious American self-flagellation.

Last of the Red Hot Lovers

(February 14, 1970)

Neil Simon's new comedy, *Last of the Red Hot Lovers,* is a smash hit. It has one setting and a cast of only four. Simon is reportedly the chief financial backer of the production and is also the owner of the theater in which it is playing. Perfection is rare on earth. The perfection with which all the elements in this phenomenon complement one another, from the play's original concept to the real-estate data, is awe-inspiring.

My point is not sarcasm alone. Simon exemplifies Broadway at its current top level of operation. If there is going to be a commercial theater—and there certainly *is* going to be one of some kind—it might as well be adroitly practiced. If the machine is going to be around, it might as well run smoothly instead of creaking and wheezing as it does most of the time. Simon is, on evidence, the optimum operator.

As a writer, he is in some ways the theater equivalent of a current cinema trend that I've called the film of make-believe meaning: the sort of film written by William Goldman or the team of Benton and Newman, or that is directed by Sidney Lumet or Robert Mulligan— seemingly sharp and fearless but essentially tame and pat. For instance, there is a scene in *Lovers* in which the hero, a fat, fortyish husband, makes a confession during his first extra-marital rendezvous. He tells the woman that his life has been "nice" but that now he feels the reality of the fact that he will someday die, that he wants more out of living, that the only sex experience he has had outside marriage was one youthful encounter with a middle-aged Newark whore, after which he threw up all night. This account, with which the hero attempts to wring us, is to me morally and egotistically repellent, but a popular playwright of ten or fifteen years ago—say, Paddy Chayefsky—would have left it there. Simon is too clever. The woman, a cynically philandering wife, replies that she is not much impressed with this recital because, first, that Newark whore might well have been her mother and, second, the fear of death is not all that exceptional or winning. In the play's give-and-take—not between the characters but between Simon and us—he has scored a point. It takes a while longer to see that the whole operation, within which the point-scoring is enclosed, is basically sentimental and consumer-flattering, that only the incidentals have been sharpened. Below the polished, sophisticated surface there is just as little as we have been conditioned to expect in Broadway comedy smashes.

But since this kind of material is exactly what the Broadway mechanism needs at the moment and since there are, evidently, very few writers who can supply it, some limited gratitude is in order. *Lovers* is a hundred times more welcome than *Coco,* which was supposed to be an oxygen pump for ailing Broadway but which is itself gasping in every department and also presents Katharine Hepburn in her first vulgar performance. (Her limitations are not news; her vulgarity is.)

As usual with Simon, his three-act play consists of a one-act play with addenda. The three acts are three assignations that the hero has, each with a different woman. The first act contrasts, to some point, a realistic woman who centers on a bitter hedonism as her sole reason for living and a romantic man who disguises his menopausal sex panic as a quest for poetry. She isn't having any of his self-deception, and she leaves—twice, in fact. In boxing terms, this first act is very clearly the woman's round. It is also a complete drama; when the first-act curtain comes down, everything that was started in that act has been finished. But Simon can't leave the play there: it is both too short and too unsoothing to be commercially viable. As variations on the first act, he supplies two more meetings—one with a kooky actress-singer, another with an unhappy wife in the hero's circle of friends. No sexual intercourse in any of these meetings, of course; the most daring innovation is that in Act Two the hero smokes pot with the actress—the familiar Act Two drunk scene except that this time it ends with the hero holding two joints instead of two glasses. The play finally works around to the assurance that the hero is basically a decent man—what's more, that what he has really been looking for is not an extra-marital lay but this very assurance that he is decent. After all the modern décor, the curtain comes down to the chime of old-fashioned cash registers.

The tone of the play is New York Jewish. The hero and two of the women play with Jewish inflections, although only the hero is (more or less) said to be Jewish. This assumption of Jewishness as fundamental to comedy is common on Broadway—implicit even when non-Jewish names and types are used, as in Simon's *The Odd Couple.*

Since the Broadway audience is assumed to be at least half Jewish, this flavor is not surprising.

The diction of *Lovers* is fake realism. The characters are supposed to be a restaurant-owner, two different kinds of housewives, and a silly girl; they speak in well-modeled aphorisms and punchy one-line gags, as if every restaurant-owner and housewife in New York had a personal gag-writer—Jewish. But this too satisfies a hunger in the audience; they have been listening for two generations to Benny and Berle, and they wish that their own conversation, in their own apartments, could be carried on in snappy comebacks.

James Coco, the hero, is a big, fat man who made a great success last season in a one-act play Off Broadway that I didn't see. I can understand the success; he has sufficient technique and variety and truth to get him through a one-act play. In *Lovers* he has some trouble. He repeats tricks (a grimace when he drinks whiskey, a nervous shake before he opens the front door), but that's possibly the director's doing. More serious, he repeats patterns and phrases of emotion and gesture in such a way that eventually we are conscious of them as techniques. He has a small resemblance to Zero Mostel. (Emphasized by a gag repeated from *Fiddler on the Roof*—Coco states some puzzling questions to which, instead of an answer, he gives a shrug and says, "I don't know.") He is much less erratic and self-centered than Mostel, but neither does he have Mostel's brilliance.

Linda Lavin gives a generally good performance as the toughie. She is a superb entertainer (*The Mad Show, Superman*) but has had difficulty with "straight" acting in the three plays I've seen her in. All through them she seemed to be fighting for crevices into which she could insert her funny little "acts." She hasn't entirely shaken the habit here; occasionally she ends lines with a widening of the eyes and a head-cocking that gets laughs and which are Linda Lavin's vaudeville interludes. But most of the time she tries hard and successfully to deal with the character's cool, measured bile. Marcia Rodd, who plays the actress, is too much like a young Phyllis Diller to appeal to me. Doris Roberts as the conventional housewife is appropriately commonplace.

Robert Moore keeps the action front-and-center in nice, square Broadway style. (There is a large dining alcove in Oliver Smith's setting that is hardly ever used.) As he did with *The Boys in the*

Band, Moore imposes obviously artificial pace and changes of pace. Most of the show is whipped along, including some bits of business that are repeated as running gags. Moore makes a dramatic point by a sudden stop, then a resumption of the dialogue in slow, spaced speech—before it whips up again to another stop, and so on. But he has got Lavin's best acting from her, and he has given Simon's play the requisite lacquer. A better director would have been out of order. Moore too is part of the event's glossy perfection.

The Gingerbread Lady

(January 16, 1971)

Neil Simon's new play is his second of the year, which is the most notable thing about it. More of that later. First, the play itself.

When the curtain goes up on *The Gingerbread Lady,* a man bustles out of the kitchen into the living room with a vase of flowers and tries placing them in various positions. Immediately this defines the play's imaginative level. Stock opening "business," while the audience settles in their seats, to tell us something of character and anticipation. (There is a similar opening in *Last of the Red Hot Lovers.*) This is the West-Seventies-brownstone apartment of an ex-singer named Evy Meara, and the man is a homo actor friend readying the place for her return. She has just spent some weeks getting dried out in a Long Island home for drunks.

We know that she has to relapse or there would be no play, and we wait around for the causes to be manufactured (the misfortunes of the actor, the marital troubles of a fading-beauty girl friend). Evy's seventeen-year-old daughter, who comes to live with her, is the rock to which she finally clings.

This is certainly Simon's least skillful play to date: the first act is a great gob of exposition. It is also his least credible: we are asked to believe that Evy's ex-husband sends their daughter to live with his nymphomaniacal ex-wife just out of an alcoholics' hospital; that the girl has no revulsion or panic, is a never failing fount of wisdom, and finally clasps her mother to her filial bosom to save her. No, we're not *really* asked to believe all this, we're asked to accept it so that we can

have the play as it trudges through predictable mechanics to an ending that is devoid of surprise or (even) tear-jerking resolution.

A good deal of this loud-voiced opus takes place with the apartment's front door open—at one point the door is broken down—yet
we never hear or see a sign of the neighbors, who are apparently
stone-deaf. This is supposed to be Simon's first "serious" play (in
point of fact, *Red Hot Lovers* was—comparatively—much more serious), but it is insured with wisecracks—the usual barrage of jokes
built on misinterpretation or distortion of a phrase someone else used
in the preceding line, or built on cozy recognition points: Schrafft
cocktails, Tareyton commercials, Bloomingdale's department store,
etc.

Robert Moore, who also directed *Lovers,* has attended to this play
like a brisk chiropractor familiar with Simon's case. Maureen Staple-
ton, as Evy, clumps and clutches all over the stage—clutching presumably for a straw of reality in the sea of staginess. Her daughter is
played by Ayn Ruymen, one of the worst debutantes in some seasons.
Michael Lombard delivers a smooth theater homo, but the most valid
performance is by Charles Siebert, as Evy's former lover. Siebert,
who was good as the paunchy, tyrannical Willy in last season's
Colette, gives solidity to an aging hip musician. He is a genuine
actor.

But this ungainly, trite, and finally pointless play is a revealing
cultural instance. The show had spotty reviews out of town, was
(falsely) announced to be closing, and had mixed reviews in New
York. According to *The New York Times*'s Sunday summary on
December 20, the play "pleased five critics, got mixed reviews from
two and was turned down by four." All during these events there was
a feeling of incredulousness in the air, as if this could not be happening to Knockout Neil, the undefeated champ, as if some sort of
appeal or effort could reverse the decision. It began on December
23, ten days after the opening, only three days after the *Times* had
published the very skeptical critical consensus on that opening. On
the twenty-third the *Times* ran an interview with the author under
the headline "Simon Traces Path from 'Flop' to Hit." The word Hit is
not in quotation marks, presumably because Simon doesn't use the
term; it's the *Times* that insists on it. Even *Variety,* the weekly
evangel of show biz, could say only that *The Gingerbread Lady* had
"a passable first week . . . the window sale has been so-so. . . ."

Yet despite these facts, despite the critical reaction, the *Times* insisted on planting the word Hit in a headline and in the story itself.

I'm not interested in proving that the play is a failure or in predicting that it will close—I don't care if it runs ten years. I'm interested in why the B'nai Broadway Anti-Defamation League, of which the *Times* seems to be president, has rallied to Simon's support.

The reason isn't obscure. He is, apparently, the last of his breed—the last regular, prolific manufacturer of plays for Broadway. In the high days Broadway had many people writing regularly for it, at various levels. Numerous playwrights had eight, ten, twelve plays produced during their careers, and there were some astonishing front-runners. Maxwell Anderson wrote over thirty plays in a career of thirty years, Philip Barry did twenty-four plays in twenty-six years, George S. Kaufman did one solo play and well over thirty collaborations in a career of thirty-five years. Simon is on his way: since 1961 he has written ten plays and musicals, all successful—including this new one, if we believe the *Times*.

Plenty of people are writing plays that they would like to see produced on Broadway, and, conceivably, they might write more successes if they had initial success. This is conjecture: very few of those who made a first hit in the last ten years have followed with another. (Where are the careers of Leonard Spigelgass, Frank Gilroy, William Goodhart, James Goldman?) Still, even allowing for the conjecture, even allowing for some reduction of present high production cost with a new "middle contract" for certain theaters, there are cultural reasons, I think, why really prolific Broadway playwrights won't appear again.

Not many new talents have confidence in the forms of Broadway plays or a desire for a lifetime dialogue with the Broadway audience. If they have serious ambitions, they do not aspire to Broadway as the best dramatists did in the past (O'Neill, for prime example). If they have popular ambitions, Broadway is so strait a gate that they are forced to try elsewhere. The hit play still has a great deal of glamour and "clout," but there's a shrinking of the belief that one has not proved himself as a writer until one meets the Broadway challenge. The role of Broadway script-supplier is not ached for, as it used to be.

At bottom there's a limited analogy with what is happening in Hollywood. Recently we've read a lot of discontented comment about current American films, a lot of nostalgic prattle about the good old days when the studios turned out good entertainment films (which, generally speaking, is true) month after month. But there's a barrier of enormous change between then and now. World War II happened, Hitler, Hiroshima, and Stalin; Korea and Vietnam happened; several domestic upheavals happened and are still happening—Youth, Black, Feminist. It's hard to imagine a gifted young director aspiring to the fictitious fiction-making career of a John Ford or George Stevens, however gifted those men were; or a screen writer embarking on a life of romantic concoctions as Philip Dunne and Norman Krasna did. Hollywood's reactions to social change have so far been overwhelmingly stilted and/or meretricious, and we have to hope that we are en route to some small percentage of wheat amidst the polemical chaff; but to hold up the taboo-ridden, fantasy-fed past as model is fruitless.

These social changes have had similar effects on recent generations of playwrights. The serious ones, many of them, are willing—anxious—to work elsewhere than Broadway. The others are faced with a crazy psychological-commercial paradox: in order to become a hit-producing playwright, the best thing is to have been one before you start out. The entertainment writers can't sell themselves as easily on Broadway as elsewhere. Television and films, though hardly blooming at the moment, are relatively more healthy.

So, for the people whose lives still depend on the commercial theater—the ticket-brokers, theater-owners, theater-party managers, Broadway restaurateurs, all the thousands in the shadows behind the bright marquees—the health of Neil Simon is important. He is one of the last who can work comfortably for Broadway on this side of the changes mentioned above and whose future is ordained, almost metaphysically, by his past. He is the sole survivor and must be safe-guarded. He's becoming the whooping crane or passenger pigeon of Broadway, and the Department of the Interior, as well as *The New York Times,* may be asked to help preserve him.

The Sunshine Boys

(January 27, 1973)

For years I've been saying that Neil Simon is not a playwright but a sketch-writer. Now, with exemplary courtesy, he has taken the trouble to prove my point. *The Sunshine Boys* is the apotheosis of a sketch. An old-style vaudeville routine is the center of the evening, with what amounts to a series of sketches leading up to and away from the main act in the middle.

The two old vaudeville troupers of the title were evidently suggested by Smith and Dale, whose Dr. Krankheit sketch I saw a half-dozen times during its long life. After forty-three years in vaudeville, Simon's duo quarreled, and have not seen each other for eleven years. Now they are being brought together for a big TV "cavalcade" of old comedy. The setting, except for the second-act TV studio where they run through their sketch, is Jack Albertson's dowdy hotel room. To it comes his old partner, Sam Levene, who now lives with his daughter in New Jersey, brought here by Albertson's nephew.

There is no play, in any organic sense. There are some maneuvers, there is a heart attack, there is a final twist, but mostly we are (in effect) backstage before the sketch, then backstage again after it. It's a good sketch—Simon's variation on the Krankheit theme—and Albertson even imitates the way Dale used to jump up and down in cartoon-pansy style. But if you can think of this evening without the sketch itself, you see that it simply wouldn't exist.

The tributary sketches are about an old man and a TV set; the crusty old man and his eager-beaver nephew; two crusty old men fencing at a reunion; crusty old man in bed, being tended by a buxom black nurse; and more. Simon gets his laughs from two series of recognitions: first, the show-biz knowledge that is now common currency among "civilians"; second, the details of "civilian" life, made funny, apparently, just by being reproduced on stage. For instance, when the curtain rises, Albertson is watching a TV soap opera. The night I was there, this brought a few titters at once. Then there was a break and on came the same Lipton's Tea commercial that you can hear at home. This brought a loud laugh. Thus Simon sets the key for the kind of humor that's to follow: nudge jokes. A nudges B, implying, "Isn't that just like so-and-so, or such-and-such?"

I certainly don't mean that Simon has no ability. If what he is doing, year after year, were easy, thousands would do it, because he seems to be making more money than any playwright in world history. He keeps his ears and eyes open, to a small superficial area of experience at least, and he knows how to phrase a crack. He is the cleverest man around Broadway. But his plays never hold up as well as those of George S. Kaufman, who was the cleverest man before him, because Kaufman—also essentially a sketch-writer and gag man—had sense enough to collaborate with others who could provide something like the body of a play.

Sam Levene has fine flavor and plays some of his bits the way Alan Arkin (who directed) used to play his old Jewish street vendor in a Second City sketch. Jack Albertson is much more of a performer than an actor, and although he has the ease of an old pro, he doesn't quite have Levene's richness and credibility. Arkin has used revue tactics throughout. The pauses, the "takes," the business—in and around the central sketch—are those of sketch-performing, not realism.

Kaspar and Other Plays

(February 28, 1970)

A fascinating and distinctive theatrical talent from abroad makes its American debut on paper. Peter Handke, an Austrian who was born in 1942, wrote his first play in 1966. Since then he has written six plays, short and long, two novels, a book of poems, and two collections of prose pieces. Now his full-length play *Kaspar* is published here with two short plays,* and they reveal that Handke has his own clear voice and vision.

His plays are difficult to describe: there are no stories and no characters in the usual sense. The lines (in translation) mesh like gears, and the cumulation is not only progressive in the usual way, it is also a tensile structure of contradictions. The *whole* is all.

The two short pieces are called *Sprechstücke,* which is translated as "speak-ins." The first, *Offending the Audience,* calls for four speakers who have no roles, only a good deal of material which they are asked to divide among themselves equally. They bid us welcome, then proceed to tell us what to expect in the piece and what not to expect; they anatomize patterns and formulas in theater-going and theater conventions, they anatomize the audience's delegation of responsibility to safe, aloof representatives, they tell us our tiny secrets so convincingly that they can command us to blink or to swallow, or

---

* By Farrar, Straus and Giroux.

not to blink or swallow, having broken down our resistance and privacy by being us. Then the speakers proceed to offend us, as a means of fiercest communication: excoriating us from every angle— political, sexual, social, ethical, hypochondriacal. One by one they cut off our escape hatches, our solace that the epithets don't apply to us; sooner or later some epithets come along that *do* apply to any one of us. After a crescendo of abuse, the speakers again quietly bid us welcome, the curtains close, and roaring applause is piped in through loudspeakers.

The power of the piece is in its calm, ruthless progression, its arrogance, and its humility. (The excoriation ends with the term "fellow humans.") The effect is like an acid bath to eat away the corrosions of cultural torpor, to reveal the mind patterns that produced them:

This piece is a prologue. It is not the prologue to another piece but the prologue to what you did, what you are doing, and what you will do. You are the topic. . . . It is the prologue to the plays and to the seriousness of your life.

The second *Sprechstück,* called *Self-Accusation,* is for two speakers, male and female, and is a kind of middle ground between the first piece, in which speakers deal with the audience, and the third, in which speakers deal with another figure on stage. Here the speakers' subject is themselves, an "I" composed of both of them, male and female, who proceeds from the sentence "I came into the world" through the acquisition of awareness, physical abilities, moral education and remission, habits, self-doubts, to the conclusion:

I am not what I was. I was not what I should have been. I did not become what I should have become. I did not keep what I should have kept.

I went to the theater. I heard this piece. I spoke this piece. I wrote this piece.

Kaspar, the major play in the book, is based on the idea—not the story—of Kaspar Hauser, whose life was also the subject of a once-famous novel by Jakob Wassermann. Kaspar was a boy of sixteen who suddenly appeared in the streets of Nuremberg one day in 1828, without a word of any language and with no name. After being taught language and acquiring a name, he said that his only recollection was of being in a dark hole all his life. He died five years later of a knife wound, possibly self-inflicted. There is no reference to the story in Handke's play, no historical setting; the idea is used only as a metaphor of delayed "birth."

Most of the play is printed in double columns: one column for Kaspar's actions and words, the second for the (simultaneous) words of the "prompters"—at least three speakers who are never seen and whose voices, says Handke, may be pre-recorded. Those voices relate to Kaspar as teacher, chorus, censor, mocker, torturer—creating a largeness in which he is invisibly contained. Kaspar arrives with only one sentence in his mouth, which he repeats frequently: "I want to be a person like somebody else was once." Through the course of sixty-five brief sections, the prompters educate him in speech and cognitions, deliver him from the womb of relative wordlessness into the world of words, and their consequences. He splits—under pressure—into several other Kaspars who move and gesticulate around him; and growing more and more eloquent, he bursts at last into a huge outburst about his new power-weakness. He ends—as the curtains jerk closed in five steps—with five statements of Othello's towering cry of disgust: "Goats and monkeys." There is also an intermission, during which Handke suggests that fragments of speeches by presidents and popes and by writers and poets at official functions should be piped over loudspeakers into the lobby and even out into the street. He supplies a possible text.

This last suggests Ionesco, but it is the only section that does suggest him: Handke does not generally work with a mosaic of banalities to depict horror. Artaud, too, might seem nearby because of the attacks on traditional theater and the air of torment that hangs over these works; but Handke renounces neither literature nor psychology, nor the culture that contains them: he is working *through* that culture as through a cavern or a tunnel. It is Beckett, I think, who has been strongly influential on Handke, but not *Waiting for Godot*—with which *Kaspar* has been compared abroad: rather two novels, *The Unnamable* and *How It Is*. In those two books Beckett moved from volubility to painful broken gasps; Handke reverses that order, but the theme is similar: there is no way to be conscious without being conscious of the agonies of consciousness.

Handke's dramatic technique seems to me less related to *Godot* than to *Play,* interwoven and polyphonic in verbal structure, rather than serially progressive. All three of the plays in Handke's book present marvelous opportunities for directors and actors who have eyes and ears and imagination and courage and who are fed up with the theater as is—even with most of the proposed improvements.

Michael Roloff has carefully translated what must have been difficult material—not only because of usual matters of nuance but because of necessary synchronizations and sound patterns. I cannot comment on the result specifically, not really knowing German; the English as such seems taut, nicely modeled, speakable. But a young friend of mine who made a translation of Handke's first piece three years ago, for study purposes, suggests that "speak-in" is a rather modish translation of *Sprechstück*, which literally means "speaking-piece"; and that *Offending the Audience* is not quite the sense of *Publikumsbeschimpfung*, which is harsher; *Beschimpfen* means to insult, to revile, to abuse.

There will be more to be said of Handke as these plays are produced and as more work of his is translated. Meanwhile the good news is that we have a new dramatist of genuine significance, who is very much a product of his age but who has found his own way to reach the bright burning point at which existence begins; to see how terrible and precious that point is; and who has the gift to put his vision in theatrical modes that cry out for performance. Caliban says to Prospero:

> You taught me language; and my profit on't
> Is, I know how to curse.

Handke seems to agree; but he also knows that language cannot be unlearned and that cursing is one way of clarifying self and being.

The Ride Across Lake Constance

(*February 5, 1972*)

Audience uproar at Lincoln Center. The press reported that preview audiences at this Peter Handke play hissed and booed and thumped their seats, and when Jules Irving, the artistic chief, made an appearance, he was forced into the lobby for a debate. The news cheered me up. Signs of life, in our town's largest anesthesia clinic!

I was even more cheered when I saw the play. It *is* disturbing and, for many, must be enraging. Not sexually: the sex content is very mild. Not politically or religiously: no overt mention of these matters. The rage doesn't even come from direct affront, as in Handke's earlier play *Offending the Audience*. It comes simply from his utter contravention of what an audience expects from a play.

Handke is Austrian, twenty-nine, a playwright, poet, and novelist, whose volume *Kaspar and Other Plays* marked for me the arrival here of an exceptional talent. These plays, and others, have had Off-Broadway production since then, none quite adequate.

The title of this new play comes from an old German tale about a man who rides across the frozen lake at night, finds out later how thin the ice was, and dies retroactively of fright. So it connotes a person who has been in great danger and doesn't know it until afterward— until *words* make the danger, and kill him.

It's a long one-act play, set in a living room. Each of the eight actors is listed, at the author's direction, as playing himself. (Thus: "Kathleen Doyle . . . Kathleen Doyle.") There is no story: a series of relations is established among people, then juggled, in brief sequences and fragments. Then it stops.

A cosmeticized middle-aged man (Stephen Elliott) is sleeping in a chair. A maid (Doyle) comes in, vacuum-cleans the whole room and plays a record, but he never stirs. He wakes when a younger man (Paul Hecht) enters, over whom he seems to have some domination. After a while another middle-aged man (Keene Curtis) comes in with two women in evening gowns (Salome Jens, Priscilla Pointer). Incidents, questions, objects are seized as means of conversation. (Hecht suddenly lifts a teapot; Elliott asks "What are you trying to say by that?") Little "acts" are performed. One woman is whipped, playfully; the other goes to sleep. Toward the end two girls (the Howell twins) come in, do a symmetrical tap-dance routine, then disappear. The maid returns with a crying baby, which she takes to each person; the baby grabs the women's breasts and the men's genitals. She takes the baby out. Curtis leans over Jens, and the lights fade.

The first impression is that we are back at the Cabaret Voltaire in the Zurich of 1916 and the Dada theater is on again. But it's quickly apparent that nihilism is not the point: something is being *got* at. Not the absurdism of Ionesco (though platitudes are used pointedly), not Pinter's embodiment of the unconscious, not lack of communication in any *Weltschmerz* sense. It's the spirit of Wittgenstein, I think, that touches this play, as it touched previous Handke plays and other postwar German writers—the relation of language and reality. David Pears writes of Wittgenstein:

. . . His aim was to understand the structure and limits of thought, and his method was to study the structure and limits of language. . . . He wanted to discover the exact location of the line dividing sense from nonsense. . . . The nature of language dictates both what you can and what you cannot do with it.

This is Handke's subject, I think. He is testing—with parodies and incongruities—the relation between what we present, in words and related actions, and what we contain: and how one affects the other.

Now, since he has chosen to do this in an art form, the act of testing is not enough. The question arises, and should arise, "Is the play any good?" The honest answer is, "How can we tell?" An exploratory playwright requires flexible criticism. The hecklers, and the people who left the night I was there, were unwilling to examine the standards by which they were judging the play; but assuming that Handke is neither a fool nor a charlatan—and he is very certainly neither, in my view—then we serve ourselves by a willingness to respond.

He's neither fool nor charlatan because he quickly shows a power of selection, a sense that the pranks and nonsense arise from a mind that encompasses a good deal more than prankishness, that the foolishness has a consistency of texture and a purpose, that the abrasion of everything we expect in a play is not only deliberate (any idiot can be deliberately anarchic) but has an esthetic rationale. Handke is showing us that the way we expect plays to operate is tied to our concept of the reliability of language: to question the latter means questioning the former.

All this is descriptive. What of effect? In vitality, the play came and went for me like a radio fading in and out: I was sometimes amused, sometimes amusingly disturbed, sometimes merely waiting for the reversals and discrepancies to get disturbing again. On the way in, the audience passed a sign saying that the play had no intermission and would run an hour and forty minutes. So, before it began, I had in mind a time space for the play to fill. This proved to be a controlling factor; it helped me through the sags by providing a shape that the play otherwise wouldn't have. I don't know any intrinsic reason why Handke's game couldn't have been played for an hour less or more. For me, it was played by the clock rather than by content—more like football, say, than baseball.

The players must be called just that: acting in any traditional sense or in any Grotowskian "matrix" sense does not apply. These people seemed to me to supply the materials they were asked for. Carl Weber, the director, articulated the play (translated by Michael Roloff) with some ingenuity of phrase, physical and verbal. I don't know why the maid was painted like a ballet doll and the others were realistic, but on the other hand I don't know why not.

Sags and all, I was glad of the evening. Which is to say, I think I understood what Handke was after, most of the time I enjoyed the game he was playing with me, and I liked exploring with him the mystery that, of course, he's not able to fathom.

Landscape/Silence

(April 25, 1970)

Harold Pinter's new short plays reveal a new Pinter. He doesn't produce much, but usually a new Pinter work means some sort of development. Each of his successive long plays—*The Birthday Party, The Caretaker, The Homecoming*—has shown, within the realm of Pinter's temperament, differences in control and interest. These two new short pieces are Pinter's first works of gentleness.

Neither play has a story, not even a logically eccentric one like *The Homecoming*. It's possible, retrospectively, to put together something of a story for each, but it has to be done merely as outline, not explanation. Otherwise the implication is that Pinter thought up a plot, then jigsawed it into a puzzle and scattered the bits out of sequence for us to rearrange. This approach brutalizes two sensitive plays. In essence they are not coded stories, they are evocations from certain lives that have been lived in certain juxtapositions, and the evocations include silence. The plays are not concerned with alienation or difficulty of communication, two facile Pinter "labels" that have already been trotted out by people who finally got a pigeonhole carpentered for Pinter and keep trying to shove this changing man back into it. The silences in these plays are between people who *have* communicated.

Silence has three characters, two men and a woman who sit on widely spaced chairs. (The woman approaches one man at one point.) They are presumably older people (no makeups are worn). One man lives quietly in the country with animals, the other man lives surlily in a noisy rented room in town. Both of them focus on the woman as an object of affection—as woman, as girl, even as child—and time flows back and forth for all of them as carelessly as light flickers. The two men address the woman only occasionally but each other never. Pinter lifts out segments of three lives as they may have brushed and entwined now and then, and from them draws quintessences of moments and moods, not narrative. At the Forum Theater in New York the evening begins with *Silence,* which is repeated in its entirety after *Landscape,* and this gives the evening a double design since *Silence* is itself cyclical in shape.

With the very first line of *Silence* a different language comes from Pinter. The quiet man begins:

I walk with my girl who wears a grey blouse when she walks and grey shoes and walks with me readily wearing her clothes considered for me. Her grey clothes.

Later the woman remembers a younger day in the country:

I turn. I turn. I wheel. I glide. I wheel. In stunning light. The horizon moves from the sun. I am crushed by the light.

Pinter has always *placed* words exactly: for verisimilitude, for rhythm, for silhouettes of banality that enclose horror or, very often, humor. Now his language is evolving new lyric qualities, poignant, still, compassionate. Most of his characters have been on their own, fighting for prerogatives of self against others, fighting even for their desires against the persons desired. In this new play there are acknowledged weaknesses and dependencies.

It is further apparent in *Landscape.* In the kitchen of a large country house sit two characters, presumably man and wife, presumably a "pair" in service there. He addresses her throughout, she never addresses him and never seems to hear him; her utterances are all memories. Neither person rises during the play. Again it is possible to reconstruct something of a "story," more than in the other play. We can infer that she has had some mental trouble, that it had something to do with a confession of unfaithfulness by him, that her devotion to him—exemplified by a day on a beach when they made love to have a child—is where she still resides; that his devotion to her, suggestive of contrition, consists of telling her details of his daily doings on the farm and in the pub. He speaks in rather more expected Pinter terms, in detail made large, like Oldenburg's sculpture—all excellently molded. The play's effect is of a protector caring for an injured person whom he injured, but without anguish. She and he take their lives as they have happened, and the last line is hers, spoken to the man no longer present, the man on the beach that day: "Oh my true love I said."

The Forum is the small "experimental" theater underneath the large Vivian Beaumont at Lincoln Center, where I have gone frequently in the past few years only to be disappointed frequently. Not so with these Pinter plays: they are small, delicate additions to our drama. The Forum production itself is another matter. The settings and lighting do little, which would not matter if the performances did more. (I read the plays after seeing them and now have a better idea of what they might mean in performance.) Peter Gill, a young English director, has a sense of phrase and seems to have worked with his actors on the essential imaginative foundation to "base" their lines, to govern their tempos and pauses. But these plays depend greatly on the very flavor of the performers, and these casts are indifferent. James Patterson, as the unquiet man in *Silence,* has the greatest chance for flamboyance and can make something of it; but his part is easier than the others. Barbara Tarbuck, the woman in *Silence,* is blandly adequate. Robert Symonds, both the quiet man in *Silence* and the "husband" in *Landscape,* is one of the Lincoln Center reliables. Here again he is competent and intelligent, but he is insufficiently rich. The two roles together emphasize how much Symonds relies on that rustic dryness which was good in Kit Carson (*The Time of Your Life*) but is getting to be something of a prop for him.

The chief disappointment is Mildred Natwick as the "injured" woman in *Landscape.* But then Natwick's career is, sad to say, a disappointment. She began some thirty-five years ago as one of the most original and creative young actresses of her generation and has since given good performances (Madame Arcati in *Blithe Spirit,* for instance). But in general she has not developed and, in fact, has diminished. Her recent performance in the New York production of *Our Town* was like an entry in the Helen Hayes Sweepstakes for Audience Love. Here she is straining for color, but the depths that might provide it are not there.

Pinter, on the other hand, does develop. These new plays are not works of major scope and force, like *The Caretaker* and *The Homecoming*, but they are lovely, and they certify that he continues to inquire his way through experience of the world and of imagination. *Silence,* in particular, sounds haunting chords, made of three lives combined like notes of music. "Elected Silence, sing to me," said Hopkins in one of his best poems. Pinter has elected a rather different silence, but it sings to him.*

Boesman and Lena

(July 25, 1970)

A ragged colored man with a huge bundle on his back appears on top of a rocky knoll and throws a big hunk of galvanized tin down to the ground. That is the first sound and, as it turns out, the perfect opening note. The man comes down, followed by a little brown woman, also burdened. They are carrying all their possessions. Here, on the mud flat before us, they build a small shack, cook a meal, and bare their lives. An old black man comes out of the dark to their fire, and dies beside it. The pair take up their burdens again and move on, continuing their lives. That is the whole play—the whole beautiful, shaking, unforgettable play.

Boesman and Lena is the third work by the South African dramatist Athol Fugard to be produced in this country: the previous ones were *The Blood Knot* (1964) and *Hello and Goodbye* (1969). Fugard is white and, as writer and director, has devoted himself to theater with "non-Europeans" in his country. Two and a half weeks before this latest play opened in New York his government refused him a passport to come here for the production. This action caused an outcry in the press, including a *New York Times* editorial, and I mention it at once because, though the refusal was characteristically

* See p. 335.

hateful of that government and the outcry deserved, it tends to distort the quality of *Boesman and Lena*. This is not a protest play, though the pain of race hatred flames through it; it becomes, quickly and surely, a drama of all human beings in their differing captivities, suffering from and inflicting hate. Boesman and Lena are brown, the old Kaffir man is black, and the specifics of their wretched lives are caused by the history and policies of their country; but Fugard makes very clear that, within the circumference of their lives, they represent the larger world. He is not saying—not by the wildest stretch of self-coddling imagination—that racial injustices do not signify; he is saying that those injustices are an extremity of the cruelty in all men. The reason that his play achieves towering height—as in the main it does—is because it *includes* the agony of *apartheid* and shows that *apartheid* is not devil-inflicted but man-made, and that Boesman is a man too.

Fugard works with small means: his previous plays had two characters each, this one has three. The influence of Eugene O'Neill has always seemed strong in him, particularly in *Hello and Goodbye,* which dealt with some rather egregious symbols of a (white) family's doom. O'Neill's influence seems strong again here—but here it is the later, greater O'Neill, not the patent symbolist. What is this play but another long day's journey into a very dark night? And the quintessential dynamics is like that in late O'Neill: drama not by the encounter of obstacle but by the stripping naked of lives. This "moment" of two hours is an ontogeny that recounts our phylogeny: because Fugard has seen that by telling crystalline truth about these wretches, with no clutter of theatrical device, he could not possibly leave us out. He has embraced these people so fiercely and lovingly that in their rags and drunkenness and cunning and persistence they move through a small epic of contemporary man. I can think of no naturalistic play since *The Lower Depths* that—far from using its subject for clinical study—so completely converts almost protozoan characters into vicars for us all.

And this is the only production I can recall in which the ground is important. The Circle in the Square is a theater-in-the-round, so all the spectators can see the floor; in addition to the rocky outcropping at one end, Karl Eigsti's setting provides a ground, the dry, cracked mud flat of the river Swartkaps. On this mud, out of which we all come, Boesman and Lena make their camp. They were evicted from their last shack that morning by the white man's bulldozer. They have been tramping the road so long together that they have had a number of stillborn babies (one child lived six months) and reckon their lives in terms of the towns they have passed through.

Their campfire attracts an old black man out there on the mud flats. Lena welcomes him, but Boesman's first word to him is "Nigger"! When Lena says that things are hard for "us brown people," Boesman says, "He's not brown people, he's black people." Lena replies, "They've got feelings, too."

They've got feelings, too. This act of pity—from a homeless brown woman who happens to have some white blood toward a Kaffir who is all black—alters the whole scale of the play.

The old man speaks a language they cannot understand and speaks little of it, but he learns Lena's name. He sits in his ragged greatcoat, still, unsurprisable, a seer living in his fate; and Lena gives Boesman her bottle of wine, out of their store of two bottles, to persuade him to let the old man stay. In the course of the long night—the quarrels, songs, near-splitups of the two—the old man sits quiet; and finally Lena, huddled with him under a blanket by the fire tells Boesman that the old man is dead. Just died, that's all. Boesman usually takes out his fury on Lena; now he beats the dead old man for the nuisance he has caused. They must move on before his death is discovered. They scrape together their pots and blankets, and leave—leaving the old man even quieter now in the mud.

In this frame we get a brute-strong, childish, frightened, frustrated, angry man; a beaten, wise, loving, courageous woman. The play's epic quality derives from the wide and simple arch of its compass: shelter, food, fire, children, quarrels, dependence, ego needs, death, endless pilgrimage. The rubbish that this pair gather and carry is the detritus of experience. It has its factual meaning—"We wear the white man's rubbish," says Boesman, "we eat it, we live in it"—and it also tells us that *they* are the white man's rubbish, trapped in the excremental vision of dark skins that psychologists have lately suggested is the root of prejudice. All true, but, in this drama, not limited: Fugard has struck so deep that his epic moves past indictment of oppressors to anguish for us all.

The language sometimes verges on the literary. For instance, I wish the word "freedom" had never been used—the concept was implicit —but there is a section in the middle that works ironies on "freedom." Most of the dialogue, however, belongs to Boesman and Lena, rarefied only enough to make them characters instead of case histories. "It's a long story if you've lived it," says Lena of her life.

This play comes before us sublimely innocent of the news that this kind of theater is supposed to be dying, as many (including me) have said with reason enough. *Boesman and Lena* is the kind of play that "nobody" writes any more, representational, sequential, mimetic; but it is rooted in such a felt need, its symbolism is so thoroughly assimilated, its tragic view so whole-souled, that it again proves a sometimes forgotten truth: no art form is dead so long as it fits the purpose of a committed and talented artist. There are at least two ways in the theater to reach the elemental: by going forward from the moribund present or by going back from it. In formal terms, Fugard has done the latter.

As Boesman, James Earl Jones gives a good, forceful performance with fissures in it. When he first entered, I thought he was the other actor, so well had this big man imagined himself small and tired. Soon, however, there were some facial and physical grimaces in the part, and occasionally the accents of Jones can be heard in Boesman's speech. As the old man, an African actor named Zakes Mokae is like an ancient black angel. But the glory of the production is Ruby Dee's performance of Lena.

Four summers ago, in the middle of a converted baseball field in Ypsilanti, Michigan, I saw Dee as Cassandra in a production of *The Oresteia,* her tiny form filling that huge space, prophesying death in the king's house and a future for herself.* Lena fulfills that latter prophecy. When Dee enters, her eyes have taken command of her being, have taken it somewhere else. Her body can do anything she asks of it, and she asks a great deal, but it is her voice that she has now developed to heroic range, from simper to demonic fury. With an imagination that conceives largely, with completely reliable techniques, with fire and pity and powerful spirit, this little woman becomes a giant, making this mud creature into a protean figure. It is the best performance I have seen in the American theater since Judith Anderson's Medea.

John Berry has directed with passion and skill. The costumes by Margie Goldsmith and the lighting by David F. Segal are perfect. To them, to all involved in this production, thanks and praise. To Athol

* See p. 103.

Fugard, off there in the South Africa that is at once his prison and his reason for artistic being, greetings, honor, love.

Sizwe Banzi Is Dead / The Island

(December 21, 1974)

Athol Fugard's *Boesman and Lena*, which was presented in New York four years ago, is one of the best new plays I have seen in my life. I saw the play again in London as directed by Fugard himself. (Here it had been John Berry.) Then Fugard spent an afternoon showing me color slides of a production he had devised back home in South Africa with a few actors—white, like himself—and no predetermined script. They had all collaborated on working out a play based on a tragic event in their country's racial agony.

Since then Fugard has devised two more plays with South African actors—black this time, two men, who are the only members of the company. John Kani and Winston Ntshona joined Fugard in 1972 and with him worked out *Sizwe Banzi Is Dead* and *The Island,* which were first presented in Cape Town, then brought to London, were afterward toured around Britain and Ireland and back to London, then were brought to the Long Wharf in New Haven and thence to an Off-Broadway theater which is right in the Broadway area.

Both plays, now alternating in repertory, are done with minimal scenery—some bits of furniture, a few props, some modulated lighting. Apparently, and effectively, a parallel is intended between the productions themselves and the austerity of their subject. The two plays have now presumably been articulated to the full but without in the least becoming works of rote, as conventional plays may do after long runs. Except for a brief improvised section at the beginning of *Sizwe Banzi,* the plays are fixed now; but the pitch of intensity in them—partly due to the fact, I'm sure, that Fugard travels with them—is extraordinary.

Both plays are drawn from the innermost feelings of three gifted and committed men. So it's something more than sad to report that, for me, both plays are disappointing. *Sizwe Banzi* is about a black man who is constrained by the passbook laws to leave Port Elizabeth, where he might make a living, and return to his native town, where he will not. He and a clever friend find a valid passbook on a dead man, and switch photos. Sizwe Banzi is thus able to remain, send for his wife and children, and support them. The price he pays is his identity: he must become Robert Zwelinsima, as per the dead man's book.

Now this might make a good ironic short play of thirty minutes or so. But it begins with a very long monologue, about two fifths of the play, by the Port Elizabeth photographer who eventually takes a picture of the "new" man. This photographer has been a Ford employee (as has John Kani, who plays him), and he rambles on about his experiences at the white man's factory, his struggle to become a photographer, and his pleasure in doing pictures of black families. Buried in this ramble are a few glints of relevance, but mostly it seems a consciously theatrical attempt to break down formal realistic theater by addressing the audience and bringing members of it up on stage briefly—devices by now so familiar that their triteness works against the freshness that is aimed at. And Kani's deliberately over-smiling presentation hovers between parody of actor-salesmanship and the thing itself.

The convenience of the dead man, in Sizwe's path just when he needs a passbook, is another theater contrivance that distracts us from the truth of the subject. And, in a quite different way, so does the harassed Sizwe's long speech in which he declares that he is a man like any other man, stripping off his clothes as he tells us and holding up his penis to prove it. The starkness seems as strained as the contrivance of the dead man, just another device.

The Island is Robben Island, a penal colony off Cape Town. The two men are cellmates. The play begins with a long pantomime passage of excruciatingly hard labor to which the convicts are condemned, followed by a scene of close physicality in their cell, in which they tend each other's aches and ailments—both scenes reminiscent of the work that the Open Theater has done under Joseph Chaikin, fortified here by grim fact and the actors' commitment to proclaiming it. (That may not be artistically "fair," but it happens.) Ntshona is in for life; Kani, whose sentence is much less, is told in the course of the play that his sentence has been reduced to only three months more.

The two men are going to do a two-character version of *Antigone* at the prison "concert." I found this incredible. I don't maintain—

how could I?—that two such black prisoners would never have heard of the play or would never have wanted to do it; but as presented, it was incredible, a touch of extrinsically applied analogy. Their preparations for the play—Kani trying to teach the slower-witted friend the scenario, the horseplay with fake bosom and straw wig—were, to speak gently, attenuated.

Yet, paradoxically, Kani and Ntshona do their imaginative best once they get into the *Antigone* scene, the former swollen with pride of place as Creon, the latter managing dignity at last in the silly wig and padding.

But after both evenings I was left with a few memorable moments and, as noted, much disappointment. The chief trouble is simultaneously the chief emotional asset: the conditions out of which these plays grow. The facts of South African *apartheid* are as well known, in essence, as they are ever going to be to those who are interested in knowing them; and these plays do little more than elaborate those facts without deepening our insight into them. And even those facts are interfered with by the staginess, old and avant-garde, described above. Even more disappointing, because more centrally relevant to the work of making plays out of this material in the first place, is that they illuminate so little imaginatively. One of the rare examples in both plays of what I had expected is a speech of Ntshona's in *The Island,* in which he spills his resentment at the fact that his friend will be released in three months while he will remain in this cell forever— a speech that ends with the line "You stink of freedom." With that line I knew more about being a prisoner than I had known before I came to the theater, and knew it through the theater's means.

The two actors are in themselves more significant than the plays they are in. As for Fugard, I've known no one in my lifetime who has worked with greater passion in the theater, but apparently his very passion can misguide him. I presume to think it has done so here. He is a director of strengths, but he is a writer of much greater strengths. He has opted in these past few years to work with actors in "devising" plays: he had his reasons—passionate, I'm sure—for doing this, but the result is wasteful of his best talents. This devising of plays with actors is a function of directors who cannot write original work —sometimes greatly gifted ones like Andrei Serban. But I hope Fugard, a writer, will write. In these plays devised with actors he has slipped into theatricalisms like none I can recall in his other work.

These new works, compared with *Boesman and Lena,* are somewhat superficial because they are artistically insecure and essentially didactic, and are thus only about the troubles of South African blacks.

I'm aware of the risks in that "only," but I stand by it, particularly after rereading *Boesman,* which has just been published here in a volume of Fugard's work called *Three Port Elizabeth Plays* (Viking). The other two plays in the book, *The Blood Knot* and *Hello and Goodbye,* are works of erratic power. *Boesman* is, if I may quote myself, "a small epic of contemporary man."

MacGowran in *Beckett*

(December 12, 1970)

In Paris last April the Irish actor Jack MacGowran presented a one-man show of readings from Samuel Beckett. MacGowran arranged the text, Beckett advised and approved. In the weekly *Le Monde* of July 8 the philosopher and critic E. M. Cioran praised the show highly. (With a writer's bias! "Even if [MacGowran] had been the author he could not have shown greater conviction or fervor.") Now MacGowran is presenting his Beckett production in New York, and if it has some of the limitations of one-man-showmanship, it is a sad, funny, beautiful evening.

The setting, by Ming Cho Lee, is excellent: mottled gray-brown hangings that curve in at the bottom to suggest the womb of an immense, petrified monster; and one small rock. The lights come up on MacGowran, his gray hair close-cut, wearing a long ragged great-coat held together by pins, no socks, scuffed black shoes. He looks like an ancient fetus dressed for a long-delayed birth. (If you saw Lester's film *How I Won the War,* you'll remember MacGowran as the soldier-turned-clown.) He stands there a moment, then words grumble out of him, resonant, wry, tinged with Dublin, and the Beckett world begins.

The evening consists of selections from the novels and poems and plays, arranged in suites and sequences. It is less a *tour de force* than a tour of climate and mind. Between selections MacGowran shuffles to a different place (rarely sitting on that rock), muttering inaudibly before he decides to let us hear once again what he is saying. He begins with the opening of *Malone Dies* and ends with the last lines of *The Unnamable,* and the gist of the evening is indeed, as Cioran says, an examination of the wisdom of having been born, "when one reflects on the advantages of never having existed, on the miracle of virtuality uncontaminated by action." This nearly Buddhist principle, as Cioran calls it ("There can be no liberation without meditation on the futility of birth"), hangs over the stage in invisible, inescapable letters; but at times through the just-long-enough evening there are touches of quite conscious self-parody, because both Beckett and MacGowran know that there is only so much nothingness that the human mind can face in two hours—two hours of the theater, at any rate. During that time one of the many things that occurred to me is that three of the greatest apocalyptists of the century have been Irish—Yeats and Joyce and Beckett—and none of them has been quite able to keep a straight face about it. Tenderness and lyricism and, above all, ridiculousness keep breaking in.

Often I rocked, really rocked, with laughter at the Beckett one-man show of the One Man: the account of the sixteen stones (from *Molloy*) which bitingly satirizes scientific method; the line (from where?) "Ideas are *so* alike when you get to know them"; or the passage (from *Molloy*) in which the narrator tells how he communicated with his blind, deaf old mother by knocking on her skull. "One knock meant yes, two no, three I don't know, four money, five goodbye."

And there is the exquisite: the love memory from *Krapp's Last Tape;* the lines from *Cascando:*

> saying again
> if you do not teach me I shall not learn
> saying again there is a last
> even of last times

In short, there is everything—but everything seen from the Beckettian view. And let's remember two points about this wonderful language. First, almost all of it was first written in French and then in English by the same man. Second, Beckett shares with Shaw and Joyce the Irish inability to write a line that cannot be spoken well, that cannot be *improved* by being spoken aloud.

One-man shows come in two kinds: the recital of separate selections, such as the shows that Ruth Draper and Cornelia Otis Skinner used to give, where it is easy to like or dislike one item or another; and the "woven" show, such as Roy Dotrice playing John Aubrey in *Brief Lives* or MacGowran here, which has to be seen more or less as an organic work. There are occasional lags of interest and tension in this Beckett evening, simply because the material was not written for the organic purpose to which it's being put, but if the lags were cut out, the evening would be too short, and there seems little likelihood that, if they were replaced, the inherent structural contradiction would be overcome. We simply have to take the show as what it is for the good that it gives us.

MacGowran himself is always legitimate, which I mean as a compliment to the authenticity of his impulse and method and understanding, but never overwhelming. Now I'd like to see him in *Waiting for Godot* or *Endgame* so that the touch of stunt would be absent and so that he could concentrate on the wholeness of a role instead of the wholeness of the author.

He is being presented on one of the four stages of the Public Theater, whose producer, Joseph Papp, whatever his defects, is certainly not short on energy and enterprise.

Not I

(December 16, 1972)

Samuel Beckett's new play runs about fifteen minutes and is for two "characters": Mouth and Auditor. As produced by Alan Schneider in its world premiere, the setting is an arena of large, almost total blackness. A small bright beam of light picks out the very red mouth of a woman at one side; on the other side a dim beam picks out a grotesquely tall, hooded and draped dark figure. A mouth and a pillar of dark presence, both in a black cosmos; that is all. The mouth begins to speak before we see it, speaks without pause while the light is on it, and continues to speak as the light leaves.

That's really what the play is about, the images that are described above. Much has been said of Beckett's distillation of language and action until his writing is, figuratively, just this side of nonexistence.

Little is said of the gift with which his plays begin: his ability to *see theatrically*. I'm not about to legislate on the creative sequence, in his mind, of philosophy or language or dramatic imagery; I doubt that Beckett himself could decide. But I'm positive that the catalyst in the process is his power to conceive of images in a theater that will make the intangible visible.

The words that pour in torment from the woman's mouth are not nonsense, although the sequence of sentences is disjointed often. On first hearing, without a script for reference, the talk seems to be concerned with an Irishwoman, who thinks she is "sixty—no, seventy," who has been involved in some sort of legal trial, and who keeps talking on and on—in a self-convolution—against the wishes of her own mouth, who wishes "she" would be quiet. The tone of voice is pure agony. From time to time the high, hooded figure across the arena raises his hands and drops them in helpless sympathy.

From the verbal torrent, though perfectly lucid phrase by phrase, comes not content but pattern—of rhythm and repetition, like themes in music. These rhythms and returns seem to be the purpose of the long utterance. Presumably, if he had thought the audience could be kept from giggling, Beckett would have used *vocalise* such as singers use, mere sounds on certain notes and in certain rhythms.

The tormented tone, the mysterious picture, these are what the play is "about," I think. My own further view, not provable as Beckett's intent but still one for which I'm grateful to him, is that the blackness is the inside of the mind, the voice is that of "she" herself, which "she" cannot stop, and the hooded figure is a testament of failed control. A Freudian might call it a portrait of a wounded id and an impotent ego.

"Portrait" is the apt synesthetic term here. This play is just long enough temporally to make it register spatially. The final effect, to which the words themselves contribute, is of abstract painting: a band of bright red-and-yellow (the mouth and chin, which seem to move in a horizontal sweep, although they are fixed, of course) and a vertical band of grayish black (the hooded figure), both laid across the ground of depthless black. Rothko and Newman are the names that come first to mind. For all I know, Beckett may never have heard of either, but that surely is irrelevant. The worlds he inhabits include theirs. Out of it all he has fashioned a brief, sharp, visible cry of loss.

Jessica Tandy, unseen except for her mouth, gushes the words very well with a sustained pitch of anguish and clear phrasing.

Home

(*December 12, 1970*)

David Storey is probably best known in this country as the author of both the novel and the screenplay of *This Sporting Life* (1963), the film directed by Lindsay Anderson. Storey's play *Home,* also directed by Anderson, inevitably suggests Beckett and Pinter and suffers very badly in the comparison. It deals, mainly, with four people in late middle age who are staying in what seems to be a resort hotel but turns out to be a mental home. Their inanities are meant to delineate the inanities of existence, and there are hints toward the end that the mental institution represents England and that these people represent its attrition.

For this purpose, the mental hospital is a much less vivid metaphor than the music hall in John Osborne's *The Entertainer.* Besides, the madman or madhouse as a comment on the sane world is an old device (Pirandello, Weiss, Witkiewicz, among others). Storey's version simply shears away plot or development and has pointlessness as its point. It is not enough. This play exists for no reason except to make clear that it is not about what it seems to be about.

Put Beckett aside as too cruel a comparison, and Storey shrivels next to Pinter. Much of *Home* sounds like a revue-sketch parody of Pinter—the hemstitching of banalities. But, like those revue sketches, what it omits is the other five sixths of the Pinter iceberg, the submerged text of ambiguity or cosmic hilarity or horror of which the clichés are only the glint. There is nothing to Storey's people besides what they say, and the only substantive differentiation among them is that the two men are middle-class and bland, the two women are lower-class and gamy.

This production is from the Royal Court Theater in London and is fine. John Gielgud and Ralph Richardson play the dodderers; both give vocal performances of extraordinary delicacy, both understand the interplay of eyes in a play liberally laced with silences. The two women are Mona Washbourne (whom we've seen in such films as *Billy Liar* and *The Bed-Sitting Room*) and Dandy Nichols (*The Birthday Party*), and both are, as usual, flawless. Graham Weston is adequate as a moronic young ex-wrestler.

But the most interesting aspect of the production for me is Lindsay Anderson's direction. Among my most uncomfortable reviewing moments have been the adverse comments I had to make on his two feature films, *This Sporting Life* and *If . . .* , because I've been very aware of the unusual directing talent even when these films go structurally awry. Every moment of *If . . .* , for instance, is beautifully made; I just wish that some of the moments weren't there. Still I can't think of another film director in British history who is his superior in skill and style.

I've longed to see his work in the theater, where he has spent more of his time and where the shape of his projects is defined—or more largely defined—by an author other than himself. My hunch has, in this instance, proved out. Where the text is more or less a given and where Anderson's job is primarily that of interpreter, he is excellent. Storey's play is fairly vacuous, but Anderson has seen clearly how it needed to be done, has *heard* it. And he has understood that showpieces for today's virtuoso actors are written not like *Cyrano* or *Virginius* but in prosy prose, and he has helped Richardson and Gielgud to an actors' holiday. Now I'm greedy to see Anderson's work on a better play.*

Subject to Fits

(*March 6, 1971*)

Robert Montgomery, the author of *Subject to Fits,* and A. J. Antoon, the director, were in courses of mine last year at the Yale Drama School. I mention this to declare my interests, which are warm, not to claim them as students in any substantive way, which I wish I *could* do because of the quality of this production. With a scene design by Leo Yoshimura (like Montgomery, still at Yale), *Subject to Fits* marks the professional debuts of three potentially significant talents.

* For quite different Storey plays, see p. 329.

Montgomery began with Dostoevsky's *The Idiot,* but, as his program note makes clear, his play is not a dramatization, it's a "response" to the novel—"smacking of *The Idiot,* dreaming of *The Idiot,* but mostly taking off from where *The Idiot* drove it." That statement itself, attesting a life born of essence and dream and compulsion, highlights the best elements in the play, its fantasy and flickering fires. I suppose that, in a highly synoptic manner, the play conveys the novel's story, but the dialogue (there are exactly three lines from the book in the play), the sequence, the emphases and distortions, the occasional songs and incidental music—which Montgomery wrote himself—all summarize what the novel did to him.

The first thing we see is a quick flash of Prince Myshkin sitting cross-legged on a platform. He smiles, brays like a donkey, and the play begins. With a cast of nine, Montgomery then gives us his crazy-mirror vision of the epileptic prince who has "seen an execution," who returns from abroad to Russia and, in its society, dares to be good, who has sentenced himself to Christianity. Because of his epilepsy, he lives always on the edge of blinding moments of serenity, which are a sign that he is about to plunge into fits of animalistic groveling. His disease—an epitome of the range of human possibility—helps create values in him that embarrass, anger, fascinate, humiliate others. The play ends with Myshkin back on the platform, cross-legged again, this time seated inside a glass cube.

Montgomery's purpose is to put Dostoevsky's theme through the mind of a young Christian today, to trace the question of possible good, expressing through the texture of the play, through the music, through the *fact* of the songs and the distortions, the modernity of his inquiry. Near the end comes the line: "It's really what we don't know that gives us a perfect reason to go on living." In its whirling-prism way, the play moves toward the consolations of that mystery.

Can it be understood by those who haven't read *The Idiot?* My first response is, What if it can't? Why can't there be a play once in a while for people who *have* read books like *The Idiot?* But I think that any viewer can understand the play's inner consistencies and tensions and will feel—possibly from the mere knowledge of its origin—some of the novel's resonance. (As with the opening donkey bray, for example, which is rooted in the book but not literally explained here.)

In its nature the play is exploratory, not steadily cumulative. Its big moments—such as the burning of the money, Ippolit's bungled suicide, Rogozhin and Myshkin over Natasha's body—are attempts at epiphany, not dramatic climax. The play examines states of being that are in contrast but not in theatrical conflict. This is a difficult mode to sustain in the theater, once all the combinations and harmonics have been sounded, and it's not fully sustained here. One mechanical matter that hurts the play is the intermission; to have the audience go out and chat and come back and then resume is more of a burden than this mood structure can easily bear. And with the latter portions condensed, the play would run ahead of our familiarity with its method. The chess and card games with Aglaya, for instance, add little. I felt some strain to keep the play off the ground between the beginning of the second act and Natasha's murder. If, unimpeded by a break, the play ran a direct hour and a half, it would have no chance to sag or to invite comparison with traditional plays; and it would sustain to the end the feeling of the first half—that this is possibly not going to be a play at all, that we are sitting before a pit in which imagination is blazing.

A. J. Antoon's direction shows lovely, strong gifts for using the stage (and is aided by Ian Calderon's fine lighting). But there's something more, something primary. The French Catholic film director Robert Bresson triumphs, in his best work, because we feel that he has infused his actors with a spiritual state. Bresson spent every Sunday for a year talking with the leading actor in *Diary of a Country Priest* before they began work. Antoon had no year, but it's this sense of communicated spirit that I got from his cast, and the sense that he has a spirit to communicate. The actors are mostly adequate, but he has lifted them—particularly Andy Robinson, the Myshkin—into otherness, into largeness.

Leo Yoshimura's setting could hardly be more simple or more helpful. A huge, fantastic, dim portrait of a haunted face hangs on the back wall. Before it there is a small arrangement of platforms and steps, with rods sticking up at the angles. The rods apportion space for us vertically, the platforms fragment horizontal space just sufficiently to provide "places" and enrichment. I've rarely seen so restrained an effort that resulted in a set begging to be *acted* on, which is one attribute of good design.

All Over

(*April 17, 1971*)

We're still expected to take Edward Albee seriously. Broadway has one comedy writer, Neil Simon, and one serious writer. Now that Williams seems withered and Miller seems all munched out, Albee is the high-art jewel of the Big Time. If we had a healthy and fruitful theater, Albee might be tolerable as one among many, a formerly vital, now weakening mediocrity. As it is, the news that Albee has written a play makes Broadway throb, makes the Ph.D. candidates slaver, and makes the general audience—or what's left of it—gather round like the crowd outside a palace waiting for word that a son has been born to keep the royal line alive.

But ever since *Who's Afraid of Virginia Woolf?*—Albee's last good play—all we've been getting from the royal bedchamber are abortions: two plays and three adaptations that are all varyingly bad and two one-act plays that are Absurdist imitations. In fact, those two imitations, *Box* and *Mao,* were the best of this poor lot because at least they showed that Albee was listening to something besides his own purr.

With his new play, *All Over,* the purr begins again with the very first lines, the feeling that the author thinks he's very high-toned indeed. Some people are sitting in the huge bedroom of a dying man: his wife and his two (grown) children, his mistress, his best friend, a doctor and nurse. The wife asks, "Is he dead?" and his mistress says that the man always objected to the use of the verb "to be" with the word "dead" because he felt it a contradiction, that the question should really be "Has he died?" At once we are in the presence of a playwright who wants us to know that he is not one of your run-of-the-mill theater dumbbells.

Throughout the play Albee obtrudes this pygmy-mandarin style. When the daughter interrupts the mother, the latter says, "Do not deflect me." Later the daughter, who is disliked, says, *"Non grata* has its compensations." And Albee may be the only dramatist now writing who uses "for" as a conjunction. "We cannot avoid them, for we are no longer private." That's class, folks.

But this classy tone isn't even consistent. There are gags. The nurse says of death, "It gets us where we live." In a quarrel the daughter says, "Fuck yourself," to the mistress. The mistress says musingly, "I've often wondered just how one does that." (Whenever a rude word is used, it's couched in genteel archness.)

I've dwelt first on the language because it's a screen between us and the play. What lies behind the screen? An allegory, about dying and life. At one point Albee gives us oblique advice not to take his play as allegory, but this is just kittenish. No one has a name in this play: the program lists them as The Wife, The Daughter, etc., and no one is ever addressed by name. The setting is heavily symbolic. (Designed by Rouben Ter-Arutunian in the mode of a smart jeweler's shopwindow.) Two huge cubes of black velour connected with chromium rods, and in the space between them, the deathbed, hidden by a hospital screen. No cyclorama or backing; these units are set against the visible bare walls of the theater. (The absence of backing makes for very bad acoustics in the barny Martin Beck. The actors have either to strain or be inaudible; all of them are both at different times.)

Allegory is a risky form because it directs our attention so fiercely to content. Other forms can thrive on style, and Albee has sometimes attempted them, but allegory implies that the author had something so large to say that only by abstraction could he handle the magnitude of his message. Yet all that really happens in *All Over* is the exact opposite of allegorical intent: we learn specific details of the characters' backgrounds and relationships. They might as well have been called Ethel and Fred and Cora, the setting might as well have been realistic to the last tack. We learn that the wife has been married fifty years, that she dislikes her thirtyish son and daughter, that she had a brief affair with the friend; that he's a lawyer whose wife is in a mental hospital; that the mistress is noble—mistresses are always noble if they're present at deathbeds; that the old nurse had an affair with a man who was on the *Titanic,* and so on. The method is bastard Chekhov: everyone gets at least one aria. A few of the arias are modestly effective, though always self-conscious, full of balanced phrases and artful dying falls; but the play remains an anthology of set pieces, generally tedious.

Not to belabor Albee with Chekhov, one difference between them is that none of Albee's material comes from or tends toward a central idea. Under the attitudinizing style and the unrevealing strokes of psychological candor, there is a vacuum. Just before the end, the wife says, "All we've done is think of ourselves," a thought that had struck me about an hour and a half earlier. We listen to them think about themselves all evening, in largely predictable terms. (I longed for the dying husband to shout behind the screen: "Will you all kindly shut up and let me die in peace?" And why, even in an allegory, doesn't the doctor object to all this chatter in a dying man's chamber?) The wife finally confesses that she loves no one but her husband, the daughter confesses that she knows no one likes her and she doesn't like herself much, the mistress faces loneliness; with these and similarly unsurprising revelations about all these uninteresting characters, the play ends.

Now it's not enough to say that all this is not enough: it's worse. The trumped-up revelations, the unproductive confrontations retroactively reveal Albee's real bankruptcy, that he knew he had nothing to say *before he started*. There is no hint in this play that Albee was genuinely on fire to say something and that he misconstrued his own depth. Rather, the impression is that he thought of the mechanism— the death-chamber symbolism—and simply began, assuming that the magic of the mechanism and the weight of his reputation would supply Art. A playwright must write, I suppose he thought, and this structure would give him the chance to show again his velvet way with words and his penchant for symbols that are provocative so long as you don't question them. In my view, this was the genesis of *Tiny Alice,* an even more complicated piece of symbolic gymnastics and the most ludicrously over-explicated play of our time. *All Over* is somewhat simpler, but is just another somewhat arrogant display piece, puffed up with sophomoric diction, a desperate grab at something to keep its now vacant author busy. Death as a catalyst on the lives of survivors is always a promising idea. The contemplation of death, as Tarleton says in Shaw's *Misalliance,* is "a delightful subject." But Albee's play is like its setting: chic upholstery stuck in the middle of a bare stage.

John Gielgud has directed with Chekhov in his ears, which helps, and with an eye searching for pictures. The characters move from one set of poses to another, as if there were someone out front clicking a camera every thirty seconds. It's hard to blame Gielgud for this, however, because there are so few dynamic currents on which to base his direction; pictures were what he was left with. He confirms this by adding a "picture curtain": that nineteenth-century device in which the final curtain rises again, not on the curtain calls but on the actors still in tableau of the play's last moment. Then it descends, and *then* we have the curtain calls.

Jessica Tandy is the wife, a competent actress suffering as she has done all her life from the insufficiencies of her voice. Colleen Dewhurst, the mistress, is a strong stage figure, but *her* voice gets hoarser and less useful all the time. George Voskovec, the friend, is still not comfortable in English after playing here some twenty-five years; one feels his insecurity of inflection. Madeleine Sherwood and Betty Field are commonplace as the daughter and nurse, James Ray is vague as the vague son. As the eighty-six-year-old doctor, Neil Fitzgerald is charming.

Seascape

(*February 22, 1975*)

In 1959 Edward Albee wrote a short one-act play called *The Sandbox* which takes place on a beach and has four (speaking) characters. It's a fantasy about the sterility of contemporary life and the relative authenticity of an older generation expressed in banality *à la* Ionesco. Now Albee has written a short two-act play, *Seascape,* which takes place on a sand dune overlooking an ocean and has four characters. This new play starts realistically, then becomes a fantasy. It too is about some sterilities of contemporary life. It too is expressed in banalities, but this time there is no reason to think that the diction is satirical.

When the curtain rises, a middle-aged couple, Nancy and Charlie, are sunning themselves. Almost the first line is Nancy's "Can't we stay here forever?" There, one thinks instinctively, is a hope for some banality-satire. But Charlie's reply, instead of being in a consciously banal pattern, takes that first line seriously. "You don't really mean it," he says sagely. Banality rolls in as the very medium of the piece, and we are off on a trite anatomy of middle-class marriage and spiritual menopause.

They are a typically typical couple: have made some money, have loved and liked one another through ups and downs, have loved and disliked their children, etc. One welcome change in Albee: as against his recent plays, he has here eschewed fake mandarinese. This dialogue is undistinguished, but at least it is decorated only with artifical broken sentences, not with artificial flowers. However, he has clung to his pseudo-Chekhovian mode: a chief ingredient of this early section is reminiscence, in wistful voice, recalling one's silly but lovable past self. Charlie in particular recalls how, as a child, he loved to sit as long as he could on the bottom of lakes and the ocean when he went swimming, worrying his parents but enjoying himself.

Then two human-size, lizard-like creatures, male and female, appear. Their sudden entry into this realistic play is pleasant: I felt that perhaps the long, basically familiar dialogue up to now was intended to lead somewhere. Anyway I found the lizard folk at least as credible as Charlie's knowing the author of *The Man Who Married a Dumb Wife,* which Nancy had asked him. (Anatole France.) The lizards speak English, and we soon learn that they live on the ocean bottom. Since it has been very carefully explained—planted, we can say—that Charlie used to love to sit on the ocean bottom, it becomes apparent that these two creatures are meant to symbolize hidden aspects of Charlie and perhaps Nancy, who has also expressed interest in the ocean floor. (See the importance of water in Freud and Jung.) Presumably, at middle age, various buried elements in the earth couple have surfaced to be reckoned with.

This is hardly a startlingly original idea for a play, but it's not a bad one. The play itself *is* bad—because it is nothing more than its idea. The conversation before the lizards appear is only remastication of well-chewed play-film-TV cud. The conversation of the foursome is mostly sci-fi cuteness of a slightly refined take-me-to-your-leader kind, two alien societies sniffing at each other. It leads only to some sentimental affinities and some quarrels (meant to alter the tone briefly), with a final imposed determination of the lizards to learn and improve. In short, the play never demonstrates in any degree a real necessity to exist. All it demonstrates is that Albee wants to exist, as a playwright. He cooked up an idea—worth maybe a half-hour instead of a bloated hour and a half (including intermission)—and then forced some arbitrary trite points into it in order to justify using it. In character, in texture, in theme, *Seascape* is an echoingly hollow statement of bankruptcy.

I think it's fair to make an inference about Albee's career since

Who's Afraid of Virginia Woolf? I think that he is caught in a modern trap. He wrote some good plays when he was young; thus, by the conventions of our society, he is sentenced to be a playwright for the rest of his life, whether or not he has anything more, really, to write. This wasn't always so: Congreve, Wycherley, Vanbrugh, Sheridan all wrote some fine plays when they were young; then, for differing reasons, quit to do other things. Nowadays this doesn't seem possible if one has been successful early and then begins to run dry. (And it's not just an American phenomenon; see the work of John Osborne since *Inadmissible Evidence*.) I have no gifts of prophecy and wouldn't want them if offered; but Albee's work since *Who's Afraid of Virginia Woolf?* (1962) seems so much more the product of compulsion to be a writer than to write, that there is no reason to hope for improvement. He's still relatively young and could do a lot of other things if he weren't shackled by fear of being thought a burned-out rocket. (For instance, as many of his comments show, he could be a perceptive critic.)

Albee himself directed *Seascape* with very mixed results. Deborah Kerr plays Nancy as if she were suspended in a noose of arch inflections and expressions. Barry Nelson, one of the last of the standard Broadway leading men—a player with a ready repertoire of "bits"—plays Charlie with modest technical competence. The she-lizard is Maureen Anderman, who, completely covered with animal costume and grotesque makeup, still conveys sexuality with her voice and quivering thigh. The he-lizard is Frank Langella, who gives a good stylized performance. (If you saw the PBS telecast of the Williamstown production of *The Sea Gull,* you saw Langella play Trepleff, sensitively.) The lizard costumes by Fred Voelpel are excellent.

Sticks and Bones

(December 4, 1971)

David Rabe, who made his playwriting debut last year, now has two plays running in New York—both at the Public Theater, both directed by another comparative newcomer, Jeff Bleckner. *The Basic Training of Pavlo Hummel,* produced last spring, seemed to me a rather run-of-the-mill unconventional play, concerning another latter-day Woyzeck trapped in a militaristic society, like Toller's *Bloody Laughter,* Green's *Johnny Johnson,* Brecht's *Schweik in the Second World War,* with the touches of expressionist fantasy that such works often have. Rabe strained for quirk and originality, as in the hero's name and some of his characteristics, but fundamentally it was a repetitive work: another sincere anti-war play which proved that sincerity is not enough.

Bleckner's work was more impressive. He cast the play acutely, directed many of the many brief scenes with surgical delicacy, and made all of it move fluently across the stage.

Now comes *Sticks and Bones,* reportedly written earlier—which is a bit disturbing because it's a considerably more interesting play. A Vietnam veteran comes home to his average family: mother, father, guitar-playing younger brother. There's joy when they hear that he's coming, but when he arrives, he's blind. His presence soon becomes an accusation—and a not so silent one—that gradually disturbs and agonizes their lives.

The mode of the play, the best of it, is pop art. Dad and Mom are called Ozzie and Harriet, the boys are David and Rick, which places the play at once under a radio-TV magnifying glass. Much of the dialogue is hi-mom-hi-dad-how-about-a-piece-of-nice-chocolate-cake?, whirling about the blinded veteran intensely, almost insanely, and the effect is of trivia swollen into threat, like Claes Oldenburg's gigantic hamburgers and light-switches. When the play works this vein, it has some frightening moments, spotlighting the frenzy with which coziness is defended.

But unfortunately it also has a river of rhetoric running through it. The soldier's accounts of Vietnam horror, his memories of his Vietnam girl are all college-dormitory purple of a kind not even to be found much in dormitories nowadays. The father's arias about his young days as a runner are faded Tennessee Williams. And the device of the phantom Vietnamese girl, who wanders through the house unseen by any but the vet, is one more use of what's been an unfruitful cliché ever since *The Return of Peter Grimm* (1911).

When the dialogue is deliberately corny, it's appropriately grotesque. When it tries to be "fine," it's corny.

There are other troubles. A string of ironies runs through the play, each of them trite: the blind man is the one who can really see, the "healthy" people are really sick, the priest is really un-Christian, the Vietnamese girl, maligned as a whore, is really pure; and so on.

These defects point to the basic shortcoming: Rabe's vision is insufficient. As in *Pavlo Hummel,* he has seen little that every member of the audience hasn't seen for himself. In *Sticks and Bones* many of his theatrical devices are striking, but the gravamen of the play is quite familiar, imaginatively and cognitively: the frantic self-defenses, the deliberate myopia of comfy middle-class morality.

Still Rabe is worth hoping about. If he can develop a *merde-*detector for his dialogue and if his perceptions grow to match his sympathies, he can be a valuable playwright. There's good reason to encourage the man who devised the last scene of this play, in which Mom and Dad and Rick, in their living room around the TV, chatting away, bring the blind David a razor and basin and encourage him to cut his wrists, complimenting him lovingly on the way he does it. But at present Rabe generally has more skill in the way that he says things than perception in what he has to say.

Bleckner's direction again shows an exceptional eye for movement, a good ear for phrasing, a feeling for development and texture. But I disliked his use of the harp for "bridge" music. The sound was wrong. Why not an electric organ—to fit the soap-opera satire? And I disagree with two of his casting choices. David Selby, the blind soldier, has a very limited voice, which only emphasizes the fact that he is burdened with the worst lines. Tom Aldredge, the father, is simply swamped by a large part. Aldredge has been adequate in smaller roles; here he almost turns himself inside out trying to supply the resources of technique and person that his part requires.

But Elizabeth Wilson, the mother, is excellent—a comedienne who knows how to use comic techniques for more than comedy.

Older People / That Championship Season

(June 3, 1972)

John Ford Noonan, a name I'll remember, is a young man who has written a play about old people. It comes coincidentally when the subject is much in the air, but Noonan is not treating a social problem; nor is he building stage traps for pathos. Insofar as heartstrings are tugged in this play, it is only because we insist on it, against the tenor of the work itself, as in Peter Nichols' *A Day in the Death of Joe Egg*. Our seemingly independent insistence is, of course, part of the playwright's design, but it's an agreeable, mature collaboration.

Noonan's play is a series of thirteen playlets, with only some small internal connection, principally connected by the fact that all the roles are played by the same six actors in a continuous, overlapping production. The subjects of the sketches are not in themselves terribly important, but here are some of them: an aging couple who must now spend nights apart because the husband's bad back forces him to sleep on the kitchen floor; a fading, fattening woman who tries for a last show-biz boost from a former boy friend who is himself a faded film star; a pair of aging homosexuals who try to part but don't; two old songwriters (they are in two sketches) who try to remember the words of one of their songs and subsequently meet the woman who once inspired it. There are three sketches, each about three old ladies, which, in their poetic abstraction, reminded me of that other (and stronger) play about old people by a young man, John Arden's *The Happy Haven*. Noonan's old ladies speak always in phrases ending in the vowel "ay"—it could have been any vowel; he had to choose one—as a metaphor of the reduction of powers and the floating-away from reality of many older people.

Those three rhyming sketches are the most explicit instances of the scheme and theme of the play. It is not a play of sentiment but of hate: hatred for the very idea of age, posited in moments of parting or attempted parting or reunion. Noonan's animus rests, obvious, on love, a love of life; one can't really hate age, one couldn't really loathe all that nonsense about serene sunset years, if one didn't enjoy living and hate the idea of seeing it constricted. The grotesquerie, which lies ahead of all of us, is seen here with humor and inevitable fellowship by a young man—in an era when, more than usual, most young people believe they will be young forever.

The most attractive esthetic element in the play is Noonan's modal distortion. Every playlet except the rhyming ones starts off fairly realistically; then actions and language stretch it slightly out of shape, in or out or sideways, and the seeming realism begins to distend like Modigliani. Noonan is interested in refraction rather than representation, and he uses the theater as a place to bend realities in order to sting our consciousness of the event. A conventional scene of a couple at an airport, flustered and excited, becomes a revelation of worried vulgar people vulgarized further by a situation strange for them. The first scene of the second act starts out as a conventional visit by one old man to another; then it turns into a replay of a scene we saw earlier. Roger pays Stanley to replay a scene with him in which a woman left Roger for Stanley. The very last scene starts out with a scientist's widow about to deliver her late husband's post-humous lecture, and it slides into an exposure of her own despera-tion in the gathering shadows.

The evening is a series of intelligent, vitally *theatrical* probes. (The last one is the only really weak one, and a poor way to finish.) It is never uninteresting because Noonan attacks from various angles and always with well-controlled, well-phrased, incisive rudeness, but it is finally not satisfactory because it is a demonstration of these qual-ities, rather than a thoroughly absorbed, self-effacing use of them. His play is a series of esthetic-surgical dissections, which could be longer or shorter, which, for all its poetic genesis, is observed, not engaging. Still it is an evening of discrete rewards. Work of this quality is far from commonplace.

Noonan has had two other Off-Broadway productions, which I missed. I will certainly try not to miss further Noonan.

The six actors are Will Hare, Bette Henritze, Barnard Hughes, Polly Rowles, Stefan Schnabel, and Madeleine Sherwood, all to be mentioned because all of them have a good time being imaginatively effective. Ming Cho Lee designed a reticent backdrop which has a high open window looking out on blue infinity—beyond life, presumably. Mel Shapiro directed, and I mean no slur when I say that it is the sort of play that is easy for a gifted man to direct well. The world of the play is exactly what he decides it is; the free-flowing form makes his work easy.

A. J. Antoon had a harder job directing *That Championship Sea-son,* in another of the Public Theater's theaters, because he was dealing with a naturalistic play, and his rhythms and emphases and lifts of imagination had to be found within the play, not rhapsodized from it. I think Antoon was completely successful. Last year he did a fine job with the surreal-fantastic *Subject to Fits* (and a less success-ful job with a Central Park production of *Cymbeline*). Now he has served a quite different style of play very well and shows that he is a director of range and exhilarating promise.

The script itself, by Jason Miller, is much more neatly turned than Noonan's and much less interesting. It deals with the reunion of a champion high-school basketball team twenty years later, at the home of their former coach in a Pennsylvania town. One of the four who show up is the blustering blockhead mayor of the town, one a pale junior-high-school principal, one a plump predatory businessman, the fourth is an alcoholic drifter. Just about the "cross-section" that might have been jotted down for the first draft of such a play. (The fifth former member does not attend, for dark reasons, later revealed.)

The dramaturgic pattern that Miller uses has been successful for decades. A group of people come together who are not usually together. (Sometimes it's a party, sometimes a country weekend, it's even been an air-raid shelter during the war.) What they seem like at the beginning is not what they are revealed to be at the end. Wow.

The initial impression here is poured on so heavily that we know it is being set up for destruction. The moment the coach tells them what a great team they were, what wonderful men they have become, and how marvelous it is to see them, our immediate reaction is: "You mean they *weren't* true champions? They're *all* rats? They *all* hate one another?" The play brings out different degrees of rattiness and deception and venality and disintegration in each, together with glib revelations of race and religious prejudice that are all small reverse pats on the back for the superior audience. Even John O'Hara would have dug deeper into his Pennsylvania. This is the sort of script that, with a little sex censorship, makes "controversial" television.

But the evening is only partially boring, and the division is not by segments, it's lateral, horizontal. At the same time that the pattern and purpose are tedious from the start, the dialogue is briskly speakable and the acting is good. So the performance has a contrapuntal effect: good surface against dull foundations and a dull overall form.

Pound for pound, this is the best cast I've seen in a Public Theater production. Charles Durning is the mayor, Michael McGuire, the principal, Paul Sorvino, the wealthy man, Walter McGinn, the sidelines wisecracking drunk. (McGinn takes a drunken tumble downstairs that is the best stage fall I've seen since Ekkehard Schall of the

Berliner Ensemble.) Only Richard A. Dysart seemed out of place as the coach; I couldn't believe he had ever set foot in a gym.

Santo Loquasto, the designer, captured oppressively the darkwood, closeted feeling of a middle-class home built around 1900. That was, essentially, a painterly act. Where Loquasto showed his specific theater sense is in his excellent arrangement of space and levels. Like all good realistic sets, it only looks like a room; it is really a theater set.

The Creation of the World and Other Business

(December 23 and 30, 1972)

Going to Arthur Miller's new play is like going to the funeral of a man you wish you could have liked more. The occasion seals your opinion because there is no hope of change.

Miller's reputation is chief among several paradoxes in the American drama of this century. Several playwrights, such as Elmer Rice and Robert Sherwood and Maxwell Anderson, had large reputations during their lives, here and abroad, and all during their lives there were a few qualified critics who dissented. (Now those reputations do nothing but diminish.) Excepting Eugene O'Neill and Tennessee Williams, Miller has the largest international reputation of any American playwright ever, and he too has had a similar group of dissenters. There have always been two Millers: the great dramatist in general opinion, and the much lesser one in the opinion of the best critics.

One reason I have always assumed for his success in most foreign countries is that his language improves in translation. One reason I have always assumed for his success everywhere is that he makes people feel they have gone on daring intellectual-spiritual expeditions when they have really stayed cozily at home the whole time. He supplies the illusion of depth without endangering anyone, and he gives his audience a painlessly acquired feeling of superiority just by their having been present at his plays.

This is not an accusation of cunning; Miller has not tried to put anything over on anyone, like some of our present-day "serious"

American film-makers. Generally his plays suffer from fuzzy concepts, transparent mechanics, superficial probes, and pedestrian diction; but he has done the best he could. True, *After the Fall* is tainted with a wriggly feeling of exculpation for some matters in his private life, but usually the falseness that crops up in his work is of another sort—the peculiar falseness of honest writers who are not talented enough to keep free of dubious artistic means.

Now the "double" Miller presents a new play. Whatever his admirers think of it, those who have thought less of him cannot now think more. Almost five years after his last play, *The Price,* almost nine years after *After the Fall,* Miller gives us a comedy based on the story of the original Fall, the first two chapters of Genesis. Hardly an unhackneyed subject, but that in itself is no bar: when Shaw wrote the first part of *Back to Methuselah,* he knew about Milton, among others. The only pertinent question is: What does the new user have to say or show us about the subject? What new insight or freshened experience of old insights does he give us? The answer in Miller's case is "None." I got nothing more from his play than that it was by a writer starving for subject matter, anxious to keep busy, who grabbed at an available classic subject and, to mask his desperation, treated it comically, to make it seem as if he had just managed to find time, in the midst of a busy schedule, for a little philosophical *divertissement.*

The program provides rubrics for each of the three acts, "Three Questions on the Human Dilemma," but since they only overload a frail work, I won't quote them. The first act takes us through the expulsion from Eden, the second through the birth of Cain, the third through the murder of Abel.

Like Milton, Miller introduces Lucifer and some angels into the scriptural story, and, like Milton, he makes the Genesis story resemble the Book of Job: we see the effect on human beings of a contest between superhuman beings. There the resemblance ends. We have no right to expect Miltonian grandeur or original theology of Miller, but we have a right to ask *something*. What does he give us? The Genesis-Milton story, reduced and distorted, and put in comic terms; and his comic method is nothing but anachronism. Adam knows it's Sunday because Eve serves him croissants. People tell Lucifer to "go to hell." When Adam misbehaves, God calls him a "schmuck." An angel tootles a bit of Beethoven on a bassoon. God mentions Notre Dame. He waltzes with Eve—to Strauss and Ravel. The anachronisms might be engaging (as they often are in Shaw) if they were used to some purpose, but all we get here is a rehash of homiletics, inconsistent and stale, in language that mixes King James and Kingsbridge Road. If Neil Simon had decided to treat the Fall, he could not have skimmed more shallowly, could not have been more cheaply referential, and would certainly have been a lot funnier.

For his own reasons, I suppose, Miller omits the fact that there were *two* forbidden trees in the Garden, one of the knowledge of good and evil, the other of life. To put the Genesis account briefly: God lies to Adam, telling him that if he eats the fruit of the first tree, on that very day he will "surely die." This doesn't happen when Adam and Eve eat. Why was God so anxious to frighten man off from that first tree? He tells us himself, after they eat the fruit. "Behold, the man is become as one of us, to know good and evil." So God expels the pair lest the man "put forth his hand, and take also of the tree of life, and eat, and live for ever." Quite explicitly, this is the story of God protecting his monopoly on moral authority, godhood, and immortality. Man was expelled by God to keep God in power.

Miller was not obligated to write this play, of course. He could have omitted the second tree, he could have contradicted the Bible (which he does: his Adam and Eve *begin* immortal), he could have done anything he liked if the result had at least been intelligible and entertaining. But what he gives us is muddle, aching along from one glib irony to another, without any internal consistency. For instance: although his Adam and Eve begin immortal, his God still wants them to multiply. The only reason given is that God would like a grandchild. Adam and Eve have no real sexual impulses before they eat the fruit, so Lucifer, deviously doing good, decides to help God get a grandchild. He induces Eve to eat the fruit and get sexy, then she does the same for Adam. And then Miller's God is angry at the pair because they *will* multiply—which is exactly what he said he wanted!

The continual muddle arises, I think, because Miller doesn't know what he wants to say. He improvises and patches, in speech that mixes borscht circuit and Bible. This suggests one more evasion with which Miller might be indicted, his evasion of Jewishness in his career. Many have noted that the tonalities of speech and character in *Death of a Salesman* are Jewish, yet Miller refused to acknowledge this. There are clues all through this new play that it was meant to be a Jewish domestic comedy on Biblical themes, something like Odets' *The Flowering Peach,* but once again Miller faltered.

And there is greater, deeper failure, best illustrated by a comparison with O'Neill. All through his life O'Neill had buried in him, like a secret fire, the story of his early life, his relation with his parents, their relation with each other and with his brother. He flirted with this material in various disguised and adulterated ways, and when at last he could confront it and plumb it, he wrote his one indisputably great play, *Long Day's Journey into Night.* All through Miller's career his dominant theme has been father-son conflict and love. Here he has gone back to the *first* father-son story, God and Adam, which, one might have thought, is the absolute epitome of what has been impelling Miller all his life, the fundamental source of what has concerned him most. But in Miller's case, as against O'Neill's, when he faced the heart of the secret, he fiddled and fumbled.

Miller's general indecisiveness is reflected in the casting. (I know the cast was changed several times in the out-of-town tryout tour, but that's none of my business here.) Bob Dishy makes Adam a sweet, patient, Jewish revue-sketch comic. Zoe Caldwell, as Eve, is like the Second Coming of Greer Garson. Stephen Elliott, as God, is like the boss in a '30s play about labor troubles, punching hard, crabbed in vocal and physical line. George Grizzard has the right sliding insinuation as Lucifer, but his speech ("whaddabout," "byoodiful") is distractingly vulgar. Gerald Freedman took over the direction in midtour, not very firmly. I can't remember ever having seen a wholly satisfactory Freedman production, even one he has directed from the beginning. His ear is imperfect, or (for instance) he would not have permitted some of Elliott's readings. His eye for simple traffic management is not very good, either. Much of the staging looks merely uncomfortable.

There *is* one creation in *Creation of the World,* and that is Boris Aronson's setting. Using colors (especially blue) out of early Italian Renaissance painting, using two giant gem-like rocks as periphery, using a raked stage so that we can see how it sometimes glows with spots of light from beneath, Aronson convinces us that this is how things looked when it all began. And, except for God's pajamas, I also liked Hal George's witty costumes.

The River Niger

(*September 29, 1973*)

I saw *The River Niger* when it was first produced by the Negro Ensemble Company last winter Off Broadway, but other urgencies kept me from reviewing it. It has since moved—successfully—to Broadway, the script has been published (Hill and Wang), and a second company is rehearsing for a tour that opens in Philadelphia in October, followed by Washington, Chicago, and Detroit—at least. So I went to see the play a second time.

The first time, last winter, was in fact my second encounter with the author, Joseph A. Walker. I had gone up to Harlem several years before to see, in a school auditorium, a musical play of his called *Ododo,* a dramatic-musical-dance history of white oppression (later produced downtown by the NEC). Amidst an almost completely black audience, I felt like that minimal white person whom Genet wants spotlighted at every performance of *The Blacks;* still, through the lumpiness and blatancy of the work, I got singed by some genuine theatrical fire.

The River Niger, in its form, came as something of a surprise after *Ododo:* it's a conventional domestic drama. Its subject is Harlem life. A housepainter, middle-aged and alcoholic, is a frustrated poet. (He's writing a poem about the Niger; hence the title.) He has a devoted wife, a mother-in-law, an old drinking pal, a son coming home from the Air Force, and a newly met prospective daughter-in-law. Out of these people's relationships and conflicts, along with others, comes the meat of this very long, overstuffed play. A second viewing made its glaring defects glare stronger, but also, happily, helped me to localize its strength. It's a terrible play; but it's not *just* terrible.

As for the first part of that statement: I haven't in a long time seen a realistic play so clumsily built, so naïvely motivated, so arbitrarily whipped to climaxes, and so ridiculously concluded. Walker is intent on cramming into his script everything he knows and feels about contemporary black life: family troubles, attitudes toward white people and toward military service, young love, job frustrations, militancy, police oppression, drugs, homosexuality, even black snobbisms about color. (Grandma resents being called black, says she's half Cherokee.) The way that Walker carpenters and shoves to get all this (and more) on stage when he wants it there makes the clumsiest nineteenth-century opera libretto look like Chekhov.

Again *à la* nineteenth century, he is addicted to stock-company hokum. (His director abets him.) The opening pantomime with Grandma and a whiskey bottle—which must take a full two minutes at the beginning of a very long play—would have been corny in Pocatello in 1890. The last-minute gunplay, into which all the characters move as naturally as if they were commandos, lacks only tremulous swelling music underneath.

The division of the stage into kitchen and living room, with people on one side often slipping into dumb show or paralysis while people on the other side finish a scene, isn't poetic or imaginative; it simply plummets out of the realistic fabric, again unhelped by the director— or by lighting that might at least dim on the waiting side. Time after time Walker's people spell out facts to people who already know them so that we may learn them. And the language ranges from the sharp and salty—the obsessively salty—to the sound of a typewriter clicking. ("No matter what you and I might think about Mo's activities, he certainly does not deserve betrayal. I could not live with myself knowing that I had an opportunity to help and didn't.")

Laden with this erratic language, this dramaturgy so clumsily clever that it's not primitive but bad, tortuously serpentine in its progress, devoid of any sense of emphasis as to which scenes should be long or short, the play nevertheless has a certain insistent life. That's the other half of the contradiction. First, it has a current of veracity, constantly battered by Walker's spurious theatrics but nevertheless there. For a white viewer, this veracity is informational—a peek behind closed doors. For black viewers, as I have seen twice with black audiences, there is warm recognition. Clearly *The River Niger* is doing for many black people what hundreds of realistic plays have done for whites for a century: quite apart from its quality, the play certifies the audience's existence. This is not a negligible function, particularly for American blacks, who have so long been deprived of accurate theatrical vicars.

But Walker's play is not unique in this by now, nor in any of the subjects that he treats. The play does have one quality that, without compensating for its horrendous faults, glows through them: the truth of affection. People *care* for one another in this play in different alliances and affinities, and the evening gets its truest life, not from plot or rhetoric or social criticism, but from the bonds of affection between husband and wife; between husband and old doctor-friend; between parents and son; between son and girl friend; between son and boyhood pal. Walker writes at his best when he's dealing with these feelings.

The director, Douglas Turner Ward (himself a playwright), played the housepainter when I first saw the play, and filled the theater with effortlessly overflowing vigor. His Broadway replacement, Arthur French, is good but not quite as effortless. His wife, Barbara Clarke, seems a touch less affecting than Roxie Roker, who played it before. The rest of the cast is unchanged. The actresses who play Grandma and the son's girl friend are the same—so bad that they are beneath criticism. Graham Brown and Neville Richen as the old doctor and a young militant are true and easy. The best performance comes from Les Roberts, the son. Roberts, along with Albert Hall of last winter's *Wedding Band,* is among the strongest young black actors in New York.

Ward's direction runs a parallel course to Walker's writing. Never really first-class, it sometimes projects life. But often he pushes people into poses and stage "pictures" that are ludicrous. He's the sort of director who is reluctant to let people sit down in their own home if they have a scene to play, and he's never really comfortable with more than two people on stage at a time.

Ward is also the artistic director of the NEC, some of whose other productions I've seen, and has said that he is interested in "a theater of Negro composition and of Negro orientation." I hope that "Negro orientation" won't mean being satisfied with laughs and handclaps of recognition, such as one can hear in any Broadway audience at a play designed for the white suburbs. The usual reply by black people to white critics is that black theaters don't care for their views because they are working for black audiences. To which I would reply that black audiences deserve work as good, by general theater criteria, as any other audience. I hope that Ward and the NEC, and Walker in his writing, will not let valid blackness, about which I have no comment, justify theatrical shoddiness, about which I do.

Short Eyes

(*April 20, 1974*)

There's some temptation to hate yourself at a play like *Short Eyes*. Here is a drama cut right out of some urgent social troubles of our time, performed by people (for the most part) who know firsthand what they are talking about. And yet, within the framework of an art, it's defective—even a trifle boring. Occasionally you feel a twinge of conscience for not capitulating to it. But no. At the last, no: if it was worth doing in the theater, then the theater is worth something; and theatrically *Short Eyes* is flawed.

It's set in a dayroom of a House of Detention, presumably in New York. Most of the characters are prisoners awaiting trial on drug and burglary charges. Most are black or Puerto Rican. Most of the performers and the author, Miguel Piñero, are ex-convicts. (The bio notes in the program are a sharp change from the usual stuff.) These actors got together as a group called The Family, a theater workshop in the Bedford Hills Correctional Facility in Westchester County, working under a director named Marvin Felix Camillo. Some of the original members dropped away; these men kept together after release, and under Camillo kept working at the Theater of the Riverside Church in New York, where Piñero was playwright-in-residence. Earlier this year they produced *Short Eyes,* which was seen by Joseph Papp and was transferred to one of the theaters in the Public Theater building.

The term "short eyes" is prison slang for a child-molester, a kind of criminal despised by other criminals. This group of prisoners has its racial antagonisms—black against "Rican," both against the one white man—but they all unite in dislike of the white newcomer, Davis, when they learn he is a "short eyes." With the connivance of a white guard who also loathes him, they murder Davis and get it accepted as suicide. They are told later that Davis was a victim of mistaken identity, but there is a double switch: one of the prisoners, an older Rican, knows that the mistaken identity is itself a mistake—because Davis confided in him at length about his psychosexual history. He *was* guilty. But the Rican—possibly because he promised Davis confidence, possibly out of deference to Davis' widow so she can at least believe her husband died innocent—keeps mum.

The writing of the play is schizoid. The banter, teasing, homo-sexual play, and fights are pungent, vital. They give the impression of extemporizations that have been taped and preserved, according to a scenario, rather than of dialogue written and memorized. In clumsy contrast are such passages as Davis' long confessional narrative and the examination of the prisoners by an officer, which were written on a rusty typewriter. The interest of the performance—and it does work up some interest—comes entirely from the work of the group as group under Camillo: a free-flowing, colorful essay in the self-histrionism of the characters, who are perhaps not so terribly distant from the performers—the creation of a kind of jungle of nativity into which Davis comes like a stranger. That atmosphere, compressed by David Mitchell's grim prison walls, is the best thing about the evening.

But because the evening wears on and makes efforts at art that become strained, the attention wanders. One critic said that attention wanders at *Short Eyes* because the audience is busy testing out the characters' emotions in themselves. Odd how infrequently that sort of wandering occurs at *Oedipus Rex*. My attention wandered because I had faced these emotions, in these renderings, so often before—on TV, in the press, on film, and in other plays. The hard, admittedly cold truth is that people who get in trouble and suffer, like people who fall in love, tend to think that because it affected them so drasti-cally, it will automatically interest others. Once the facts are famil-iar—and Piñero's facts are by now very familiar—only the telling can be interesting. And Piñero hasn't much skill in telling.

There *is* a strong irony in his play, but I'm not convinced that he's aware of it. These prisoners very badly need some sort of superiority. The "short eyes" gives it to them, in a surge that floods across their racial and personal differences. But the inhumanity they then practice toward their "inferior" is simply an extension of the very inhumanity, the social cruelty, that put them here in the first place. So, funda-mentally, they are their own persecutors.

Because this underlying truth is left murky, because Piñero relies so naïvely on facts that have by now lost their shock value, the viewer soon conquers his impatience with himself at not being overwhelmed by the play.

Jumpers

(*May 18, 1974*)

The curtain rises, and the heart sinks. On stage is a huge mirror reflecting the audience. Thus *Jumpers* begins, with a metaphor not only superficial but stale—Harold Prince used it twice in the last decade, in *Cabaret* and *The Visit*. (And Genet uses it all through *The Balcony*.) Then we get a long splash of vaudeville. A master of ceremonies comes out and introduces a woman who appears in cabaret costume to sing and who muddles the words. (*"Achtung!"* says our already wary mind. "This is a dream.") Out comes a troupe of acrobats, introduced as the "Radical Liberal Jumpers." (Ho *ho!*) Then comes an "iron-jaw" act, a girl hanging by her teeth from a swinging trapeze, shedding her costume as she swings. Then more muddled singing by the first woman, then the jumpers come back and perform at length—so long that even their obvious function as symbol disappears while we concentrate on their act as act. They form a pyramid, a shot rings out, and the top man falls; the lights fade and come up in the fancy boudoir of the singer, who is in fact a professor's wife and who has indeed been dreaming all the above. Except that—and here our metaphysics begins to strain at the leash—the murdered jumper is in her boudoir.

Tom Stoppard, the Englishman who wrote this play, is the author of *Rosencrantz and Guildenstern Are Dead,* which was hailed for its novelty and its existential explorations. The latter seemed to me even more tenuous than its novelty: W. S. Gilbert wrote a *Rosencrantz and Guildenstern* in 1891. Stoppard's *R&G* was only a bright undergraduate's one-act prank waffled out to three acts. Then we got a bill of his one-act plays, *The Real Inspector Hound* and *After Magritte,* which showed the undergraduate being less bright, merely facetious. In 1972 we read about Stoppard's new play, *Jumpers,* produced at the (British) National Theater and hailed as a work of philosophical richness and wit.

Sorry. *Jumpers,* in proof, is a work of copious philosophical *allusion,* written in that rhetorically ornate style brandished by a dramatist who has more wish than need to write and who takes the offensive stylistically in order to cow us. (Latter-day Albee is another example.) But Stoppard slides even further. He tries to fob off one more example of a stage-worn shallow genre: the play in which the author shows that he has cosmic itches and tries to scratch them with a mixture of facile intellectual rotundities and self-conscious theater mystique. Examples: Philip Barry's *Here Come the Clowns,* Thornton Wilder's *The Skin of Our Teeth,* Max Frisch's *The Chinese Wall.*

Stoppard attempts a triple counterpoint between his vaudeville, a murder-mystery farce, and an intellectual comedy. A professor of moral philosophy (Brian Bedford) is in his study trying to dictate a lecture on God's existence to his secretary, while his wife (Jill Clayburgh) in her boudoir is frantically trying to get rid of a body while dallying with her psychiatrist lover, who is also a philosophy don and her husband's boss. The corpse is clothed in one of the tumbler costumes; the husband's secretary is the "iron-jaw" stripper, now clothed and wigged. This braiding of vaudeville-farce-cogitations is supposed to stun us into perception of the relation of one to the other: the acrobats as visual equivalent of moral flip-flop, the murder-farce and sexual innuendo as gloss on the professor's moral speculations and vice versa. Not one shadow of a hair of such relation or supportive resonance is established. The elements are merely juxtaposed, that is all; and the mere juxtaposition is itself supposed to create weight—more, to bully us into fear of doubting that weight. Some physical connections (the corpse's tumbler costume, the stripper-secretary) are made; but there is no thematic resonance whatsoever between the scurrying antics in the boudoir and the intellectual meanderings in the study. And those meanderings end with the usual bland cop-out in this kind of purportedly probing work. It turns its back on query after the appropriate two and a half hours, and accepts the universe so that we can all go home. From the closing speech: "Do not despair—many are happy much of the time. . . . No laughter is sad and many tears are joyful."

I won't dwell on the triteness of the characters: the bumbling pedantic older husband, the frustrated wife who used to be on the stage, the smoothie lover, the comic detective, the humble houseman who turns out to be a juggler of philosophic jargon himself. The last is rather like the housemaid in Muriel Spark's comedy *Doctors of Philosophy,* produced in London in 1962, published here by Knopf in 1966—a play similar in tone to *Jumpers,* though not in plot, with dialogue more wittily polished.

Stoppard's dialogue has some sheen and a degree of donnish wit, but it is less amusing than Spark's and much less surgical than Simon Gray's in *Butley,* another play about English faculty people. While the professor is dictating, his wife, trying to get attention, screams from the bedroom: "Murder—Rape—Wolves!" He goes to his study door and shouts: "Dorothy, I will not have my work interrupted by these gratuitous acts of lupine delinquency!" Then, returning to his God lecture, he dictates: "My method of inquiry this evening into certain aspects of this hardy perennial may strike some of you as overly engaging, but experience has taught me that to attempt to sustain the attention of rival schools of academics by argument alone is tantamount to constructing a Gothic arch out of junket." In content the line is Stoppard's coy comment on his own method. In style the deliberate circumlocution, lolloping along to a point of heavy comic contrast, is the fake mandarinese of decadent Albee. If you throw in references to Bertrand Russell and such freshman chestnuts as Zeno's paradox of motion, you reduce the starved theater audience to quivering cries of gratitude for such profundities, cries mixed with gasps of wonder at a mind that can play so lightly with such deep thoughts.

The play is fake, structurally and thematically. All through it some recent similar experience kept nagging at me, and at last I remembered: Lindsay Anderson's film *O Lucky Man!* The film is on a quite different subject, but it too was a vehicle, groaning with effects, which toppled to show that Anderson, like Stoppard here, had absolutely nothing inside. But at least Anderson is a master of his craft as such; Stoppard is not. He is just one more half-baked egoist anxious for a cosmic grab, who thinks that the size of his ambition will certify his seriousness, particularly if he is comic, most particularly if he is reflexively theatrical.

My low opinion of the script would be no higher if it were well performed, but at least I would have had the pleasure of good performances. Brian Bedford nibbles his way busily through the mouthy dialogue like a long-haired chipmunk chewing his way through cheese. I have rarely been so conscious of an actor's teeth. To judge by *Jumpers* and Molière's *School for Wives* (1971), Bedford seems on his way to being the present-day Maurice Evans—Broadway's English star by virtue of elocution. Jill Clayburgh, the wife, is stripped at one point and we get a glimpse of her behind. Nothing else she shows—in technique or understanding—is so well rounded. The rest of the cast is beneath comment, except the acrobats, who are pretty good.

Peter Wood, who directed, also did the first production in London with Michael Hordern and Diana Rigg, who must have got everything possible from the parts. The effect here is as if Wood had been content to put together a road company, making do for the provinces.

The sets—two rooms that swing in and out and some backdrops—are by the celebrated Josef Svoboda of Prague. I have bad luck with Svoboda. A book published by Wesleyan in 1971, *The Scenography of Josef Svoboda,* contains some stunning designs of his, done at home. The work of his that I have seen on stage—two previous productions at the National, the revival of *I Vespri Siciliani* at the Metropolitan Opera, and now *Jumpers*—seems the product of a middling design student at a middling drama school.

The National Health

(*November 2, 1974*)

Peter Nichols is English, forty-seven, and prolific. *The National Health* is his third play to be done in the U.S., and by now we can discern a profile. He's intelligent, witty, mordant, and lazy-minded. *A Day in the Death of Joe Egg,* which was also made into a film, had a strong central premise: two young parents with a mute immobile child and the comedy-fantasy life they build around her. Having got the premise, Nichols thought he had the play, and after he had gone on for an act, he had to patch together a story out of rags and tatters. *Forget-Me-Not Lane* was the narrator's memoirs of his youth and didn't do much more than exploit the (British) audience's recollections of period minutiae and the trite poignancy of characters who, we know as we watch them, have since died.

Now comes *The National Health,* set in a North London hospital (the Sir Stafford Cripps Ward!). Again Nichols' assets are plain, including his ability to write good parts. (He was an actor for five years and he knows how to write for actors.) But again the laziness. Here he leans—with some talent but nonetheless just leans—on the inevitable horrors and comedies and ironies in a hospital ward. In an assorted cast of characters, some die, some leave, some come back, and they don't all behave predictably in relation to those facts. But *that's* predictable: and Nichols doesn't go much further. Maybe he thought the title itself would help, with its connotations of, well, of national health. No luck. It doesn't fill the hole at the center of the concept.

He does filigree his play with two devices. The first is show-biz fantasy. He interweaves a series of episodes called "television time": romance between a young Scots doctor and a Puerto Rican nurse, as well as one between the doctor's doctor-father and a Scots nurse, done as a cartoon of TV soap opera but really as a cartoon of pop adulation of the people in whose hands the lives of the patients rest. An orderly steps out of the play frequently to act as caustic inter- locutor. Vaudeville of the serious is not exactly new and Nichols doesn't use it as well as, say, Charles Wood did in his script for Lester's film *How I Won the War,* but the montage of deathrattle and raillery has its effect.

His second device is mode-mixing in the straight scenes. He ruth- lessly combines barrack-room gags (inopportune farts), realistic horror (a cancer patient's chilling screams), glib religious satire (a missionary and a chaplain lampooned), insightful humor (a woman doctor so overworked that she falls asleep on a patient's chest while listening to his heart), and moving moments (an ulcer patient trying not to worry about his young son). He also revives a few antique jokes ("If my old friends were alive to see me now, they'd drop dead"); still the constant changes of key give the play a tart, unfooled air.

But neither they nor the fantasy sequences redeem it. In all his work so far Nichols has shown irreverence for sentimentality and theatrical taboos but, fundamentally, not much more. He *seems* to bite bullets—in *Joe Egg* the anguish of having a brain-damaged child, in this play the implacability of the hospital bed waiting for every one of us—but he just mouths them for a while before he spits them out, he never really crunches. We keep waiting for the author's gravity as distinct from the subject's. And waiting and waiting. Nichols' talent so far is for choosing subjects and modes, not in what he does with them.

He's pretty lucky in his American production. *The National Health* was first done here at the Long Wharf in New Haven last season, under Arvin Brown's direction, and with one important change the same show has been brought to New York. Brown has become our main importer of new British plays and has developed a company reasonably adept in, among other things, various British accents. The Long Wharf first did (in the U.S.) David Storey's *The Contractor* and *The Changing Room* and Nichols' *Forget-Me-Not Lane,* and they deserve our gratitude for giving us a look at interesting new work in the British theater. (They've also done first American productions of Gorky and Lawrence plays.)

Brown has given us a particularly good look at this play. I don't know whether he was influenced by the London production, which I didn't see, but he has certainly directed a vigorous, nicely varied show here. (A director can remember arrangements and even some readings, but he can't really remember tempi and rhythms.) He has also made the best use so far of the misbegotten playing space at the Circle in the Square, which ought to have *been* a circle, not an oval. Nothing can be quite comfortable there, but at least Brown has integrated the necessary long-distance running into the play's dynamics.

His Long Wharf company has been well deployed, including those admirable older actors William Swetland (a good Shotover in the LW's *Heartbreak House*) as a daft doctor-patient and Emery Battis (a good Larry Slade in the LW's *Iceman Cometh*) as the cancer victim. Notable too are Olivia Cole as a Jamaican nurse, Richard Venture as the ulcer man, and Rita Moreno as the Latin-tootsie nurse. The biggest role, the interlocutor-orderly, is played by a new member of the cast, one of my favorite young American actors, Leonard Frey. (He was Motel in the *Fiddler* film.) He has the sardonic-heartbreak quality and the campy fluency that the part needs.

A few of the actors are weak, but this is inevitable in a large cast—too large for a regular commercial production these days—and the average is above average. Brown has handled them all with sympathy and imagination. In fact, I think he's somewhat more serious than the play he's working on. Still I'm glad he let us see it so clearly.

Absurd Person Singular

(November 9, 1974)

Alan Ayckbourn has been trumpeted as the Neil Simon of England. Untrue. Neil Simon is a master of middlebrow, smart-cracking social comedy, a manufacturer of character comment that probes just enough to make us laugh indulgently and like ourselves a wee bit more. To judge by *Absurd Person Singular,* the first Ayckbourn play produced here, he has no such interest. (He has had several other big London successes besides this one.) *Singular* shows him to be much more the Mack Sennett of England—fifty percent of Sennett, anyway.

Ayckbourn calls his play a comedy, but it is farce; and essentially it is not theater farce, it is film slapstick. The great farces of Feydeau and Courteline and Pinero are complicated machines of egocentric desire in monochromatic characters, people who desperately want something or other and bump violently into or frantically evade or breathlessly deceive others. Ayckbourn makes no such machine. His characters are monochrome, all right, but few of them *want* anything very much: they just behave in certain ways that are sharply and quickly defined. One wife is a compulsive housecleaner who has an addiction to cleaning, no matter whose house she's in. Another wife is a compulsive, socially pretentious drinker. And so on. The result is a series of situations that lead to physical complications that lead to more physical complications. The play is so much like a series of Sennett set-ups that it could very easily be played completely silent with fifteen or twenty subtitles.

Ayckbourn understands the secret of this kind of laugh-building. Each of his nests of structures begins with an action that is perfectly credible for its doer and then proceeds perfectly logically: the comedy comes from the fact that this logic has nothing to do with the logic of the other people. For instance, a husband angrily sends his wife out to buy the soda she forgot to get for the party going on inside the living room. They are both anxious that the guests—business big-shots whom they are eager to impress—should not know of the lapse. The wife goes out the kitchen door, into pouring rain, with raincoat and big hat and boots, her evening dress underneath. When she returns, the kitchen door is locked, and she hovers outside the window like a wet ghost, ducking when one of the guests comes in from the living room. Finally she has to go in the front door pretending to be someone else until she can get to the kitchen and change. She has behaved perfectly logically according to her pattern: that pattern simply has nothing to do with what the others, or we, would call sensible.

The three acts are three Christmas Eve parties with the same three couples (and one couple who never appear), each party in the home of a different couple. It's suburbia, but there's no more attempt at suburban satire than is inescapable, in our culture, in merely choosing the setting. The charms of these bourgeoisie remain discreet. The first act is in a climbing couple's kitchen, with the guests leaking in from offstage (an eccentric device previously used by Wolfgang Bauer in *Party for Six*). The second act is in the home of a philandering incompetent architect and the wife he is driving batty. The third act is in the home of a moldering middle-aged banking couple. During the play the first couple get prosperous, the second have domestic turbulence, the third molder more as the wife boozes more, but none of this is closely related to or caused by the action of the play we see.

Except for the batty wife's non-suicide. Her attempts to self-destruct are the basis of the funniest act, the second, in her home. The laughs come from the fact that no one—except her husband, the cause of her trouble, who has gone to chase down a doctor—understands how neurotic she is or what she is trying to do. She just moves mute and doggedly doomed through their busy, chattering incomprehension. She leaves a suicide note on a table: someone else, who needs a scrap of paper to write something on, grabs it and turns it over to use the other side. She sticks her head in the oven preparatory to turning on the gas: the compulsive housecleaner friend thinks she's worried about the dirtiness of the stove and immediately helps out by cleaning it. The neurotic stands on a table to hang herself from a light-fixture and pulls off the socket: the banker thinks she's trying to repair the fixture and climbs up on the table to help. By the time the distraught husband returns, everything has proceeded to a point, with strict logic, entirely disconnected from the point at which he left.

As hinted above, most of the dialogue itself is quite unfunny. Ayckbourn almost seems to flirt with the idea of an Ionesco-like barrage of banalities, which may be the source of the "absurd" in his title, but the dialogue never quite gets to that level of self knowledge.

If this play were not well *done,* it would be worse than unfunny, it would be embarrassing.

But it is well done indeed, which brings us to the other fifty percent of Mack Sennett—the director. (Sennett wrote *and* directed his films.) Eric Thompson has got the shortest end of any stick that I've seen in a long time. His name occurs in most reviews of *Singular* in a subordinate clause about the direction near the end. I speak strictly proportionately but quite seriously when I say that Thompson's contribution to *Singular* is no less than Peter Brook's was to *Marat/Sade.* I never expected to see such good farce playing again on our stage. I have seen these six actors before, some of them many times, so I know how much Thompson has done with them.

Ayckbourn himself may have helped: he has been an actor and he directs the first tryout productions of his plays in Scarborough, far from London. But Thompson, also an ex-actor, directs the plays in London and has built this one with the frivolous ingenuity of one of those huge matchstick castles. Timing is precise; concentration is utter. And Thompson has solved the age-old problem of theater farce that Sennett never had to face. When there are two or three or ten actors in a film scene and only one of them is doing something, the director just cuts away from the others, closes in on the main man so that the others won't be standing around with the proverbial egg on their faces. But the stage director can't send the other actors offstage: he has to find some way to keep the others both neutral and supportive of whatever Number-One-at-the-moment is doing. Thompson handles this well in every case, and there are lots of cases. Mostly it's a matter of eyes. Thompson has given his actors careful instruction about what they ought to be thinking about and looking at when they are not figuratively center, so that they are really in the scene, not just actors waiting for cues, without being distracting. The whole thing is put together with superlative craft.

So there are good farce performances from Carole Shelley, the only English member of a cast that does well with English accents; Richard Kiley, that fine romantic actor who almost made *Man of La Mancha* bearable; Larry Blyden; and Geraldine Page, enjoyably over-articulating her platitudes as the lush. Even the oleaginous Tony Roberts is tolerable (he's the architect). And, heaven be praised, I have lived long enough to write a favorable word about Sandy Dennis. As the glazed neurotic, wandering around her kitchen, trying patiently to kill herself, she is very, very funny.

Half the laurels at least, then, to Eric Thompson. If you never expected again to see a play in which a man carrying a bowl of potato chips is startled and whooshes them up into the air; in which another man is repairing electric wires when someone accidentally turns on the switch and the current makes him do a skeleton dance; and certainly never expected to see such things done well, then *Absurd Person Singular* will refresh you. Historically, it's interesting too: silent-film comedy fed on the theater of its day, and now it's feeding back into its source.

Equus

(*December 7, 1974*)

Equus is by Peter Shaffer, who belongs to an English playwrights' club that includes Tom Stoppard and Peter Nichols, the Latter-day League of Middle Seriousness. Shaffer is best known here for *Five Finger Exercise* and *The Royal Hunt of the Sun,* two plays that aimed heavy thematic artillery but then, like Chaplin's cannon, fired their shells only a little plopping way. *Equus* does better, but not enough.

It was first produced last year by the National Theater in London, and the American production, which is generally admirable, is based on the earlier one—the same director, one of the original two leading actors, the same costume and scene design. The setting is a low rectangular platform with low rails that have benches inside them. It's used principally as a psychiatrist's office but is obviously meant to suggest a boxing ring. Behind the platform are two small arcs of bleachers. Members of the audience occupy most of those bleacher seats, helping to form a circle with the rest of the audience in their conventional places out front; but all of the actors also sit in those seats, or near them, when they are not actually "on." The lights are mostly boxing-arena white.

So the play, which deals with a doctor and a young patient, is presented as a match between them. This is clever enough but fundamentally irrelevant—or at least no more relevant than in any analyst-patient relationship. The virtues of the production lie elsewhere.

Shaffer notes in the program and in the book (Atheneum) how he got the idea for the play. A friend told him about a shocking crime. Shaffer then "modified" it for his purposes. As he presents it, a seventeen-year-old boy, employed on weekends at a stable in southern England, one night blinds six horses. The magistrate before whom the boy is brought asks a psychiatrist to take the boy on. Though the play is interwoven with enacted memories and enacted fantasies, it's essentially a chronicle of that analysis: how the doctor breaks through the boy's defenses, with the aid—somewhat unwitting—of the boy's parents, and finally uncovers the reason for his barbarous act.

Since this is not a Hitchcock psycho drama, there's no reason not to reveal what is discovered. The boy's religious mother had put a picture of a flagellated Christ in his bedroom; the boy's atheist father had taken down the Christ and put up a photograph of a horse, head-on, eyes large. The boy had developed a combined religious-sexual fixation about horses (it does sound a bit like a pat Hitchcock psycho script) and used secretly to go galloping naked at night on a particular horse, having orgasms as he went. One night the girl who had got him his job in the stable took him back there. They attempted to make love, but he was impotent because he felt that the horses were watching. He frightened the girl off; then, frenetic and ashamed— more ashamed because he "betrayed" the horses than because he failed the girl—he blinded the animals who figuratively watched the act. His ability to reveal the story at last is said by the doctor to cure him, more or less, of his troubles. (Shaffer says he has had expert advice, but this conclusion seems, medically, rather neat.)

Now the author sensed, quite rightly, that this chronicle was not enough. In fact, during the first half of the play not much more than this psychical detective story is begun, and at intermission the play seems somewhat gauzy. During the second half, texture gets laid on. Shaffer has characterized the doctor as unhappily and frigidly married, and during the second half we learn that the doctor, who is an amateur of ancient Greece and its myths and rituals, is fundamentally jealous of his patient's passion. Crippling and painful though the boy's fixation is, it's at least hot and consuming, says the doctor whose job it now is to excise the boy's passion and render him normal.

"That boy has known a passion more ferocious than I have felt in any second of my life," he tells the magistrate. He describes his life, with its three-week planned tours of Greece every year, the rest of the time spent with a woman he hasn't even kissed in six years. Bitterly he concludes: "Then in the morning I put away my books on the cultural shelf, close up the kodachrome snaps of Mount Olympus, touch my reproduction statue of Dionysus for luck—and go off to hospital to treat him for insanity."

The speech is flashily effective (like the boxing-ring gimmick), but my own reaction was: "And quite right, too. You *should* treat him. He's sick and you're a doctor, and you're well and you know it." The moment summed up for me a conviction that the doctor's jealousy was only Shaffer's fabrication—R. D. Laing diluted and ladled in to fill the dramatic vessel to the top. The original murder story had apparently struck Shaffer not only with its horror but also with its singularity, and he had tried to mine some mythic significance out of it. (Horses loom large in myth.) Then, realizing at halftime that the play was thin and the mythic addenda insufficient, he had worked in this doctor's-jealousy theme. I'm not trying to criticize telepathically or by the standard of intention but by what is given us. The doctor to whom the passionate boy is brought just happens to be passion-starved (he says) and just happens to be a devotee of the myths that the patient's case adumbrates. Neatness, neatness all the way—as when one builds from the end forward. And we are asked to believe that the one doctor to whom the magistrate will entrust the boy, the only one who has the magistrate's confidence, has faulty faith in his profession, has no passion about it. I couldn't believe it. The man we see *is* a man of passion: it's Shaffer who imposes on him the things he says, contrary to the passionate life we see him leading, because it's Shaffer who needs those statements for his neat recipe.

Peter Handke (as a contrary example) took the story of Kaspar Hauser for a play because it provided a dramatic means for Handke's philosophy. That process, on internal evidence, seems reversed here. Peter Shaffer hears a shocking story, then dredges around for some materials—Apollo-Dionysus, lurking Pan, lurking Laing—to give it body and to "serious" it up. The result is certainly not dreadful or boring. I've noted only a few of the many effective moments; and Shaffer's writing as such, though he can't be said to have developed a distinguishable style, never falls below that minimal adroitness with which most British writers apparently are born. But the atmosphere of manufacture, of utilization, makes Shaffer seem a creator of modish dramatic interiors, smartly furnished with whatever ideas happen to be going at the moment.

A few things in the production are unfortunate. The device of having all the actors always remain on stage at the sides is a trite and quite pointless trick (and a dreadful strain on the waiting actors' attention). Roberta Maxwell, whom I've liked greatly in *Slag* and *Miss Julie,* is miscast as the stable girl. She's too old and too complex for the part. But John Dexter, the director, has made the play swirl and flare. He has used his six "horses"—young men in leotards with wire stilts and wire equine masks—with a centaur's eye. He has got a stunning, elemental performance of the boy from Peter Firth, who also played it in London. And he has helped that good actor Anthony Hopkins (of such films as *The Girl from Petrovka* and *Juggernaut*) to model his immense role with depth and idiosyncrasy. I wish that Hopkins wouldn't say "chooldren" for "children," but I'm grateful for practically everything else that he does. How well he times pauses with his *thoughts,* how well he balances dedication and humor and embarrassment about his own emotions. Michael Higgins is solid as the boy's father, and blessed Frances Sternhagen has one of the best moments: a speech in which the boy's pious schoolteacher-mother rejects the doctrine of absolute parental responsibility for a child's psyche, puts some of the burden on the boy himself, and declares her belief in the devil.

The Taking of Miss Janie

(June 1, 1975)

Ed Bullins is one of the most talented of contemporary black playwrights. In fact, he is one of the few genuine talents among a group of playwrights—the blacks—who are even more flagrantly pampered by critics than are younger American playwrights in general. I've had an eye out for Bullins ever since I had the chance, eight years ago, to read the manuscript of his early play *Goin A Buffalo.* The work of his that I've seen since then has affected me much like that first play: ragged but raging; raging but ragged; a strong personal voice that often lapses into clichés of dialogue and construction. A grimmer way of saying this is that his talent is now no less but his art is no greater. He has neither dwindled nor significantly developed. His latest play, *The Taking of Miss Janie,* is a case in point—indeed, it's more of a case in point than a play.

The idea is theatrically attractive: a view of the American '60s built on the relationship between two college students, black man and white woman, including the woman's conscious wish to be a friend and her less conscious wish to be taken; the man's perception of this; his loathing of it combined with his liking of her, and his ultimate revenge on both of them, on the world, by succumbing to her wish to be raped by him. (I'm not assuming, any more than Bullins is, that all women are just dying to be raped: I'm talking about some psycho-sexual myths in a specific time, place, situation.) The play opens with the rape just finished, near the end of the decade, and closes with the rape just beginning. Between, we get the events leading up to it: their meeting at UCLA; her introduction to his black friends, male and female, and his Jewish friends, a hippie girl and a zonked-out beat poet; their meeting of her boy friend at the time, a guitarist, also Jewish. Bullins wants to examine the texture and movement of the '60s at a focal point of the decade's dynamics: socially and politically radical college students. We see examples of black nationalism, black intellectualism, the growth of women's lib, drug culture, rock culture, and so on.

But there are two troubles, quickly apparent: (1) all we are getting is examples, not drama; (2) Bullins has absolutely no *ideas* on his subject, he can only present bits of it as evidence. As the play progresses, he seems to become aware of this, to become frustrated and panicky; so he "opens up" the play, makes it become conscious of itself as play, makes the characters address the audience in quasi-historical tone with references to the future. But the device doesn't work: it stands shivering as a naked attempt to give depth to a play that hasn't really reached it. Like other Bullins work, the trouble with *Miss Janie* is that Bullins never decided, in artistic terms, why he wanted to write it and what he was going to do about it. Some dramatists, even such an unlikely one as Shaw, have told us that they start with characters and let the characters "write" the play. If true, which I beg leave to doubt somewhat, the difference in Bullins is that his characters aren't equally resourceful. He needs to help them more, in advance.

The framework—the fated "rape"—is good. Much of the funky dialogue is rhythmic, sharp, pungent. But when Bullins leaves the funky, he often leaves the true. For instance, the white girl says, "Why are you forcing your will on me?" Or a black girl says of love, "Even the pain was sweet, though bitter." Bullins' character-drawing fluctuates, too. The heroine and the Jewish beat (well played by Hilary Jean Beane and Robert B. Silver), the black nationalist and intellectual (well played by Kirk Kirksey and Darryl Croxton) are all vividly drawn. But the hero moves in and out of the "literary," a black sexpot is a howling stereotype, and the (eventual) lesbian never comes to life.

Gilbert Moses staged the play adeptly within the flexible setting designed by the always ingenious Kert Lundell. The play was first done by the New Federal Theater of the Henry Street Settlement, which specializes in ethnic work, and the production was then moved by Joseph Papp to the basement theater at Lincoln Center. Papp subsequently announced an agreement with Henry Street "to develop plays that will be presented first at Henry Street and then at Lincoln Center or at the Public Theater, downtown." Translated, this means that Papp has delegated part of the preparation of his work elsewhere, relying in some degree on the taste and initiative of others.

PART III

notes on music

Jesus Christ Superstar

(*November 6, 1971*)

Jesus Christ Superstar was preceded by an LP sale of three million. (Or was it three billion?) The advance ticket sale for the show is immense, and a film is being planned. Trade talk is that this "rock opera" will make more money, in all versions, than anything ever. And some people say that God is dead.

The New York opening has met with strong protests from different religious groups, Jewish, Catholic, and Protestant, each one criticizing the show from its own perspective. Without getting into the specifics of the objections, I think there has been a little over-reaction on their part. Certainly the show will be seen by millions, as it has already been heard by millions, but is it anything more than a *rock* experience? Does it have even as much spiritual effect as, for instance, some of the best Beatles songs? On the basis of what I saw, I would doubt it.

I had never heard a note of the score, by Tim Rice and Andrew Lloyd Webber. I had deliberately not bought the record so that I could go to the show virginal. Here's what happened there. First, I heard a lot of sound. In many huge theaters, sound is amplified to make sure everyone hears everything. At the Mark Hellinger, sound is amplified to put your head in a barrel of decibels. Every performer carries a mike—wrapped with rope to keep it in period! Nevertheless I missed about one third of the lyrics, which were over-amplified and poorly enunciated.

What I saw wasn't much less confusing. The Christ figure was conventional enough: white gown, long fair hair with a center part, and trim beard. But the Mary Magdalene was apparently just out of *Hair,* the Pilate had been watching Basil Rathbone on late-night TV, and the Judas, who was less the Iscariot than a reincarnation of St. Vitus, revealed himself at last in a sparkling silver jockstrap. They were all surrounded at times by writhing dancers and singers inherited from vintage Cecil B. de Mille.

I recognized versions of various Gospel scenes, including an Elevation of the Cross in which Jesus wore an immense shiny train that would have made Florenz Ziegfeld drool, and a Crucifixion in which

Jesus was pushed out at us horizontally on a sort of triangular plate. But, as presented, I couldn't connect one scene with another and certainly got no whit of religious intent.

If one *wants* to worry about this show, one could note that, for instance, the high priests, dressed in circus costumes and hanging in a scaffold, chortle about how they're going to make Jesus bleed; or that Jesus kisses the Magdalene. But will this make Jew-baiters or de-deifiers out of millions? Everything, heterodox or otherwise, seems too weak, too ineffectual. How dangerous can a show be when it has only one memorable tune?

The real agony manifested here was not that of Jesus but of Tom O'Horgan, the director, as he struggled to give drama to a story that, in its very being, is undramatic. The whole point of the Passion is that, though Jesus questioned, he did not struggle. As for the décor, Robin Wagner's design had one good idea: the stars over Jerusalem came down in a large Christmas-present box.

My own professional disappointment, differing from the objections of the professional religionists, is that the show fails to live up to its title. Like (apparently) everyone else, when I first heard that title, I thought it was a knockout. I thought that we would get a highly topical version of the Passion in which the modern machineries of celebrity and glamour would be used to show: (a) that the Jesus story was a shrewd put-on; or (b) that its truth could be brought closer to us through the vocabulary of today's show biz; or (c) that the great poem of Jesus' life and death would naturally transcend any attempt to put it down by vulgarization (in both senses). But what did we get? Only a very feeble contemporary oratorio, no more than a termite's attempt to do in today's musical lingo what Bach and Handel did in their way. Not only non-religious but not even fulfilling of its title. The word "superstar" is used in one song, the metaphor never.

Jews, Catholics, Protestants of the world, relax. The religious crisis of our time is not at the Mark Hellinger Theater, only some of the Jesus Generation. I admit that they are sickening. Imagine a lot of people who think that love means licking everyone like a puppy, that true Christian belief will make life *easier!!!* Sometimes one does indeed feel like crying, "Savonarola, where are you now that we need you?" But *Jesus Christ Superstar* will flow on, if only at syrup's pace. Religion and atheism will both survive it.

Gisela May/*Berlin to Broadway*

(*November 11, 1972*)

Gisela May is an East German actress who sings Brecht songs. Those are the four paramount facts about her. She is very much the product of a particular culture; she acts her songs; she doesn't "speak" them, she has a rich contralto singing voice; she focuses on the greatest theater artist of her society. After those facts, an opinion: she is absolutely first-class.

May has just made her second American visit—from East Berlin, where she has been a member of Brecht's theater, the Berliner Ensemble, since 1961. (Her singing programs are something *else* that she does.) She spent most of her time in New York, with a few dates elsewhere, and will be gone by the time this appears. These comments are both a record of a real theatrical event and an appeal for her return.

She is somewhere in her forties, I'd say, broad-shouldered and quick, with full page-boy blond hair. She strides out on the café stage in a smart black pants-suit, and before she has finished her good-evening-and-thank-you-for-coming, you know you are in the presence of about 150 years of rueful, wry, Middle European history couched in pleasantly knowledgeable show biz, projected with sure talent. You feel simultaneously relaxed and expectant.

She delivers. Her program consists entirely of songs with lyrics by Brecht, the music by three composers: Kurt Weill, Paul Dessau, and Hans Eisler. ("Mack the Knife" is saved for a second or third encore.) Of these three musicians, it's clear that Weill was the best songwriter, though the others are theatrically at home. As May works her way from a *Happy End* group through *Mahagonny* and *Threepenny Opera,* you see that she is using her material as Maggie Teyte used the French song or Chaliapin the Russian. Each song is a small play, yet without any arty "transformation": she simply sings each one from the inside out. "Surabaya-Johnny" becomes a small melodrama because the heroine knows she is trapped in a melodrama, so the hairs on your arms prickle. "Pirate Jenny" is done quite differently from the (good) Lotte Lenya style of dark bitterness. May sings it with a fixed smile, rather quickly, mechanically, like a transfixed victim of Fritz Lang's Dr. Mabuse. When the pirates ask Jenny how many of their captives she wants killed and she says, smilingly, *"Alle,"* it's prickle time again.

Then, in a moment that for her may be the easiest but for us is the most striking, she takes a great piece of ugly gray cloth and covers the pants-suit and the hair, and with the aid of lighting (well handled throughout) she becomes Mother Courage. She sings three of Dessau's songs from the play. There is probably no such thing as Instant Mother Courage; still if you know the play, you feel that, in quintessence, you have seen it again.

May sings mostly in German. Some songs are translated, but a friend who speaks no German said he understood her best in her own language. This is more than a pretty conceit: she can use her own language as an illusionist uses his hands; and in her own language she makes the most of her cabaret-cosmos voice. Henry Krtschil, also from East Berlin, conducted the five-piece band sharply.

It's a commonplace that Weill was at his best when he worked with Brecht. My own heretical opinion is that Brecht was at much of his best when he worked with Weill. Together they make the *idea* of musical theater.

By coincidence there's an Off-Broadway show called *Berlin to Broadway with Kurt Weill* which presents exactly a reverse view: we follow Weill's career with various lyricists. The Theatre de Lys, where it is playing, is also where *Brecht on Brecht* played a few years ago, as well as *The Threepenny Opera* some years before that; time has brought ultra-sweetness to the house.

The set for that small stage is a busy little monster, the staging is fussy and pompous, and the best that can be said for the four singers who, with the narrator, comprise the cast is that they are somewhat effective in the American Weill, which is sadly inferior to the German.

The title of this show is, unwittingly, the core of the matter. Weill began in a German theater that, esthetically and ideologically, was the enemy of Broadway; he ended up the composer of *Lady in the Dark* and *One Touch of Venus,* which are good glittery musicals, and of *Street Scene* and *Lost in the Stars,* which are vacuous pop "operas." Moral judgments are out of place. Weill, like many other European artists, went through severe personal and cultural shock because of Hitler and the enforced emigration. I note only that

Brecht, unappealing though he seems to have been personally, went through no comparable esthetic change.

It was pathetic to hear these four young Americans fumbling with the Brecht-Weill songs the day after I heard Gisela May, but they did passably with later Weill. I particularly liked Margery Cohen singing "That's Him," with those spry lyrics by Ogden Nash.

The Faggot

(*August 11, 1973*)

Al Carmines is a minister of the Judson Church on Washington Square in New York and is now well known for his theatrical productions there, most of them with music by himself and often with himself in the cast. Some of the shows have subsequently moved to Off-Off-Broadway houses; some of them have toured to other cities. Through the last seven or eight years his productions have become less and less covertly homosexual; his latest, *The Faggot,* which was moved from the church to an OOB theater, is a declaration.

When Carmines began, particularly with his adaptations of Gertrude Stein material like *What Happened* and *In Circles,* he struck a fresh and old-fashioned note. His stagings and adaptations charmingly disregarded conventions; his music—with himself at the piano —had an old vaudeville beat and his melodic invention bubbled. He has poured out musicals and adaptations during the years, and I'm sorry to report that, as he has become better known, he has become somewhat stale and certainly less taking. The musical patterns have become repetitious, the melodies undistinguished and sometimes undistinguishable. Worse, as he has become more sexually frank, he has sometimes crossed over into the exhibitionistic and tasteless. I haven't seen all Carmines' productions because there are only seven days in the week, but the last I saw before this—*Joan,* about a modern Joan of Arc in the Village—was a rotten show and sometimes an offensive one.

The Faggot is a revue—songs and sketches about homosexuality, male and female. The general thesis is one that—*pace* the Supreme Court—is trite even by community standards: homosexuals are entitled to the same comforts and discomforts as any other sexual being. The one partly fresh statement in the show is that some homosexuals will miss oppression if ever they become fully accepted, just as some heterosexuals want sex to be a sin because it's the only way they can enjoy it.

But even the triteness of the ideas wouldn't matter—who goes to revues for intellectual enlightenment?—if the songs were good and the sketches pointed. Musically Carmines is scraping the bottom of the barrel organ. The sketches are even worse. Sometimes he steps away from the piano (the only instrument) to go into a sketch as Oscar Wilde (with Bosie) or Gertrude Stein (with Alice B. Toklas). Anticipation rises; but these sketches, like almost all the others, simply trade ungiftedly on their choice of subjects, with no wit, poignance, or purpose. And there's one song about Catherine the Great and a stallion (literally) that seemed to me a hernia of sexual liberty, a failed attempt to show that all sex, if one wants it, is equally good. (What's the ASPCA position on this?)

Aside from the increasing sterilities in Carmines' material, his new production exemplifies an aspect of Off Off Broadway that is now solidifying into a rationale: amateurism as an esthetic. When OOB began to grow, in the late 1950s, it was welcome for many reasons. It offered freedom and flexibility as the original Off Broadway began to get expensive and careful. OOB, which performed in lofts and churches and cafés and converted stores, was free of union rules and obligations, operated on half a shoestring, could do what it liked and do it quickly. No long, stomach-rending waits for production. European plays, previously unseen, were seen; U.S. playwrights, very many of them, began to be produced, and were induced to write more and more because they had a ready stage. Spontaneity had returned to the theater, from which it had been absent almost since the nineteenth century. Polish, in acting as well as in scenery, became suspect by negative logic. Since money couldn't be spent on competent actors and good scenery, the *absence* of good acting and of good décor became a talisman of authenticity, of non-corruption.

All this was happy because it was a free-spirited beginning. Now, from the production view, it looks like the end. Inadequate acting and direction and setting now seem the level where Off Off Broadway is going to stay. Improvement, either by training its people or by getting trained people, seems to be the last thing in anyone's mind, particularly Carmines'. Inadequacy has now become the standard.

I went to his church often, and often saw bad amateur acting and heard hooty singing and didn't mind, if the work was interesting, because I couldn't possibly have seen the show otherwise. Besides, there was something touching in the devotion of these men and women, not all of them young, to Carmines. I'm no longer so grateful. Many of the people in *The Faggot* are performers I have seen for years at the Judson Church, and since they are no better than they used to be, they are in effect worse. The audience has developed a coterie feeling between themselves and the stage, not the feeling of community that is the optimum but of conspiracy, cheering established inadequacies they would resent elsewhere, I believe. The level of acting and singing and staging in *The Faggot* would probably be blasted in a Broadway theater. Here it is tolerated, no longer as growing pains but as achievement, as proof of non-commercial purity. But if one takes a clear look, the emperor is not only naked, he looks pretty terrible in the buff.

Candide

(March 30, 1974)

The musical show based on Voltaire was first produced in 1956, failed, and has since become a Sacred Cause among its admirers. (I was out of the country that year and missed it.) Now it has been greatly revised, and revived. Lillian Hellman's book has been replaced by Hugh Wheeler's shorter, lighter one. Stephen Sondheim has added some lyrics to the already good ones by Richard Wilbur, all of which patter neatly through Leonard Bernstein's prettily adequate operetta score. Hershy Kay has apparently done new orchestrations, skillfully, for a smaller group. Eugene and Franne Lee designed costumes and setting—the crucial matter, see below—and Harold Prince directed. The show does not begin to be a dramatization of the whole novel, but it does get something of Voltaire's essence: a blitheness so persistent in the face of terrible facts that it becomes more wistful than ironic. Skimpy, poked about, sometimes flashily theatricalized, this *Candide* at least does better by the spirit of its author than *Man of La Mancha* did by Cervantes.

The Chelsea Theater Center produced the revival a few months ago in their Brooklyn home; now it has moved to Broadway. Therein lies a tale almost as interesting as the hero's.

The CTC, founded in 1965, is an institutional theater operating principally in a large upper-floor room in the Brooklyn Academy of Music. They have done a number of new and old plays of high quality, and have produced most of them (that I've seen) unsatisfactorily. To direct this revival of *Candide,* they engaged Prince, an experienced producer and director of Broadway musicals. Prince, a member of the CTC's board, has lately started to diversify his activities. And, of course, he has known Sondheim and Bernstein at least since *West Side Story,* which he co-produced.

One feature of the CTC productions in Brooklyn has been the varied use of their rectangular room. Sometimes they have done plays conventionally: rows of chairs across the narrow axis of the room with an elevated stage at one end. Sometimes they ranged the rows the long way and played the show on a stage along one of the long sides (Gay's *The Beggar's Opera*) or, having banked the rows high, acted on the floor (Genet's *The Screens*). This idea—varying the physical relation between actors and audience as is helpful to the play, instead of fitting the play into a fixed relation—has been an "advanced" concept at least since Okhlopkov's work in the U.S.S.R. in the 1930s; and it got renewed currency with the momentous productions of Grotowski's Polish Laboratory Theater.*

For *Candide* Eugene and Franne Lee went further than the CTC had gone before. The Lees have previously designed for Peter Brook and André Gregory and Richard Schechner, and their work here reflects that experience. They made the CTC space into a rough, ripply amphitheater of benches, with audience stools also on the "pit" floor; with three small stages, one in the center of that pit and others on two of the sides; with an undulating runway making an O around the pit and connecting to the center stage with two little drawbridges. (Someone has to come out before each performance, even on Broadway, and warn the audience, first, that the show will run without

* See p. 63.

intermission and, second, to keep feet and coats off the scattered playing spaces.) The musicians were split into four groups stuffed into various nooks of the setting, with the conductor visible to all choirs.

All this was quintessential to the show's success. Prince's staging took brisk advantage of the setting, so briskly that the audience gets slight chance to see how undistinguished the cast is. Mark Baker, the Candide, is a slovenly speaker, a mediocre singer, simply young and energetic. Lewis J. Stadlen, who has more to do than Candide because he combines narrator and Dr. Pangloss and several other parts, has a lot of confidence based on very little talent and an unattractive personality. Only Maureen Brennan, the Cunegonde, is really satisfactory—with a nice operetta voice and a wide smile of innocent sexiness. (A sample of how Hugh Wheeler italicizes elements in Voltaire: Cunegonde gets raped by one Bulgarian regiment instead of one Bulgarian.)

But as energetically as Prince has moved the show, as brightly as it has been revised, I think it's fair to say that its success came from the design concept. Of course Prince is presumably responsible for engaging the Lees; it's part of the eclecticism that marks his production— the overtones of Brook and Gregory, the U-shaped curtain from Carmen Capalbo's *Threepenny Opera,* even the release of streamers from the ceiling *à la* Jerome Robbins in *West Side Story.* (This last was eliminated when *Candide* moved to Broadway.) All these elements, some of them avant-garde, were selected by Prince knowingly, blended carefully, and served up tastily. The show might have been a success with relatively conventional production, on a stage in front of an audience; but this unconventional method gave the audience a sense of adventure even before the show began, gathered them into a community of—I'm afraid it's the right word—cuteness: which is to say, adventure without any risks.

The Brooklyn production, put on for a limited run, was sold out very quickly. Prince and the CTC made plans to move it to Broadway, and they understood the quintessence of the show's success. They rented the cavernous Broadway Theater and converted it into a much amplified version of the CTC playing space. The whole setting described above has been reproduced, except that rows of benches now stretch away much farther in two directions—a p.a. system must be used.

So now we have an unconventionally staged Off-Broadway show that has become a hit on Broadway by remaining an Off-Broadway show. Some six years ago I saw *Hair* twice, once down at the Public Theater, once up on Broadway. *Hair* wasn't exactly a failure uptown, but, for me, it was much weaker when it was stuck up on a platform in front of the audience. Downtown the audience had surrounded the show, had seemed to compress and increase the youthful energy in it. I think Prince and friends may have learned from this difference. They realized how integral the shape of the production of *Candide* was to its success—commercial success even more than artistic fulfillment.

Now, despite backless benches, the big-money audience ($15 top on Saturday night) can go, is flocking, to Off-Broadway adventure right on Broadway itself. Some of that audience used to get kicks from searching out novelty and experiment in the Village and elsewhere; now the adventure is being silver-plattered up by the ticket agencies. This is not the first time that Off Broadway has fed the Main Stem; nor was *Hair* the first time. But, to my knowledge, this is the first time that "Off-Broadwayness" has been preserved in the commercial move, has been transported whole to the big time.

And this is yet more evidence of the great shift in the American theater since World War II. Up to 1950 or so, Broadway fed the theaters of America and supplied American plays to the world. It was the source of virtually all new American plays of any importance and of production ideas. Now Broadway is the source of almost nothing. Its musicals come from films or Off Broadway or are revivals; its plays come from abroad or Off Broadway. Now Off Broadway *itself,* so to speak, has come to Broadway, to provide a new kind of Broadway hit. Dr. Pangloss would have been pleased; by his standards it would have only proved further that this is the best of all possible worlds.

A Chorus Line

(*June 21, 1975*)

Credit where credit is certainly due. I haven't been shy about criticizing Joseph Papp adversely, so I underscore at the start that his hospitality and support helped to make *A Chorus Line* possible. Apparently he had little to do with the creation of the show (and hasn't claimed otherwise), but he provided the place for Michael Bennett and his collaborators to evolve it over a period of months as a workshop production. Many of the Public Theater workshops never see the light or much light. Once in a good while, as with Jack Gelber's version of Mailer's *Barbary Shore,* the results are as interesting as any in Papp's far-flung—and still flinging—empire. A scattershot policy occasionally pays off if you keep it up long enough. Papp persists; and this is one of the happier results.

Michael Bennett is a Broadway choreographer and director whose previous work, as I've seen it, has ranged from fair to foul. His choreography for *Company* was smart, for *Follies* less smart; his direction of Neil Simon's play *God's Favorite* was a mistake. Most of his work has been in musicals—he began as a chorus dancer at seventeen and is now only thirty-two—and the experience of the chorus call has been central to his life, the process of trying out for jobs in shows, getting and not getting them. That experience is a microcosm of cultural comment. Out of it Bennett has made a good show, using a method that is a further cultural comment.

The Broadway musical performer is a special, rarefied breed. He (please also read "she") was much in demand in the first half of this century when musicals were produced in great numbers. It's paradoxical that as the number of musicals has drastically declined, their job requirements have risen in stringency. Formerly a show might have a singing group, a group of show girls (who only had to be tall and gorgeous), a dance group whose work was mainly tap, and occasionally some ballet dancers as well. From about the time of *Oklahoma!* (1943) and Agnes de Mille's choreography therein, the character of Broadway dancing has changed; this, combined with money tightening, has made it necessary for fewer and fewer people to do more and more. The same ensemble must now do the dancing (tap *and* ballet), sing, look sexy, and also play small parts when necessary. The competent Broadway musical performer is one of the best-trained people in the American theater—and has become so just as his job opportunities have dwindled. ("Don't tell me that Broadway is dying," wails one of the girls in this show. "I just got here.")

With all that's required and with so few chances to use it, the chorus call for a Broadway show has become a special circle of hell.

To explore it, to explore why some people insist on preparing and heading for it, Bennett conceived the idea of *A Chorus Line.* His helpers, all skillful, were the co-choreographer Bob Avian, the writers James Kirkwood and Nicholas Dante, the lyricist Edward Kleban, and the composer Marvin Hamlisch. Robin Wagner's setting is just black drapes with a huge mirror as backdrop which splits into sections on pivots and can disappear—not a fresh idea but useful for a dance show. Tharon Musser's lighting is highly responsive to situations and does more to "dress" the show than any other element.

The strikingly different fact about *A Chorus Line,* and its most illuminating cultural aspect, is that it was evolved through months of rehearsal. Bennett has said that the entire cast—a very talented group —was engaged before the show was written. The book, the songs, and the dances were worked out as they went along, from materials that came out of rehearsals, including the lives of all the participants. This is clearly the appropriation by Broadway musical people of a method that has been developed, not by Off Broadway but by Off Off Broadway—in "matrix" groups, such as Joseph Chaikin's now disbanded Open Theater, which evolve their productions out of the contributions in rehearsal of all the participants, with writers and composers (if used at all) as collaborators in the evolution. In fact, one device near the beginning of *A Chorus Line*—when a dance ends with the line of dancers holding up their photographs in front of their faces—is strongly reminiscent of a similar device in the Open Theater's *Mutation Show* (1973). In further fact, this show's overall method, winnowing out the performers' autobiographies to juxtapose them against what they are now, is also reminiscent of *The Mutation Show.*

As the lights come up on *A Chorus Line* (no curtain), a group of twenty-three men and women—called "boys and girls"—are dancing in rehearsal clothes, led by the director and his assistant. The director soon eliminates six. Then, seated at the back of the auditorium, he tells the remaining seventeen that he will finally select eight, "four and four"; that he wants a strong unit who can also play small parts; and that he must know more about them. This public self-revelation, not exactly run-of-the-mill at chorus calls, is the central device. Each of them steps forward in turn and talks, and/or sings and dances, about "himself." Each of them is actually dealing with a fictional character, but all of this material has obviously been mined from firsthand observation or experience, worked over and "set" by Bennett and his colleagues. Finally the director chooses eight.

Two common denominators apply to most of the stories. First, these dancers hated their families and home towns. (One of the boys grew up in Buffalo, which so depressed him that he once thought of killing himself; but "to commit suicide in Buffalo is redundant.") Second, as one number says, "everything is beautiful at the ballet." They are mostly refugees who dread having to return to the outside world either by failing or by aging. The border between psychic needs and creative impulse is always fuzzy; and this show makes clear that most of these people are here, have suffered to get here, are suffering to stay, at least as much out of hatred of their pasts and past selves and the glare of daylight as out of their love of dancing and the theater.

None of this is startling or deep, some of it is show-biz corn, but most of it is authentic, even some of the corn. And almost all of it is well done. Carole Bishop as an aging dancer, Priscilla Lopez as a cockily clear-headed Puerto Rican, Sammy Williams with a riskily sentimental scene about a homosexual who has finally been acknowledged by his parents are outstanding. The low point is a plotty scene between the director and his ex-girl, who was almost a star and now needs a chorus job, but Donna McKechnie dances the part with dazzle.

Bennett's problem with these successive "case histories" was variety of presentation, which he handled so well that we're never conscious of the problem. Hamlisch's music, though there are no hummable tunes, is sculpted to its occasions neatly and danceably. And there is an ironic payoff. In the latter part of the show (two hours plus, no intermission) the dancers learn a number from the new show for which they're trying out. For the curtain call of *A Chorus Line* all seventeen come out in the new show's costumes and do that new number. The costumes are pure Busby Berkeley, the song is peppily inane. *This,* Bennett and friends seem to be saying, is what these people were dying to get into, what they have trained for.

So *A Chorus Line* is the result of a Broadway institution going to Off Broadway to examine itself, using Off-Off-Broadway methods to do it (whether or not Bennett saw the Open Theater), and finding some futility to report. The irony is compounded because this show, a smash success, will move up to Broadway. Well, the successful move of *Candide* from Off Broadway to a huge big-time house proved that there was big money in unconventional staging of conventional material. Now this good new musical, made by a process absolutely antithetical to big-time procedures, is going up to be a big-time success. It's no news that commerce feeds on art, but the joke here is that this show, which fundamentally tells us how sterile the whole Broadway business is, is going up to help sustain it.

My Verdi

(Horizon, *Winter 1975*)

Many millions of people in the last century might have written an article with this title. Here is mine, about the Giuseppe Verdi who belongs to me, with some of the facts of his astonishing and endearing life. I am not a musician, only someone who is pathologically jealous of the worst musician he has ever heard. But I have had some five decades of pleasure in listening to music and have never enjoyed any music more than Verdi's. I use the word "enjoyed" as carelessly and unambitiously as the old man himself might have enjoyed a cup of black coffee before getting to work at four o'clock in the morning. He is my Verdi because he made my scalp tingle when I was twelve, because the more I learn about the theater the more I worship his genius, because the famous photo of that black-suited, white-bearded peasant standing in his garden with his rolled umbrella behind his back is the grandpa of blessings that all of us would have liked.

When I was thirteen I began to do some writing for the old Metropolitan Opera House program—biographical notes and verses and fillers. There was no money; I was paid in tickets. Those days, in the late 1920s, were the days of vocal splendor (as phonograph records prove) and of empty houses. Very many times that boy of thirteen or fourteen or fifteen attended performances over which opera-lovers now weep, and sometimes he sat in a box alone, his feet extended on a gilt, red-cushioned chair, listening to Ponselle or Gigli or Rethberg or De Luca or Pinza, watched Tullio Serafin conduct. And often, very often, it was Verdi. The Aga Khan could not have had opera in greater luxe or glory.

I began then to read about Verdi, and although I am nothing like a Verdi scholar, reading about Verdi is still one of my happier obsessions. His music was what brought me to his life, of course, particularly because it is theater music—none better as such. The life itself is a story of such courage, size, simplicity, love and pain and honor that I have to tread warily, lest I be tempted to the fallacy that great artist means great man, always. (Was Wagner a great man? Was Proust?) But if you are looking for support for that theory, Giuseppe Verdi's life leads.

He was born in the hamlet of Le Roncole in the broad Po Valley near Parma on October 10, 1813, the year of Wagner's birth. Beethoven was forty-three. When Verdi died in 1901, Wagner had been dead eighteen years, Debussy was now thirty-nine, and Stravinsky was nineteen. To say that Verdi encompassed the nineteenth century is something more than a figure of speech.

This prototypical Italian was born French, in a divided Italy. His birth certificate states his given names as Joseph Fortunin François. A few months later French rule over the region gave way to Austrian rule; Austria was the power against which Verdi later joined in the struggle for Italian independence. So he was born, to put it not the least bit hyperbolically, into drama.

His father was the local innkeeper and grocer. I have seen Le Roncole, and as late as 1956 it was only a crossroads with a few houses, a sort of general store and post office, and the Verdi birthplace, unchanged but now, naturally, a monument. In Verdi's childhood there was also an organist, because it was he who gave the boy his first music lessons after Verdi had been thunderstruck by church music and his father had bought him an old spinet. Not a great deal is known about Carlo Verdi, but he must have had some perception, because he soon saw that his son was too good for the local teacher and transferred him to a school in Busseto, a town three miles away. (Busseto, the town where—on a Verdi pilgrimage—I ate a meal that gave me near-ptomaine! Verdi, who grew to hate Busseto later in life, would have warned me not to eat there.) There Verdi met the man who can be called the single most important influence in his life.

Antonio Barezzi was a prosperous grocer—in fact, the supplier of

Verdi's father—and a devout amateur of music. A couple of years after the boy began studying in Busseto, Barezzi took him into his home, employed him, and helped his studies with a man who was the organist of Busseto Cathedral and director of the Philharmonic Society. The young Verdi also played duets with Barezzi's young daughter, Margherita.

In the historical tradition of composition up to that time, Verdi began to write music on commission for specific use. As his biographer Francis Toye says:

> . . . Verdi was a practical musician, a craftsman writing music to meet the current requirements of the day. In his youth those current requirements were represented by the cathedral, the military band, and the Philharmonic Society of Busseto; in later days by the opera houses of Milan, Paris, Cairo, London, and St. Petersburg. The principle, however, remained the same.

A wonderful principle, that operated for Michelangelo and Shakespeare as well: the dailiness of filling an order like an artisan, fused with the anomaly of doing it with genius. Terrible artists have filled commissions, great artists have worked without them. But that unique, somehow humorous combination of a great artist running his career like a tradesman busily pleasing customers is a special pleasure in Verdi's career. Years later he was offered a three-year contract by a London theater and declined it because, among other reasons, he didn't like being limited, as this contract would have done, to writing only one opera a year. He had other customers to serve.

Still young, only eighteen, Verdi went to Milan in 1832, partly financed by Barezzi and partly by a Busseto institution, in order to enter the Milan Conservatory. He was rejected. He went to a private teacher in Milan and worked hard, perhaps especially hard to demonstrate the conservatory's error. Then in late 1833 or early 1834 came a stroke of luck—"luck" being defined for an artist as a chance to show the talent that has nothing to do with luck but might wither without it. A group of Milanese amateurs were rehearsing Haydn's *Creation,* and Verdi used to attend rehearsals. One day none of the three conductors appeared, and the young man sitting in a corner of the hall was asked simply to sit at the piano and fill in as accompanist. "I accepted," he wrote some forty years later, "and sat down at the piano to begin. I remember very well the ironical smiles that passed among those dilettantes. My youthful face, my scrawny figure, and my poor clothes commanded but little respect. However, the rehearsal began, and little by little I began to warm to it. Then as my excitement grew, I stopped merely accompanying, and began to conduct with my right hand while I played with my left." Result: the absent maestri were forgotten, and Verdi was asked to conduct the public performances. Further result: he was asked to compose an opera for this society.

Verdi was delighted, but he was delayed. His old teacher back in Busseto died, and Verdi, who had obligations to the town, was recalled to take over the local Philharmonic Society. During the four and a half years that followed, his future might have seemed predictable: a provincial musician had gone up to the big city for training and had returned to his home town to spend his life. Verdi composed more occasional music and ran the Philharmonic Society, but continued working, when he could, on his opera. Also, he resumed playing duets with Margherita Barezzi. In 1836, when she was seventeen, they married, and even that seemed like one more strand in a conventional tale: rising home-town boy weds wealthy patron's daughter.

But Verdi was Verdi, and the story altered. He finished his opera, *Oberto, Conte di Bonifacio,* whose libretto by one Piazza was revised by Verdi's friend Temistocle Solera. He finished his contractual obligations in Busseto. He took his wife and his baby son to Milan. (An earlier child, a daughter, had died just after the boy was born.)

Oberto was produced at La Scala, Milan, in November of 1839 with moderate success—enough success to bring Verdi a contract for three more operas from the director of La Scala. Then came a cruel paradox too horrible to be called ironic. His small son had died just before *Oberto* was produced. The first of his new operas was to be a comedy. While he was writing it, Margherita died, in June of 1840. He managed to finish the comic opera *Un Giorno di Regno (A Day's Reign)*, and it was produced in September. The wonder is not that it was not very good but that he was able to finish it at all. It could not have surprised Verdi, possibly it did not even interest him much, that it was a failure.

Again it might have seemed that his future was predictable. He thought his career was over. What was worse, he didn't care. Here, one might have thought, was a young musician who had had a flurry of attention but had been broken both by professional failure and by personal tragedy. Perhaps he would go home to Busseto and survive by giving music lessons, perhaps he would not survive.

That winter he was still in Milan, in obscure lodgings, doing nothing. (He himself told the story, in the autobiographical sketch he wrote in 1879.) One evening, as snow was falling, he was walking through the streets and accidentally met Merelli, the head of La Scala. Merelli, who had refused Verdi's request to be released from his contract with the opera house, asked Verdi to walk with him as far as his office. On the way Merelli told him about a "pig-headed" composer who had just declined a libretto by Solera and wanted something else. Verdi offered a libretto that had been prepared for him and that he would never need. Merelli, whose mind was obviously spinning away busily, said that this was a marvelous idea, and while they talked, he talked Verdi inside the theater to the office. There he took out the manuscript that the other composer had rejected, and suggested that Verdi take it along with him.

"What should I do with it?" Verdi replied. "No, no, I am not in the mood for reading librettos."

"Eh! It won't bite you, will it? Read it and then you can give it back to me." Merelli forced the manuscript into Verdi's hands.

The young composer left and started back through the snow to his lodgings. He says:

On the way home I felt a kind of indefinable malaise, a very deep sadness, a distress that filled my heart. I got home and with an almost violent gesture threw the manuscript on the table. . . . The book had opened in falling on the table; without knowing how, I gazed at the page that lay before me and read this line:

Va, pensiero, sull' ali dorate.

"Go, thought, on golden wings." It is the first line of the chorus of exiled Jews—in *Nabucco*. That line served as the slender filament that tugged Verdi back to life. Although he made another effort to return the libretto, something had stirred again in him: "One day one verse, another day another, here a note and there a phrase, little by little the opera was composed."

Here is a simple dramatic fact to which no flourish need be added. Sixty years later, at Verdi's funeral, the immense crowd spontaneously began to sing that chorus of exiled Jews—singing, at the very end of his giant career, the lines that had brought him back to music.

He finished *Nabucco* (which was his own irreverent shortening of *Nabucodonosor*—Nebuchadnezzar) in the autumn of 1841. It was produced in March 1842 and—to keep this story incredible one need only stick to the facts—was an overwhelming success. "The public went mad," says Toye.

Verdi's career, from that point, went up and up, though not unvariedly so. *Nabucco* made him famous in Italy: ties, hats, and sauces were named for him. His next opera, *I Lombardi alla Prima Crociata* (*The Lombards at the First Crusade*), also from a Solera libretto, was produced eleven months after *Nabucco*. (*I Lombardi* was, in curious fact, the first Verdi opera produced in America—New York, March 1847.)

His next opera, *Ernani,* marked two changes in his career. It was his first opera based on a famous play—his new librettist, Francesco Piave, had drawn the book from Victor Hugo's *Hernani*—and it was the first opera he wrote for a theater outside Milan. *Ernani* had its premiere at La Fenice in Venice in March 1844. A few months later it was produced in Vienna, where Donizetti was director of the Italian Opera, and soon after was performed in other countries. *Ernani* was the work that made Verdi an international figure, but it ensured his stature as a hero in Italy, particularly since his work continued to get in trouble with the Austrian governors' censors. (One chorus in *I Lombardi* had evoked a patriotic demonstration.)

Before the year was out he emphasized these two career changes: he produced *I Due Foscari* (*The Two Foscari*) in Rome, November 1844, and his librettist Piave drew the book from Byron's play. No other composer that I know drew so consistently on established dramatists. This is no guarantee of successful operas, but it certainly shows some sense of dramatic aspiration. Among Verdi's sources are Schiller (*Giovanna d'Arco, Don Carlo, I Masnadieri, Luisa Miller*), Voltaire (*Alzira*), Victor Hugo again (*Rigoletto*), Dumas *fils* (*La Traviata*), and of course Shakespeare (*Macbeth, Otello, Falstaff*).

Note, too, an element common in his day and country, uncommon in ours. He wrote for specific theaters, for specific use. The condition of composers' writing and then looking for outlets only came into being during Verdi's lifetime. Composers in various countries still wrote for various uses, and in Italy the dominant form was opera. The writing of new operas for opera houses every year was almost comparable to the writing of new plays for dramatic theaters today. In 1820, for instance, La Scala had eleven works in repertory, four of which were premieres—today an unbelievable proportion. In the biographies of Verdi there is no clear statement of what first attracted him to opera, except his own comment that he was delighted when the first libretto was offered him in Milan; but it could almost be said that, for an Italian talent of his day, it would have been more remarkable if he had *not* been drawn to opera.

This theatrical vocation meant for Verdi, as for all composers to whom opera has meant more than grinding out of stage fodder, a concern with story, structure, characterization, and language that surprises those today who vaguely assume that the librettos were somehow always "there" and the verses unimportant. Verdi's correspondence with his librettists quickly proves the opposite. ("The phrase must have a turn that grips you!" he wrote to one. "Theater . . . theater!") More to the recurrent point of theatrical excruciation was his continuing struggle with production problems, especially a continuing struggle with singers. As soon as he had enough reputation to stand up to opera stars, who were accustomed to alterations by composers at their whim, he did so.

This insistence on production control was for Verdi a matter not of ego but of quality, and sometimes his perfectionism had regrettable effects. For much of his life he dreamed of an opera on *King Lear*. His letters of the 1850s contain scenario outlines and suggestions. In 1856 he started negotiations with the San Carlo Opera of Naples to write the *Lear* opera, but the project foundered because he would not accept the San Carlo soprano as Cordelia. If this is the debit side of the ledger—that we now have no *King Lear* of Verdi's because of premiere conditions—the credit side is that his concept of theatrical quality (whether or not always maintained subsequently) gave us the works we have.

After his Roman production it was all of three months before Verdi produced another opera—in February 1845 at Milan: *Giovanna d'Arco* (*Joan of Arc*), based by Solera on Schiller's *Maid of Orleans*. (This is where my own experience enters the chronicle, the first of the works so far mentioned that I have seen staged. I saw *Giovanna* in Paris in 1951, with a new singer named Renata Tebaldi, and three things are memorable about it for me: Tebaldi was wonderful; a love scene between Giovanna and King Charles was so inappropriate that it had a naïve charm; and I can't recall one note of the music.) The most interesting point about *Giovanna* is that, like so much of Verdi's work in those days, it had censorship trouble. It dealt with a subjugated country struggling for freedom; so when it was done in Palermo in 1847, the libretto had to be revised, the setting transposed to ancient Greece, and the title changed to *Orietta of Lesbos*.

One reason more that I love Verdi is that his next opera, called *Alzira* and based on Voltaire's tragedy *Alzire* or *The Americans* (set in sixteenth-century Peru), is by common consent his worst. This was Verdi's eighth opera (discounting an early lost opera, before *Oberto,* called *Rocester*), and I respond to the fact that this man was human enough to do his worst work after he was already famous; and I respond too to the fact that seven months later, in March 1846, he produced *Attila* with somewhat more success.

Just a year later came the premiere of his tenth opera, *Macbeth,* his first from the dramatist who was his lifelong passion. "I prefer Shakespeare to every other dramatist," he said once, "the Greeks not excepted." Verdi's *Macbeth* may be the earliest work of his to have life still in the world repertory; I have seen two productions, one in New York (not at the Metropolitan) and one in Rome. In addition to its intrinsic virtues, this *Macbeth* makes a good test of one's ability to accept and thrive on operatic convention. If it is stupidly easy to laugh at any opera as unlifelike, it is less stupidly easy to laugh at an opera from a titanic play. But if one can, for instance, listen to the three choruses of witches in *Macbeth,* instead of three witches, and understand how Verdi and Piave were not merely setting Shakespeare to music but were translating one set of theater conventions into another set, then one can appreciate Verdi's rendition as acute rather than vulgarizing.

Verdi was now in his mid-thirties, and the operas poured out. His next, *I Masnadieri,* based on Schiller's *The Brigands,* was written for Her Majesty's Theater, London, and was produced there in July 1847, four months after *Macbeth* in Florence. (One more reason for loving Verdi: I share his opinion of London. "If only London had the climate of Naples," he wrote, "there would be no need to sigh for paradise.") A whole enormous fifteen months elapsed before the next premiere (*Il Corsaro, The Corsair,* Trieste); then only three months until the next (*La Battaglia di Legnano, The Battle of Legnano,* Rome); eleven months until the next (*Luisa Miller,* Naples); eleven months until the next (*Stiffelio,* Trieste); then after four months, the next, Venice, in March 1851.

It was *Rigoletto*—his second opera based on Victor Hugo with libretto by Piave. Because it is the earliest of his works that is still widely played, we think of it as early Verdi. It was his seventeenth opera. He was thirty-eight.

Staggering though these figures are, it's important to remember that Verdi was only an outstanding example of what was happening in his time, not an exception. Donizetti, to take another such example, wrote some seventy-five operas between 1816 and 1843, at least three of which—*Lucia di Lammermoor, L'Elisir d'Amore,* and *Don Pasquale*—will last as long as some people can sing and others want to listen. The particular joy of this epoch's theater culture was that it gave a genius every chance to grow. The opportunity to write so much, the demand that he do so, strengthened and deepened Verdi.

Take, as instance of his developing theater sense, the very subject of *Rigoletto.* To us today it is simply "an opera." But the play itself had caused a scandal when it was first produced in Paris; and to choose as protagonist of an opera the hunchbacked accessory to a libertine's vices, a father who unwittingly assists in his daughter's ravishing and then her murder—that called for convictions about the theater in advance of contemporary acceptances.

Take, as musical instance of that same theater sense, just one example. In Act Two the hunchbacked jester arrives at the Duke's court pretending to be at work amusing the courtiers but is actually trying to learn where his daughter is; then, discovering that the Duke has her inside, he bursts out in rage at the courtiers; then, realizing his impotence, he breaks down and appeals to them for help. Any composer could have written music that was first bantering, then irate, then suppliant. The distinction of Verdi is that his music goes far past the appropriate basic colors: he has the power to invent melody that is in itself lovely at the same time that it takes the theatrical requirement of the moment to its quintessence. The only reason we don't gasp with wonder every time we hear this three-part scene of Rigoletto's is that it is so good. We now take its power so familiarly that we somehow assume it was easy to do.

Shortly before this premiere Verdi's personal life began to be "visible." He had been a widower since 1840: about 1848 he began to live with an ex-singer named Giuseppina Strepponi, whom he had known since the *Oberto* days and who had become his friend when she sang in the first production of *Nabucco* in 1842. For reasons of health she had eased herself out of an operatic career and moved to Paris, where she gave singing lessons. When Verdi was in Paris on business, they met again, joined lives, and remained joined for fifty years.

Peppina, as Verdi called her, was three years younger than he and, according to Frank Walker, a Verdi scholar, had borne two illegitimate children to a man from whom she was long separated. (Little is known of those children; they did not live with her and presumably died young.) Certainly Verdi loved and honored her; eleven years later he married her.

The delay in marriage may, in a sense, have been Peppina's doing. In his thirties Verdi had no liking for life in the countryside, but she persuaded him otherwise, at least to live in Busseto. There it may well have been the proximity to his adored former father-in-law, Barezzi, that inhibited Verdi from remarrying. It was during this period that he grew to dislike the people of Busseto for their behavior toward Peppina. Nevertheless he bought an estate, the Villa Sant' Agata, near Busseto and eventually married Peppina, and they made Sant' Agata their principal residence from then on.

To visit Sant' Agata, as I have done, is to realize forcefully a particularity in Verdi. He was born in Le Roncole, grew up in Busseto, and spent much of his life at this villa—and all of these places are within a few miles of one another. Avoiding sentimentality about his love of the people (he had his troubles with them) or his love of the land (he went through some disaffection with it), still we can see how important the countryside of his birth was to him, and can infer what a rooted feeling it gave him—maybe just because he could quarrel with the townsfolk in their own dialect. I don't argue that one can hear the Po Valley in his music. But I think it reasonable to believe that his sense of identity was linked with this region and that his identity gave him assurance, just as his (larger) Italianness gave him affinity with an age of opera that this very identity enriched.

Technically Verdi was a citizen of the Duchy of Parma until Italy was united, and it was as such a citizen that he—without fancy—can be said to have written. In 1873 he composed his glorious *Requiem Mass* in honor of the Italian novelist and patriot Alessandro Manzoni. (But Verdi was no devout Catholic. I think it not blasphemous to say that the "theater" of the mass was more sacred to him than its theological components.) When the score was published, Hans von Bülow, the conductor associated with Wagner, disparaged the mass as operatic. Johannes Brahms then sent for the score, studied it, and said, "Bülow has made an ass of himself. Verdi's *Requiem* is a work of genius." What I think Bülow deplored and Brahms recognized was the Po peasant of genius singing the timeless texts in his own specifically Italian voice. This is what a visitor feels —or at least believes he feels—as he stands at the gates of Sant' Agata.

Verdi lived and worked. Then when people thought that he might die or that at least he was played out, he lived and worked some more. After *Rigoletto* came *Il Trovatore* (*The Troubadour*), now a war-horse of the repertory—but how many composers have supplied war-horses? Then came another great act of daring, *La Traviata*. (Hard to translate—*The Strayed Woman,* perhaps.) Alexandre Dumas *fils* had produced his play *La Dame aux Camélias* in February 1852 in Paris. Verdi saw the play and reportedly became wildly enthusiastic about it at once. Today we have small appreciation of the daring it required in 1852 to, first, make an opera of a contemporary play and, second, to choose a drama of the sufferings and sacrifices of a sympathetic courtesan. Frank Walker cites an Italian critic who "has suggested a possible reflection, or sublimation, in this opera of Verdi's personal relationship" with Peppina and with Barezzi, who was not yet reconciled to her. They were quite unlike Violetta and Germont senior, but what does apply, certainly, is the opera's recognition of worth in a woman who lives unconventionally. Francis Toye says that *La Traviata* (done in Venice, March 1853—one year after the play's premiere) "became the symbol of revolt against current sexual conventions." Today that aspect of the work is antique; the importance of *La Traviata*—for me, at any rate—is that it is Verdi's first perfect work, absolutely unflawed, crystalline genius from first note to last, a musical rendition of romantic drama, not realistic rebellion, so pure that its romance becomes real.

With previous Verdi works and even with some that follow, there are moments when I think, "Ah, yes, that's where he came from and what he was better than." In a way I can even enjoy those moments—what better example than the Anvil Chorus in *Il Trovatore?* —because they are such *good* old-fashioned stuff and also because, by contrast, they reveal the dimensions of the material around them. But there are no such moments in *La Traviata*. Every moment is nineteenth-century Italian opera, but every moment is that school of opera at its purest pinnacle. The Prelude to Act One, after its opening moment that asks gently for our attention, sings its famous theme in the strings, but is it a mere lush "operatic" melody? Only in the hands of a ham orchestra. Otherwise it is the very idea of the dramatic-through-the-lyric, the module of which so many other composers provide only barrel-organ imitations. (And Verdi's prodigality of invention is exemplified by the fact that he later uses this theme only once, very briefly, when Violetta says goodbye to Alfredo in Act Two. Just suppose Puccini had been lucky enough to think of that theme. We would have had it banged at us recurrently for three hours.)

The drinking song in Act One, Alfredo's declaration of love, Violetta's suspicion that she may love him—all these enlarge what might have been conventional exercises into music drama because the composer takes the scene with utter seriousness and has the gift to go beneath conventional musical strophe to make the scene quintessential of the feelings it contains. I have no favorite passage in *La Traviata*, but let us look at one more moment: the scene between the elder Germont and Violetta in Act Two. Dramatically it represents the complete conversion of Violetta's attitude toward her affair with Alfredo in a relatively short time. The material, in the harsh glare of textual analysis, is sheer lavender: a courtesan being asked to give up her lover for the sake of his innocent sister's good name. But Verdi, with his intensity of conviction (remember, it was daring material then) makes the scene survive as viable theater; then, with breathtakingly *specific* invention, takes it past the merely viable to the overpowering with one unbelievably beautiful theme after another. This is what I would call perfection in opera: the dramatic, fixed and magnified through music.

Between 1855 and 1867 Verdi wrote the five works sometimes called the "dark" operas, *I Vespri Siciliani* (*The Sicilian Vespers*), *Simon Boccanegra, Un Ballo in Maschera* (*A Masked Ball*), *La Forza del Destino* (*The Force of Destiny*), and *Don Carlo*. (Of *La Forza* Pierre Boulez has said, "If anybody asked me to conduct [it], I'd much rather go for a walk." Permission granted!—by anyone who has ever heard Toscanini's recording of the overture.)

To explain why Verdi produced only five new works in twelve

years, one could say that he also did extensive revisions of two earlier operas and that *La Forza* was commissioned by the Imperial Theater of St. Petersburg, to which Verdi had to make two arduous journeys. But there are other reasons, I think—both for the reduced output and for the melancholy tinge, indefinable but recognizably different from the drama of the earlier days. First, middle age. Verdi entered his fifties during this period, presumably with the energy changes and rue of spirit that often attend that age. Second, the 1860s were a period of tremendous political turbulence and warfare in Italy, too complex to summarize here. (Audiences under Austrian governors used to shout "Viva Verdi" with two meanings: first, the obvious one; second, his name happened to be an acronym for Vittorio Emmanuele Re d'Italia—Victor Emmanuel, King of Italy—the man whom they wanted as king of a free and united homeland.) In fact, during this time Verdi took a relatively complete holiday from music for two years to devote himself to politics. After Parma was joined by plebiscite to Piedmont, Verdi was induced, much against his will, to run for office in the Chamber of Deputies at Turin. He was elected, and served from 1860 to 1865 as a devoted follower of the great leader of the *Risorgimento,* Count Camillo Cavour, whose policies he supported even after Cavour died in 1861.

Another possible reason for the diminution and darkening of activity was purely musical. Verdi for a while had been a god in Italy, in much of Europe. Through the 1860s a rival god appeared in the north, Richard Wagner. Admiration for Wagner's work began to infiltrate Italy, particularly among the young, and increasingly Verdi was mocked, even calumniated. He held himself above the battle—and indeed, years later, wrote a very touching letter when Wagner died—but he was certainly disturbed.

For some or all of these reasons there were four years of musical silence after *Don Carlo,* the longest silent period in Verdi's career up to that time. In 1868 he was approached by the Khedive of Egypt to write an opera for the opening of the Suez Canal. Verdi got a libretto in French prose from Camille du Locle which was turned into Italian verse by Antonio Ghislanzoni, and at last *Aïda* was produced in Cairo in December 1871. Two months later it was produced at La Scala, Milan, with gigantic success, although—much to Verdi's hurt —some attributed his fuller, richer use of the orchestra to the influence of Wagner.

Under everything, however, Verdi remained the stubborn, dryly humorous peasant. When *Aïda* was performed at Parma in May 1872, Verdi got a letter from a man who lived nearby saying that he had made two trips to Parma, had seen *Aïda* twice, hadn't liked it, and was enclosing a bill for two round-trip tickets, two theater tickets, and two "detestable suppers" at the station. Verdi instructed his publisher, Ricordi, to pay the bill, deducting only the price of the meals, which the man would have had to eat anyway, all on condition that the man sign a formal document promising never to attend any Verdi operas in the future. The document was drawn up and executed, the money refunded.

In 1873 he wrote the *Requiem,* easily the best of his few works outside the theater, conducted it in Milan in 1874, then conducted it in Paris, London, and Vienna. He was sixty-two. Vittorio Emmanuele, now King, made him an honorary senator; though Verdi accepted, he never attended parliamentary sessions. Many thought, and he more or less agreed, that his public life of every kind was finished. He revised *Simon Boccanegra,* he conducted *Aïda* in Paris, but he wrote nothing new.

Yet again Verdi surprised the world. In 1879 he met an extraordinary man twenty-nine years his junior—Arrigo Boito, half Italian, half Polish, poet, and in his own right a composer. (His opera *Mefistofele* is still performed.) He had once written an anti-Verdi poem, but was now not only contrite but thoroughly converted to Verdi's music. He and Verdi were brought together to discuss the possibility of an opera on *Othello.* Three days later Boito produced a sketch for the libretto. Seven years later the opera was finished. Many think, with justice, that Boito gave Verdi the best opera libretto ever written. As for the music, the least that can be said of it is that it is worthy of the libretto. (Bernard Shaw wrote that Verdi's success with *Otello* "proves, not that he could occupy Shakespeare's plane, but that Shakespeare could on occasion occupy his." Well, by such a measure from such a measurer, that seems praise enough.)

Otello was first performed at La Scala, Milan, in February 1887. Toye records that the oldest of theatrical tributes was accorded Verdi after the premiere. "When the composer left the theater, a crowd of admirers, who throughout the day had lined the streets to applaud his every appearance, unharnessed the horses from his carriage and drew it to the Hotel di Milano, where he always stayed."

And *still* he was not finished. Let us acknowledge the last miracle quickly. With the aid of another superb libretto from Boito, Verdi six years later produced *Falstaff* (from *The Merry Wives of Windsor*)— again at La Scala, February 1893. He was seventy-nine. Remember that not only when the music's comic vitality bursts at you from the very first phrase but when you hear Fenton's love song in Act Three, that lifting lyric of poeticized desire. (Evidently, and this is not rare, Verdi felt brighter at seventy-nine than at fifty-five.)

He lived another eight years. He died on January 27, 1901, in that same Hotel di Milano. Peppina, wife and strength of most of his life, had been dead four years.

He bequeathed most of his money, the future royalties from his operas, his piano, and his first spinet to the home for destitute musicians that he himself had built in Milan; and he directed that he and Peppina were to be buried side by side in the oratory of that home, which is where they are.

Wholeness: that is a prime quality in the life sketched above, the sense that the artist in that life moved right *through* it to the end. Some still speak of the split Verdi, the early "Rossinian" and the later "Wagnerian." I have always thought of him as one, growing man. Incompetent to comment musically, I cite three professionals.

Georg Solti, that excellent conductor: "Even in the operas of the 1850s certain passages anticipate the next stage of development. They demonstrate Verdi's genius for expressing human tragedy by understatement."

Donald Francis Tovey, prince of critics: "The remarkable thing in Verdi's later development is that it shows no conflict of style. Verdi once said of himself, 'I am not a learned composer, but I am a very experienced one.' That is the word of power. . . . All of his experience went into his music and enlarged it, crowding out what it superseded, without demanding transplantation and without injuring its foundations."

Igor Stravinsky: "Verdi's gift is pure, but even more remarkable than the gift itself is the strength with which he developed it from *Rigoletto* to *Falstaff,* to name the two operas I love best."

In 1876 Verdi wrote to a friend: "It may be a good thing to copy reality; but to invent reality is much, much better."

It is the statement of a man who understands that reality is not necessarily mimesis of actuality: reality, in art, may lie in constructed systems that deploy experience at the maker's will in order to illuminate our lives. And Verdi understands, in contrast to the usual cant, that life is not necessarily "more important" than art. First, art is inseparably part of life; second, it is the part of life where the best that man can conceive is attainable—design, purpose, meaningful comedy, meaningful tragedy, instead of the kinds which we usually face in the world around us.

Verdi's life was hardly an ivory-tower existence, as we have seen, yet there is the feeling that art is where he really existed. He was in some ways modest—he often said he was "not a learned composer" or some variant thereof; but he was furiously committed. And underneath his painstaking work with librettists, his difficulties with managers and singers and conductors, his passion for finish in every detail, there lies, I think, this passion for the "real" reality. Life, he says, is nonsense without art, and art is nonsense unless it is absolutely the best that one can make it. The possibility of perfection is the reality of art, available only in art.

That passion drives through the story of his life. But other great artists—Rembrandt, Keats, Joyce, to name a random few—had the same passion. Why the special appeal of Verdi? Why, to speak personally, is he "my" Verdi, as evidently he has been to millions? (Stravinsky said: "How I would like to have known him!")

One reason is that Verdi was a true man of the theater. That phrase is often cheaply used, as if it were grandly self-justifying. Here is one attempt to explain it: the man of the theater is an artist for whom experience is clarified and consciousness is extended through conflict, for whom agon is the means to order out of chaos. Unlike such artists as the lyric poet and the novelist, the theater artist's radical perception is of truth approached through a line of rising tensions to conflict and to change. Fundamentally, the test of the theater artist's quality is whether he sees experience that way, inevitably and surely, or whether he has to adjust experience to that perception, to work on it. Fundamentally, it is this vision of life as truthful through drama, rather than as material for drama, that distinguishes the great theater artist from the merely good or worse.

Nietzsche said, "Only artists, and especially those of the theater, have given men eyes and ears to see and hear with some pleasure what each man *is* himself. . . . Only they have taught us . . . the art of staging and watching ourselves. . . . Without this art we would be nothing but foreground and would live entirely in the spell of that perspective which makes what is closest at hand and most vulgar appear as if it were vast, and reality itself." That truer perspective, which tells us where reality begins to exist, was in Verdi.

But why is it so powerful in Verdi? Why is his theater art, practiced through music, so commanding and irresistible? Foremost in the answer, so far as the answer can be made in words, is his melody. We are supposed to be a bit embarrassed about that term these days; the term "theme" is more chic (and often the theme is an arrangement of sounds that could be otherwise arranged without harm). But if Verdi's melodies, as melodies, did not appeal—at once and always— we would not be talking about him. His work would be as dead as that of his jealous rival Mercadante, whose sixty operas are completely forgotten. All discussion of Verdi's gravity and growth, even of his orchestral virtues on which Solti and Tovey insist, would not exist without the first, immediate appeal of his melody.

It is dynamic melody. It comments and characterizes as it moves. It delights, but is meant to do more than delight: it is intended to grow, to take you from one point to another like a passage of poetic drama, to leave you changed. What the great Verdi singers know, what Toscanini knew so wonderfully, is that no aria, no phrase of Verdi is over until the very end. The *line* must be held, rising to the conclusion. He writes, so to speak, in periodic sentences. All of it is beautiful, but none of it is fully beautiful until it reaches the end for which it has been made beautiful, and the dramatic reality is complete.

We often say, rightly, that Verdi touches the heart, that his music embraces the whole range of feelings in us. This swift immediacy, this ease of access to us exists—in his case, at least—because he was a popular artist working in a (then) popular art. Essentially that is what comes through his music, I think, through his life. He was (like Shakespeare) a popular artist in both senses—of the people and for the people. Excepting a few film-makers in the century to come, he was the last great genius in Western cultural history to create for a wide audience, not for a cultivated elite. He wrote with such intensity and depth that he transcended popular conventions without forsaking them; he built on them (like Shakespeare) to grow from a national artist very much of his time, to a world artist for all foreseeable time. When we love Verdi, possibly we are responding to the fact that he was of an age when the very best could be for the most; possibly we are responding to the warm sense of community that supports and empowers him.

The FM radio plays while I read and, absorbed in my book, I stupidly "waste" the good music. Then they put on a Verdi record— Claudia Muzio singing *"Addio del passato"* from the last act of *Traviata*—and the book drops in my hands. The composer has given the singing actress the means to tear me away. The little squash-hatted peasant has included me in his command that we leave our lives for the truth of our lives through drama. Muzio sings her last sudden high note—no, utters her last cry—and the strings beat softly, quickly, to a close. And I am left, hungry, in the reality outside that music, the lesser reality in which, most of the time, I live.

PART IV

stages of discussion

homosexuality

Homosexual Drama and Its Disguises

(The New York Times, *January 23, 1966*)

A recent Broadway production raises again the subject of the homosexual dramatist. It is a subject that nobody is comfortable about. All of us admirably "normal" people are a bit irritated by it and wish it could disappear. However, it promises to be a matter of continuing, perhaps increasing, significance.

The principal complaint against homosexual dramatists is well known. Because three of the most successful American playwrights of the last twenty years are (reputed) homosexuals and because their plays often treat of women and marriage, therefore, it is said, postwar

291

American drama presents a badly distorted picture of American women, marriage, and society in general. Certainly there is substance in the charge; but is it rightly directed?

The first, obvious point is that there is no law against heterosexual dramatists, and there is no demonstrable cabal against their being produced. If there are heterosexuals who have talent equivalent with those three men, why aren't these "normal" people writing? Why don't they counterbalance or correct the distorted picture?

But, to talk of what is and not of what might be, the fact is that the homosexual dramatist is not to blame in this matter. If he writes of marriage and of other relationships about which he knows or cares little, it is because he has no choice but to masquerade. Both convention and the law demand it. In society the homosexual's life must be discreetly concealed. As material for drama, that life must be even more intensely concealed. If he is to write of his experience, he must invent a two-sex version of the one-sex experience that he really knows. It is we who insist on it, not he.

There would seem to be only two alternative ways to end this masquerading. First, the Dramatists' Guild can pass a law forbidding membership to those who do not pass a medico-psychological test for heterosexuality. Or, second, social and theatrical convention can be widened so that homosexual life may be as freely dramatized as heterosexual life, may be as frankly treated in our drama as it is in contemporary fiction.

If we object to the distortion that homosexual disguises entail and if, as civilized people, we do not want to gag these artists, then there seems only one conclusion. The conditions that force the dissembling must change. The homosexual dramatist must be free to write truthfully of what he knows, rather than try to transform it to a life he does not know, to the detriment of his truth and ours.

The cries go up, perhaps, of decadence, corruption, encouragement of emotional-psychological illness. But is there consistency in these cries? Are there similar objections to *The Country Wife, Inadmissible Evidence, The Right Honorable Gentleman* on the ground that they propagandize for the sexually unconventional or "corruptive" matters that are germane to them? Alcoholism, greed, ruthless competitiveness are equally neurotic, equally undesirable socially; would any of us wish to bar them arbitrarily from the stage?

Only this one neurosis, homosexuality, is taboo in the main traffic of our stage. The reasons for this I leave to psychologists and to self-candor, but they do not make the discrimination any more just.

I do not argue for increased homosexual influence in our theater. It is precisely because I, like many others, am weary of disguised homosexual influence that I raise the matter. We have all had much more than enough of the materials so often presented by the three writers in question: the viciousness toward women, the lurid violence that seems a sublimation of social hatreds, the transvestite sexual exhibitionism that has the same sneering exploitation of its audience that every club stripper has behind her smile. But I suggest that, fundamentally, what we are objecting to in these plays is the result of conditions that we ourselves have imposed. The dissimulations and role-playings are there because we have made them inevitable.

Homosexuals with writing ability are likely to go on being drawn to the theater. It is quite the logical consequence of the defiant and/or protective histrionism they must employ in their daily lives. So there is every reason to expect more plays by talented homosexuals. There is some liberty for them, limited, in café theaters and Off Broadway; if they want the full resources of the professional theater, they must dissemble. So there is every reason to expect their plays to be streaked with vindictiveness toward the society that constricts and, theatrically, discriminates against them.

To me, their distortion of marriage and femininity is not the primary aspect of this matter; for if an adult listens to these plays with a figurative transistor-radio simultaneously translating, he hears that the marital quarrels are usually homosexual quarrels with one of the pair in costume and that the incontrovertibly female figures are usually drawn less in truth than in envy or fear. To me, there is a more important result of this vindictiveness—its effect on the basic concept of drama itself and of art in general.

Homosexual artists, male and female, tend to convert their exclusion into a philosophy of art that glorifies their exclusion. They exalt style, manner, surface. They decry artistic concern with the traditional matters of theme and subject because they are prevented from using fully the themes of their own experience. They emphasize manner and style because these elements of art, at which they are often adept, are legal tender in their transactions with the world. These elements are, or can be, esthetically divorced from such other considerations as character and idea.

Thus we get plays in which manner is the paramount consideration, in which the surface and mode of a work are to be taken as its whole. Its allegorical relevance (if any) is not to be anatomized, its visceral emotion (if any) need not be validated, and any judgment other than a stylistic one is considered inappropriate, even censorious. Not all artists and critics who advance this theory of style-asking are homosexuals, but the camp has a strong homosexual coloration.

What is more, this theory can be seen, I believe, as an instrument of revenge on the main body of society. Theme and subject are important historical principles in our art. The arguments to prove that they are of diminishing importance—in fact, ought never to have been important—are cover for an attack on the idea of social relevance. By adulation of sheer style, this group tends to deride the whole culture and the society that produced it, tends to reduce art to a clever game which even that society cannot keep it from playing.

But how can one blame these people? Conventions and puritanisms in the Western world have forced them to wear masks for generations, to hate themselves, and thus to hate those who make them hate themselves. Now that they have a certain relative freedom, they vent their feelings in camouflaged form.

Doubtless, if the theater comes to approximate the publishing world's liberality, we shall retrace in plays, as we are doing in novels, the history of heterosexual romantic love with an altered cast of characters. But that situation would be self-amending in time; the present situation is self-perpetuating and is culturally risky.

A serious public, seriously interested in the theater, must sooner or later consider that when it complains of homosexual influences and distortions, it is complaining, at one remove, about its own attitudes. I note further that one of the few contemporary dramatists whose works are candidates for greatness, Jean Genet, is a homosexual who has never had to disguise his nature.

On the Acceptability of the Homosexual

(The New York Times, *February 6, 1966*)

My thanks to all correspondents—well, almost all—who commented on my remarks about homosexual dramatists two Sundays ago. Most of the numerous letters expressed antipathy to my remarks, but I cannot quite call them letters of dissent because they did not often disagree with what I actually said. They dealt more with matters inferred than with statements made in the article.

The subject is self-evidently important and worth further exploration. Rather than try to answer individual letters, I have extracted for comment (and have italicized below) the principal themes that run through the letters.

In the light of modern knowledge, it is impossible to draw a distinct line between homosexuals and heterosexuals. This seems to me a socially sentimentalized version of some psychological truths. We all know that everyone contains elements of hetero- and homosexuality and that some individuals lead both kinds of sexual life. Indeed, in a notable article called "Homosexuality and American Theater" (*Tulane Drama Review,* Spring 1965), Donald M. Kaplan, a psychoanalyst, writes that "the distinction between heterosexuality and homosexuality in the world of current theater is a thin line of illusion." But Dr. Kaplan is discussing the generally *unconscious* forces in our society that have bred, even encouraged, the growth of homosexual elements in our theater. This does not controvert the fact that those who live consciously as homosexuals know society's estimate of them and the legal strictures aimed at them; and know that in order to write plays about life as they experience it, they must in some degree disguise that experience. The plain fact that I could not name the three dramatists I was discussing is proof of their technically outlawed position.

To state that I, for example, presumably have homosexual components in my psyche is irrelevant to the social fact that my marital life is legally and conventionally acceptable, while the homosexual's life is restricted by law and convention. To claim that this social fact has no influence on the homosexual writer is to argue an insensitivity in him that is not credible.

An author does not have to murder in order to write of murder, does not have to be a woman to write of women, etc. Why cannot a homosexual write of marriage? Obviously, all artists write of more than they actually experience, or the world's imaginative literature would be strictly autobiographical, would in fact not be imaginative. All that we ask for is conviction. When an author writes of areas in which we are personally inexperienced—murder (for most of us), femininity (if we are men)—we ask to be convinced by correlation with what we have observed and imagined. When he writes about matters of which we have experience—such as marriage, if we are married—our standards are firsthand, though of course not encyclopedic.

But this comment by readers is an example of imaginary inference from that first article. I made no suggestion that homosexuals be barred from writing about heterosexuals, any more than the reverse. The homosexual scene in *Inadmissible Evidence* by the presumably "normal" John Osborne is one of the most touching passages in the play. I said only that homosexuals should be allowed to write about life, all of life, as they honestly see it.

There seems to me a cosmic difference between a homosexual's writing about marriage, if he chooses, and a homosexual's being forced to disguise his own experience as marriage in order to write about it.

Many heterosexual dramatists have written vituperatively of women. I did not suggest that only homosexuals have written of women as destroyers; or that amiability toward women is in itself a criterion of either a dramatist's sexuality or his worth. But, again, there is a wide difference between a writer's straightforward truth on the subject of women and a pretense to one kind of reaction on that subject when he is motivated by another.

Many homosexual authors have written warmly and beautifully of women. Accepting this as common knowledge, I specified that in the work of three contemporary American dramatists there seem to be some disguises and distortions about women and marriage.

Many homosexual artists have been geniuses. Michelangelo, da Vinci, Shakespeare, and Proust were the four most frequently named. As for the first two, the arts of painting and sculpture can be practiced with fewer references to details of character and psychological color than writing must use. (Music can be composed entirely without environmental reference.) With all respect to Freud's psychosexual analysis of Michelangelo and da Vinci, one can look at their works for years without raising the question of the makers' sexuality. (Possibly excepting such figures as the sibyls in the Sistine ceiling.) The work of novelists and dramatists, which must use words, ideas, details of living, cannot be so abstracted.

Shakespeare's presumptive homosexuality occurred in a context so different from ours—a theater in which all female roles were written for boys and were played by them—that it is difficult to reconstruct the Elizabethan creative and emotional environment. (For a stimulating fictional attempt, see Anthony Burgess' novel *Nothing Like the Sun.*) Shakespeare's creation of female characters, or that of Proust (whose Albertine was probably an Albert transvested), is not neatly explicable. But explication is not called for here. Why need we cite these towering geniuses in connection with the American dramatists in question? Do the achievements of Shakespeare and Proust justify the social attitudes that produced distortions in the work of these lesser men?

Homosexual subjects have already been treated on the Broadway stage. Yes, earlier than any correspondents mentioned: Edouard Bourdet's *The Captive* (about lesbianism) was produced—and censored—in 1926. But the subject is still surrounded by an air of exceptional daring and controversy. More important, the point is not an argument merely for homosexual subjects but for the freedom of the homosexual writer—a much broader argument.

A play should be judged on its merits, not by its author's sexuality. With this thundering truism, who would disagree? I would only add that if one sees elements in a play that keep it from complete realization and if one believes, on purely internal evidence, that these elements come from homosexual disguise or distortion, then, with equal truism, one is not only permitted but also obligated to express this view.

But I want to leave rebuttal and close with the positive intent of the earlier article. The homosexual dramatist ought to have the same freedom that the heterosexual has. While we deny him that freedom, we have no grounds for complaint when he uses disguises in order to write. Further, to deny him that freedom is to encourage a somewhat precious esthetics that, out of understandable vindictiveness, is hostile to the mainstream of culture. It seems to me that only by such freedom can our theater be freed of homosexual "influence"—a mis-

nomer for the stratagems that homosexuals in all branches of the
theater are now often forced to use in order to work.

One well-known writer on the theater has asked whether I mean
that I want to see homosexual intercourse on the stage. No more, I
would say—and rather less, in fact—than I want to see heterosexual
intercourse. I mean simply (to repeat) that homosexual dramatists
need the same liberty that heterosexuals now have. If this is too much
for us to contemplate, then at least let us all drop the cant about
homosexual "influence" and distortion: because we are only complaining of the results of our own attitudes.

Find Your Way Home

(January 26, 1974)

The last six or seven years have brought a flood of Off-Broadway
plays about homosexuality. The biggest hit was the slick *Boys in the
Band* by Mart Crowley, and the most recent was *The Enclave,* abysmal, by Arthur Laurents. Now there's a homosexual play on Broadway.

Find Your Way Home is by no means the first play on the subject
to be performed on Broadway. Edouard Bourdet's *The Captive,*
about lesbianism, was produced in 1926 (and was closed by police
action). The first time I ever saw Laurence Olivier he was the object
of an older man's pursuit in Mordaunt Shairp's *The Green Bay Tree*
(1933). One of the best homosexual plays I've seen, also about
lesbianism, was Dorothy and Howard Baker's *Trio* (1944). But this
new play is much more explicit than anything I've seen on Broadway.
Broadway's daring was, as usual, prepared by Off Broadway, and, as
is also usual with Broadway daring, the play is an import.

The author is John Hopkins, an Englishman who has made a
serious reputation in his country with his TV dramas (imagine *that*
here!) and has a new play to be directed by Harold Pinter this spring.
To judge by *Find Your Way Home,* Hopkins' first U.S. production,
his reputation is running a bit ahead of his achievement.

A middle-aged married man has learned that his homosexual interest is stronger than his interest in his wife or his (many other) girls.

He returns to the young man he loves after a year's absence, and his wife secretly follows him. She thinks he is meeting a girl. The wife, after shock, after recovery of equilibrium, implores him to return; the husband, apparently, decides to remain with the youth. (It's a somewhat ambiguous ending.) The most engaging of the trio, by far, is the young man, who has been driven by his socio-sexual position and his forlorn love for the older man over the borders of degradation and prostitution.

Hopkins is utterly serious and is concerned only with the effect of emotional developments on these three people. But he has made the mistake of assuming that the choice of this still-daring subject is in itself dramatic, will itself supply the "meat" of a play; and that his honesty will itself provide fresh insights. The script that followed, after he chose the subject and licensed himself, is at best adequate and is a good deal of the time banal. If one imagines this play as dealing with a conventional triangle, something that's frequently easy to do, then such a scene as the wife's confrontation of the husband, her fears of loneliness, her references to the children, her progress through various sorts of pride are all extremely familiar. Most of the dialogue is more cliché than vernacular. (Phrases occur like "Time passes" and, about a job, "I was a glorified office boy.") Also some of the sexual data seem rather obtrusively explicit. Perhaps this is the characters' bravura, rather than Hopkins'. Concede that, and we are still left with a play that means, rather than does, well.

But the evening is memorable, the play worth seeing, because of Michael Moriarty. (His only important previous New York appearance was as a replacement.) Moriarty has been working his way up through and around regional theaters; I saw him first in Minneapolis in 1966 and thought he had talent. He played the lead in the recent film *Bang the Drum Slowly* quite competently, if not overwhelmingly, and in Katharine Hepburn's recent TV production of *The Glass Menagerie* he gave the only good performance, as the Gentleman Caller. In Hopkins' play he has the first really demanding role I have seen him in and, as is often the case with gifted people, the more demanding the role the better the performance. Moriarty seems to *etch* the portrait of this young man with incisions of semi-suppressed agony and forced facetiousness. Every pause, every inflection, every jagged gesture seems the consequence of a turbulent and continuous internal process, revealed to us in slivers and flashes. He is fine; and, especially as he reveals a full voice in his occasional brief outbursts, he could have a very considerable future.

The wife is played by Jane Alexander (who was the girl in *The Great White Hope*) with intelligence, but her faintly adenoidal suburban sensitivity intrudes somewhat between her and me. The husband is Lee Richardson, a competent, experienced craftsman who, alas, seems the actor the producers had to settle for when they couldn't get the one they wanted originally. Edwin Sherin has directed generally well, although he does leave people standing about quite a lot, and he has quite obviously planted a chair downstage left for a listener to sit in while others have long speeches, so that the speaker can play front.

people

An Actor's Life*

The Autobiography of Joseph Jefferson, edited by Alan S. Downer. Harvard University Press. Originally published in 1890 by the Century Company.

(May 6, 1972)

I have a recording so old that it begins with an announcer's voice. He says: "Mountain Scene from *Rip Van Winkle* by Joseph Jefferson. Columbia Record." Then we hear Rip in the Catskills, meeting the queer little man (whom we don't hear) with the keg of schnapps. The

* Written for a series of "Reconsiderations" of old books.

voice is a light baritone with little upward breaks for intimacy and fun, the accent a friendly stage German. On the other side is the Return Scene, twenty years later, between Rip and his daughter (whom we don't hear), with the sentiment as sure and unabashed and therefore effective as in a Chaplin film.

What an eerie, fascinating feeling to put down the autobiography of a man born in 1829 and then hear his voice, a man who knew such actors as Forrest, Macready, Cushman, and Booth, who met Holmes and Longfellow and Stowe, Trollope and Browning. The record supports the central impression of the book: that it is a strand of cultural history leading from a remote age—more than 140 years in effect, if not in actual time—to the beginnings of the present.

Jefferson's autobiography is one of the few "classics" among lives of actors, which term I would define as biographies that can be read for pleasure even by general readers. On the evidence Jefferson was a wonderful one-part actor. He played numerous other roles besides Rip, but several good critics wrote that he was Rip, and wonderful, in all of them. His book lives, not as a memorial of a great artist, which he never claims, but as a picture of an intensely active theater, a compendium of observations on acting, a sketchbook of a changing nation, and a journal of an open-eyed traveler abroad.

Jefferson, who died in 1905, was the son and grandson of actors. So far as his autobiography or his editor, the late Alan Downer, tells us, he had very scanty formal education, so the writing, which is competent Victorianese, is especially remarkable. He started it at the instigation of William Dean Howells, who may have helped, and also had help from Richard Watson Gilder, the editor of *The Century Magazine,* who serialized it before book publication; but their help, whatever it was, was unintrusive because the tone is personal and consistent.

Jefferson's parents were poor and may not have been very good actors: their engagements were usually short and they spent most of their time as strolling players. He was born in Philadelphia, but had no fixed residence until much later in life. He made his debut in Washington at the age of four in blackface, doing a Jim Crow song. (Among other matters, his book reflects current prejudices against blacks, Jews, and Indians—all points of etiquette, even in a good-hearted man, during Jefferson's lifetime.) His childhood included a tour through the Erie Canal to the new town of Chicago, population

2000; travel by open wagon and sleigh down to Springfield, where the company was aided by a young lawyer named (but it's *true*) Lincoln; literal barn-storming in Mississippi. His youth included a tour following the American army into Mexico in 1846, where he had his first romantic encounter. About sex and love and marriage—he was twice married—he is reticent. Modern readers are conditioned to supply what he leaves out.

He leaves out a good deal, in fact. The book skips many transitions and, of course, does not conclude his career. He lived and worked for fifteen years more, and got honorary degrees from Yale and Harvard. It is a chronological collection of memoirs, rather than a seamless account.

For instance, in 1856 he made a trip to London and Paris—"not the Paris of today [!], with its gilded domes and modern grandeur, but the old, quaint, dirty, gay, strange city in the early days of the Second Empire, with its high, toppling buildings, narrow streets, and lively people." He says he wanted to see France because his mother's family had come from there, but it still seems an unusual and unusually expensive jaunt for a quite modestly successful actor of twenty-seven to make with his family in those days. In 1861 he went to Australia, without any reason given. Downer says that Jefferson was not in good health and that, after the death of his first wife in that year, he needed to travel. But he stayed in Australia and New Zealand four years, acting much of the time. Is it mere coincidence that his exile was precisely during the years of the Civil War? He does not say; but his book reveals great affection for the South—in later years he had a home in Louisiana, as well as in Massachusetts—and one can speculate that he had Northern affiliations but Southern sympathies and used his wife's death as an excuse to avoid decision.

There are dozens of general anecdotes, mostly vivid (including a murder he witnessed in his youth), but the book's uniqueness is in its view of a nation and a time from a life in the theater of the day. Here, as unselfconscious cultural history, one can discern four principal themes.

First, the American theater was dominated by English or Irish actors until well along in the nineteenth century. Downer's annotation tells us that the vast majority of the actors whom Jefferson knew were born in the British Isles and often returned there. (And as Francis Hodge says in *Yankee Theatre,* the authors of Jefferson's two big

"Yankee" hits, *The Octoroon* and *Our American Cousin,* were an Irishman, Dion Boucicault, and an Englishman, Tom Taylor.) Imagine the mixture of accents in a performance. Jefferson himself says of his first appearance with Laura Keene in 1857 on the "western side" of New York: "It was looked upon as a kind of presumption in those days for an American actor to intrude himself into a Broadway theater; the domestic article seldom aspired to anything higher than the Bowery."

Second, there was, in the sociological sense, a society of actors. Actors lived everywhere, figuratively speaking, because there were companies everywhere, as well as strolling troupes that played "in between" and stars who traveled to the resident companies. In 1868 Jefferson was one of the first stars to employ a "combination," a company of actors who traveled with him, instead of appearing with a local company who supported him; and he feels it necessary to justify this startling innovation at length. There are now some dozens of resident theaters in the U.S., but they do not yet constitute such a national society of actors because they are not a natural, inevitable product of our culture, they are an attempt to counteract some of its centralizing, polarizing impetus. All hopes for their success; but they make quite a different case from Jefferson's going to Boston or Philadelphia or Louisville or St. Louis and finding old actor friends living and working there, getting their satisfactions or dissatisfactions where they were.

Third, connected with this, was the status of theater as popular culture. Film critics and historians tend to think that the glamour and mythologizing of actors began with film, but when the only performing idols available were live actors, *they* were mythologized. Instead of, say, James Stewart being available in every city simultaneously, every city had an actor doing James Stewart roles. On a South American visit, Jefferson ran into an American who recognized him and pumped him with questions about actors back home, name after name after name. "They seem like old friends to me," says this theatergoer. He sounds like a modern movie buff.

Fourth is Jefferson's discovery that, through the years, the audience was getting impatient with words and was more interested in visual effects. "Why should this be? Is not the audience of today as intelligent as that of a hundred years ago? This may be so, but by degrees it has been accustomed to a supply of entertainments for the eye, rather than the ear. . . ." This supports the thesis of A. Nicholas Vardac in *Stage to Screen* that the nineteenth-century popular theater was unconsciously moving toward film, that its audience unconsciously demanded the invention of film. (Vardac also notes that in 1896 Jefferson filmed a few minutes of Rip.)

Forty years ago, when I first read the *Autobiography,* I was filled with regret for an era I had missed. Now I'm more suspicious. Great as the best actors probably were, most of the productions, as ensemble work, must have been horrible by our standards. Still, to read the book now is to see a theater that, tackiness and all, had one quality at its height that our theater must regain: it was essential. Outside of religious bigots, very few nineteenth-century Americans would have dreamed of *not* going to the theater.

Obviously, it was more widely available, proportionately, than now, and it satisfied appetites that are now satisfied by most films and almost all TV. But one definition of the challenge to our theater today is that it must find a way of being necessary without being popular, since the pop hunger, which is in all of us, is fed otherwise. Not hard-breathing "relevance" or preening "uplift" but essentiality is what our theater needs; and the task is complicated because today's audience is more experienced, more wooed, more selective than earlier ones. Yet there are recurrent occasions—a new play here, a new production there—to believe that the theater can still be a certification, an enlargement, of our existence, unduplicated elsewhere. When those occasions can reasonably be hoped for by a prospective audience, the theater becomes essential. Jefferson's book is no blueprint, but it describes a desirable norm: a time when a theater and its audience depended on one another.

Bernard Shaw: Collected Letters 1874–1897*

(November 27, 1965)

What an especially irritating world it must be for those who dislike Shaw. During his lifetime, there he was, with irrepressible regularity, in their newspapers and magazines and theaters and bookshops. He is

* Published by Dodd, Mead.

still very much in theaters around the world and, as a subject as well
as an author, is still very much in the bookshops. (At least five new
Shaw books in this season alone.) Of course one need neither see his
plays nor read those books, but to the antipathetic, the fact of their
existence and the effort of ignoring them must be a small crown, if
not cushion, of thorns.

The most important book of these five latest, and the most important of the post-mortem Shaw industry, is, with maddening inevitability, by Shaw himself. Dan H. Laurence has previously edited three
collections of Shaw material—on music, polemics, and Ireland—
which had been justifiably uncollected by the author. Now Laurence
has embarked on the huge task of editing Shaw's letters for publication in four volumes, of which this is the first—ending in 1897 when
Shaw was forty-one. Laurence has had a considerable job of selection. There is supposed to have been a total of well over a quarter-
million letters, postcards, and so forth, not now all extant or available. Of the available correspondence in this first period, Laurence
has published 691 items. He has selected intelligently, with an awareness of context, inner sequences, overtones, and pertinences, and he
has annotated the letters thoroughly with biographical and other data.
As a reading volume, it is surprisingly interesting; very little tempts
one to skip. As a reference work, it is invaluable, particularly since
there is no completely satisfactory biography. (Of the major attempts, Henderson is out-of-date and incomplete anyway, Pearson is
gossamer-brained, Ervine is all polarized adulation-and-jealousy by a
dramatist-critic-friend who knows he was inferior but keeps trying to
prove that he wasn't.)

The proportion of letters to calendar year naturally increases as
time goes on and as the subject's life becomes more full. The entries
for 1887 fill only twenty pages, those for 1897 fill 125 pages. Not all
of the entries were previously unknown; 235 had already been published, at least partially, but their inclusion here (like those to Ellen
Terry) was necessary. In future volumes the letters to, for example,
Granville Barker and Mrs. Campbell must be included. Laurence has
had access to the much publicized but still unpublished diaries that
Shaw kept from 1885 to 1897, now in the possession of the London
School of Economics, and makes several helpful references to them.

In the letters there are dozens and dozens of engaging details,
anecdotes, and small insights; there are also revelations of larger

matters. A sampling of the former: applying for a job at twenty-three, he speaks of his one previous position:

In this post I sulkily distinguished myself so much that when, a year later, the cashier, an elderly man whose testimonials were quite as flattering as that which I enclose, absconded, I took his place. . . .

By 1885 he was playing down his first name, probably out of dislike of his father, also a George.

There is an assortment of extensive advice on, among other topics, novel-writing (before he had published a line of fiction); interviewing; how to form a newspaper syndicate; speech lessons; how to write libretti; how to play Shakespeare (this to Ellen Terry).

There are stabs of history-alive. In letters to William Archer he asks the Ibsen translator to "go to headquarters and consult Ibsen" for advice on a production of *Little Eyolf* in 1896. On a lower scale, we can also observe such matters as the arrival, trial, and acceptance of the telephone and typewriter.

There is an account of a bicycling collision with Bertrand Russell in 1895 that contains tiny sketches of the two not-yet-eminent men:

Russell, fortunately, was not even scratched; but his knickerbockers were demolished. . . . As for me, I flew through the air for several yards, and then smote the earth like a thunderbolt. . . . "All right," I shouted . . . "I am not hurt" and bounded up, pulling myself all together instinctively. "You *must* be," said Russell, glaring at me in consternation.

Essentially this book is the record of a birth. In 1876 Shaw, at the age of nineteen, emigrated from Dublin and his father to join his mother and his surviving sister in London, where they had gone three years before. His reasons were a blighted romance, an aversion for his father and an affection for his mother, and a sense of possibility in London as against one of suffocation in Dublin. This book details the hatching of London Shaw. He said many years later that he was Irish by birth, English by conquest, and this volume contains the plans of campaign—the blithe but unshakable self-assurance that is the mark of the genius or the pathetic crank. Either a man fulfills these youthful assertions and assumptions about himself, or he ends up as a graying figure of fun in bohemian cafés. The general image of this book is that Shaw erected a dream edifice and then slipped in realities underneath to sustain it.

There were two main sources of those realities. His first efforts at creative writing (as the phrase is) were failures—five novels that bounced dismally from publisher to publisher in London and New York. Then, while still supported by his mother's singing lessons, at the age of twenty-seven, he met William Archer in the British Museum reading room, and Archer got him his first critical post. At about the same time he heard Henry George lecture, became interested in economics and socialism, and soon joined the newly formed Fabian Society. These twin avenues of critical journalism (art, literature, music, drama) and political activity (lecturing, pamphleteering, debating) were the happiest of outlets for his pent-up teeming powers. He struck London like a combination of lightning and one-man flood. His work gave him entry to the society he wanted, gave his congenital highhandedness a greater flourish, gave his garrulousness added fuel, and completed the persona that he wanted at that time. It also provided the inner confidence that he needed to begin work as a dramatist, for although his public confidence was not a façade, he seemed to need some certifications—justifications to himself and acceptances by others—in order to start writing plays.

The link between genius and extraordinary energy has never been more notable than in his case. In 1893 he declines a social invitation:

The fact is, I have to be at so many places that I never can go anywhere. Musical criticism, though it takes all my time, is quite a minor activity of mine. I have my article to write, four picture exhibitions to criticize, a political conference to attend, and a lecture to deliver before Sunday night.

In 1897 he writes to Ellen Terry:

. . . What with the preparation of the plays [*Pleasant and Unpleasant*] for publication and the ever returning Saturday windmill sail [now of drama criticism] that strikes me down before I have stumbled to my knees after the last blow, and the Fabian with its two weekly committees, and now on top of it all the Vestry with *its* two committees [he had been elected a vestryman—a borough councillor—of St. Pancras] and the Webbs's great new treatise on Democracy which I have to help in revising, I cannot even write to you. . . .

. . . he says in a lengthy letter! The famous letter to Golding Bright, separately reprinted as *Advice to a Young Critic,* with which he enclosed a review of Bright's that he had edited in inks of two colors, ends:

I find you have got an atrociously long letter out of me. I have been blazing away on the platform this evening for an hour and a half [a political speech] and ought to be in bed instead of clattering at this machine.

It is perfectly patent that these remarks, and many others like them, are, first, brags, and, second, have a strong touch of compulsion, even of refuge, about them. But also—which latter-day clear-sightedness often overlooks—they are true. This man *did* all these things, and continued to live at this prodigious pace of work of all kinds for about another forty years, when he slowed down to a normal, full-time writer's life. (What is also patent—though often prejudicedly ignored—is that, along with all these labors, he was consistently generous with time and money, considerate, utterly loyal.) This early spate of work included some of the best music criticism ever written, by fairly general consent of the musical; some of the best theater criticism ever written; *The Quintessence of Ibsenism,* a pioneer book in its field; the editing of the classic *Fabian Essays,* to which he contributed two of the eight essays; activity as one of the chief proponents and founders of the Labour Party; and the composition of his first seven plays, two of which, *You Never Can Tell* and *Candida,* will, I believe, still be revived 500 years from now to a chorus of criticism still explaining—quite logically—why they ought to be dead.

The subject of Shaw's sex life, a matter of both interest and latter-day derision, is marked in this book. He himself stated that he was *virgo intacta* until he was twenty-nine; then he either did or did not have a large number of affairs in his thirties. He had at least some mistresses. A curiosity is that one of them, the actress Florence Farr, played a role in *The Philanderer* that Shaw had modeled on another, Jenny Patterson. (Especially illuminating about Shaw the amorist is a letter from the painter Bertha Newcombe, who was unrequitedly in love with Shaw in the '90s and who wrote about it in 1928.)

In this vein there is the lyric tendency of his famous correspondence with Ellen Terry, whom he did not even meet until some years later:

. . . My Ellenest . . . love me hard, love me soft, and deep, and sweet, and for ever and ever and ever.

There is his equally lyrical, simultaneous correspondence with his future wife:

I have an iron ring round my chest, which tightens and grips my heart when I remember that you are perhaps still tormented. Loosen it, oh ever dear to me, by a word to say that you slept well. . . .

And he says with a wink (to Ellen Terry) that he is adept at all this:

My pockets are always full of the small change of love-making; but it is magic money, not real money.

A great deal of his "love-making" was indeed play-acting; and even when it was real, he tried to convert it into pretense, into stances and attitudes that would keep the women from getting over-serious about him. (Said Bertha Newcombe: "The sight of a woman deeply in love with him annoyed him.") The woman he married—for a long and devoted marriage—insisted on prior agreement to a sexless relationship. All these facts provide a field day for the literary psychoanalyst, particularly when one adds that Shaw was an almost too pat opposite of that shiftless drunkard his father, that he was raised a Protestant in Catholic Dublin, that he lived a bachelor with his mother until he was in his forties.

But the shortcoming of such analysis is in its implied conclusion. If only poor Shaw had had a stronger and more admirable father figure, had been raised in a happier home, had not had so many environmental and familial stimuli to puritanism . . . But if all those undoubted benefits had been his, then what? Can we be sure that they would have made him an even better artist? As it is, he is the greatest dramatist in English since Shakespeare.

In an age when more and more is known about people and is subjected to closer and closer scrutiny, the relation between life and art is taken to be increasingly direct. But the ever intenser minings of scholarship and the ever more complex apparatus of psychology frequently lead us past initial seeming revelations back to pretty much where we were before. The connection between biography and works seems highly flawed. These letters depict fascinatingly the shape and style of the life without which Shaw's work would have been impossible, but can they do more? It is argued, for example, that Shaw, as thinker and dramatist, is less thoroughly revolutionary than Ibsen, and a case can be made for that belief. But was it Shaw's congenital instinct to tidiness that made him a Fabian instead of a philosophical anarchist? If so and if it is argued that Ibsen could never have joined any political party, let alone a gradualist one, how explain that Ibsen was a petitioner for royal favors, an accepter of royal decorations, and an infatuated ass with young girls as an old man—none of which Shaw, the party functionary and repressed romantic, could have been? At the last, the facts of an artist's life, sexual and otherwise, are not of great explanatory "use." If we care about the man's work, then the life is interesting, particularly as encasing what Leon Edel calls "the history of an imagination"; but as direct explanation, it is strewn with snares of facile assumption and with howling incongruities.

The burden of the biographical process has become so heavy that, in this case, the facts of Shaw's life tend to make his detractors gloat, his admirers feel embarrassed. But rather than being a proof in itself, this phenomenon seems to me only to underscore another truth, simple, irrational, fundamental: finally, one's reaction to a writer depends less on demonstrable intrinsic qualities in the work and more on one's own temperament (to use an old-fashioned word). Shaw is a talkative busybody, a nagging preacher, a would-be encyclopedist; he has a faint smell of soap and water, of Jaeger woolens, of Right Living. (He was a vegetarian before 1897.) One can, if one chooses (which is the root of the matter), stop there. Others, myself included, see these facts as the mortal manifestations of a demi-urge, a titanic being so huge, so insistent, so demonic, that he frequently overrode human practices of work and dedication. The basic discomfort for us with Shaw is not the usual pathos of genius, that he was ahead of his time, but that he seems to have come from another planet: that he viewed the human race with incisive perception but a bit clinically; that, in addition and in contrast to his myriad immediate activities, he had a disquietingly long-range historical view. One can find hints already in these letters of the perhaps over-objective logic that led him to see the virtues, as well as the faults, of Franco, Mussolini, and Hitler. One can find the deliberately disturbing dogmatism that led to his untenable statements on Stalin and Soviet Communism. (Although some of his critics on this point are blessed with the best of hindsights.) What is worse for some people, both the objectivity and the pronouncements are attended by wit.

Yet Yeats's familiar description of Shaw as a smiling sewing-machine stitching steadily away is, as these letters show, not large enough to be even a half-truth. There is not, in this early volume, sufficient basis to discuss the well-known charges against Shaw of unoriginal philosophy, incomplete revolutionary theory, dated economics, and puppet drama. But what is evident in this book—and what scales down the Yeats comment—is the unleashing of a multitude of forces, the birth of a heroic figure who stitched, certainly, but who also soared and gamboled, who saw life as a totally consuming, inescapably amusing, but nevertheless holy game. Even on this side of our century's cataclysms, we can feel the force of his *being;* we can feel that if our connection with his views and art is no longer completely contiguous, yet the fact that such a man once really existed is a subtle source of strength.

*Bernard Shaw: Collected Letters 1898–1910**

(World, *October 10, 1972*)

I don't know anything quite like it. There are collections of letters by great writers—Keats, Flaubert, Chekhov, Joyce, to name a random few—that are treasures, without which life would be perceptibly duller. But the letters of Bernard Shaw, treasures though they certainly are, are also something else. The process of publication, now in its second volume, combines an electric sense of intensification with the feeling of discovery of a huge posthumous work. Out of an enormous amount of material the editor is hewing what amounts to the longest autobiography of a great author in print. To follow these volumes is almost to watch a new, fuller birth, as if Shaw were progressing through his career again, this time seen more completely, more roundly, in his size and in his crankinesses. These letters, unlike cognate volumes by others, do not merely enlighten or explain or divagate interestingly: They enlarge all the dimensions of their author.

The first volume covered the years 1874–97, ended when Shaw was forty-one, and contained 691 letters. This volume, which covers only

* Published by Dodd, Mead.

the next twelve years, contains 644 letters (two thirds of them previously unpublished). Dan H. Laurence, the entirely admirable editor, says that Shaw wrote about a quarter of a million letters and postcards, some of which have disappeared, so that when the projected four volumes are finished, only about one one-hundredth of the correspondence will be included.

Probably, if we rely on Laurence's reliable judgment, these will be the pieces most worth reprinting of those that survive; still these figures make the cardinal point. Quite apart from everything else, Shaw is a focus of blazing energy in Western cultural history. This present volume represents a rigorous selection from a correspondence carried on while the author was writing ten plays; supervising very closely (with scenery sketches and casting advice) the productions of his plays at home and abroad; scrutinizing intensely the French and German translations of his work; acting mainly as his own publisher in Britain; writing long essays and short books on a wide range of subjects; serving with devotion on the council of the borough of St. Pancras; campaigning for the Labour Party; and participating in the affairs of the Fabian Society (all while being knocked out by migraine one full day a month). The list is incomplete.

But to list these activities in this way is almost to belittle him—as if he were the world's most dazzling intellectual juggler. The specific miracle, from the aspect of this book, is the quality of the letters: the fact that while Shaw was writing *Man and Superman* and *The Doctor's Dilemma* and *Caesar and Cleopatra,* among other plays, while he was writing *The Perfect Wagnerite* and various political-economic brochures, he was creating a huge supplementary *literature,* which, as far as he knew, was destined to remain fragmented and private.

Of course, not all these letters are equally interesting; some of them, particularly those about internal Fabian maneuvers, are quite skimmable. Of course, too, he must have suspected increasingly that some time, somewhere, some of these letters would see the light; from a relatively early date he ran his life not merely as a career but as the care and feeding of an institution. ("I am by a very great deal the best English-language playwright since Shakespear," he said, quite accurately, in 1900.) Of course, too, some of the material in these letters comes from or ended up in plays or articles or books. But these letters are, in sum, an act of intellectual and literary largess that staggers the merely mortal.

The recipients range from theater colleagues to Auguste Rodin (to whom he wrote in French), from a moonstruck girl to August Strindberg. In 1898, when this volume begins, he got married with his left ankle in a cast, where it remained for some eighteen months. The comment of *The New York Times* on his marriage:

Mr. Shaw, having become the husband of a lady who possesses both wealth and amiability, will no longer be under the necessity of writing slashing criticisms or plays in which he rails at human nature. He can now settle down and become a respectable, middle-class gentleman, devoted to charitable pursuits and his wife.

The *Times* was partially obeyed: Shaw did give up theater criticism, at which he was simply the best who has ever written in English. He felt he was getting on in years; it was high time to concentrate on other matters. All through this volume he refers to himself as an ancient, and he particularly bemoans his fifty-fourth birthday—exactly forty years before he died. He became, as he saw himself later, an exponent of his convictions about the Life Force: an extraordinary example of a man's person responding in dynamics to a philosophical belief.

I have neither space nor competence to deal with all his ideas, from those on Marx's theory of value to those on land reform. He has often been severely criticized, and it still goes on, for his views on many of these subjects. I see no reason to doubt that much of this criticism is justified. But what most of the critics ignore is the fact that while each has usually spent his life in the particular field wherein he attacks Shaw, that subject was just one of the strings to Shaw's bow, and, as they often admit, he made some contribution to it.

However, I can point out his prescience on a number of subjects, stated with a courage that came to him quite effortlessly—one may say, uncourageously. When the Boer War broke out, many of his fellow Fabians rallied to the South African side and berated British imperialism; but Shaw called it a war between two predatory animals and foresaw the Boer mentality that would produce *apartheid*. He foresaw what would happen in India. He understood the then moral innocence of the United States. On a more practical level, he investigated photography and also foresaw, via the phonograph, what is now called oral history.

His own correspondence is not enough for him. He supplies people with long letters for *them* to send in certain situations, as well as a detailed scenario with which he hopes to induce his beloved enemy Chesterton to write his first play.

The wit—well, Shaw is laughing the whole time. Laurence points out rightly that "Shaw's epistolary art, like his dramatic art, was essentially a comic one." The comedy ranges from the humor of a letter complaining about the lack of heating in the Royal Court Theater to this conclusion of a letter about *Man and Superman* to Tolstoy:

> You said that my manner in that book was not serious enough—that I made people laugh in my most earnest moments. But why should I not? Why should humour and laughter be excommunicated? Suppose the world were only one of God's jokes, would you work any the less to make it a good joke instead of a bad one?

Can you *not* love that man? (I suppose the answer is yes; Tolstoy didn't.)

The essence of Shaw's prose derives, as he says, not from literature but from music. This is clear in his sensitivity to rhythm, to interlocking rhythms, the ability to build small cumulative phrases as he rolls along in a large over-arching crescendo; and especially it is clear in the fact that he wrote *vocally*. He wrote always with his ear, a gift that never wavered even in his extreme old age, when other assets failed him. From socialist pamphlets to plays to letters, his prose can be spoken—indeed, is not savored fully unless it is at least heard in one's head as speech, not merely read as print. (Try the Tolstoy bit above, as a speech from a high comedy.)

Shaw had one other habit that he, presumably, acquired from his adored Mozart and Beethoven: he tried things out before he used them finally. For those who know his work, these letters are sprinkled with motifs that appear in the plays. A passage about encountering a snake and becoming friends suggests Androcles' "A pet snake is the best of company." A passage about the public flavor of Dickens' private letters foreshadows Tarleton's remarks on the subject in *Misalliance*. An actor's assumption that a reference to Stevenson (R. L.) was to a theatrical hack named Stephenson clearly is the model for confusion between Lord Byron and a hack named H. J. Byron in the prologue to *Fanny's First Play*. His comments about the reliability of

Jews in business foreshadow Warwick's similar comment in *Saint Joan*. (And a line on a card from his sister in Germany—*"Wie lange, ach du Herr, wie lange"*—became the last line of *Saint Joan*.)

This busy reveling in utterance, this eternal playing testing hearing speaking, leads to the central fact and crowning paradox of Shaw, perhaps the one that ensures his monumental stature. Often in these letters he animadverts against "pure" art, against the society of artists, and, most notably in an exchange with Henry James, says he would never have bothered to put pen to paper in his life for purely esthetic reasons. (His definition of an Elizabethan author: "A man with an extraordinary and imposing power of saying things and with nothing whatever to say.") Yet despite all these proclamations, which were very likely calculated propaganda against the hyperestheticism of his time, there is no writer of English prose who lives more thoroughly in his language than Shaw—not through it, but beautifully *in* it. The social-intellectual argument pales in some of his plays; the springy, lifting eloquence still invigorates.

This is the fundamental reason for the incredible life's work. To count up Shaw's writings is almost like counting the breaths he took. He was not living except when he was using words. Words, no matter what he may have said tactically about language as an end in itself, were the *way* that he lived—words that, on paper, speak. When his plays falter in comparison with his great peers', Ibsen and Strindberg, in their spectrum of fire, of visionary madness, of view beyond the edge of order, still they can never, for readers of English, be utterly undone—because of their language. Germans and Italians sometimes tell us of Goethe's and Dante's overshadowing of Shakespeare; abstractly just or not, this can never finally be true for those born in English. So proportionately can it never be entirely true of Shaw as against the two men with whom he is usually measured, and for the same reason.

The platitudinous babblers of the daily press tell us today as they always did that Shaw's characters are only his mouthpieces. Read Shaw's remarks on that subject to William Archer in 1904. (And, of course, read the plays—with eyes and ears.) His respectable critics tackle him on the thoroughness of his revolutionary philosophy. Whatever their arguments, I have always felt that basically they object to Shaw because he was an optimist, the last truly great writer who was truly optimistic. Yet these critics who are suspicious of optimism as essentially frivolous, whose philosophies are oriented to bitterness if not despair, in their own lives work, write, beget children, teach—in their actions testifying to Shaw's credo of the Life Force even as they quarrel with it intellectually. Shaw, like all the real giants, ultimately embraces those who disagree with him, whether they know it or not, admit it or not, like it or not.

There are two more volumes of these letters to come. Strength to Dan Laurence! As I have tried to show, he is engaged, excellently, on an important task: helping to bring forth a posthumous masterwork.

The Lives of Granville Barker

(Horizon, *Autumn 1975*)

In 1971 the Royal Shakespeare Company came to New York with Peter Brook's production of *A Midsummer Night's Dream,* which was hailed as revolutionary.* In some ways this was true, but what was generally unknown was that Brook's production was in a revolutionary tradition, a tradition begun before World War I by the English director Harley Granville Barker. "Barker's productions at the Savoy from 1912 to 1914," Robert Speaight has written in *Shakespeare on the Stage,* "looked ahead in a pretty straight line to Peter Brook's *A Midsummer Night's Dream* at Stratford more than fifty years later." It was Barker who had pioneered in stripping Shakespearean production of overblown nineteenth-century scenic and musical and stylistic baggage.

My point is not to diminish Brook, who has inherited from the past as all alert artists must, but to identify and explore that inheritance. Granville Barker is one of the most extraordinary and extraordinarily versatile figures in the history of the English-speaking theater, an artist whose influence, long after his death, remains strong on both sides of the Atlantic even when his name is unknown. (The very spelling of that name is a bit of a muddle. After his second marriage Barker hyphenated his middle and last names, so some indexes list him as Granville-Barker, Harley. His biographer, C. B. Purdom, calls him Barker, and I'll follow suit.)

* See p. 55.

Early in his life Barker reportedly said that he planned to spend ten years as an actor, ten as a director, and the rest of his life as a writer. He did hold more or less to that schedule, though the decades overlapped somewhat. Presumably he meant that in his later years he would concentrate on playwriting, which he had begun early, and he did indeed write some plays and translate many in those years; but what he did not foresee was that he would spend his last twenty-five years quite out of the working theater—as a scholar, principally concerned with the essays by which he is now best known, his *Prefaces to Shakespeare*.

All four of these careers had their true distinctions. His acting made a strong impression on many critics. Max Beerbohm wrote of one Barker performance in 1904 that it had "just that mastery of climax and anti-climax which makes an artistic whole." Of his directing, John Gielgud, who worked with Barker in 1940 in one of his rare returns to the theater, said: "I never saw actors watch a director with such utter admiration and obedience. It was like Toscanini coming to a rehearsal." Of his playwriting, J. B. Priestley said in 1967 that Barker "is undoubtedly one of the most original, intelligent, and sensitive English dramatists of this century." And of his *Prefaces* Arthur M. Eastman said in *A Short History of Shakespearean Criticism* (1968) that Barker, as no one else in that history, "helps us to a sense of the stage actuality of a Shakespearean play."

It is possible—possibly easy—to fault Barker in each of his four professions, but the fact that he achieved genuine eminence in all four of them stamps him a genius. What makes him relevant today, not just a rueful-fascinating historical figure, is the way he affected the theater in which some of us work and which all of us attend. What makes him biographically interesting are the elements of tragedy in his life, tragedy that is endemic to the theater.

Barker was born in London in 1877, the son of a rather nebulous real-estate agent who was descended from clergymen. His mother, much more influential on him, was the granddaughter of an Italian physician who had emigrated to England. (Bernard Shaw, who met Barker at the turn of the century, said that the younger man "had a strong strain of Italian blood in him and looked as if he had stepped out of a picture by Benozzo Gozzoli.") Mrs. Barker was the chief bread-winner of the family by means of a then popular entertainment, the poetry recital. She toured Britain and America. Her son could not have had much formal education—the first anomaly in a career marked by intellectual rigor—because he spent much of his childhood traveling with her and sometimes recited items on the program.

He made his first appearance as actor in a provincial English theater in 1891, and the following year, aged fifteen, made his London debut as a "3rd Young Man." Evidently he showed some quality, although he was no immediate sensation, because he kept finding work and kept progressing. One noteworthy encounter came in 1897 when he played in a suburban production of *She Stoops to Conquer* with Gordon Craig, who himself became a theater revolutionary in quite a different vein (and who disliked Barker).

About this time Barker began writing plays. His first, a collaboration called *The Weather-hen,* was produced in London with some success in 1899. Barker was twenty-two. That year he read a minor role in a copyrighting performance of Shaw's new play *Caesar and Cleopatra.* In those days the copyright law was such that at least one public performance of a play had to be given in order for the author to hold his rights. (Sometimes he would merely get some friends, actors or otherwise, to come to a hall one morning, tack a hastily scrawled performance notice on the board outside, and have his friends read the script aloud on stage.) The importance of this particular performance was, first, that Barker was selected for it, and, second, that it brought him together with the forty-three-year-old Shaw and thus helped to initiate a great era in the English theater.

In 1900 Barker played the poet Marchbanks in the first production of Shaw's *Candida,* and this really sealed an important friendship between Barker and Shaw and Mrs. Shaw. It was cruelly breached sixteen years later by Barker, and it is clear that the breach was a wound that Shaw carried, however jocularly, all his life. A volume of his letters to Barker has been published (few of Barker's letters to him have survived) and he lived long enough to write an obituary of the younger man. As for Barker, his playwriting was strongly influenced by Shaw and so, apparently, was his intellectual and personal life.

The meeting of Barker and Shaw helped to change the latter from a published but rarely performed dramatist into a famous theater artist in Britain and, soon, the world. Barker did this partly by his acting of important Shaw roles. Shaw said he was, "humanly speaking, perfect" as Marchbanks, and subsequently Barker played in the first productions of *Man and Superman* (John Tanner), *John Bull's Other Island* (Father Keegan), *Major Barbara* (Adolphus Cusins), and *The Doctor's Dilemma* (Louis Dubedat). He influenced Shaw because, quite inferably, the author had him in mind when writing those roles and because his performances contributed substantially to the productions that ensured Shaw's theatrical place. That might have been monument enough, to have been inspiration and executant for a great dramatist, but it was a lesser part of Barker's career, even of his contribution to Shaw's career.

Barker had begun directing in 1900, and by 1904, at the age of twenty-seven, he had done five productions, including a bill of short plays (two of them by Maeterlinck) and a full-length play of his own, *The Marrying of Ann Leete.* His own play, set in the eighteenth century, has stylistic resemblances to Maeterlinck. Then came two significant events. He married Lillah McCarthy, a lovely and stunningly gifted actress with whom he had once toured; and she became part of the second event. He joined forces with a manager named J. E. Vedrenne to run the Royal Court Theater (nowadays known as the home of the English Stage Company, producers of John Osborne and other prominent playwrights of the last twenty years).

The Barker-Vedrenne partnership was no ordinary managerial move. It was, as it turned out, the major effort of Barker's life toward the goal that mattered most in his life: the establishment of a permanent theater of high quality. He and the critic William Archer had already written a book-length study called *Scheme and Estimates for a National Theatre* that set forth, in ostensibly practical terms, the means to realize a vision.* The means was not forthcoming, so Barker sought another avenue. He and Vedrenne, who was the manager of the Royal Court, decided to do a series of matinees of plays of merit. They began in October 1904 with some backing from friends, including Shaw, and by the following February they took over the theater completely.

The Barker-Vedrenne management of the Royal Court lasted until June 1907, when money troubles intervened, but during that relatively brief time it changed the shape and intent, even the frustrations, of the English theater. From that time on, the level of playwriting, of

* See p. 357.

general artistic tenor, was affected by the Royal Court venture; achievement and disappointment were measured by the Barker-Vedrenne record.

In the course of those three years the Barker-Vedrenne management gave 988 performances. Shaw loomed largest in the list with 701 performances of eleven of his plays. They also produced plays by Euripides (in Gilbert Murray's new translations), Ibsen, Galsworthy, Hauptmann, Schnitzler, Yeats, Masefield, and Barker himself. He directed many of the plays and acted in many, sometimes in those he also directed.

Seasons of serious new plays are not unfamiliar phenomena these days (partly because of Barker's effect, here as in Britain), but in those days such seasons were virtually unknown. The previous century had been one pre-eminently of acting, usually star-centered rather than ensemble work, and of generally abysmal playwriting, usually tailor-made for stars. The intellectual and esthetic changes that were already roaring through the other arts and that had already blown away much of the fustiness in continental playwriting had left the English-language theater almost untouched. This director-actor-playwright, twenty-seven when he joined with Vedrenne, changed all that in just three years. He did not move our theater *en bloc* to Parnassus, but from then on it could at least know what it was missing. Further, perhaps foremost, it established Bernard Shaw in the position from which he has not yet been budged: as the greatest dramatist after Shakespeare in our language.

It also established Barker. At thirty he was now a figure of first consequence. The end of the Royal Court days marked the end of the ten years as actor that he had "scheduled" for himself: he acted very little thereafter. Now he concentrated on directing, which profited enormously from his acting talent and experience, and on writing plays. His first play of lasting worth, *The Voysey Inheritance,* had been produced at the Royal Court in 1905, directed by himself with himself in the leading role. The plot concerns a respected solicitor who, just before he dies, informs his son and partner that the firm is operating fraudulently. The son must then decide whether to expose matters and bring about ruin for the firm and its clients or keep up the fraud until he can set things right. In 1907, came *Waste,* again directed by Barker with himself in the leading role, a play about a brilliant young politician who has a casual affair that wrecks his career and prevents him from doing the great good he might have done his country. In 1910 came *The Madras House,* directed by Barker but without him in the cast (as part of the next major London effort to establish a quality theater, Charles Frohman's celebrated tenancy of the Duke of York's). *The Madras House* too deals with inheritance of a sort—the passing of a successful fashion house from father to son—but thematically it deals with changes in men's view of women and with women's changing view of themselves. All three of these plays have elements of, in Max Beerbohm's phrase, "breadth and brilliancy." All three of them show, again in Beerbohm's phrase, how "deeply influenced he was and is" by Shaw. Still, of all the dramatists influenced by Shaw, Barker is easily the best, and if his "original contributions to our dramatic literature" are not quite the "treasures" that Shaw called them in his obituary article, they are still far too good for oblivion.

Paradoxically, his plays, his works in permanently available form, have had less effect on the theater than his work in ephemeral form: his directing. His production of new plays at the Royal Court and elsewhere had demonstrated his diamond-bright intelligence, his hatred of stagy cliché, his great sensitivity to character nuance, his extraordinary ear. Now he began to apply these attributes to Shakespeare. To some his work seemed raw and disturbing, but his intent was to unite the best of what he took to be the Elizabethan manner with the best of the modern. He believed in suppleness of verse-speaking (music but not music for its own sake) and the speed of speech and action that are implicit in the very structure of the Elizabethan stage; he believed in simple design and costume and lighting, chaste and strong rather than lots of stage freight and upholstery.

With the aid of a rich peer, Barker was able to make one more attempt at establishing the beginnings of a theater close to his ideal, at the Savoy. He was highly dissatisfied with the job-lot life of the commercial theater, so much so that he had even talked about emigrating to Germany and becoming a naturalized citizen there. Several visits to that country had strongly impressed him with German regard for the institution of the theater and willingness to subsidize it (which is still true). But he was at least able to begin work at the Savoy. His productions of Shakespeare there began with *The Winter's Tale* in September 1912. Critics said it was not Shakespeare, it was post-impressionism. Amid the uproar, writes C. B. Purdom, "there were those who recognized new factors . . . freedom from subservience to the actor-manager, freedom from elaborate staging, faithfulness to the text, and the conviction that Shakespeare was not a dead classic but a dramatist for the twentieth-century theatre."

Two months later Barker produced *Twelfth Night* at the Savoy. Other work intervened, and he did his last Shakespeare production, *A Midsummer Night's Dream*, at the Savoy in February 1914. (A wry note: it was the Germans who helped to alter his theater plans, and his subsequent life, in 1914.) In his entire career he directed only four Shakespeare plays—there had been a production of *Two Gentlemen of Verona* ten years earlier—but they have touched the theater's thinking about Shakespeare ever since.

His ten years as playwright were overlapped by his ten as director. And those years in turn were overlapped, were ended at last in a way that wrenched him out of his whole style of life.

In the winter of 1915 Barker brought three productions to New York: Shaw's *Androcles and the Lion,* Anatole France's *The Man Who Married a Dumb Wife,* and Shakespeare's *Dream.* Press and public were startled but engaged, as they were by the two productions of Greek plays that Barker did in American college stadiums in the summer of 1915. Then a change, sudden and profound, came in Barker's private life.

In a sense not at all cynical, this change might be said to reflect a desire, perhaps unconscious, to emulate Shaw even further. Barker's playwriting, as noted, was indebted to Shaw. He joined the socialist Fabian Society, in which Shaw was prominent, and he resigned from the executive board of that society when Shaw did (although Shaw remained a socialist all his life while Barker filtered away). The very example of professional versatility, though Barker's was much less, was set by Shaw. Now a different sort of example may possibly have affected Barker: Shaw's marriage to an adoring rich woman.

Barker's own marriage to Lillah McCarthy had seemingly been good. They had worked together at the Royal Court and the Savoy, and she was with him in America playing leading roles for him. But in New York Barker met Helen Huntington, the wife of an American multimillionaire, and they fell in love. His affection for her was genuine: there is no more reason to doubt that in his case than in Shaw's. (More reason to believe it in Barker's case, perhaps, because, unlike Charlotte Shaw, Mrs. Huntington was not rich in her own right. Her husband endowed her generously when they parted.) But given the importance of Shaw in Barker's life, it is hard to believe that some idea of living *à la* Shaw did not occur to Barker.

The effect on Lillah was cruel, devastating. She left America with Barker in June 1915 believing that his relationship with Helen was over. But he was back in New York in September without her, and in January of 1916 Lillah got a letter from him asking for a divorce. "She went at once to Shaw," says Purdom, "who said that he, too, had heard from Barker by the same post." Years later Lillah described that evening in a passage from her memoirs that was omitted from the published book. (All references to Barker were deleted, at his insistence, from Lillah's manuscript.)

I went [she wrote] all frozen on a cold January night. . . . Shaw greeted me very tenderly and made me sit by the fire. I was shivering. Shaw sat very still. . . . How long we sat there I do not know, but presently I found myself walking with dragging steps with Shaw beside me . . . up and down Adelphi Terrace. . . . He let me cry. Presently I heard a voice in which all the gentleness and tenderness of the world was speaking. It said: "Look up, dear, look up to the heavens. There is more in life than this. There is much more."

If that sounds unlike the usual image of Shaw, it fits the image of a protective parent, which is how he saw himself in relation to the young genius and his gifted, beautiful wife. After Barker returned to England, Shaw saw him as often as he could, despite his sympathy for Lillah, but the friendship could not continue. Barker's new wife detested both Shaw and the theater itself. She felt that the workaday theater was an unworthy place for a man of Barker's intellect and writing abilities, and she disliked Shaw, possibly because he was a link with and reminder of Lillah but more surely because he was happy in the theater, appreciated Barker's gigantic theatrical gifts, and wanted him to keep on using them.

Unquestionably Shaw was grievously hurt by the breach, though he sometimes spoke lightly of it. He wasn't even informed of the second marriage, which took place in July 1918. A month later Shaw wrote to Barker: "It would be convenient occasionally to know something about you. I surmise that you are married; but it is only a surmise. . . . I have refrained, with an exaggerated delicacy, from asking you questions for a year or so. Now I do ask them bluntly." The reply is not known (although they met later that year).

Unquestionably Shaw had looked on Barker as a son-in-art. (At one time there was even a rumor in London that Barker was his natural son.) In his biography of Shaw, the Irish critic-playwright St. John Ervine says that a few years after the second marriage he was driving in the country with Shaw and they passed the road that led to Barker's palatial new home. "I said to G.B.S.: 'Harley Granville-Barker lives up that road.' He looked at it in the odd way he had when he was moved, and, almost as if he were indifferent, said, 'Oh, Harley!' But when G.B.S. was as terse as that he was under deep emotion."

Thus, if Barker had made his second marriage because he was consciously or unconsciously modeling himself on Shaw, the result was to split him from his model. It was a Shavian irony.

In 1930, twelve years after their marriage, the Barkers moved to Paris, which was their place of residence, except for their exile during the Second War, for the rest of their lives. Barker hyphenated his name to please his new wife and they established themselves in a grand duplex Parisian apartment that had a staff of eleven. From his second marriage until his death in 1946, save for a few excursions, most of them quite brief, he did nothing in the theater. He wrote about the theater, principally a book called *The Exemplary Theatre* in which he restated his aims for the theater he had not been able to make and argued for the closer relation between the university and the theater that has since come about in Britain and America. He lectured from time to time. He translated—some French plays on his own, some Spanish ones with his wife. He finished his fourteen illuminating *Prefaces to Shakespeare,* each one an essay on a particular play, the one on *Hamlet* so long that it is a book in itself. And he wrote two more plays, of debatable quality but of high vicarious interest. *The Secret Life* (1923) is about a retired English politician who is persuaded to run again for Parliament and a probable Cabinet post, but who quits the campaign to visit the woman he loves who is dying—in America! *His Majesty* (1928) is about an exiled king who makes an effort to regain his crown but is sent again into exile. It is hardly intrusive to see these plays as devices of psychological projection.

Of Barker's brief returns to the theater, the chief one was the ten days he spent, at John Gielgud's invitation, attending rehearsals of the latter's *King Lear* production in 1940. Gielgud devotes a chapter to this experience in his autobiography *Stage Directions* (1963) and says: "[Barker] had only ten days to work with us on *King Lear,* but they are the fullest in experience that I have ever had in all my years on the stage." To read Barker's preface to *King Lear* is to read intellectual exegesis at its most practical, a theater mind intent on exploring the text with performance as its imperative. (Speaking of isolated scholastic Shakespearean study, he says: "There is great delight, there is much profit in such study; but it is a study of causes rather than effects, not a study of the work of art itself.") To read the nine pages of notes that Gielgud made of Barker's specific suggestions for voice and movement—Gielgud gives them as an appendix—is to glimpse the theatrical gifts that underlay the essayist's gifts. To read both is to perceive the breadth of the man and the extent of the loss in his virtual retirement from a directing career at the age of thirty-eight.

During the Second War the Barkers lived in New York, where he did some work for the British Information Service. He lectured at Yale, Harvard, and Princeton, and his book *The Use of the Drama* grew out of his Princeton lectures. Before he came to America he had already become a legend, remote from almost all of his former theater associates, especially his former closest friends, the Shaws. In 1943 Shaw sent a postcard, one of his favorite literary forms, to Barker in New York: "Charlotte died last Sunday, the 12th September, at half-past two in the morning. She had not forgotten you. . . . You will not, I know, mind my writing this to you. She was 86. I am 87." Three years later Shaw wrote his obituary article about his former friend, twenty-one years younger.

Why did Barker leave? Why, before he had begun to reach the height of his one gift that can inarguably be called great, did he forsake the theater? He sometimes answered that question. He wrote to Gielgud in 1937 that he had pinned his faith to the establishing of a permanent national theater and, "finding it . . . no go, I got out." He had said in 1915, "Since we cannot do away with the theater, let us make it as good as we can." So he had tried, in epoch-making fashion; but, frustrated by the war and increasingly wearied by frustration, he allowed himself to be led away.

There are reasons beyond his theater idealism, of course, that help explain his susceptibility to persuasion. "When Barker was young," says Purdom, "it was the thing to be a writer, while to be an actor was to belong to a despised profession. He never grew out of this state of mind." He always preferred the company of other kinds of artists, of politicians and intellectuals, to that of people only in the theater. There was certainly an appetite for misconstrued gentility in Barker that made him vulnerable to Helen's immense loathing of the theater. But fundamentally it was his inability to realize his visions that made him willing to give up. In 1916 he even wrote a one-act play called *Farewell to the Theatre* about a famous actress who gives up her career because she can't have it at the level she wants. That and his two subsequent full-length plays are his apologia in disguise. The history of the theater contains other successful people who felt themselves cursed with theatrical talent, gifts they could exercise only in a place they disliked. William Charles Macready, the English actor, was an international star for three decades until he retired in 1851; the last two words of his voluminous diaries, after the entry noting his retirement, are *"Thank God!"* (Italics his.)

The tragedy of the English theater was that it could not give the right home to an artist of Barker's vision. The tragedy of Barker is that he looked for the excuse to leave: that a residual Victorian ache for propriety aggravated his artistic frustration and sapped his will to fight further. And the tragedy is compounded because it is quite clear that, in the library of his Paris apartment, he was "directing" on paper, putting into his Shakespearean and other essays the force and wisdom that might have gone into the establishment of a history-making theater.

The oddity is that he nevertheless did make history; that, despite his disproportioned career, he has had a huge influence, seen and unseen: on those who knew from whom they were learning and on those who learned from him without knowing the source. In 1967 the English critic Ivor Brown said: "Barker established the status and proved the value of the [director] in this country." In one way the statement is exaggerated; Barker was not the first. In another it is too modest; he also affected the United States—directly by his productions and writings, continuingly by the cultural osmosis that brings important artistic influences from England to America and vice versa. Whenever we see a director concerned with unity of concept, a company concerned with authenticity of style and the idea of a permanent ensemble, we can know that they are in some degree the progeny of Barker. Whenever we see a university supporting a professional theater and professional training, we can know that the program is to some integral extent the result of Barker's *The Exemplary Theatre*. As for Shakespearean scholarship, few competent Shakespeareans would deny the vitality that Barker pumped into that body.

In his early play *Waste* the young politician-hero, Trebell, objects to high-flown talk about the influence of God on man's search for knowledge and says that he wants to converse in prose. His opponent in discussion says: "What is the prose for God?" Trebell replies: "That's what we irreligious people are giving our lives to discover." The theater proved too prosaic for Barker to discover his god in it, but before and after he left it, he did work that still helps those stubborn enough to hope.

themes

Notes on Naturalism: Truth Is Stranger as Fiction

(Performance, *March/April, 1973*)

Naturalism is dead, of course. Everyone knows that. The French, who invented it in the eighteenth century and pioneered its practice in the nineteenth century, dethroned it about 1900 and sentenced it to death. During the twentieth century it has been re-sentenced by numerous people as inimical to esthetic adventure, as incongruent with our era, as subservient to bourgeois "recognition" appetites in art and, no matter how bald in detail, inevitably confirmatory and pat.

But it's curious that people have to keep *on* sentencing naturalism to death. And it's curious, too, that few have bothered to look at the theory in the new light of new times. I have been forced to do so by two plays seen in the past year, both by the English playwright David Storey, both performed at the Long Wharf Theater in New Haven, which gave them their American premieres. My purpose here is not to discuss Storey as writer but to examine the results of an esthetic impulse to which he responded.

Here are the two plays in brief. In *The Contractor* a wealthy builder in the North of England is marrying off his daughter. A group of local workmen erect a large party-tent on his lawn, the ceremony is held, and the tent is dismantled. Some story elements are interwoven, but the putting-up and the taking-down of the tent, in complete detail, are the central actions.

The Changing Room is set in what we would call the locker room of a football stadium in the North of England. (Rugby football, the tougher kind.) In the first act the players—a predictable assortment—drift in, dress, with horseplay and conversation, and go out to play. The second act is between halves, when the team rests, and during the second half, when an injured player is brought out. In the third act the players shower, dress in street clothes, with horseplay and conversation, and drift out.

There is virtually no story in *The Changing Room,* less even than in *The Contractor,* which is hardly "plotty." The football play has only two elements that depart from the reportorial: the old sweeper, who somewhat too symmetrically opens and closes the play, has a "character-cameo" touch of Russophobia; and the injured player has a stagy bit about an electric power kit that he has just bought and brought with him and about which he is worried. Other than these matters, *The Changing Room*'s dialogue, as far as I can tell, could have been tape-recorded during an actual game. Jonathan Marks used an apt analogy for these Storey plays in a seminar at Yale: the Disney studios have artists who do foregrounds—the story elements—and artists who do backgrounds. It is as if the foreground men had little to do in *The Contractor* and weren't used at all for *The Changing Room.*

Leaving aside some complaints about the generally competent Long Wharf productions, I was almost always interested in the first play and was completely held by the second. Trying to understand why this had happened, I made some notes.

1. The "purer" the naturalism became, the less story that was

involved, the more interesting it became. The common definition of naturalism is "the slice of life": the clinical presentation of a segment of life as it is, without alteration or embellishment or contrivance. And it occurred to me that I had never seen or read a naturalistic play that really satisfied that definition. All such plays that I know use naturalism as a medium for presenting a story devised by the author for the author's purposes: Gorky's *The Lower Depths,* Fugard's *Boesman and Lena,* Hauptmann's *Die Ratten,* and so on. It was Storey's impulse to purity of style that was intriguing me, that seemed a true act of daring.

The closest previous approach to absolute naturalism, by the definition above, that I know of occurred at Madison Square Garden in New York on June 7, 1913. John Reed, financed by Mabel Dodge and aided by (among others) Robert Edmond Jones and Walter Lippmann, staged a pageant that recreated a conflict between striking silk workers of Paterson, New Jersey, and the police which had actually taken place in the previous April. Two thousand of the Paterson workers, their wives and children re-enacted the events of April. (And the newspapers called it "a new art form.") But *The Changing Room* is purer naturalist *art* because it doesn't use football players, it uses actors.

2. The dramatic naturalists of the nineteenth century operated within the province of the theater and were, in general, warring against romanticism *in the theater.* The dramatic naturalist today knows that, in a real sense, his work cannot be limited to a theatrical action. Naturalism can no longer be a war against falsification of the theater.

Nor can it war against falsification of the world to the audience: no factual revelation is possible to the naturalist who deals today with an audience saturated—via film and TV and the mass press— with the veristic minutiae of the world around them. Because society and society's consciousness have altered so radically, naturalism has inescapably altered in texture and in motive.

Today, who doesn't know—or know sufficiently—the facts of men's behavior in locker rooms? If we grant that Storey is intelligent enough to recognize this, then we must grant that he had a motive other than factual revelation. I think that motive was purely esthetic. Stripped of any possibility for factual revelation, and stripped of any story (the Disney story men have gone home), naturalism becomes perforce as sheerly esthetic a mode as any that would have pleased Pater or Wilde.

3. Thus the pleasure in watching *The Changing Room* was a pleasure in abstraction, not in reproduction; in stylistic exercise, not in any of the historical "scientific" aims of naturalism. And thus that pleasure, rather than being dusty with century-old courage, became ultra-contemporary and free: the creation of a para-world that merely resembles, more than is usual in the theater, the world outside but whose purpose is to reward by *not* being the world outside, by being created by artists within its own perimeters. A valid comparison is with ballet. One might enjoy a ballet of a locker room, which could not possibly be "real," as one watched the physical arcs and motifs meet the exigencies of pattern and musicality. The "reality" here is simply a different mode, and one enjoys watching the physical and verbal arcs and motifs meet the demands of theatrically projected verism.

4. The New Naturalism, new because of the changed context, has long been an accepted mode in the contemporary graphic arts—in the sculpture of Kienholz and Segal, for example. Their work has at least two effects: their painstaking reproduction of reality becomes, by their act of reproduction, an abstraction from reality; and the quality of their particular vision is an avenue to fresh speculation on that hardy perennial: What is Beauty?

The New Naturalism of the theater shares those effects, but is different because the aspect of time enters in. The work is not permanent, and its creation must coincide, or seem to, with the real time involved in dressing for a game, undressing and showering, and so on. This temporal aspect, while seeming to be a difficulty, is actually an asset over the graphic arts because there is an esthetic pleasure in seeing the temporal requirements met. The split-second fulfillment of time imperatives is a source of theatrical excitement, an integral part of the artistic reward in this mode.

5. "Happenings," already a term with a slightly antique ring, might seem to be part of the New Naturalism, but are not. They are not recreations. They occur at the moment they are seen.

6. It is generally assumed that the film took over naturalism from the theater and dwells in it. Some film estheticians from Lindsay to Kracauer have talked about film as mediator and/or redeemer of reality. Documentaries aside (and they are a very mixed question),

the assumption is decidedly questionable. Nothing makes this clearer than the film versions of certain plays. The creaky mechanisms of *Sleuth,* for instance, were just barely acceptable, or "real," in the theater; on the screen that reality is dispelled. The makeup disguise that is crucial to the plot becomes utterly ridiculous in the film. This is not because film *achieves* greater reality but because it needs greater reality with which to *begin.* (This may be why so many poor plays that impose on middling theater reviewers—like *The Subject Was Roses* and *The Effect of Gamma Rays on Man-in-the-Moon Marigolds*—do not impose on equivalent film reviewers.)

Films that ostentatiously employ naturalistic devices rarely result in valid naturalism. Cassavetes' *Husbands* was boring and self-defeating because it was not the recreation of the events it was supposed to be about but simply a record of actors extemporizing on a scenario. If there was any naturalism in it, it was that of an actors' studio, not of bedrooms and bars.

Occasionally a film-maker understands naturalism and moves toward it from the core outward. Rouquier's *Farrébique* (1947), even though it was made (in the director's words) "with some cheating," used a French farm family to re-enact the events of a year on their farm. An American film called *David Holzman's Diary* by L. M. Kit Carson and Jim McBride (1970) starts with a young film-maker named David Holzman sitting in his room with a tape recorder next to him, addressing the camera, saying that he is going to keep a journal of his life with camera and tape. Only at the very end do we find out that he and everyone else in the various lifelike episodes are actors.

This revelation greatly upset some audiences, and their reaction points to an inherent shortcoming in film naturalism, even when well employed. As Pudovkin and Bazin pointed out, the essence of cinema is the difference between the real object and its film image. The closer a fiction film gets to facsimile—without that "difference"—the more it entails a kind of deception. The film medium does often record actuality, and naturalistic film fiction tends to come deceptively close to that actuality. The theater is always made before your eyes, so is congenitally free of any factual deception.

Also, since film action is all finished before we begin to see it, film naturalism cannot provide the temporal "balletic" rewards described above.

7. Expanded modern consciousness has expanded the domain of any play. It is no longer contained within the borders of the "script" or the action; it frequently includes the dramatist himself. Speaking of irony, which for him includes a wide spectrum of drama, Bert O. States says:

> . . . the old character-driven (or "flaw"-driven) plot, in the strain from the Greeks through Shakespeare to Ibsen and beyond, is no longer of much use to [the modern ironist]. It is replaced by what we might call the author-driven plot, or the plot in which the author becomes the silent and invisible antagonist of his own fiction.*

This wider embrace of the modern audience, which predicates the "participation" of the author in ironic drama, includes the world itself in naturalistic drama. At a naturalistic play today, the pressure of your neighbor's arm, the laughter of the audience are part of the event, since the author is positing his play as visually indistinguishable from the reality in which you exist at the same time that, paradoxically, he wants esthetic connections between you and an art work created and dissolved in two hours' time. So the world around his stage is involved in two ways: modern consciousness strips naturalism of everything but its stylistic function, yet the viewer's reality, which begins at the stage's edge, provides some of the dramatic tension for what is happening on stage.

8. Considered solely as style, naturalism today has some links with non-naturalistic modes. The "beefy" feeling of the players lining up and running out onto the field one by one, the way they exploded back into the locker room at the half, muddy and noisy, gave me the greatest sense of physicality in the theater, of body presence, since Grotowski. The other night at Foreman's Ontological-Hysteric Theater I saw certain repeated phrases of movement that reminded me of the unhurried way in which the referee had examined each and every one of the players before the game in Storey's play. The two different moments were linked by a scrupulous attention to detail whose use on stage was grounded, ultimately, in wit.

These stylistic linkages indicate once more that naturalism now can be seen only through eyes conditioned by (historically) post-naturalist theater.

* Bert O. States, *Irony and Drama* (Cornell University Press, 1971), p. 113.

None of the above is an argument to drop everything that has happened in the twentieth-century theater in favor of the New Naturalism. I wouldn't want to see endless naturalist works about locker rooms or restaurant kitchens—but then I wouldn't want to see endless works in any one or two or three modes. I have simply tried to analyze responses from a playwright of whom I expected little. (His *Home,* in a quite different style, I found vacuous.) And in that analysis perhaps there is a hint, not of a new Way of Life for which all others should be abandoned, but of one more path of possibility.

Pinter and Sexuality: Notes, Mostly on *Old Times*
(American Poetry Review, *July/August 1974*)

Considering that this has been a century of increasing sexual candor, it's strange that this increase has been so little reflected in the work of the century's leading dramatists. Many of them have dealt frankly and radically with love, with ideas of marriage and equality, but this is hardly more than to say that one can't write plays without using men and women in them and that man-woman relations are inevitable. (Even those relations have reached a minimum in Beckett and Handke.) Outside the theater, however, the air of the century has become redolent with sexuality as such, the musk of sexual attraction and power, as distinct from love and marriage. Only a few important playwrights have been interested to explore sexuality itself as a dramatic field; the ones I think of—not of equal stature—are Wedekind, García Lorca, Williams, **Genet,** and—to judge by *Divine Words,* the one play of his now available in English—Valle-Inclán.

And Harold Pinter. The sexual aspects of Pinter's work, though certainly not ignored, have not been much discussed. Here are some notes on the subject, principally about his latest play.

The moment one underscores the word "sexuality" in relation to Pinter, almost his entire body of work takes on a different light. Even the trite but true idea of menace in earlier Pinter, of formless fear, becomes differently galvanized.

The majority of his short plays and all of his long plays except *The Caretaker* are concerned with sex in some degree. Even *The Birthday Party,* that thriller with the plot left out, is tinctured strongly by the incidents with the girl next door. (Named Lulu. A deliberate echo of Wedekind?) In the short play *A Slight Ache* the dirty old match-seller outside the house is patently—perhaps too patently—a symbol of the lost sexuality inside the house. One of the most erotic moments I have seen on a stage was in the Off-Broadway production of this play several years ago when the filthy creature was finally admitted to the house and Frances Sternhagen, seated before him, put her arms around his hips. Sternhagen, a very good actress, is not my idea of a sexy personality; the old man was a bundle of rags. Yet when she embraced him, saying, "Hmm, you're a solid old boy, I must say," it eclipsed most orgies in pornographic films.

There is an unmistakable difference in Pinter after *The Caretaker.* That play, a small masterpiece of hate and fear and desolation, so sure of itself that it often includes comedy, seems to cap a series of variations on materials and moods contained in *The Room* and *The Dumb Waiter.* Each of these plays deals with an enclosed space, a seeming refuge, into which menace and hostility seep. Through those early plays, *The Birthday Party,* and a number of short works, sexuality had also been a theme, though not always the dominant one. After *The Caretaker,* sexuality takes over.

The dynamics of *The Homecoming,* Pinter's next long play, is *non sequitur*—in interchange, within long speeches, in action, in continuity of scenes. This method, applied to the subjects of family, marriage, and the family's relation to a son's wife, shocks us with disjuncture. One of its effects is to reveal the suppressed—both in the characters and in our own social composition. Also, because of the outrages calmly committed and calmly accepted, the play is very funny. Peter Hall's production for the Royal Shakespeare Company was beautiful, as was his subsequent film; but sometime I would like to see *The Homecoming* performed *à la* Marx Brothers, with the pauses taken as freeze-frames.

Pinter's next plays, two short works called *Landscape* and *Silence,* were innately sexual, as was the brief play *Night,* unproduced here. An important point about all three of these plays is that the writing shows a gentleness unprecedented in Pinter. This gentleness continues as part of the complex mix in *Old Times.*

I concentrate here on *Old Times* partly because it has been so casually stuffed into the old Pinter "formless fear" bag, partly because it has been underpraised (in my view) even by Pinter admirers, but mostly because it takes Pinter even further into sexuality.

There are three characters. Deeley, a film director, lives in the country with his wife, Kate. They are visited by Anna, who shared a flat with Kate in London twenty years before and is herself now married, living in Sicily. The play moves in its dialogue—never in physical place—into and out of that twenty-year-old past. The text is full of contradictions and ambiguities, which has led to the opinion that they are themselves the subject matter—the unknowableness of the past, the interfusion of past and present. I think that all the contradictions, even the ambiguities, tend toward a virtually explicit agon: a contest between the husband and the returned Anna for sexual possession of Kate.

This became clear to me, as I believe it *is* clear, only after seeing the play a second time with a different cast. The first time, in the original London production, the play was disappointing; the second time, in the New York production, I knew why. The London production left me thinking that the past-present fusion might be what the play was *for* and that, though it was extraordinarily well written, it was somewhat insubstantial. But the New York cast—Mary Ure, Rosemary Harris (Anna), and Robert Shaw—had much more sexual charge than Dorothy Tutin, Vivien Merchant, and Colin Blakely. (Particularly the last.) The New York cast made the play resonate much more fully.

And, paradoxically, this cast made the setting, by John Bury, seem quite wrong. Bury had done the excellent set for *The Homecoming,* gray, slab-like, a house of seedy males. His design for *Old Times* had a similar cold, geometric feeling. In London it seemed passable as another "Pinter setting." But in New York the same set seemed utterly wrong. The place where the play figuratively takes place is Kate's loins. The setting should have a sense of enclosure, warmth, curve. In London the setting mastered the actors; in New York the actors battled the setting.

What follows is not a report on the New York production. It's my own view of the play, stimulated by that production but based on subsequent readings.

There are two acts. The first act has three major sections or strophes, I think. The act begins with Deeley and Kate as they discuss Anna, whom they are expecting. But she is in fact already on stage, standing in the shadows upstage, a mystery and a threat from the very first moment. (And her presence is a subtle dramaturgical stroke, to tell us from the first split second that this play is only seemingly realistic.) Deeley questions Kate about Anna, and Kate says, among other things, that her friend was a thief. Anna used to steal "bits and pieces. Underwear." Deeley questions Kate about Anna as if he had never met her; indeed, Kate says he hasn't. This, eventually, is seen as the first contradiction in the play. There are many contradictions. This whole process of contradiction can be viewed as a compact, the sort of agreement that people often make, especially husbands and wives, to revise the past, as in Orwell. Or it can be viewed, less gravely, as pretense and teasing. Or it can be viewed, less literally but more seriously, as part of Pinter's method of inclusive tensions, including untruths as well as truths, letting us sort them out as we go, as part of his intent to encompass both the conscious and the unconscious and to make his language more dangerous than factual. One can say of the language here, as in other Pinter plays, that nothing is to be believed of the words spoken except the effect they have. This doesn't mean that the characters could say anything; the effect would then be quite different. The language is most carefully selected, but it lives and works by overtone, by movement away from the literal, not by conventional cognitions.

The first strophe of the act ends and the second strophe begins when Anna "comes in"—that is, steps forward and is lighted, is seen by Kate and Deeley. Anna's first speech is a model for playwrights: that first word, "Queuing," which helps her to cut into the scene; the colorful, happy flow that pours through immediately, as she recreates in a minute or so the busy, giggly life of two young women in London ("innocent girls, innocent secretaries," lilted by Rosemary Harris, is not a sound I will forget), swirling out her memories of the city in which she and Kate were young, ending with three small questions that rein in the rush gently to a halt: " . . . does it still exist I wonder? do you know? can you tell me?"

A slight pause. Then Deeley says, with purposeful banality, "We rarely get to London." It's a pointed refusal to support Anna's mood, an attempt to puncture it, a disclosure that he suspects at once that she is planning an invasion. Kate overrides his intervention; she insists on joining figurative hands with Anna. As she rises and pours coffee, she says, "Yes, I remember." With these flickers and counter-flickers, the battle begins—and quickly develops—between Anna and Deeley over Kate.

In the course of casual conversation about living in the country, Anna says that if she did it she would miss London, but "of course I was a girl in London. We were girls together." Deeley, further in the vein of contradiction-cum-truth, says, "I wish I had known you both then." After a moment Anna speaks the most quoted (and most obvious) line in the play. They have had a casserole for dinner; and, after a small pause, Anna says: "You have a wonderful casserole."

DEELEY: What?
ANNA: I mean wife. So sorry. A wonderful wife.

Anna's slip of the tongue is of course a judgment on Deeley's attitude toward Kate, true or not.

The second strophe ends with the interchange of old popular songs between Anna and Deeley. At first it seems merely a comic bit—the game in which one memory of pop culture prompts another—but soon it takes on the quality of a tussle for possession of the past. These lines, all from songs about loving a woman and being loved by her, are sung by Anna and Deeley in the presence of Kate. Then Deeley says, "They don't make them like that any more." A silence; and the third strophe begins.

He launches into the first long, ambiguous recollection of the past. (Anna's opening speech was unambiguous.) He tells about going into a London film theater years ago to see *Odd Man Out*. (Note the title.) He recalls that there were two usherettes in the foyer, one of whom was stroking her breasts while smiling at the other, who watched in a kind of unwilling sexual communion. But, in the play's vein of transmutation and purposeful contradiction, he says there was only one *other* person in the theater, "and there she is"—Kate. It is as if he knows Kate was the other usherette, but in his mind, at least, he wants to separate her from that communion.

Anna joins in his praise of the film, seemingly to certify the occasion rather than the picture: then says, "There are some things one remembers even though they may never have happened. There are things I remember which never happened but as I recall them so they take place."

These lines have sometimes been cited as the very meaning of the play. I disagree. They are the *mode* of the play, the way (already demonstrated) in which it functions—Anna says "so they take place," the present tense, not the past; but the mode is used to plunge on into sexual mysteries. Deeley replies, "What?" bewilderedly, perhaps in fright of discovery, of similarity between Anna and him. Then Anna goes at once—her oblique reply—into a story of a man she once found with Kate in their room, crying and sobbing. Certainly-probably, as it eventuates, this man was Deeley.

Soon Kate says, "You talk about me as if I were dead," and after more reminiscing about her by the others, she says, " . . . you talk about me as if I *am* dead. Now." Anna replies with what is almost an overt advance:

How can you say that? How can you say that, when I'm looking at you now, seeing you so shyly poised over me [Kate is offering her a cigarette], looking down at me—

Sharply Deeley interrupts. "Stop that!" It's as sharp an outburst as any he makes in the play.

In a moment, quite calm again, he takes the conversation back to the time when he was thinking of marrying Kate, as if to remind Anna that decisions in this matter were made "twenty years ago" (the words with which he finishes). After a silence, Anna says—her first utterance since Deeley shut her up, and it's as if she wanted to placate him now—"When I heard that Katey was married my heart leapt for joy." She then talks knowingly about Kate's nature, how Kate had always been interested in the arts, and in a speech that is a dark counterpoint to her very first speech, she reminisces about their London outings, ending with a memory of how they too once went to see *Odd Man Out*.

Deeley soon turns the focus, purposely, to Anna's husband. They talk about Sicily. Then Kate, who rarely asks questions, asks Anna some questions about Sicily, all rather sensory—about sun and heat and bare feet—and Deeley keeps trying to intervene with recollections of some filming he did in Sicily. To no avail. Kate keeps questioning: she asks Anna, "Do you like the Sicilian people?" Deeley tries again to intervene, but Kate repeats her question. After a silence Anna plunges the dagger into Deeley. She goes into the first "flashback" dialogue of the play—not reminiscence but dialogue, soon joined by Kate, as if the two women were back there again in their London flat. Deeley is excluded.

He tries to fight his way in, with a feeble remark about the casserole. Again, no avail. The women remain in the past, talking about some men they might ask over to their flat that night. Then Kate, joining past and present, rises and says she'll have a bath. She leaves.

Anna turns to Deeley, who, except for his one bootless interruption, has been shut out of the dialogue for some minutes. She looks at him. The stage direction does not say that it's a look of triumph, but what else could it be? The first act ends.

During the intermission Kate's bath is transposed from the past to the present. There is also a significant physical change. The scene shifts from the living room to the bedroom, but, more important, there is another transposition. The bedroom contains two divans that also serve as beds, and an armchair. Pinter's stage directions: "The divans and armchairs are disposed in precisely the same relation to each other as the furniture in the first act, but *in reversed positions.*" (Italics added.) The visual effect of that simple physical reversal is to underscore other reversals.

In this act too, there are three main strophes, I think. The first is between Anna and Deeley, while Kate is inside bathing. As they drink coffee, Deeley states the other side of his truth-contradiction tension about the past. He says he *did* meet Anna twenty years before, first in a pub, then at a party. She sat on a sofa, and he "gazed" up her skirt. He says: "You found my gaze perfectly acceptable." His use of the word "gaze" is a dig at her; in the first act he singled out her use of that word as extraordinary.

Deeley says that a girl friend of Anna's came into that party—he is still using that circuitous, smoky way of describing *and* blurring events—and they left together. After which he had looked at the indentations that the girls' buttocks had left on a sofa. These references to looking up skirts (with black stockings) and to imprints of buttocks help to charge the already sex-laden air even further.

Anna teases him ("I've rarely heard a sadder story"), then changes the subject to Kate now, inside, bathing. Both she and Deeley go into descriptions of Kate's washing and soaping so that her nakedness, unseen, becomes a voluptuous presence. They discuss the drying of Kate, an experience they have both had; then in a small, quiet frenzy Deeley says that *he'll* do the drying, he's the husband. He adds ironically that Anna can supervise and give him some "hot tips." He pauses, then says bitterly, "Christ." Some counter-attack against Anna, some territorial defense, seems urgent. He looks at her slowly, and says: "You must be about forty, I should think, by now."

The second strophe begins as Kate comes out of the bathroom, already dried, of course, wearing a bathrobe. She walks to the window, her back to them. Deeley and Anna softly sing alternate lines of "They Can't Take That Away from Me." They both admire Kate as she turns to look at them, and Kate, utterly centered on self, preening like a cat who deserves no less than the adulation she is getting, speaks (one of her longest speeches) about luxuriating in the senses, ending with her pleasant memory of rain on her eyelashes in the city.

Anna, to whom "city" means herself and Kate twenty years ago, is quick to say that there are other nice things in the city, like a nice room and a hot drink waiting for you. And after a pause there is another "flashback" conversation *in* that London room. Deeley interrupts, much sooner than he did the last time, working in a reference to *Odd Man Out,* but Kate and Anna reweave the "flashback" and begin again to talk about the men they might invite over. They agree that "Christy" is the nicest and they'll ask him around. Deeley cuts in: "He can't make it. He's out of town." This time Kate replies *as if Deeley himself were in the past:* "Oh, what a pity." Perhaps Christy is Deeley? At any rate, this last intrusion of Deeley's washes away the past-in-the-present. There are no more "flashbacks" in the play. Deeley's successful penetration into that time-plane finishes them.

Now the third, final strophe. In it Anna's grip grows tighter on Kate, Deeley begins to thrash. Deeley tries to suggest that Anna leave, by asking whom else she intends to visit in England. Anna says that she knows no one else, and turns the conversation again to Kate, to her shyness, to the fact that once she, Anna, borrowed some of Kate's underwear and wore it to a party where a man looked up her skirt. (Like the reverse arrangement of the furniture, speeches all through this play refract previous speeches at odd angles.) Again Anna is emphasizing intimacy between her and Kate. Deeley picks up a remark that Anna has made about Kate being a Brontë "not in passion but only in secrecy." He asks Anna, "What was she in passion?" Anna replies coolly that this is his province, and he says, "Of course it's my bloody province. I'm her husband." A pause. He seems frightened, backed into a corner. Almost pathetically he says: "I mean I'd like to ask a question. Am I alone in beginning to find all this distasteful?"

Anna pretends to be surprised at the question. All she has done, she says, is to fly from Rome to see her oldest friend. This mention of Italy is a welcome cue to Deeley, who seizes it and brings up the subject of Anna's husband, waiting in Sicily for her. The speech is long (one interruption by Anna) and full of funny *non sequitur,* but not *really* funny because it carries an undertone of panic, a panic that drives Deeley at last to speak gibberish:

I mean let's put it on the table, I have my eyes on a number of pulses, pulses all round the globe, deprivations and insults, why should I waste valuable space listening to two—

He never gets the noun out. Kate interrupts swiftly—her only swift speech in the play—before Deeley can speak it. "If you don't like it, go."

This, almost, is a decision: by Kate. Deeley makes some weak, broken jokes about not having any place to go. Pitiable. Anna almost pities him. She says to Deeley: "I would like you to understand that I came here not to disrupt but to celebrate." What she is celebrating, she says, is an old and treasured friendship that was forged before Deeley knew them, that all she wanted—and still wants—for Kate is her happiness.

Now, after a pause, Deeley contradicts what he told Kate at the very beginning: he says he *had* met Anna before: except that, with the evocative double-exposure vision of this play's language, he tells Kate he met Anna when "she was pretending to be you at the time. . . . Wearing your underwear she was too, at the time." This juxtaposition, or interchangeability, of crotches intensifies what we can call the genital ambience. Deeley pursues the double-exposure theme by saying that "She thought she was you. . . . Maybe she was you."

He invites Kate's censure for having looked up Anna's skirt. Kate declines to censure. He continues the ambiguity:

DEELEY: If it was her skirt. If it was her.
ANNA: (*Coldly*) Oh, it was my skirt. It was me. I remember your look . . . very well. I remember you well.
KATE: (*To Anna*) But I remember you. I remember you dead.

(Here is another mirror image, another reversal. In Act One, Kate said that Anna talked about her as if she, Kate, were dead.)

Then Kate speaks her longest speech, the longest speech in the play, the final words of the play. In this speech the contest, the drama, shifts from conflict between Anna and Deeley over Kate to conflict within Kate herself. She remembers their room twenty years ago and remembers Anna dead, her face "scrawled with dirt," Anna trying to smile when dead. Then Kate says: "I had quite a lengthy bath, got out, walked about the room, glistening, drew up a chair, sat naked beside you and watched you."

She pauses. The words "glistening" and "naked" shimmer in the air, Kate *knowing* her sexual magic.

She continues, with her own variation on the story in Act One about the man in their room. She brought him home, she says, and plastered his face with dirt from a window box:

He resisted . . . with force. He would not let me dirty his face, or smudge it, he wouldn't let me. He suggested a wedding instead, and a change of environment.
Slight pause.
He asked me once, at about that time, who had slept in that bed before him. I told him no one. No one at all.

Those are the last words. This last speech seems to me a figurative but resonant statement of the pain that Kate had felt twenty years before in leaving a lesbian lover for a husband, with the dirt as a (puritanical) metaphor of that lesbianism.

But it is not the end of the play. Kate sits on her divan, the contest for her still not quite decided. Anna walks to the door, then stops. (Defeated? Teasing?) Deeley starts to sob quietly, as the man in that London room had sobbed twenty years before. (Not sure he is not defeated? Not sure of anything?) After a moment Anna returns, switches off the lamps, then lies down on her divan. (At least she is hopeful.) Deeley stops sobbing. He looks at both divans, then *he* goes to the door; then *he* stops and turns back. He goes to Kate's divan, sits on it, and lies across her lap. (An "echo" of her last speech? A plea by kinetic memory?) Then he gets up and goes to the armchair, apart from the two divans. To await, with resignation, the decision.

After a silence the lights suddenly come up brightly: on Deeley in his chair, Anna lying on her divan, Kate sitting on her divan. The swift surge of light is like a flashbulb for a photograph. The last contradiction: the picture that here is fixed is unresolved. Thus the play ends.

Note the similarity to *The Homecoming*. At the end of that play, two men kneel to a woman who entered the house meekly but has become a central force. At the end of *Old Times* the one man prostrates himself before a quiet woman who is the central force.

If one accepts this "map" of *Old Times,* as I do, what does it make of the play? Is it about a husband trying to defend his marriage against the recurrence of his wife's youthful homosexuality? (Deeley never leaves the two women alone together.) Well, even in this age of broadened acceptances, that could still be a legitimate drama, depending on its depth of character, on its honesty about the fears involved on *every* side. But I think that *Old Times* goes further, encompasses more, becomes something other than a battle between hetero sex and homo sex.

As noted, Pinter has lately moved more and more fully into the field of sexuality. But he has no social thesis, no psychological bent. Sexuality is to him a territory of powers and mysteries and paradoxes. *Old Times* no more says that we've all got to stand fast against homosexuality than *The Homecoming* warns us against creeping prostitution. In *Old Times* the particular arrangement of elements in the sexual field—a husband, a wife, a former girl friend of the wife's—appealed to Pinter, I would venture, only as colors and masses do to a painter, tone and harmonies to a composer. They had to be people, not nameless charade figures, or, Pinter's dramatic method being what it is, they would not have become "colors and masses" in his eyes. But it was feelings that he was after, rather than a schema, the powers of sex expressed through these exponents, in these tensions and attractions. That sense of sex power over lives— shaking and shaming and exalting them—is what remains after the play. The agony of affinities, unchosen but irresistible, is what Pinter has caught in the slender filaments of his exquisitely distilled dialogue, his pauses and silences. Deeley and Kate and Anna are very much themselves; they are also manifestations of a giant invisible force.

It is this ability to dramatize the invisible that characterizes Pinter's theater. Many have noted that his work hovers on the edge of the rational, that he likes to tease at the border of the irrational and unrational. To me, it is as if Mistah Kurtz's "horror" had long ago left the Congo and Pinter was a supersensitive watchman of its advance. This aspect of the irrational, apprehension of the "horror," is signified often by physical threat (*The Dumb Waiter, The Birthday Party*), but the threat and the fear are only symbols for the tissue-thin security of life itself, the immanent condition of mortality, whether one is patently threatened or not. Every moment of our lives, every single moment, we are threatened by death, and the subconscious awareness of that threat keeps the deep-buried animal growling in even the most civilized of us.

But there is another aspect of the irrational in us, an aspect linked with living—sheer sexuality. This second aspect of the irrational is not separable from the other—how can living be separated from the possibility of dying?—but the two are quite distinguishable. Sometimes sexuality works its way out through that relatively recent Western invention, love, sometimes not. More and more in recent years Pinter has concentrated on this second dark force, not in any Laurentian sense of ecstasy or wisdom of the blood but as mystery, not as fantasy or daydream or even liberation but as fundamentally frightening vulnerability.

And it is this, finally, that holds us in *Old Times*. Under its music, its wit, its contest, its sculptured form, it is our empathy with fellow victims that holds us. We too have felt or dreaded the sovereignty of loins like Kate's (transpose the sex as you like), the waking and dreaming continuance of that threat. We too have seen this sovereignty held by people so *saddled* with it that, even as they dominate us, we almost feel a kind of pity for them, as if they were children bearing weapons that burden them even as they threaten us.

That sexual vulnerability in us, immanent as the vulnerability to death, acknowledged or not, struggled against or submitted to, is what Pinter has circumscribed in this play. His delicately modulated, chromatic, contradictory writing, spaced and bound by silences, is like a series of colored markers sent up to the surface of a sea by a danger deep below, the mere surface index of a huge buried presence in us that has nothing to do with reason or explanation.

"I do so hate the becauses of drama," Pinter said in an interview in 1966. "Who are we to say that this happens because that happened, that one thing is the consequence of another? . . . The most we know for sure is that the things which have happened have happened in a certain order. . . . Life is much more mysterious than plays make it out to be."

Not *his* plays. In one view, my "map" of *Old Times* might be taken as an intrusion on a work that Pinter wants to leave unexplained. But I persist with it because, first, I think that in any view the play has been underestimated and underconsidered and, second, I have not "explained" it, I have only tried to identify the surface markers of a deeper, inexplicable action. The great gift of Pinter is that his words and actions demarcate the inexpressible without needing to express it. The patterns of demarcation in *Old Times* are more important than the "becauses"—inevitably so, since the "becauses" do not exist.

Pinter likes to write poems about the themes of plays that he is working on. In his book *Poems* (1968) he includes "A View of the Party," written in 1958, the year in which *The Birthday Party* was first performed. The poem is a variation on themes of that play.

Here is a poem that Pinter published in the (London) *Times Literary Supplement,* December 11, 1970, presumably written at about the time he was writing *Old Times.*

All of That

All of that I made
And, making, lied.
And all of that I hid
Pretended dead.

But all of that I hid
Was always said,
But, hidden, spied
On others' good.

And all of that I led
By nose to bed
And, bedding, said
Of what I did

To all of that that cried
Behind my head
And, crying, died
And is not dead.

The Idea of Repertory

Hardly a month goes by without one more definitive article on the fate of the American theater, and almost every one prescribes the repertory system as the solution to all problems—or at least the requisite first step toward solution. Few of these articles give more than the sketchiest idea of what repertory really is, and none that I have seen treats it historically. Harold Clurman, who knows this important subject, said when he was addressing a group of theater people in 1964: "One of the primary problems is to make people understand what a repertory theater is. . . . You would be surprised how many people, sometimes in very high positions—and sometimes trustees of a board!—who support the theater, have to have explained to them what the word means."

I begin my own comments by taking Clurman's hint and examining the word itself. It doesn't mean what it looks like. "Repertory" doesn't mean "repetition." A repertory theater does indeed repeat plays, but the word comes from the past participle of the Latin verb *reperire,* to find. The O.E.D. gives three meanings for repertory; abridged, they are (1) an index; (2) a storehouse; (3) repertoire. If we look then under the most pertinent meaning, "repertoire," we find: "A stock of dramatic or musical pieces which a company or player is accustomed or prepared to perform."

This definition is a small miracle of compression. It not only gives the quintessence of the idea, sometimes misrepresented even by presumed repertory supporters, it also includes the term with which repertory used to be interchangeable and with which it is now often confused: stock. Today a stock company may or may not have a permanent ensemble; it performs plays successively, for one or two or however many weeks, then discards them. Through much of the nineteenth century a stock company was a repertory company—a stock of people, in a relatively permanent ensemble, who had a stock of plays to perform and could choose from among them as needed. The only element left out of the O.E.D. definition is alternation: a repertory company varies its bills, rarely giving any one play more than five or six performances in a row, bringing it back after having performed other plays.

This system, which may now strike some readers as a fancy idealistic plan, was for centuries *the only form of theater practice*. That is the prime historical point. The idea of repertory is not a professorial or critical theory; less than a century ago it was universal and commonplace in Britain and America (as it still is in Europe). We'll explore the reasons why it was abandoned, but what we are discussing is a return, not a novelty.

To trace its history, I begin on this side of the Middle Ages and emphasize English tradition. The theater of antiquity, of Greece and Rome, is not ancestral of ours in forms of operation; and virtually everything in the American theater—language, classic repertoire, theatrical customs—derives from England.

During the first thousand years or so of the Christian era, the formal theater was under the Church's interdiction, but traveling players kept working "underground." As Jacques Burdick writes, "Forced together by circumstance, mimes, actors, acrobats, rope dancers, and musicians joined forces to survive." After the Church began to use formal theater for its own purposes, around 1000 A.D., and began to draw on surviving professionals to assist, actors moved out of the figurative underground to prosper in the new sunlight; and by the middle of the sixteenth century they were familiars of the continent and of England. Actors traveled. Audiences didn't. Many people might never go ten miles from home in their entire lives; they had neither money nor transport nor, often, permission. Actors had to be vagabonds, or starve. There simply weren't enough people in any one place to make up many audiences. Even if actors wanted to stay a week in one place, they had to have seven plays in repertoire, a stock of goods to offer like any other traveling tradesmen, so that the available audience who came on Monday could come again on Tuesday and the rest of the week. Traveling with just one play would have been stupid, and staying in one place would have been unthinkable.

But the latter idea became thinkable as the Renaissance wore on, as towns and cities grew larger, as economic and social currents altered because of—O worn but unavoidable phrase!—the rise of the middle class. Since there were now more people with more money to spend and more leisure time, living in larger compact areas, at least some troupes could stop traveling, or could vary their traveling with extended engagements in one place. But just because companies now were, or could be, fixed in one place, they did not alter the "stock of wares" idea of their traveling days. Partly this was because repertory (a term they never heard) was the only form of theater practice they knew. Theater *meant* repertory, as water means wet. Partly it was because there was no kind of audience pressure to change. In Britain —therefore in America too, as the colonies built theaters and developed a profession through the eighteenth century—audiences were conditioned to the scheduling of Play A on Monday evening, Play B on Tuesday, C on Wednesday, with perhaps A back on Thursday.

And beyond the matter of custom on both sides of the footlights, there were economic reasons to continue the "traveling" practice in one place. Cities, though growing, were still not large enough to support extensive straight runs of one play at a time. If a new production was a success, it took time for news of it to travel among the maximum potential theater audience; the spacing-out of performances of that production allowed that time. Besides, the bulk of any theater's repertoire was "standard" works, not new plays. If Smith made a hit as Othello, it was only Smith whom people were coming to see, not a new play, and it was better business to "tease" the audience by spacing *Othello* out among other standard plays, rather than to plunk down fifteen or twenty performances in a row. Further, Smith would have objected to an extended run because he was used to variety in his acting, an alternation of roles, and would have felt that a long unbroken sequence in one role was freakish and possibly harmful. (When Edwin Booth scored a success as Hamlet in New York in 1864, the manager persuaded him to give 100 straight performances of the part—probably a record at that time for an old play. Booth acceded reluctantly; he was afraid it would ruin him as an actor.)

"In the early period [of the nineteenth century], the stock theater was the only form of professional theater organization." So says Edward William Mammen in the best work I know on this aspect of the American theater, a monograph called *The Old Stock Company School of Acting,* published by the Boston Public Library in 1945. "A system in which a single group of actors presented many plays during a season was obviously well adapted to the comparatively small and isolated communities of these years." (Mammen's "comparatively" applies to the future, not the past.) But change was coming; change had in fact already come, unperceived at first, and had begun to work its way. This change had two components, one theatrical, the other general. The first, like so much in our theater, arrived from England, quite literally. Beginning in 1810 with George Frederick Cooke, English stars began to tour the United States, often traveling alone, simply taking over the leading roles in a local theater's productions of standard plays. The number of these English star tours increased, as if, under the political distinctions, the United States were still a cultural dominion of the Old Country. By 1835, wrote William B. Wood, a Philadelphia theater manager of the day, "that system was now at its height; the regular actors no longer forming a joint stock company, but being reduced to the condition of mere ministers or servants upon some principal performer, whose attractions it was now their sole and chief duty, to increase, illustrate, or set off."

Lesser actors, both British and American, also tried to set themselves up as touring stars because such tours quickly became cachets of eminence. Increasingly, local managers had trouble drawing audiences to productions done solely by the resident company, without some glamorous visitor.

To compound this intrinsically theatrical problem came the invention and extension of the railroad. In 1849 there were fewer than 6000 miles of track in the United States; one could not go directly by train even from New York to Albany. In 1860 there were over 30,000 miles of track, much of it west of the Mississippi. In 1869 the Golden Spike was driven in Utah, and transcontinental trains began.

This immense technological development had a huge impact on the theater. Stars could, of course, now travel farther, more easily and quickly; and now they could take some of their own supporting players with them, to make sure that important supporting roles were played as they wished in a local theater. This led, in short order, to what was then called the "combination" company: the *complete* acting company with star(s), along with all costumes and scenery— what we would today call a road company. These combination companies, for reasons of economy, usually traveled with one play, so each successful company amounted to a long run of one play, done in numerous places. Joseph Jefferson, in his autobiography, said somewhat guiltily that he was one of the first to use a combination company, with *Rip Van Winkle* after the Civil War; but the practice had actually begun in the 1850s, had lain dormant during the war, then had exploded in the 1870s.

The railroad made it possible and inevitable. The railroad even influenced scene design: pieces of scenery, called flats, were now built to fit through freight-car doorways. Doubtless the railroad had another effect, less marked by theater historians: now the audience could travel too. People from small towns now went much more frequently to cities, where they saw grander theater productions, which they could then compare with local fare. The "small and isolated communities" that Mammen mentioned became larger and less isolated. The public did not exactly become a national band of connoisseurs, but in some ways—standards of polish and luxe, for instance—they became too demanding for what must have very often been the shoddiness of local theaters.

Because of these cumulating factors, the decline of the stock company was catastrophic. In 1860, Mammen says, there were more than fifty stock companies around the country, and in 1871 there were still some fifty. But by 1878 there were only twenty; by 1880 seven or eight. By 1887 there were four, three of them, paradoxically, in New York.*

They were pushed out by the combination company, which is essentially still our predominant theater practice—one play produced to run as long as possible, in one place or on tour, with a group of actors assembled only for that play, with a physical production built only for that play. For a local manager, the chance to book an entire show, complete with scenery, was a financial boon. Previously he had

* Mammen adds that in the late 1890s "a new or twentieth-century type of American stock company arose. This differed from the older form in having much smaller acting companies, cheaper admission prices, a weekly change of bill, and twelve performances a week. It filled a place in our national life somewhat similar to that of the 'movies' today and was indeed killed by them. It has been re-born, with somewhat different characteristics, as 'summer stock.' "

had to pay a corps of actors every week and provide his own scenery; now he could book "packages" as and when he needed them and when they were available, with almost no overhead in other weeks. And those packages came festooned with personalities and with proven reputations. The local manager could not match it, and the local audience much preferred it.

Thus we got the long-run system. An enormous amount has been written, with truth, about the defects and ill effects of that system, but those writers almost always scant the improvements that it brought about. The first improvement was in the direction of plays—the very birth of the profession of director. In the centuries of stock, plays were not rehearsed in anything like the way to which we have become accustomed. Most plays were standard items, and each theater had a venerable prompt book for each play—also more or less standard— containing the entrances, exits, principal movements, and "business" for the cast. The stage manager rehearsed newcomers in the fixed patterns, especially in any nuances of this particular house. When a new play was produced, the movements and effects were usually worked out in collaboration between the cast, the stage manager, the prompter (if he was old and trusted), the author (if he was present and respected), and the manager of the house. No one was expected to have the overall artistic vision and control of the present-day director.* In the main, the actors, particularly the leads, were expected to be experienced and knowledgeable, to be able to take care of themselves in the working-out of character and the devising of effects and "pictures."

Around the middle of the nineteenth century a new theater artist came into being—the director, responsible for an integrated production. Among the earliest instances of this full concept were the productions by Samuel Phelps at the Sadler's Wells Theater of London, which, admittedly, was a repertory company but which operated on true ensemble principles. As the repertory/stock method dwindled in Britain and the United States, as more and more reliance was placed on the success of one play in one production, more and more

* There were some rare eighteenth-century figures who occasionally exercised such vision and control. For an account of one such exception, see *David Garrick Director* by Kalman A. Burnim (Southern Illinois University Press, 1973).

care was spent on its preparation under an artistic mentor, such as Dion Boucicault, in Britain and America, and Augustin Daly, in New York. The theater now had a person at work who had something of the relation to a production that a conductor has to a symphonic performance. (Curious coincidence: the rise of the conductor in symphonic music was roughly concurrent with the rise of the theater director.)

That increased reliance on one play at a time led to an increased investment in scenery—of money, time, and taste. Previously most stock theaters had used a stock of scenery, interchangeable drops and wing pieces and flats, to represent the palaces, forest glades, drawing rooms, and so on, of the repertoire. Pieces would be combined and recombined; a new and distinct physical production for one play was a great rarity in those theaters. Scene design had flourished in the Italian Renaissance, and until the middle of the eighteenth century this flowering had touched the best theaters of the West; but since then design had often been romantically hack and stale.

With costume the situation had been considerably worse. Mammen quotes a rule on this subject from the regulations of the Boston Museum, which (despite its name) was one of the best American stock theaters: "Every Gentleman engaged in the Museum must provide himself with such hosiery, wigs, feathers, swords, shoes, buckles, gloves, cravats, laces and ornaments, etc. as may be appropriate and necessary to the costume he may wear. When the costume is of the present period, the whole must be provided by the performer. The Ladies of the Company furnish their own dresses in each and every case." This is a succinct description of artistic chaos. Every actor had his own costume basket as he had his own makeup, and very often one actor did not know what other actors in a scene were wearing until he stepped on stage at a performance. The long-run production, as against repertory, demanded and got more attention for unified, particularized costume design.

Once again art and economics went hand in hand. When more money was invested in scenery and costumes for a play, more performances of that play had to be given to repay the cost; the "run" system made those added performances possible. And once again theater history is shown to be inseparable from histories outside the theater: greater scenic fidelity, whether to Venice in the time of Shylock or to Paris in the time of Marguerite Gauthier, was demanded by a public whose literature was becoming more realistic and whose eyes were becoming accustomed to accurate renditions of their world. One historian of the nineteenth-century theater, William W. Appleton, points out that the box set—the setting based on the "missing fourth wall" principle—came into use around the time of the invention of photography. Before then, rooms had been represented on stage by a backdrop and a few wing pieces on either side that were parallel to the backdrop. Now audiences demanded stage rooms with walls that behaved like the walls of the rooms they knew, with workable doors and, sometimes, with ceilings.

But the most radical effect of the change from repertory to the long run was on the playwright. First and most obvious, he could make more money. Prior to about 1850 a new play might be given by a stock theater for as long as a week; then, if it was successful, it would be placed in the repertory to alternate with other plays. There were anomalies like *Uncle Tom's Cabin,* which in 1852–3 had a run of 300 consecutive performances at one theater, but in general a new play would get, in the course of a season, a maximum of some forty non-consecutive performances. The long-run system paid the playwright, when successful, much better.

The playwright's success thus became crucial to the theater's success. Previously the failure of a new play simply meant that it was withdrawn; the theater continued—with its standard repertoire and perhaps another new play or two. It was a theater of performance: people went to see the actors. They might go to see the same play twice or three times a year, at one theater or at different theaters, to see different actors in the roles, as a ballet-lover may now go twice in the same season to see different Giselles. But with the end of repertory, audience interest shifted from player to play. New plays, as such, took on an importance they had not had since Athens. The playwright's specific gravity in the theatrical compound became much weightier. Theatrical criticism, which had previously concentrated on acting, reflected this change and now concerned itself more with writing.

The search for successful new plays became the theater's prime interest. When a new play became a hit, it was often because of a particular star's performance, and he or she then clung to it, nearly to the exclusion of everything else, as long as it would draw. Joseph Jefferson in *Rip Van Winkle* was a national institution for several generations. And in *Long Day's Journey into Night* Eugene O'Neill has told us, in thinly disguised form, what a burdensome gold mine *The Count of Monte Cristo* was to his touring-star father, James O'Neill. That search for scripts, which took over at this time, is still our theater's dominant drive.

By 1900, allowing for very few exceptions, we can say that the stock/repertory theater with a relatively permanent company had disappeared as a major institution: the carefully directed and specifically designed one-show-at-a-time theater had taken its place; and a manager did a new production only when he had a new script of promise. It was a complete revolution in theater practice.

And around 1900 a great change also came about in attitudes toward repertory. As we have seen, for many centuries repertory had been virtually the only form of theater operation. It was bread-and-butter. It had needed no intellectual or esthetic justification; the tawdriest as well as the best theaters made their livings that way. Then the theater changed its way of making a living; and repertory, after it had been supplanted by the long run, became revered, yearned for, apostrophized, etherealized. It was as if the theater had practiced repertory for all those centuries out of high-mindedness, not for cold cash reasons, had somehow slipped from grace, and as if the salvation of the theater (which always needs *some* kind of salvation) depended on a return to that earlier, untainted, idealistic system.

Mournful statements began to appear about the loss of the stock company, particularly as a school for acting. In fact some of the more clear-eyed critics, like Bernard Shaw, who had seen the results of that schooling, were of quite mixed opinions about its value. True, the young Henry Irving had played 428 roles (small ones, mostly) at the Theater Royal, Edinburgh, between 1857 and 1859, and had treated it as his conservatory; but for every Irving there had been at least 100 *routiniers* who quickly learned superficial tricks, and nothing more, to get them through ill-prepared productions. Mammen, who did as reliable a study of acting as is possible through research alone, concludes that in the early nineteenth century the beginner at the Boston Museum had to learn entirely on his own; in the middle of the century, as runs lengthened, there was some balance between careful instruction and variety of roles; toward the end of the century, as the long-run system took over, chances for variety disappeared, but "the apprentice stood a far better chance of adequate instruction." Yet, despite these facts, the idea of repertory as school and as professional fulfillment became more and more hallowed.

In 1904 William Archer, the English critic and dramatist, and Granville Barker, the English genius who was actor, director, dramatist, and critic, collaborated on a book called *Scheme and Estimates for a National Theatre*. The author's assumption, based on the past of the English-speaking theater and the continuing practice of the national and municipal theaters on the continent (which, through benefit of subsidy, have not changed to this day), was that their proposed theater would have to be a permanent repertory company. Archer and Barker conceded some points skimped by other enemies of the long-run system before and since: "Beyond all doubt, the supersession of the old stock company by the long run system has done a very real service to the stage. It has encouraged a finish, both in play-writing and acting, which the older conditions never allowed. It has broken a tradition of slovenliness." But then they went on to stress the shortcomings of the new system, especially the type casting, in which actors are cast repeatedly in roles that they closely resemble and develop only narrow specialties: "Under the old system talent and skill were expected to work impossibilities; under the new system little is left for them to do." Repertory was "the only practical system" for the national theater they envisioned, with a permanent company, with plays alternated and (remember the word *reperire*) retained.

That British National Theater had to wait a long time for its birth, but in the Edwardian decade there were several attempts in Britain to establish repertory. One of the most notable, which lasted only seventeen weeks, was made in London by the American producer Charles Frohman in 1910—128 (alternated) performances of ten plays— hardly astronomical but already so unusual in the English-speaking world that a book about that season was published. The year before in New York a heavily endowed company called the New Theater launched a series of very expensive repertory productions in an immense theater; the New lasted two seasons. Less than fifty years had elapsed since repertory had been the commercial mainstay in both countries. Already in both countries repertory had to be commer-

cially cosseted and critically eulogized just to get started; but even
when good—and Frohman's season apparently was excellent—the
public's custom had changed.

Nevertheless, in Britain between two world wars the repertory
movement continued to struggle and managed to stay alive. After the
Second War the Old Vic of London became the National (at last!)
and the Memorial Theater at Stratford-on-Avon, eventually rechris-
tened the Royal Shakespeare, opened a London base. Both companies became repertory groups and, with fluctuations, have done
admired work. There is no question as to whether repertory can pay
its way in Britain: it can't. Both of these companies and others (like
the rep theaters of the continent) are kept going by government
subsidy far beyond anything the United States has ever given to the
theater. Still, they have had considerable public support and have,
additionally, become tourist attractions. By and large, they have been
true repertories with many actors remaining for many seasons. The
National in particular has retained some productions for more than
one season, sometimes for several seasons. (Again *reperire*.)

In the United States the outstanding attempt at repertory between
the wars was made by Eva Le Gallienne, who was also involved in
the first attempt after the Second War. Le Gallienne's Civic Repertory Theater ran on 14th Street in New York from 1926 to 1933.
The American Repertory Theater, with Le Gallienne as one of three
directors, ran on Columbus Circle in New York only from November
1946 to February 1947. The difference in life spans was not, I think,
due entirely to quality, although the quality of the first theater was
reportedly high—I saw only *Peter Pan* there as a child—and the
quality of the second, I can testify, was low. In the intervening years,
costs had greatly increased. Other attractions for desirable actors had
greatly increased. And the public had lost in theatergoing—as against
opera and ballet—the habit of repertory. (I mean the best available
public. There is no point in discussing people who would not in any
case be interested in Shakespeare and Ibsen.)

The money situation for repertory has improved somewhat in recent years because of more chances for subsidy. In 1957 the Ford
Foundation began its Program in Humanities and the Arts, which
has been especially helpful to theaters. Other foundations have also
helped substantially. In 1965 the federal government began the
National Endowment for the Arts, one aspect of which from the start

has been theater assistance. I have to note that the projection of the National Endowment for theater aid in 1975 was $6.5 million while West Germany's annual support of theaters stands at about $120 million. Still, partly in response to lately available financial aid, there are now some fifty resident theaters throughout the country. Some of them call themselves repertory companies, and a few of them come close to the definition, particularly the American Conservatory Theater of San Francisco and the Acting Company, which was organized in New York but spends most of every season touring. Their work, with the work of some other groups, shows at least a clear recognition of the repertory ideal and, however incomplete or abortively implemented, tries to move toward that ideal.

Why has repertory *become* an ideal? Why has the standard commercial practice of the last century become the utopia of our time?

Early in the twentieth century the long-run system, like all new systems anywhere that bring improvements, began to show its defects. Its virtues were as described, but it soon became apparent that, under the new system, the theater had been converted from modes of continuity into hundreds of separate little enterprises, each one born to die, however long the death was postponed. Actors, now usually type-cast, were deprived not only of variety but of the chance for refreshment and improvement of a role that alternation provided. If development of theater artists had never been as consistent under the old system as was now nostalgically imagined, it had become practically nil. Since the object of production was now to see how long a play could run before it was permanently discarded, most of the plays chosen were those that the largest number of people would rush to see as soon as possible and which would be least missed when they were thrown away. Further, the new system was exploiting the artistic development of centuries with little concern for sustaining or replacing it, as a paper mill might exploit a forest that took centuries to grow. The paper may be more apt to the times than the trees, but the mill, neglecting reforestation, commits ravage.

As these ravages became clearer, some of the best theater people began to argue for a return to repertory, at least in some theaters, to revive and expand its advantages. Some of them, like Archer and Barker, realized that those advantages had rarely been properly exploited; they resolved now to make amends. (Again I underscore that this argument went on only in Britain and America: on the continent the leading theaters, all government-subsidized, had never abandoned repertory.) But since repertory was no longer the mainstream, those who favored it immediately became exceptions, somewhat rarefied. The support of repertory quickly took on the color and trappings of a Cause among many theater people.

Many *theater* people. Enthusiasm on the subject, until relatively recently, was generally restricted to professionals. In the nineteenth century, repertory had, so to speak, been commanded by the audience. Now the audience was either unconcerned or satisfied with the new order. Theater people were trying to command repertory back.

Then, during the last decade or so, came further change—rather, several related changes. First, among actors. American actors had *talked* about repertory for seventy years as the ideal form, as a home, as a place to develop and sustain; but in my experience and observation they had done this talking only when they were out of work. When they had jobs, in commercial shows or films or radio or TV series, they only sighed about it ruefully or mentioned it not at all. But more and more actors, particularly young ones, developed a deeper revulsion toward commercial conditions at the same time that more resident theaters were established. I don't maintain that actors no longer want fame and big money and that no golden offers would lure them away from the Ashtabula Rep. I do maintain that more actors, particularly young ones out of university drama schools who may also have served internships at theaters abroad, have been less willing to throw themselves, as a first obligatory step, on the meat markets of Broadway and Hollywood, have tried to find rational ways to invest their theatrical lives elsewhere.

The attitude of playwrights, too, has changed. The first step happened around 1950. The best English-language playwrights became repelled by Broadway and the West End, shifted their aspirations toward Off Broadway and its London equivalent. This took them out of inhuman money pressures but not necessarily out of the long-run system. In England, which has the two best English-language reps, the next step for playwrights was especially logical because many of the most desirable actors and directors were connected with those companies. Harold Pinter gave his plays *The Homecoming* and *Old*

Times to the Royal Shakespeare Company, *No Man's Land* to the National, to be performed in a repertory schedule. Many other playwrights, in England and here, have done the equivalent.

For the playwright this meant less money, at least in this first production: and usually the first production is the most lucrative. It also meant making do with the actors in the company most of the time, instead of selecting from the whole corps of working actors. Although there were exceptions to this, where actors were jobbed in for specific new plays (as they are for some revivals), still fundamentally the playwright was moving toward repertory. What led him there, I believe, was not only the absolutely incredible financial conditions and consequent strictures of Broadway, not only Off Broadway's gradual approximation of Broadway conditions, but a growing feeling that what was good for the theater was good for the playwright, and that repertory was good for the theater. What might be lost in immediate revenue and completely free-handed casting might well be made up for by intelligence and devotion, by the length of the play's life rather than a crammed run. To help such a theater was perhaps to find actors and audience for whom to write. This, as many playwrights have learned, is becoming a hard question to answer: Whom am I writing for? Repertory theaters, organic, related to a community, may be part of the answer.

Other kinds of theater artists who at first had also benefited from the change to long runs began to see virtues in repertory. James Tilton, scene designer for the APA Repertory Company, said in 1967 that he rejoiced in the requisite discipline: "I must design scenery to fit each director's concept, scenery to fit the needs of the particular play, scenery to fit my artistic standards, and scenery to fit into, with, around, and under, or over every other play's scenery." Nancy Potts, the APA costume designer, said, " . . . working with the same company affords me an opportunity to have a better idea of what I can do with a particular costume since I know all about the actor who will be wearing it. I know what he will need in terms of adjustment, how well he wears certain colors, and so on. . . . It's a big difference from the usual [one-play, long-run] situation."

What all this seems to mean is that for every kind of theater artist an evolution has taken place. Some in every one of those arts, though they don't want to go back to the stock theater of the last century, want to go forward to an improved practice of repertory. They know that *every theatrical profession has benefited in some way from the long-run system,* but that this system has outlived, by seventy years or so, its usefulness to anything but the straight business theater. These professionals want to take what they have gained from System Two back into a bettered System One.

And that is not only not all, it may not even be the most significant development. The American audience now seems to be changing. The repertory theaters around the country, of which there are a few, and those close to repertory in method, of which there are many more, report high attendance rates. In 1972–3 the American Conservatory Theater played to ninety-percent capacity. (In form the ACT is as close to a repertory theater as any that we have; I'm not commenting here on choice of plays or quality of work.) None of these theaters is rid of the need for subsidy: on the contrary, subsidy is increasingly necessary as costs zoom ahead of ticket prices. But audience response is growing. New York is an exception. The theatrical capital of the country still, it was the last city to let go of the old stock theater and will be the last, I think, to support the new repertory. It is spoiled, both truly and falsely sophisticated, and is still hag-ridden by longings for the Broadway glitter that manages skimpily to survive, if somewhat pathetically. But in the rest of the country, things are different. People don't go to touring shows or local affairs in ritual fashion, as once they did. They are now sick of road-company dregs and jerry-built local productions. They subscribe, in great numbers, to the resident theater.

Certainly a great deal of that subscription is only a new kind of ritual, keeping up with new culture-conscious Joneses or filling in the winter evenings or doing something that may turn out to be good for the kids. But that kind of support, always present in any supported public art and not to be snooted at in peril of both our souls and our budgets, helps to keep those theaters alive; and one important group for whom they are being kept alive—possibly the most important in a long view—is the best part of that audience: those who go out of hunger, not rote. That best audience exists: I have seen a bit of it myself and I have heard a lot about it from directors and managers of theaters around the country. Spattered with television sludge, jostled by the sweaty hysteria of most so-called serious magazines, choked by the many weeds in the (essentially wonderful) garden of film, they feel apparently that they are almost being driven back in refuge to something that a theater—a good theater—can give them: and that one of the most rewarding ways in which a theater can operate, can serve them, is repertory. Possibly the ultimate power—which in Athens, Greece, or Athens, Ohio, is the audience—will opt for repertory.

Is repertory the best form?

Conceding nothing to rosy rhetoric, let's try to run an austere, summary balance sheet. For directors, what they may possibly lose in rehearsal time in a repertory schedule, they gain in chances for ensemble exploration and cumulative power, in less need for the break-in period of the one-shot production. Scene and costume and lighting designers have usually to work less lavishly in repertory but can work more ingeniously, more consistently in their general intent, with ample chance for variety. The playwright makes less money with a repertory production, but he has what serious writers want so desperately these days, a habitat.

But it's the actor who gains the most, with a theater and artistic family, with accrual of roles, and the chance to improve in them—if he can withstand, or wants to withstand, or at least can visit only temporarily the other fields that will beckon. Even though or possibly because the actor gains most from repertory, he is the theater professional least likely to remain in it. Of course he is the only one who needs physically to remain. The playwright's work can be done subsequently in other places in other ways while he remains with the theater. The designers can remain while their work is used subsequently elsewhere. Even a director can absent himself for several weeks to do a guest job elsewhere without seriously affecting a repertory schedule. A member of the acting company doesn't have these options, without interrupting his work in his own theater. On the other hand, he gets more from it. As film is predominantly the director's medium and the long-run theater is the playwright's, repertory is the actor's.

Is that all? Is that enough? Most of these advantages, allowing for some loss of refreshment through alternation, would come from a "series" season, a company that did one play for (say) a month, then another for a month, and so on. The audience would still see the work of an established company, would still have the chance to see the same actors in different roles throughout the season. Is there one inarguably unique asset of repertory?

Yes. *Reperire.* We have a heritage of great world drama. We rarely see much of it. We can never see all of it and can never have a sizable portion of it available to us in any theater's repertoire, not even as much as the average symphony orchestra performs of the musical heritage. Still a corps of repertory theaters could produce and keep on tap a growing number of great plays so that American audiences, as they came along through the years, could have the chance to see some of those titanic works at least once in their lives, even if in some cases it meant going to other cities, as opera enthusiasts often do. Reading those plays is always possible, always wonderful, but it cannot be sufficient. A good theater should prove that it is not sufficient.

This function, as "living museum," has a special hardship in America because America has contributed so little to that dramatic heritage. In the long term, at the deepest level, that fact may nag at an American repertory company. Certainly no American theater can yet be the cultural equivalent of such theaters as the Comédie Française and the Burghtheater of Vienna, where enduring indigenous works are the core of the theater's repertoire. But classics are classics not by critical decree but because they live and their life is irresistible; and the one function that no other medium can take from the art of the theater is to fulfill the life of those classics. A real "living museum" is not a dusty place.

This is not to say that a repertory's only function is to keep some classics alive; but it is to say that such work cannot be done in any other theater form. By doing it an American theater can make many other things possible for other American artists, including playwrights.

So it may be that the hour of repertory is returning. Not by using the term as an arty shield against criticism of incompetence. Not by using it as an aggrandizing label on any theater that happens not to be "long-run." But by using the method truly, better than before, both to keep the past available to the present and to give the present a better place to speak to the present. Will such theaters, such companies, such audiences be "permanent"? Mark Twain once said of something that he thought it would last forever, then added: "By 'forever' I mean thirty years." I would gladly settle for thirty years per theater in a world where constant change is daily bread.

I have to note, finally, that I don't *believe* all the above will happen. Belief, in these matters, is for rhapsodists. But it seems reasonably reasonable to hope. The ingredients are there. They can be fused with talent and by will.

PART V
on criticism

Who Did It?

(The New York Times, *March 27, 1966*)

Three recent productions, and comments received here after reviews of them were published, raise an old and painful question—one that seems unanswerable.

In the course of rehearsals or out-of-town tryouts or New York preview of a play, changes are sometimes made in personnel. Often, as in each of these recent cases, it is the director who is changed. The newcomer may prove markedly superior or (as in one of these shows) inferior to the man he replaced.

If he is superior to the first man, he is heavily burdened because he rarely has enough time in which to raze the original conception of the production and build afresh. If he is inferior to the first man, he benefits by good work that he could not himself have done. In either case, his name goes on the program as director, and he gets the blame or the credit for what happened before he joined the show.

The former case is more immediately serious, because a talented man suffers in reputation for what he did not do and could have improved if there had been time. But unjustified praise is also serious because it can lead to more engagements and future bungling.

What can be done about these injustices? Not much. A good director can't take his good work with him when he leaves a show, in order to keep a lesser man from being credited with it. The closest one can come to a tenable suggestion is that a second director can refuse to let his name be put in the program until and unless he is satisfied with the result.

But this proposal sounds simpler than it would prove in practice. No producer wants to present a play without a director's name on the program; it is too obvious an index of trouble and of eagerness to avoid blame. And many directors would not want to leave their names off, even if they were not happy about results, because work is so scarce that almost any record of employment is better than none.

Equal credit to two or more directors is not fair unless it is really a joint effort all the way through. Otherwise, how shall multiple credits be phrased? Shall a program say: "Directed for the first two weeks by Hilton Barnes and after that by Clive Kramer"? Or shall it say: "The characterizations of Sam and Louis were developed by Hilton Barnes, who also staged the first-act curtain, but who disclaims responsibility for the casting of May Wyne as Clara"? Ludicrous as they look in print, matters like these are often the facts of the case. But how can they be noted publicly?

Then too there is the actor who wants to play a character one way and is told by his director to play it otherwise. Shouldn't the eventual praise or blame be shared by the director? And what of the scene and costume and lighting designers? All of them have something less than a free hand in many cases and have undoubtedly suffered or profited unjustly in the course of events. An author can, and often does, publish his play after the opening, indicating how it was altered in production. But what can these other people do?

The critic who is familiar with the work of persons in a production can note divergences, good or bad, from the past; and sometimes the weight of the evidence compels a conjecture as to what happened. Where he does not know the past work or where the evidence is not compelling, he has no choice but to use the information in the program as given. To take account of theatrical rumor would only lead quickly to other injustices, possibly much more grave—if not to a sort of anarchy. Imagine a critical practice in which the program information could be disregarded at will.

The situation causes—and must continue to cause—hardships. I wish I could say that in the long run everything evens up, but I don't believe it. Browning's line "There shall never be one lost good" is debatable enough in most of the world, but is especially thin in the theater. Lots of good work gets lost; and much that is less good gets praise that belongs elsewhere.

This is one trouble that we cannot blame on current theater conditions. There was probably a backstage story—the real facts of the matter—about the first performance of *Oedipus*.

Why Do Critics Persist?

"We are not liked, we critics." So Max Beerbohm began "The Critic as Pariah" in 1903. "The creators of art do not like us, nor do the men in the street." For about as long as there has been theater criticism, regularly published comment on theater productions—which, in English, dates from the late seventeenth century—there has been resentment of it. In 1714 Joseph Addison wrote, "I do not indeed wonder that the Actors should be such professed Enemies to those among our Nation who are commonly known by the Name of Criticks. . . ." In 1722 Richard Steele notes in the preface to *The Conscious Lovers* how he has "suffer'd by Criticks." In 1740 Colley Cibber, writing the *Apology* for his life, calls critics "Piddlers in Wit" and compares them to highwaymen robbing him of his pittance. If it amuses you, you can even account it one more instance of Shakespeare's prescience that in *Love's Labour's Lost* he has Berowne speak of "A critic; nay, a night-watch constable."

Resentment of the "night-watch constable" is still very much alive. Every newspaper or magazine interview with a theater (or film) person, every TV talk show with such a person includes its jabs at critics. Recently a well-known theater director came over to me at a meeting and introduced himself; as we shook hands, he said with a generous grin, "I don't usually speak to critics." And I can testify to Beerbohm's comment about the man in the street. For instance, when I was a newspaper critic for eight months I got—mixed, I must stipulate, with some friendly letters—scores of adverse letters, many of them from readers who specified that they were angry at me even though they never went to the theater.

Some theater people are exceptions to the above, people as different as George Abbott and Peter Brook. Abbott, our longest-running maker of long-run shows, has said: "Each individual critic is a fallible human being subject to his prejudices and his sense of well-being at the time he is in the theater. But collectively, they are almost always right." Brook, who works on theater frontiers, says that if a critic "spends most of his time grumbling, he is almost always right."

But the majority opinion on critics is negative, and is by no means restricted to theater criticism. Poets have spoken in verse about critics of poetry. Burns wrote a two-line "Reply to the Threat of a Censorious Critic":

> With Aesop's lion, Burns says:—"Sore I feel
> Each other's blow; but damn that ass's heel."

Chekhov had something to say (according to Gorky's report) about literary critics:

Critics are like horse-flies which prevent the horse from plowing. . . . And what does the fly buzz about? It scarcely knows itself; simply because it is restless and wants to proclaim: "Look, I too am living on the earth. See, I can buzz, too, buzz about anything."

Lately Saul Bellow weighed in on this subject:

The career of a critic, when I am feeling mean about it, I sometimes compare to that of a deaf man who tunes pianos. In a more benevolent mood I agree with my late father that people must be encouraged to make as honest a living as they can.

When Baudelaire was writing art criticism, he noted that "the artist reproaches the critic with being unable to teach anything to the bourgeois, who wants neither to paint nor to write verses—nor even to art itself, since it is from the womb of art that criticism was born." In the film world one statement, out of many available ones: Akira Kurosawa has said, "I've never read a critic who didn't put false meanings into my work."

As for music, it provides possibly the best instance of an artist's dislike of a critic: Wagner's caricature of the Viennese music critic Eduard Hanslick as Beckmesser in *Die Meistersinger von Nürnberg*.

Enough. Pages of further evidence, easily available, would only repeat what is already clear: there is a venerable tradition of critic-resentment. Knowing that the atmosphere is hostile, on the part of most artists and also of much of the public, why does the critic persist?

I concentrate, in my attempts to answer the question, on the theater critic; and, further, I concentrate on the competent, serious critic. There are many critics—the majority, in fact—who are neither one nor the other. Someone else will have to explain them. The word "critic" as used below will mean the theater critic who is equipped for the work. Though he—or, of course, she—is in the minority, he encounters at least as much resentment as his incompetent colleagues, often more than the incompetent ones because he is more demanding.

The first and least important reason for the critic's persistence is that the artist's resentment is often spurious. Often it is nothing more than anger at an adverse opinion, dressed up as deep-seated hostility to the critic's profession. That anger is human enough, but is polemically spurious. It could be taken seriously only if artists were equally angry at good reviews. After a bad review the artist demands to know the critic's qualifications, but never after praise. The critic would be inhuman not to understand the artist's anger, but he would be silly not to persist in spite of it. The alternative would be to believe that the critic is qualified only when he praises.

However there *is* a resentment of the critic that obtains even when the reviews are good, a feeling longer-ranged and deeper. This is the artist's resentment that there is anyone with the power to sit in public judgment on him, to approve or disapprove his work. The objection here is not to a specific review but to the very practice of criticism. To this the critic can reply in purely utilitarian terms. In the long view, he performs services for the good artist, as publicist of the good and of the bad; as mediator between artist and audience; as historian. There is no point in the artist's arguing that the theater existed before theater criticism; he may as well argue that the theater existed before the invention of artificial light. Controlled lighting is now part of the theater's being and so is criticism. Besides, the Osbornes and the Pinters and the Albees complain of the practice of criticism (more than of specific reviews) only after that practice has helped very considerably to establish them. Brecht battled with critics throughout his life, but it was because a Berlin critic named Herbert Ihering traveled to Munich in 1922 to see a play called *Drums in the Night* by a new playwright—and understood what he saw—that Brecht's career was launched. Successful actors too numerous to mention have complained of critics after critics have aided crucially in their success. Producers who have plastered billboards and advertisements with quotations from critics have subsequently lamented the box-office power of the critic to whom they gave that power. The critic—our critic—persists because he sees that they all want to not have their cake and eat it, too.

As for the public's resentment, the fundamental rock-bottom reply is that the critic would not exist if the public did not want him to exist. Not one newspaper or magazine, however high-minded, would carry criticism one day after the editor became convinced that the public had stopped reading it. The public reads the critic and is sometimes, perhaps often, irritated with him, but keeps on reading. The irritation can come from vexation of the ego because the critic's opinions are in print and the reader's opinions are not. Sometimes the reader is irritated because he feels that the critic, by implication, is accusing him of philistinism or is indicting him for being ignorant or easy. But if the critic is a specialist, as he ought to be without being academic or remote, then he ought to know more than the general reader; in any event, he cannot apologize for knowing more about his field than the non-specialist. The critic persists because he believes in the public as educable and in himself as possible educator in his field. Less magisterially and more basically, he persists, too, because he knows that, beneath the fuming and spluttering, the public simply likes to read criticism. The medium of criticism as such is now firmly established as part of a reader's reading matter.

Often the critic is said to be a failed creative artist. Often this is true. Of course first-rate criticism has been written in all the arts by first-rate artists: Dryden and Shaw, Schumann and Berlioz, Reynolds and Delacroix, Coleridge and Eliot, James and Lawrence. Matthew Arnold said, "Wordsworth was himself a great critic, and it is to be sincerely regretted that he has not left us more criticism; Goethe was one of the greatest of critics, and we may sincerely congratulate ourselves that he has left us so much criticism." Still, despite these alpine examples, there are not many superlative artists who have had absolutely concurrent careers as critics. Most of those who have made careers of criticism have indeed been second-rate or failed artists.

I'm glad of this. It seems to me a reason for persisting, not desisting. The critic who has at least tried his hand at an art knows something of the making of that art and has more understanding of both success and failure in creation. Nowadays there are courses of study, particularly of graduate study, to prepare one for a career of theater criticism. (I have taught in such a program.) This procedure has long been standard in literature and the graphic arts, but is a relatively recent innovation in the theater. When I was a drama student, one could study any branch of theater practice except criticism. To have studied that, to have wanted to study it, would have been thought an admission of failure in a young person before he had even started. This was foolish. But I also think it a defect in the theater critic never to have done anything in a theater but sit in an orchestra seat.

For ten years when I was young I was a member of a repertory company, doing everything from acting to posting bills. I have also written some plays. I mention these matters because all this experience has been taken by some, sometimes in print, as a black mark against me. The argument was that anyone who had done all these things and was now a mere critic must be jealous. Well, I wouldn't want to swear that jealousy has never touched me, nor would I deny that I would rather be a first-class artist than anything in the world. Still I would rather be, if possible, a first-class critic than a second-class artist or worse. And is it a charge against the literary criticism of R. P. Blackmur and Yvor Winters that both published poetry of a lesser order? Only in the theater does the nuttiness prevail that experience in a critic is a shortcoming. The critic not only can persist in the face of this resentment, he can despise it.

But so far I have been defensive. There is a more important, positive case for criticism.

It has never been stated more strongly than by Oscar Wilde in his dialogue "The Critic as Artist":

ERNEST. But is criticism really a creative art?

GILBERT. Why should it not be? It works with materials, and puts them into a form that is at once new and delightful. What more can one say of poetry? Indeed, I would call criticism a creation within a creation. For just as the great artists, from Homer and Aeschylus down to Shakespeare and Keats, did not go directly to life for their subject-matter, but sought for it in myth, and legend and ancient tale, so the critic deals with materials that others have, as it were, purified for him, and to which imaginative form and colour have already been added. Nay more, I would say that the highest Criticism, being the purest form of personal impression, is in its way more creative than creation, as it has least reference to any standard external to itself, and is, in fact, its own reason for existing. . . .

Allow for the exaggerations of anti-philistinism, the luxury of wit and paradox, the bravado of *fin de siècle* estheticism, and that is still a statement of substance, particularly as it comes from a writer in no need of apologies. But Wilde goes even further:

GILBERT. Certainly, [criticism] is never trammeled by any shackles of verisimilitude. . . . One may appeal from fiction unto fact. But from the soul there is no appeal.

ERNEST. From the soul?

GILBERT. Yes, from the soul. That is what the highest criticism really is, the record of one's own soul.

This is not to be confused with Anatole France's purply dictum that a good critic is one who describes the adventures of his soul among masterpieces. How many masterpieces does a good critic encounter in a career that concentrates on new works? Besides, anyone, critic or not, can adventure among masterpieces; millions do. Wilde is, as he usually is under his consciously daring tone, more serious. He is making an analogy between the critic's exploration of art-and-his-own-life and the artist's exploration of myth-and-his-own-life. Wilde's juxtaposition would be merely amusing—or would be differently amusing—if there were not truth in the creative quality of criticism. Creation let us define for our purposes as the imaginative rendering of experience in such a way that it can be quintessentially re-experienced by others. The critic does that.

And this leads to the prime consideration, the element in criticism most often ignored or unrecognized. Criticism is a talent. Scholarship and university degrees at various levels can be helpful, surely, but they do not in themselves make good critics any more than in themselves they make good playwrights. Criticism is a talent. If one has a talent, one wants to use it. Objections cannot stop the talented critic any more than objections of a different sort can stop the talented playwright. The person who has that critical talent may or may not have equivalent talent for "original" work in the art. Some have had both. But if he has the critical talent alone, why shouldn't he use it? Setting aside commercial interests and the injured interests of inferior artists, setting aside even the understandably nettled egos of first-rate artists, what else can critical talent do, if used with integrity, other than enrich the art with which it is concerned?

In the art with which we are concerned here, there are two distinct kinds of criticism, theater criticism and drama criticism. The former deals with performance—all elements of the production including text-in-performance; the latter concentrates on text, with appropriate literary and cultural-historical comment. This distinction, between theater critics and drama critics, seems to me more helpful, less arbitrary and subjective, than the usual distinction between reviewers and critics. Talents for both kinds of criticism are not always present in the same person. Some critics, like James Agate, shine in theatrical work, some, like A. C. Bradley, in textual work. A very few, like Bernard Shaw, excel in both.

I concentrate here on the theater critic, for three reasons. First, the theater critic needs attention more than the drama critic. The drama critic is sheltered by the aegis of literary criticism, is more generally "respectable," and, since he has no immediate effect on a theatrical production, he runs into little animosity from the theater or the theater public. The drama critic does not have to understand why he persists in the face of hostility because he encounters very little of it. Second, the theater critic does have to understand, for himself at least, why he continues despite animosity. Part of it surely is that being a critic gives him an identity, just as being a dentist gives that man an identity. The Italian theater critic Nicola Chiaromonte said (as Mary McCarthy tells us) that he liked "having a part to play, a role assigned to him, that of the critic, whose mask he wears, in the common drama of society, where we all play our parts, and the theater is not just a microcosm of the real world, it is a cosmos in which all that is lived in the real world may be clarified and purified to a point where it can acquire significance." That is a sound psychological and philosophical reason for choosing, among all the "roles" that society affords, the one of critic. But not many such "roles" encounter such consistent ill will as the theater critic's, so he needs to understand his intrinsic professional reasons for persisting.

Third, the theater critic's work is, in my view, more difficult than the drama critic's and is at least equally important—in some ways more important. Theater criticism is more difficult, in judgmental essence, because it must be done under some sort of time pressure, whether of an hour or a day or a week or a month or a quarter-year, and because there is not often a useful body of precedent criticism on a production to help or helpfully irritate the theater critic. His criticism is at least as important as the drama criticism that may follow long after because, to a considerable degree, it determines what that subsequent criticism will be. The theater critic, even if he writes for a quarterly, is what I would call a front-line critic: anyone who comments on a play or production within, say, a year of its appearance is in my mind a front-line critic. He has the primary, crucial task of winnowing wheat from chaff—in effect, of selecting the materials that will eventually become the subjects for drama critics. The best of theater critics make mistakes. (See Shaw's negative review of *The Importance of Being Earnest*.) But it's in the front lines that most of the crucial decisions are made. (Luckily, in the case of *Earnest* there were other theater critics who saw its merits.) The playwright of value, even though his work can be read after a production has closed, has a long, hard pull to return, sometimes posthumously, from the neglect or disapproval of theater critics. How many good playwrights, disregarded in their time by critics, have later found the approval that their work deserved? Büchner is no example because his work was not produced at all, was hardly visible, during his brief lifetime. What fine play of a hundred years ago, produced in Paris or Rome or London or New York, is lost probably forever, could not even get published, not even preserved in manuscript, because the corps of theater critics at the time were blind to its quality? We will never know; and the mere possibility that one such play has been missed sends a shiver up the spine. That shiver confirms the theater critic's importance, responsibility, and need to be competent.

That shiver also confirms his prime motive for being: to find and foster the good. It is he, the best theater critic—as type, not as individual—who largely determines which plays will be studied, will be written about by drama critics, will be revived in the theater.

Besides his judgment on the playwright, the theater critic must, or should, make judgments on all elements of a production and must be able to discern, in some degree, how each element is being helped or hindered by the others. (Theater people other than writers have no possible recourse to subsequent reevaluation, at least as far as any one production is concerned, which naturally intensifies their dislike of the critic.) This leads to a salient fact of critical history. Some theater critics who are blatantly weak in literary judgment are valuable for their other theatrical judgments. Such disparate figures as William Winter, the critic of the *New York Tribune* from 1865 to 1909, and James Agate, the critic of the (London) *Sunday Times* from 1923 to 1947, are practically useless to us in their judgment of new plays, but they understood a great deal about other matters in the productions that they saw. For instance, Agate wrote of Ralph Richardson as Cyrano: "This is a grand actor when the part is honest; he would be my first choice for Mr. Valiant-for-truth with his 'I fought till my sword did cleave to my hand.' But Cyrano is Mr. Valiant-for-

embroidery. . . ." These few lines make Richardson's essence so vivid, and give such a quick insight into the essence of the role of Cyrano as well, that we can overlook the fact that Agate once proposed a Kafka Is Balls Club with himself as president.

These functions of the theater critic connect directly with his importance as historian and to historians. If the history of the theater is valuable, and it seems to me no less culturally and socially illuminating than the history of any other art, then the theater critic is invaluable. Compare the history of the theater before criticism was practiced with the subsequent history, and you see the difference between a chronicle fleshed out with snippets from other histories, from biographies and journals and the obiter dicta of amateurs (like Pepys), and a chronicle enriched by on-the-spot professional description and discussion. Just suppose that William Hazlitt, who makes Edmund Kean's London debut in 1814 sharp and exciting for us today, had been present at Shakespeare's Globe. Think of all the subsequent critical argy-bargy that would have been superfluous; think, positively, of the light that might have been shed.

The theater critic gives theater history its fullness of life, with no more Olympian truth than the contemporary commentator gives to the history of any other art or of politics, but with no less truth either. No one, I hope, will read William Winter for his opinion of the newfangled and scandalous Ibsen; but anyone who wants to "see" Edwin Booth as clearly as is now possible, anyone who wants to understand the character and standards of nineteenth-century theater practice, which is one fine way of learning about nineteenth-century America, cannot dispense with Winter.

The theater is a *subject*. That at last is why the critic writes and why the reader, even the one who rarely goes to the theater, reads. The theater is a complex, significant, reflective, and implicative subject. The consumer-service motive or function is quite secondary, though, like any other human being, the critic likes to see his enthusiasms prosper. Much more important, more central to his being than any box-office influence he may have is the realization that he works in a concurrent plane to the theater, not a congruent plane. He is in a kind of para-reality to the theater's reality. His criticism is a body of work obviously related to but still distinct from what the theater does; possibly influential, possibly not, but no more closely connected than is political science to the current elections. The critic learns that, on the one hand, there is the theater, with good and bad productions and, on the other hand, there is criticism, which ought to be good about both good and bad productions. Life is the playwright's subject, and he ought to be good about its good and bad people; the theater is the critic's subject, and he ought to be good about its good and bad plays.

But most of what is done in the theater—more than in any other art except film—is mediocre or worse; so the theater critic spends most of his time with trash. But the trash is as much a part of his subject as the non-trash. The theater historian A. M. Nagler has pointed out that Shaw wrote one of his best reviews about an item called *The Chili Widow*. Every critic grapples continually with *Chili Widows*. They need to be identified and at least generically understood, both as a matter of clear sight and because every critic either has a touch of John the Baptist or else he ought to quit. He ought to live in hope that the truth, the true art, is continually en route—and does in fact occasionally appear. Part of his function is to make sure that false messiahs and peddlers and charlatans are shown as such. Hope—non-delusionary, non-inflationary, non-self-aggrandizing hope—is the core of the critic's being: hope that good work will recurrently arrive, hope that (partly by identifying trash) he may help it to arrive, hope that he may have the excitement and privilege of helping to connect that good work with its audience.

Look through the index of the collected writings of any theater critic you admire, and note how many *Chili Widows* are listed, how few of the plays he discusses are ones that you have seen or would want to see or read. But the critic hoped and persisted; through hoping and persisting occasionally found good work; through hoping and persisting, even when the theater was bad, created a literature.

I don't paint the theater critic as suffering saint. I understand the resentment that he draws from professionals and public. This resentment is simply a condition of his life, not a martyr's crown, and is cognate to the difficulties that other writers and artists accept as facts of their existence. Still, no other writer or artist works in so constant an atmosphere of hostility. The critic persists primarily, of course, out of ego, as any other writer persists; but also because, if he is the critic we are talking about, in the long run he serves even those who resent him.

index